Handbook of Software Engineering

Volume I

Handbook of Software Engineering
Volume I

Edited by **Tom Halt**

CLANRYE INTERNATIONAL

New Jersey

Published by Clanrye International,
55 Van Reypen Street,
Jersey City, NJ 07306, USA
www.clanryeinternational.com

Handbook of Software Engineering: Volume I
Edited by Tom Halt

International Standard Book Number: 978-1-63240-293-6 (Hardback)

Printed in the United States of America.

Contents

Preface

Software engineering is an area of computer science engineering, which is related to designing, development, and maintenance of software. It wouldn't be wrong to say that Software Engineering is one of the youngest braches of engineering. In fact, it started only in the early 1940s and it was not before the year 1968 that the term itself was coined.

In today's world, this field has many applications in all branches of engineering. However, software engineering was initially introduced to address issues related to poor quality of software and ensure that software is built systematically and within the prescribed budget. Essentially, software engineering can be divided into ten sub-disciplines.

There are a limited set of activities involved in the production of a software development procedure. Software can never be manufactured; it is always developed with some parameters kept in mind. There is no single ideal approach to develop software. However, there are some procedural activities which are involved in the entire development process such as waterfall model, spiral model, agile model, etc. A software development process is never ending because iteration is always made to improve the quality of the product, even after it is delivered. These iterations are called updates. Software is a very essential part of computer science.

In this book, these aspects are discussed in chapters. I especially wish to acknowledge the contributing authors, without whom a work of this magnitude would clearly not have been realizable. I would also like to thank my publisher for giving me this unparalleled opportunity and my family for their continuous support.

Editor

A Stateful Approach to Generate Synthetic Events from Kernel Traces

Naser Ezzati-Jivan and Michel R. Dagenais

Department of Computer and Software Engineering, Ecole Polytechnique de Montreal, C.P. 6079, Station Downtown, Montreal, Quebec, Canada H3C 3A7

Correspondence should be addressed to Naser Ezzati-Jivan, ezzati@gmail.com

Academic Editor: Antonella Di Stefano

We propose a generic synthetic event generator from kernel trace events. The proposed method makes use of patterns of system states and environment-independent semantic events rather than platform-specific raw events. This method can be applied to different kernel and user level trace formats. We use a state model to store intermediate states and events. This stateful method supports partial trace abstraction and enables users to seek and navigate through the trace events and to abstract out the desired part. Since it uses the current and previous values of the system states and has more knowledge of the underlying system execution, it can generate a wide range of synthetic events. One of the obvious applications of this method is the identification of system faults and problems that will appear later in this paper. We will discuss the architecture of the method, its implementation, and the performance results.

1. Introduction

Tracing complete systems provides information on several system levels. The use of execution traces as a method to analyze system behavior is increasing among system administrators and analysts. By examining the trace events, experts can detect the system problems and misbehaviors caused by program errors, application misconfigurations, and also attackers. Linux trace toolkit next generation (LTTng), a low-impact and precise Linux tracing tool, provides a detailed execution trace of system calls, operating system operations, and user space applications [1]. The resulting trace files can be used to analyze the traced system at kernel and user space levels. However, these trace files can grow to a large number of events very quickly and make analysis difficult. Moreover, this data contains too many low-level system calls that often complicate the reading and comprehension. Thus, the need arises to somehow reduce the size of huge trace files. In addition, it is better to have relatively abstract and high-level events that are more readable than raw events and at the same time reflect the similar system behavior. Trace abstraction technique reduces the size of original trace by grouping the

events and generating high-level compound synthetic events. Since synthetic events reveal more high-level information of the underling system execution, they can be used to easily analyze and discuss the system at higher levels.

To generate such synthetic events, it is required to develop efficient tools and methods to read trace events, detect similar sections and behaviors, and convert them to meaningful coarse-grained events. Most of the trace abstraction tools are based on pattern-matching techniques in which patterns of events are used to detect and group similar events or sequences of related events into compound events. For instance, Fadel [2] uses pattern-matching technique to abstract out the traces gathered by LTTng kernel tracer [1]. They have also created a pattern library that contains patterns of Linux file, socket, and process operations. Waly and Ktari [3] use the same technique to find system faults and anomalies. They have also designed a language for defining fault patterns and attack scenarios.

Although defining patterns over trace events are a useful mechanism for abstracting the trace events and finding the system faults, there are other types of faults and synthetic events that are difficult to find with these techniques and need more information of the system resources. In this way, modeling the state values of a system and using them may help much in finding those complex kinds of system problems. Indeed, without a proper state model, many patterns will simply attempt to recreate and recompute some of that repetitive information in a time- and performance-consuming manner.

This paper mainly describes the architecture of a stateful trace abstractor. Using a state database to store system state values enables us to have more information about the system at any given point. Indeed, after reading the trace files and making the state database, we can jump to a specific point and abstract out the trace at that point. For example, suppose we see there is a high load or a system problem at a certain time. In this case, we can load the system states at that point, reread, abstract out, and analyze only the desired part to discover the main reason of the given problem.

The main goal of this paper is to explain how to use the system state information to generate synthetic events as well as to detect complex system faults and anomalies. In this paper, we first explain converting the raw trace events to semantic events. Secondly, using a predefined mapping table, we describe extracting system metric values from trace and creating a database of the system state values. Finally, we investigate using pattern matching technique over semantic events and system state values to generate synthetic events as well as to detect system faults and misbehaviors.

The next section discusses related work. It is followed by a section explaining the proposed techniques and also the architecture of the model. Subsequently, we discuss our method in detail and provide some illustrative examples to show how it can be adopted to generate a wide range of synthetic events. Finally, our paper concludes by identifying the main features of the proposed method and possibilities for future research.

2. Related Work

The related work can be divided into two main categories: trace abstraction techniques and their usage in intrusion detection systems (IDSs). Trace abstraction combines groups of similar raw events into compound events and by means of eliminating the detailed and unwanted events reduces the complexity of the trace [4]. Furthermore, abstraction provides a high-level model of a program and makes understanding and debugging the source code easier [5]. Several studies have been conducted on analyzing, visualizing, and abstracting out large trace files [2, 3, 6]. Trace visualization is another way to show abstractions of trace events [7]. It uses visual and graphical elements to reveal the trace events. Through their work in [8], Hamou-Lhadj and Lethbridge carry out a survey on the several trace exploration and visualization tools and techniques. Some important tools that make use of these techniques are Jinsight [9], which is an Eclipse-based tool for visually exploring a program's run-time behavior; Program Explorer [10], a trace visualization and abstraction tool that has several views and provides facilities like merging, pruning, and slicing of the trace

files; ISV [11], which uses automatic pattern detection to summarize similar trace patterns and thereupon reduces the trace size. Other tools include AVID [12], Jive [13], and Shimba [14].

Besides visualization, pattern matching technique has been widely used for trace abstraction [6, 15]. Most of the aforementioned tools use this technique to detect repeated contiguous parts of trace events and to generate abstract and compound events [8]. Fadel [2], Waly and Ktari [3], and Matni and Dagenais [6] use pattern matching technique to generate abstract events from the LTTng kernel trace events. Pattern matching can also be used in intrusion detection systems [16]. For example, STATL [15] models misuse signatures in the form of state machines, while in [17], signatures are expressed as colored petri nets (CPNs), and in MuSigs [18], directed acyclic graphs (DCA) are used to extract security specifications. Beaucamps et al. [19] present an approach for malware detection using the abstraction of program traces. They detect malwares by comparing abstract events to reference malicious behaviors. Lin et al. [18] and Uppuluri [16] use the same technique to detect system problems and misuses.

Almost all of these pattern-matching techniques have defined their patterns over trace events and did not consider using the system state information. Our work is different as, unlike many of those previous techniques, it considers the system states information and provides a generic abstraction framework. Our proposed method converts raw events to platform-dependent semantic events, extracts the system state value, and sends them as inputs to the pattern-matching algorithms.

3. Overview

First, here are some terms that will be referred to throughout this text:

(i) "raw event" is used to identify the event that is directly generated by the operating system tracer. Raw events show various steps of the operating system running, such as a system call entry/exit, an interrupt, and disk block read;

(ii) "semantic events" to show the events resulting from conversion of platform-specific raw events to environment-independent events. As will be discussed later, there is a mapping table between raw events and environment-independent semantic events;

(iii) Also the term "synthetic events" is used to identify events that are the result of trace abstraction and fault identification analysis modules and depict high-level behavior of the system execution. In other words, synthetic events are generated from raw and semantic events to explain the system behavior at various higher levels. "sequential file read," "attempt to write to a closed file," "DNS request," and "half-opened TCP connection" are examples of synthetic events. Figure 1 shows the relations of these three event types.

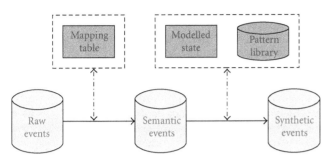

FIGURE 1: Raw, semantic, and synthetic events and conversion between them.

TABLE 1: Raw events to semantic events.

Raw events	Semantic events
sys_open event	
sys_dup event	File open
sys_create event	
sys_read event	
sys_pread64	File read
sys_readv event	
sys_write event	
sys_pwrite64 event	File write
sys_writev event	
sys_kill event	
sys_tkill event	Process kill
sys_tgkill event	

In order to support different versions of trace formats, we propose a generic synthetic event generator that uses a set of semantic events rather than versioned raw events. Indeed, having different versions of kernel tracers as well as an evolutionary Linux kernel that leads to different trace formats makes it difficult to have a stable version of an analyzer module. It means that, for each new release of kernel or the tracer and also for any change in the trace events format, the abstraction module will have to be updated. However, by designing a generic tool, independent of kernel versions and trace formats, we can achieve a generic abstraction module that will not be dependent on certain kernel or tracer version. Semantic events help in this way: we define a semantic "open file" event instead of events of both the sys_open and sys_dup Linux system calls. In the Linux kernel, there is often no unique way to implement user-level operations. Thus, by grouping the events of similar and overlapping functionalities, we reach a new set of semantic events that will be used in the synthetic event generator. Examples of such semantic events have been outlined in Table 1.

Later, for the trace formats, one must simply update the mapping table for converting the raw events to semantic events. With this table, the synthetic event generator will work without the need to be updated for the new trace formats, being independent of the specific format and version.

Another technique to make the synthetic event generator more generic and powerful is to use the system state values. In this work, we use system state values besides the trace events for extracting the high-level information. As discussed in the related work, most of the abstraction techniques use patterns over raw and high-level events to generate abstract events. However, generating some complex types of abstract events can be very time consuming and can affect system performance. It is also difficult to generate some complex types of synthetic events that deal with several system resources or under different user identities and at different levels. Thus, using patterns of trace events is somehow not enough, and there is a need to extract and use more system information. To do so, we model state values of important system resources in a database named "modeled state." This database contains current and historic state values of the system resources, keeping track of information about running processes, the execution status of a process (running, blocked, and waiting), file descriptors, disks, memory, locks, and other system metrics. The modeled state can then be used to show users the current system states. For example, each scheduling event which sets the current running process in the modeled state will be readily available for the upcoming events. Similarly, file open events can associate filenames to file descriptors in the modeled state. These values can then be used to retrieve the filename of the given file descriptor in the context of the upcoming file operation events.

4. Architecture

In this section, we explain the architecture of the proposed solution which is shown in Figure 2. It consists of various modules: event mapper, modeled state, and synthetic event generator. In the following, we will explain how each module works.

4.1. Mapper. In the architecture, the event mapper is used to convert the trace raw events to environment-independent semantic events and also to extract the state values. The mapper actually has two steps: converting the raw events to semantic events and converting the semantic events to state changes. For each step, it uses a different mapping table. The first table is used for converting the raw events to the semantic events, and the second one has been used to convert the semantic events to corresponding state changes. It makes use of two mapping tables that contain list of conversion entries for each event type. There is not necessarily a one-to-one relationship between the raw events and corresponding outputs. A raw event or a group of raw events can be converted into one or more semantic events. For example, a Linux_sched_schedule(p1, p2) event may be mapped into two semantic events: process_stop(p1) and process_running(p2). Table 2 lists examples of these mapping entries. The mapper in Figure 2 includes both the mapping Tables 1 and 2. In other words, when events are processed in the mapper, corresponding semantic events are generated, and changes in the modeled state also occur. Most

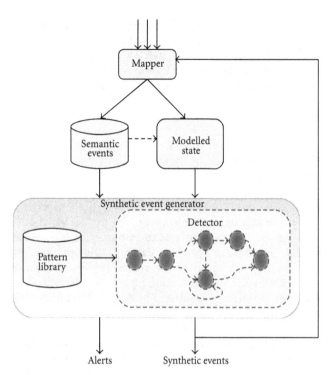

FIGURE 2: Architectural view of the stateful synthetic event generator.

TABLE 2: Semantic events to state changes.

Semantic events	Corresponding state change
File open (fd)	Changes the state of the input fd to opened
File read (fd, count)	Changes the state of the input fd to read
File close (fd)	Changes the state of the input fd to closed
Kill process (p1)	Changes the state of the input p1 to killed

of the changes take place by directly changing a state value. However, some events may have more complex effects on the modeled state. In this case, a set of changes may be queued to be performed on the state values.

4.2. Modeled State. The modeled state stores the system metrics and different state values of them. The system metrics (e.g., process name, file name, etc.) are stored in a tree-based data structure called "attribute tree" [20] or "metric tree." In this tree, each metric has an address starting from its machine name. The content of the attribute tree is similar to the tree shown in Figure 3, where names starting with $ identify the variables and can have many values. For example, $pid can be process1, process2, ...

The tree shown in Figure 3 acts like a lookup table in which various system resources and attributes are defined in a file system like path. Besides that, there is another tree based interval database to store the different values of those resources and attributes during the system execution. We store all of the extracted state values in this database that enables us to retrieve the state values at any later given time. Montplaisi and Dagenais [20] proposed a Java

implementation of the modeled state that is used in this project to store and retrieve the state values.

Different types of data may be stored in the modeled state: the state of a process, the current running process on a CPU, state of a file descriptor, and so on. System resources statistics are another type of information that can be stored in the modeled state. Examples of these statistics include number of bytes read and written for a specific file, for a process or for the whole trace, total CPU usage per process or per trace or for a specific time period, the CPU waiting time, number of TCP connections in the last 2 seconds, the duration for which a disk was busy, and large data transfers. Statistics extracted from trace events are similar to the extracted state values from events. By processing trace events, one can interpret the event contents, gather relevant statistics, and aggregate them by machine, user, process, or CPU for the whole trace or for a time duration. For that, we identify the event types and event arguments used to count, aggregate, and compute the statistics of the system metrics. In other words, when one defines a mapping between events and states, he or she may also want to relate associated trace events to the statistics values.

The statistics can then be used to generate synthetic events to detect system faults and problems. In this project, we use a threshold detection mechanism [15, 21] to detect system problems. In this approach, the occurrences of specific events and statistics values of important system metrics are stored, updated, and compared to predefined threshold values. If the values cross the thresholds, or in the case of a quick rise in a short period, an alarm is raised or a log record is generated [15]. With this approach, some hook methods may be registered and invoked in the case of unusual growth or the reaching of certain threshold. For some predefined semantic events, we store and update the statistics values of the important metrics (e.g., quantity of I/O throughput, number of forks, number of half-opened TCP connections, CPU usage, number of file deletions, etc.) in the modeled state.

It is important to mention that system state is a broad term, and it could be too resource and performance consuming to care of all system resources. For trace abstraction, we only need to store a subset of that information required to represent the synthetic event patterns and associated initial, intermediate, and final states. In other words, the amount of data stored in the modeled state will depend on the patterns and will be extracted from them. Therefore, by having created a pattern library in advance or by importing them during analysis, it would be possible to determine the required set of system attributes and metrics that should be kept track of, in the modeled state.

4.3. Synthetic Event Generator. Synthetic event generator is another module that is used to generate high-level events from trace events. The synthetic event generator may use either the semantic events, modeled state values, or both to generate the synthetic events. It makes use of a pattern library that contains various patterns for reducing the trace size and also for detecting the system faults and attacks.

```
$machine/processes/$pid/state
                        execmode_stack
                        exec_name
                        fds
                            $fd1
                                filename
                                type
                            $fd2
                            . . .
         /cpus/$cpuid/current_process
                        pid
         /disks
         /memory
```

FIGURE 3: Typical organization of the modeled state elements.

In this paper, we use finite state machine to define the patterns. In this way, we have created a set of state machines based on the semantic events and state values to abstract out the Linux kernel execution events. In addition, it contains patterns to detect Syn flood attack, fork bomb attack, and port scanning. Each state machine represents a set of states and a sequence of actions and transitions. A transition is triggered by reading an associated semantic event or a state value change. Reaching a particular state targets a synthetic event that can reveal either a high-level system behavior or a system fault or a misbehavior. In this model, we use the modeled state to store both the states of system resources as well as the state machines' intermediate states. Based on this idea, common methods are used for storing, retrieving, and exploring the states.

As an example, suppose that we want to list all "write to a closed file" synthetic events. In this case, by comparing the filename of each write event to the open files list kept in the modeled state, we can generate and list all of these synthetic events. Here, we actually have a pattern of "write to file" semantic events and a specific path in the modeled state (open files list). Another example of such a pattern is when we want to detect all sequential file reading operations. In this case, for each read event, we keep track of the last read position as well as whether all previous read operations were sequential or not. Then, upon closing a file, if the state values for all previous read operations were sequential, and the last read operation has read the file to the end, then a "sequential file read" synthetic event can be generated. In the same way, a pattern is defined over "file read" semantic events and relevant modeled state values.

The resulting synthetic events are again passed to the mapper. The mapper may have mapping entries for synthetic events as well, which means that the same way that semantic events change the state values, synthetic events can affect them. For instance, a "TCP connection" synthetic event can change the state of a socket to connecting, established, closing, and closed. Previously generated synthetic events may also be passed again through the synthetic event generator, which means that they can be used to generate complex higher-level events. For example, one can generate

"library files read" synthetic event from the consecutive "read */lib/* files" synthetic events. Figure 4 depicts this issue.

Another result is that the stateful approach enables the analyst to seek and go back and forth in the trace, select an area, and abstract out only the selected area. In other words, it supports partial trace abstraction. For instance, suppose we see there is a high load at a specific point, we can jump to the starting point of the selected area, load the stored system information, and run abstraction process to get meaningful events and to achieve a high-level understanding of the system execution.

5. Illustrative Examples

Using patterns of semantic events and system states helps to develop a generic synthetic events generator. This way, we are able to generate more meaningful high-level events and to detect more system faults and problems. Here, we provide a few examples that outline aspects of synthetic events we can generate using the proposed method.

5.1. System Load and Performance. By keeping track of the system load and usage (e.g., CPU usage, I/O throughputs, memory usage, etc.), and aggregating them per process, per user, per machine, and per different time intervals, it becomes easy to check the resource load values against predefined threshold values. Thus, by processing the trace events and having defined standard patterns, we can compute the system load and store in the modeled state. For example, for each file open semantic event, we increment the number of opened files for that process and also for the whole system. Likewise, we decrement the number of opened files for each file close semantic event. In the same way, for each schedule in and out event, we add the time duration to the CPU usage of that process. We perform the same processing for memory usage, disk blocks operations, bandwidth usage, and so on and update the corresponding values in the modeled state.

The detector module then compares the stored values against predefined thresholds and detects whether an overload exists in the system. In case of overload, a "system

Abstract level 1   Abstract level 2   Abstract level 3

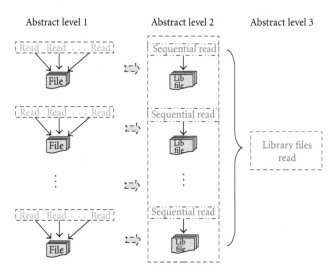

FIGURE 4: Generating several levels of synthetic events.

overload" synthetic event would be generated, and an alarm would be raised to the system administrator or any predefined monitoring systems. The Administrator or the monitoring system, in turn, responds appropriately to the problem. This solution can be extended to all types of system load and performance problems.

5.2. Denial of Service Attacks. The proposed stateful method can also be used to detect denial of service (DOS) attacks. For instance, a "fork bomb" is a form of denial of service attack which clones a large number of child processes in a short time, in order to saturate the system resources. To detect this attack, one can store the number of fork operations for each process in the modeled state. In this case, upon forking a process, value of a corresponding counter is incremented, and upon killing a process, the value is decremented. Each time the value changes, it is compared to the predetermined threshold value, and in case the threshold value is reached, it will generate a synthetic event and will send an alarm to the system monitoring module. Figure 5 outlines the state machine used for detecting these kinds of attacks.

The same technique may be used for detecting the "Syn flood attack" and for other similar DOS attacks as well. For each connection (even half-opened or established), we keep track of a counter in the modeled state, and the attack (or a possible attack attempt) is detected by comparing the value of the counter to a predefined value. The predefined value can be defined by an expert or by an automated learning technique. These values can be adjusted for different servers and applications.

5.3. Network Scan Detection. Network scanning—especially port scanning—is the process in which a number of packets are sent to a target computer to find weaknesses and open doors to break into that machine. The scanner sends a connection request to targeted ports and, depending on the scanning method, receives a list of open ports, version of operating system, and running services on the other end.

Port scanning has legitimate uses in computer networks and is usually considered one of the early steps in most network attacks. Nmap [22] is the most widely used tool for such network scanning. We used Nmap to generate the relevant kernel traces of high-level port scanning. There is actually no way and no reason to stop a user from scanning a computer. However, by detecting port scanning, one can be alerted because of a potential attack.

There are many ways to perform and accordingly detect a port scanning from network packets. A common method, which is implemented in Nmap, involves establishing a typical TCP connection and immediately closing it by sending an RST or an FIN packet and repeating it to different ports at defined time intervals. Another hard-to-detect port scanning method is sending a dead packet (a typical TCP SYN or TCP FIN instead of a regular TCP connection). According to RFC 793 [23], an open port must ignore this packet, and conversely, a closed one must reply with an RST packet. Consequently, any answer from the other end will determine the status of the port: whether it is open, closed, or filtered.

The LTTng kernel tracer traces the packets in both the IP and TCP layers. However, the proposed prototype uses socket-related events (TCP layer) to detect "port scanning" synthetic events. Simplifying the prototype, we consider every TCP connection pattern—even established or half opened—followed by a disconnection, a single port scan. Upon detecting these kinds of events, we update an associated entry in the modeled state. The scanned port number, pattern used, source address, source port, and timestamps of the first packet are stored in that entry. There is a registered method in the detector module which monitors the associated modeled state entry and, in case of detecting a successive port scanning, generates a "ports scanning" synthetic event and raises an alarm to the system-monitoring module. Due to the completeness of the defined rules and patterns, this technique can detect distributed port scanning even with different timings between packets. Figure 6 depicts

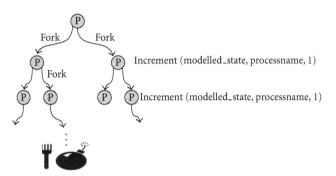

FIGURE 5: State transition for detecting the fork bomb attack.

the state machine used to detect "port scanning" synthetic events.

6. Implementation

We have prototyped a Java tool in Linux that takes the LTTng trace as input and applies the proposed techniques to create the several levels of abstract events. We use the Java library provided by Montplaisi and Dagenais [20] to manage the modeled state and other shared information. Our synthetic event generator stores all the system states as well as the states required for state machines in this tree.

We also created a prototype pattern library that covers common Linux file, network, and process operations. Using this pattern library and the proposed method, we can generate various levels of file operations (e.g., file simple open and close operation, sequential and nonsequential, file read and write, etc.), network connections (e.g., TCP connection, port scanning, etc.), and process operations (fork process, kill process, etc.). The pattern library also includes patterns of some system problems and attacks.

In this implementation, we have defined the patterns in XML format. Also we hardcoded the preactions and postactions for each state transition. Waly and Ktari [3] have developed a language for defining patterns and attack scenarios over LTTng events. Efforts are needed to extend this language to support the patterns of system states. Generally, the required language should be a declarative language with which one can declare the patterns and scenarios and mapping between events and outputs. It can, however, also be a programming-like language with which one can define state variables, pre- and posttransition actions, conditions, output formats, and so forth. Designing such a language is a future work of this project.

We have used a C helper program that simply calls the "wget WWW.YAHOO.COM" in Linux to generate the corresponding kernel traces. Figure 7 shows the highest level of generated synthetic events for this command. The count of generated raw event for this command is 3622. The synthetic event generator has converted these 3600 raw events into less than 10 synthetic events. Here, the synthetic events include reading some library and configuration files, making a TCP connection to WWW.YAHOO.COM, and writing the data read to file index.html.1, following with some other event.

TABLE 3: Number of events in different levels of abstraction.

Size (MB)	Number of events		
	Original trace	Abstract level 1	Abstract level 2
25	2279766	335362	4954
75	5420727	710052	5466
150	8872888	976672	86697
500	37328387	7668926	178426
1000	68961889	20186771	192788
2000	140507496	33924846	328430
5000	328868336	130293720	2099836
10000	621132167	159023500	2247225

7. Performance

For the performance testing, the Linux kernel version 2.6.38.6 is instrumented using LTTng and the tests are performed on a 2.8 GHz with 6 GB ram machine. We will show the results from different points of view. As discussed in the Implementation Section, we have generated two other levels of abstraction in addition to the semantic events. For the first abstract level, we have used 120 patterns, and for the second level, we have used 30 patterns. Following tables and figures show the results for traces with different sizes from 25 MB to 10000 MB. To generate these trace files, we have used "wget -r -l0 URL," "ls –R," and also "grep x.-r" commands consecutively.

7.1. Reduction Ratio. As discussed earlier, one goal of the abstraction technique is reducing the trace size. We have measured the reduction ratio of the proposed method. Figure 8 and Table 3 show the reduction of the number of events in the different levels of abstraction.

Table 3 shows the numbers of events at each abstract level. For instance, by applying the synthetic event generator over a 10 GB trace file, we could reduce it to a trace with 25% of the original size but still with mostly the same meaning. It is important to note that the content of trace files at different levels should yield the same interpretation of the system execution. In the Implementation Section, we showed that the same meaning can be extracted from different levels of abstraction. Using the same pattern-matching technique, the

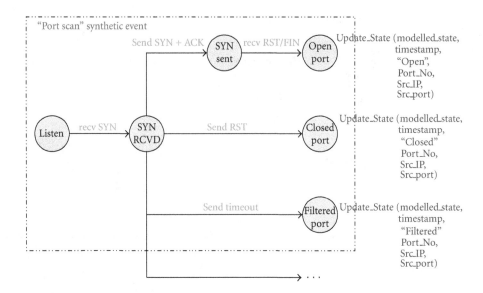

FIGURE 6: State transition for detecting the port scanning.

FIGURE 7: A view of the implemented stateful synthetic event generator.

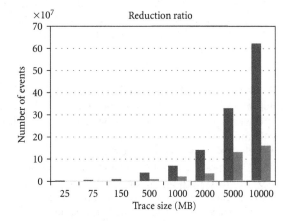

FIGURE 8: Reduction ratio.

reduction ratio is related to the number of patterns and also the number of containing events in each pattern. For that, the reduction ratio of the different examined traces is not the same.

7.2. Patterns and Containing Events. Table 4 shows the number of selected synthetic events of various trace sizes for the first abstract level. In the proposed pattern library, a set of patterns have been defined for each of these synthetic events, so that by applying them over trace events and by retrieving the current system state, the engine is able to detect those events. We have defined 120 patterns for abstracting out the trace events and generating the first level of abstraction. These patterns cover important aspects of file, socket, process, and also system wide operations. The patterns are stored in an XML file, and the system is defined in such a way that administrators can easily add new patterns to the system.

TABLE 4: Count of different event types in first level of abstraction.

| Events count | Size (MB) | Number of synthetic events in first level of abstraction | | | | | | | | |
| | | File operations | | | | Network operations | | | | |
		File open	File read	File write	File close	Socket create	Socket connect	Socket receive	Socket send	Socket close
2279766	25	2727	8401	12913	2327	150	112	4583	7911	150
5420727	75	2474	18563	30251	2122	370	718	21523	26570	611
8872888	150	86780	59108	20913	86536	154	106	7574	10767	161
37328387	500	87484	158484	1025703	88143	673	979	60880	70651	1070
68961889	1000	98583	218789	6507052	96226	159	73	57965	62003	168
140507496	2000	161458	562239	5980178	161577	2140	2500	166420	245718	2638
328868336	5000	1045710	612821	23001032	1044562	4592	5154	137733	296566	5356
621132167	10000	755647	3541833	23214444	720016	27676	20741	735271	1288181	29059

As the second step, Table 5 shows some important synthetic events for the second abstract level. To generate these events, a set of patterns were defined over the events of the first level of abstraction and also the relevant modeled state values. For instance, "check file" synthetic events contain a sequence of an open file, check file status or check file permission, and a close file. Also "sequentially file read (write)" refers to a set of subsequent file operations that consist of a file open, read from (write to) a file sequentially, and finally close it. An "HTTP (DNS) connection" is detected through a pattern of socket create, socket connect to a 80/53 port with transport protocol equal to TCP (UDP), zero or more send/receive data, and finally socket close events. However, a "network connection" synthetic event means that there is a complete connection (sequence of socket create-socket connect, send/receive data, and close socket), but that the engine could not find the type of connection protocol or the destination port. This happens because of probable missing events. It may also occur if the connection was already established at the starting time of the trace. At this level, we have defined 30 different patterns for detecting such kind of synthetic events.

It would be interesting to know the number of events participating to form a synthetic event on one upper level. Table 6 shows the average number of events from one level below contained in each synthetic event.

As shown in Table 6, "check file" synthetic events always contain three events: open a file, check a file attribute, and close that file. It is important to note that the numbers here only show the containing events from one level below. On the other hand, in this example, each of these three events can in turn contain several events from a lower level. As another example, the average number of 48 events obtained from a 5 GB trace means that each "sequentially file write" synthetic event contains 48 events on average: one for open file, one for close file, and the rest for write events. The null value for the DNS connection is because there is no such connection for those traces.

7.3. Execution Time. As discussed earlier, one of the important features of the proposed method is its execution

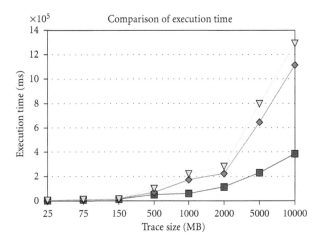

FIGURE 9: Execution time comparisons.

efficiency. In this section, execution times for different trace sizes will be shown. Table 7 shows the time spent to read the relevant events, to look for patterns, and to generate the first abstraction level.

The numbers in Table 7 show the time spent for reading the events, looking for the patterns, and generating the abstract events. The execution time for checking each pattern has a relatively minor impact when checking all patterns simultaneously. Reading the trace events and finding relevant events for each pattern takes most of the analyzing time.

Figure 9 shows the differences between execution times spent for different levels of abstraction.

In Figure 9, the blue line shows the execution time needed for reading the trace events. For this step, no pattern was specified, and the diagram only shows the time needed for reading all trace events. In the same way, the orange line shows the execution time for generating the first level of abstract events. The execution time consists of reading events, looking up the patterns, and generating the abstract events. The yellow line depicts the time needed for analyzing

TABLE 5: Count of different event types in second level of abstraction.

| Events count | Size (MB) | Number of synthetic events in second level of abstraction | | | | | | |
| | | File operations | | | | Network operations | | |
		Check file	Sequentially file read	Sequentially file write	Read write file	Network connection	HTTP connection	DNS connection
2279766	25	928	673	496	230	43	103	4
5420727	75	1117	742	253	10	372	193	46
8872888	150	66141	19742	440	213	58	103	0
37328387	500	53371	32093	1791	888	688	274	108
68961889	1000	81607	14343	207	69	139	29	0
140507496	2000	61647	96921	2505	504	1486	867	285
328868336	5000	948436	87095	8047	984	1921	3116	319
621132167	10000	395067	303452	20267	1230	11740	16668	651

TABLE 6: Average number of containing events for generating the upper level synthetic events.

| Events count | Size (MB) | Average number of containing events | | | | | | |
		Check file	Sequentially file read	Sequentially file write	Read write file	Network connection	HTTP connection	DNS connection
2279766	25	3	3	10	9	1	38	5
5420727	75	3	3	25	87	3	37	5
8872888	150	3	4	11	9	2	38	0
37328387	500	3	4	10	26	2	44	5
68961889	1000	3	3	20	67	4	82	0
140507496	2000	3	4	61	16	5	92	5
328868336	5000	3	6	48	62	3	34	5
621132167	10000	3	4	34	120	4	42	5

and generating both levels of abstract events. Differences between the orange and yellow lines with the blue line show that the time needed for analyzing and generating the first level of abstraction is more than the time needed for the second level. This is explained by the fact that the number of patterns in the first level is much greater than the number of patterns in the second level. The results show that the execution time is relatively linear with the trace size and also the number of relevant events. However, there exists other factors that affect the results. The complexity of patterns and also the number of containing events for each pattern may lead to different execution times for different synthetic events. For example, in Table 7, we see different values for different synthetic events for the same trace file, and the reason is that they have different scenarios with different complexities and different numbers of containing events.

Another important factor is the number of coexisting patterns. As shown in Figure 9, the number of patterns and the number of coexisting patterns affect the execution times for the two different abstraction levels. Since the first level deals with file and socket operations, they need to be called for each file/socket access, thus having a large impact on the performance and execution time of the analyzer. By contrast, in the second abstraction level, the analyzer works with fewer coexisting patterns, less often called during a process lifetime; thus, less time is needed for analyzing

and generating the second level of abstract events. The execution time is therefore related to the size of the trace files, the number of relevant events, the number of coexisting patterns, and also the complexity of patterns.

8. Conclusion and Further Work

In this paper, we proposed an abstraction method that uses a set of patterns over semantic trace events and system state values to generate synthetic events. Using the notion of semantic events (the events of a generic type that replace platform-dependent events) can help decouple the synthetic event generator from the system and tracer-dependent events. Using semantic events as well as system state values makes the abstraction process more generic to support different versions of trace formats and operating system kernels and also to support both the kernel and user level tracing. As shown in the Illustrative Examples Section, using proposed techniques, we efficiently generate a wide range of synthetic events that reveal more of the system behaviors and can also be used to detect a larger range of system problems.

Although most of the synthetic events can be defined by patterns and state machines, we do not support the synthetic events that are not representable using state transitions. For

TABLE 7: Execution time for generating the first abstraction level.

Events count	Size (MB)	All (ms)	Time spent (ms) for analysing and generating the first level of abstract events									
			File operations				Network operations				
			File open	File read	File write	File close	Socket create	Socket connect	Socket receive	Socket send	Socket close
2279766	25	4748	3963	4024	3995	4038	4151	3952	3871	3937	3777
5420727	75	9176	5900	6195	6394	6218	6394	6257	5884	6014	5957
8872888	150	12735	10403	10308	10183	10282	9975	10025	97125	10125	10424
37328387	500	58477	50251	50855	51928	50424	49366	47896	48962	49163	48104
68961889	1000	148284	128252	129157	138988	128186	127912	128312	127191	126915	128061
140507496	2000	226569	177913	180017	187366	178640	177389	174385	179372	178509	179097
328868336	5000	650228	513230	514012	546782	512659	510139	507873	511201	510139	512771
621132167	10000	1105124	902245	916292	941668	909893	907177	901127	899976	904227	874227

example, a dependency analysis between different processes and resources, leading to the computation of the critical path for a request, cannot be defined as a simple pattern. Another possible limitation is related to the output completeness of the tracers. Because not every state modification is logged with a tracer, this may somehow limit the proposed technique.

Using the proposed method and having defined a complete pattern library can also lead to an efficient host-based intrusion detection system. In our project, expanding the rule base and pattern library is an important future work. We have implemented a prototype pattern library that works over semantic events and system states. However, more work is needed to complete it and to support more aspects of system behavior. Examples of the patterns we should extend include memory usage and interprocess communications.

As mentioned in the Implementation Section, there is a need to further develop the supporting language. This language can be declarative or similar to a programing language and should support the requirements needed to implement the proposed method. It could be used for defining the mapping table between raw events and semantic events, as well as the mapping between events and state changes. We will focus on extending the language defined in [3] in a future investigation.

References

[1] M. Desnoyers and M. R. Dagenais, "The LTTng tracer: a low impact performance and behavior monitor for GNU/Linux," in *Proceedings of the Ottawa Linux Symposium*, 2006.

[2] W. Fadel, *Techniques for the abstraction of system call traces [M.Sc.A. dissertation]*, Concordia University, 2010.

[3] H. Waly and B. Ktari, "A complete framework for kernel trace analysis," in *Proceedings of the Canadian Conference on Electrical and Computer Engineering (CCECE '11)*, pp. 001426–001430, Niagara Falls, Canada, May 2011.

[4] J. P. Black, M. H. Coffin, D. J. Taylor, T. Kunz, and T. Basten, "Linking specification, abstraction, and debugging," CCNG Technical Report E-232, Computer Communications and Networks Group, University of Waterloo, 1993.

[5] M. Auguston, A. Gates, and M. Lujan, "Defining a program behavior model for dynamic analyzers," in *Proceedings of the 9th International Conference on Software Engineering and Knowledge Engineering (SEKE '97)*, pp. 257–262, Madrid, Spain, June 1997.

[6] G. Matni and M. Dagenais, "Automata-based approach for kernel trace analysis," in *Proceedings of the Canadian Conference on Electrical and Computer Engineering (CCECE '09)*, pp. 970–973, May 2009.

[7] L. Fu, *Exploration and visualization of large execution traces [M.Sc.A. dissertation]*, University of Ottawa, 2005.

[8] A. Hamou-Lhadj and T. Lethbridge, "Survey of trace exploration tools and techniques," in *Proceedings of the 14th IBM Conference of the Centre for Advanced Studies on Collaborative Research*, pp. 42–55, IBM Press, 2004.

[9] W. D. Pauw, R. Helm, D. Kimelman, and J. M. Vlissides, "Visualizing the behavior of object-oriented systems," in *Proceedings of the 8th Conference on Object-Oriented Programming Systems, Languages, and Applications (OOPSLA '93)*, pp. 326–337, ACM, 1993.

[10] D. B. Lange and Y. Nakamura, "Object-oriented program tracing and visualization," *Computer*, vol. 30, no. 5, pp. 63–70, 1997.

[11] D. F. Jerding, J. T. Stasko, and T. Ball, "Visualizing interactions in program executions," in *Proceedings of the 19th IEEE International Conference on Software Engineering*, pp. 360–370, May 1997.

[12] A. Chan, R. Holmes, G. C. Murphy, and A. T. T. Ying, "Scaling an Object-oriented system execution visualizer through sampling," in *Proceedings of the IEEE International Workshop on Program Comprehension (ICPC '03)*, 2003.

[13] S. P. Reiss, "Visualizing Java in action," in *Proceedings of the ACM Symposium on Software Visualization (SoftVis '03)*, pp. 57–65, ACM, June 2003.

[14] T. Systä, K. Koskimies, and H. Müller, "Shimba—an environment for reverse engineering Java software systems," *Software—Practice and Experience*, vol. 31, no. 4, pp. 371–394, 2001.

[15] S. T. Eckmann, G. Vigna, and R. A. Kemmerer, "STATL: an attack language for state-based intrusion detection," *Journal of Computer Security*, vol. 10, no. 1-2, pp. 71–103, 2002.

[16] P. Uppuluri, *Intrusion detection/prevention using behavior specifications [Ph.D. dissertation]*, State University of New York at Stony Brook, New York, NY, USA, 2003.

[17] S. Kumar, *Classification and detection of computer intrusions [Ph.D. thesis]*, CERIAS lab, Purdue University, 1995.

[18] J. L. Lin, X. S. Wang, and S. Jajodia, "Abstraction-based misuse detection: high-level specifications and adaptable strategies," in *Proceedings of the 11th IEEE Computer Security Foundations Workshop (CSFW '98)*, pp. 190–201, Rockport, Mass, USA, June 1998.

[19] P. Beaucamps, I. Gnaedig, and J. Y. Marion, "Behavior abstraction in malware analysis," in *Proceedings of the Runtime Verification Conference (RV '10)*, pp. 168–182, 2010.

[20] A. Montplaisi and M. R. Dagenais, *Stockage sur disque pour accs rapide dattributs avec intervalles de temps [M.Sc.A. dissertation]*, Dorsal lab, Ecole Polytechnique de Montreal, Montreal, Canada, 2011.

[21] M. M. Sebring, E. Shellhouse, M. Hanna, and R. A. White-hurst, "Expert systems in intrusion detection: a case study," in *Proceedings of the National Computer Security Conference*, pp. 74–81, 1988.

[22] 2011, http://www.nmap.org/.

[23] RFC 793: Transmission Control Protocol, 2011, http://www.faqs.org/rfcs/rfc793.html.

2

Formal ESL Synthesis for Control-Intensive Applications

Michael F. Dossis

Department of Informatics and Computer Technology, School of Kastoria, Higher Technological Education Institute of Western Macedonia, Fourka Area, 52100 Kastoria, Greece

Correspondence should be addressed to Michael F. Dossis, mdossis@yahoo.gr

Academic Editor: Kamel Barkaoui

Due to the massive complexity of contemporary embedded applications and integrated systems, long effort has been invested in high-level synthesis (HLS) and electronic system level (ESL) methodologies to automatically produce correct implementations from high-level, abstract, and executable specifications written in program code. If the HLS transformations that are applied on the source code are formal, then the generated implementation is correct-by-construction. The focus in this work is on application-specific design, which can deliver optimal, and customized implementations, as opposed to platform or IP-based design, which is bound by the limits and constraints of the preexisting architecture. This work surveys and reviews past and current research in the area of ESL and HLS. Then, a prototype HLS compiler tool that has been developed by the author is presented, which utilizes compiler-generators and logic programming to turn the synthesis into a formal process. The scheduler PARCS and the formal compilation of the system are tested with a number of benchmarks and real-world applications. This demonstrates the usability and applicability of the presented method.

1. Introduction

During the last 3-4 decades, the advances on chip integration capability have increased the complexity of embedded and other custom VLSI systems to such a level that sometimes their spec-to-product development time exceeds even their product lifetime in the market. Because of this, and in combination with the high design cost and development effort required for the delivery of such products, they often even miss their market window. This problem generates competitive disadvantages for the relevant industries that design and develop these complex computing products. The current practice in the used design and engineering flows, for the development of such systems and applications, includes to a large extent approaches which are semimanual, ad-hoc, nonautomatically communicants from one level of the design flow to the next, and with a lot of design iterations caused by the discovery of functional and timing bugs, as well as specification to product requirements mismatches later in the development process. All of these issues have motivated industry and academia to invest in suitable methodologies and tools to achieve higher automation in the design of contemporary systems. Nowadays, a higher level of code abstraction is pursued as input to automated E-CAD tools. Furthermore, methodologies and tools such as high-level synthesis (HLS) and electronic system level (ESL) design entries employ established techniques, which are borrowed from the computer language program compilers and mature E-CAD tools and new algorithms such as advanced scheduling, loop unrolling, and code motion heuristics.

Even nowadays, the practiced flow for complex heterogeneous (hardware + software) systems and applications is still to a large extent an empirical process. Usually, engineers and engineering managers with different technical area skills are brought together at the same group, or even from a large number of different organizations of a consortium, and they are allocated engineering tasks which are scheduled and partitioned manually and by the most experienced engineers of the team. Even during the design process, the engineers of the team exchange information between them in a nonformal and ad-hoc way. Quite often, the system designers, the engineering managers and the other engineers of the team use a mix of manual methods and tools that are fundamentally incompatible with each other. Thus, the design data need to be manually modified in order to be ported from one tool or engineering level of the design flow, to another. This of course prolongs the spec-to-product cycle and drastically increases the engineering effort which is required for the completion of the product, mainly due to the very fragmented design and development flow which is still in practice in industry. Therefore, academia and industry, for a long time, have been investigating formal and automatic transformation techniques to automatically convert design representations from a higher abstraction level to a lower level in the design process. The main contribution of this paper is formal and automatic hardware compiler system to deliver correct hardware implementations from high level, algorithmic, and directly executable program code system specifications.

The conventional approach in designing complex digital systems is the use of register-transfer level (RTL) coding in languages such as VHDL and Verilog. However, for designs that exceed an area of a hundred thousand logic gates, the use of RTL models for specification and design can result into years of design flow loops and verification simulations. Combined with the short lifetime of electronic products in the marker, this constitutes a great problem for the industry. Therefore, higher abstraction level and executable types of specifications are required to make the industry competitive. HLS started appearing as an attractive solution in the 1980s where simple HLS tools were mapping mostly linear (dataflow-oriented) applications into hardware netlists. However, the broad acceptance of HLS by the engineering community was prevented for a long time from the poor synthesis results from specifications that with hierarchy and complex (e.g., nested) control flow constructs in the specification program. The programming style of the specification code has an unavoidable impact on the quality of the synthesized system. This is deteriorated by models with hierarchical blocks, subprogram calls, as well as nested control constructs (e.g., if-then-else and while loops). The result of these models is that the complexity of the transformations which are required for the synthesis tasks (compilation, algorithmic transformations, scheduling, allocation, and binding) increases at an exponential rate, whereas the design size increases linearly.

Usually the input code (such as ANSI-C or ADA) to HLS tool is first transformed into a control/data flow graph (CDFG) by a front-end compilation stage. This involves a number of compiler-like optimizations such as code motion, dead code elimination, constant propagation, common subexpression elimination, loop unrolling hardware-oriented optimizations such as minimization of syntactic variances, retiming, and code transformations which are based on the associativity and commutativity properties of some operators, in order to deliver simpler expressions. Then, various synthesis transformations are applied on the CDFG to generate the final implementation. The most important HLS tasks of this process are scheduling, allocation, and binding. Scheduling makes an as-much-as-possible optimal order of the operations in a number of control steps or states. Optimization at this stage includes making as many operations as possible parallel, so as to achieve shorter

execution times of the generated implementation. Allocation and binding assign operations onto functional units, and variables and data structures onto registers, wires, or memory positions, which are available from an implementation library.

A number of commercial HLS tools exist nowadays, which often impose their own extensions or restrictions on the programming language code that they accept as input, as well as various shortcuts and heuristics on the HLS tasks that they execute. Such tools are the CatapultC by Mentor Graphics, the Cynthesizer by Forte Design Systems, the Impulse CoDeveloper by Impulse Accelerated Technologies, the Synfony HLS by Synopsys, the C-to-silicon by Cadence, the C to Verilog Compiler by C-to-Verilog, the AutoPilot by AutoESL, the PICO by Synfora, and the CyberWorkBench by NEC System Technologies Ltd. The analysis of these tools is not the purpose of this work, but most of them are suitable for linear, dataflow-dominated (e.g., stream-based) applications, such as pipelined DSP and image filtering.

An important aspect of the HLS tools is whether their transformation tasks (e.g., within the scheduler) are based on formal techniques. The latter would guarantee that the produced hardware implementations are correct-by-construction. This means that by definition of the formal process, the functionality of the implementation matches the functionality of the behavioral specification model (the source code). In this way, the design will need to be verified only at the behavioral level, without spending hours or days (or even weeks for complex designs) of simulations of the generated register-transfer level (RTL), or even worse of the netlists generated by a subsequent RTL synthesis of the implementations. The behavioral code can be verified by building a module that produces test vectors and reads the results and this verification can be realized with simple compilation and execution with the host compiler of the language (e.g., GNU C compiler and linker). This type of behavioral verification is orders of magnitude faster than RTL or even more than gate-netlist simulations.

Moreover, the hardware/software codesign approach, which is followed by the author's work, allows to model the whole embedded (or other) digital system in ADA (currently a C front-end is being developed as well), and coverified at this level using standard compile and execute techniques with the host ADA compiler. This also enables the building of the system under test as well as the testbench code to be developed in the same format, which enforces functional verification and debugging at the earliest steps of the product design and development flow. In this way, and by using standard and formal techniques, late reiterations in the development flow are avoided and thus valuable project time is saved, so as to focus to more important, system level design decisions such as the target architecture and tradeoffs between hardware and software implementations of the various system parts. For the system compilation, a formal IKBS methodology is used, by combining compiler-compiler and logic programming techniques, borrowed from areas such as formal compilation and artificial intelligence.

The codesign techniques of the author's work produce superior hardware module performance and their results are more adaptable to different host architectures, as compared with traditional-platform-based and IP-based approaches. This is due to the fact that platform-based design makes a lot of system and interface assumptions about the target architecture which are often found out that they are not true, and, therefore, the delivered parts are not compatible and cannot be plugged into the target system. Even in the best case, the codesign results are found to be suboptimal due to mismatching performances of the core and the interface functionality of the delivered modules. The same apply for the IP-based design, plus the time spent to understand the IP's function and interfaces, and build proper test procedures for IP verification flows when the given IP is plugged in the target architecture.

This paper presents the formal IKBS methodology, as well as the usability and benefits of it in the prototype hardware compilation system. Section 2 discusses related work. After a review of existing intermediate formats, the author's intermediate predicate format is analyzed in Section 3. The hardware compilation design flow and in particular the loading of the IPF database in the IKBS engine are explained in Section 4. Section 5 summarizes the inference logic rules of the IKBS engine of the back-end phase of the prototype behavioral synthesizer. In Section 6, the mechanism of the formal high-level synthesis transformations is presented. Section 7 outlines the structure and logic of the PARCS optimizing scheduler which is part of the back-end compiler rules. Section 8 explains the available options for target microarchitecture generation and the communication of the accelerators with their computing environment. Section 9 outlines the general execution environment for the results of the hardware/software codesign methodology of this paper. Sections 10 and 11 discuss experimental results, draw useful conclusions, and propose future work.

2. Background and Review of ESL Methodologies

2.1. The Scheduling Task. The scheduling problem covers two major categories: time-constrained scheduling and resource-constrained scheduling. Time-constrained scheduling attempts to result into the lowest hardware cost (e.g., area or number of functional units) when the total number of control steps (states) is given (time constraint). Resource-constrained scheduling attempts to produce the fastest schedule (the fewest control states) when the amount of hardware resources or hardware area are given (resource constraint). Integer linear programming (ILP) formulations for the scheduling problem have been proposed. However, their execution time grows exponentially with the increase of the number of variables and inequalities. Therefore, ILP is generally impractical and it is suitable only for very small designs. Heuristic methods have been introduced to deal with large designs and to provide suboptimal but practical implementations. Heuristic scheduling uses in general two techniques: constructive solutions and iterative refinement. Two constructive methods are the as-soon-as-possible (ASAP) and the as-late-as-possible (ALAP) approach. Both

of these methods place the hardware operations in a precedence-based list. With the ASAP method, one operation is taken from the list at a time and the algorithm tries to position the operation at the earliest possible control step. With the ALAP method, each operation from the list is moved at the latest possible control step. The operations that were placed in the same control steps of by both ASAP and ALAP methods constitute the design's critical path.

In both ASAP and ALAP scheduling, the operations that belong to the critical path of the design are not given any special priority over other operations. Thus, and particularly when the resource constraints are too hard and so only a few operations can be assigned on similar functional units in each control cycle, excessive delay may be imposed on the critical path operations. This is not good for the quality of the produced implementation. On the contrary, list scheduling utilizes a global priority function to select the next operation to be scheduled. This global priority function can be either the mobility [1] of the operation or its urgency [2]. The mobility of an operation is the difference between its ASAP and ALAP control step in absolute terms. Force-directed scheduling [3] calculates the range of control steps for each operation between the operation's ASAP and ALAP state assignment. It then attempts to reduce the total number of functional units of the design's implementation, in order to evenly distribute the operations of the same type into all of the available states of the range. This is done by using distribution graphs of operations, which are assigned to the same state.

The problem with constructive scheduling is that there is not any lookahead into future assignment of operations into the same control step. In this way, the generated design implementation may be suboptimal. In contrast to this, the iterative scheduling produces new schedules, by iteratively rescheduling sequences of operations that maximally reduce the cost functions [4], after an initial schedule is delivered by any of the above scheduling algorithms. When no further improvement can be achieved, the scheduling execution stops. The above scheduling techniques are usually applied on linear dataflow dominated sequences of operations. In order to schedule and place control-intensive designs which include constructs such as loops, loop pipelining [5], and loop folding [6], different techniques have been reported in the bibliography.

2.2. Allocation and Binding Tasks. Allocation determines the type of resource storage and functional units, selected from the library of components, for each data object and operation of the input program. Allocation also calculates the number of resources of each type that are needed to implement every operation or data variable. Binding assigns operations, data variables, data structures, and data transfers onto functional units, storage elements (registers or memory blocks) and interconnections, respectively. Also binding makes sure that the design's functionality does not change by using the selected library components. The three interdependent tasks of binding are functional-unit binding, storage-element binding, and interconnection binding. Functional-unit binding assigns operations onto functional units and operators (e.g., adders, subtractors, multipliers, ALUs) from the available resource library. Storage binding maps data objects such as variables, constants, and data structures (e.g., arrays, or records) onto hardware elements such as registers, wires (connected on the power or ground lines) and RAMs/ROMs, respectively. Interconnection binding maps data transfers onto sets of interconnection units, along with the necessary multiplexing to implement the required data routing in the delivered hardware implementation. All of these are placed on the datapath implementation of the design after HLS runs on it.

Generally, there are three kinds of solutions to the allocation problem: constructive techniques, decomposition techniques, and iterative approaches. Constructive allocation techniques start with an empty implementation and progressively build the datapath and control parts of the implementation by adding more functional, storage, and interconnection elements while they traverse the CDFG (control-data-flow-graph) or any other type of internal graph/representation formats. Constructive techniques are fairly simple but the implementations they produce are far from optimal. Decomposition techniques divide the allocation problem into a sequence of well-defined independent subtasks. Each such subtask is a graph-based theoretical problem which is solved with well-known graph methods. Three such graph-based methods are the clique partitioning, the left-edge technique, and the weighted bipartite matching technique. The three allocation subtasks of functional unit, storage, and interconnection allocation are mapped onto the problem of graph clique partitioning [7]. The nodes of the graph are operations, values, and interconnection elements. The task of finding the minimum cliques in the graph which is the solution for the subtasks, is an NP-hard problem, therefore, heuristic approaches [7] are utilized for allocation.

Because the conventional subtask of storage allocation ignores the side-effects between the storage and interconnections allocation, when using the clique partitioning technique, graph edges are enhanced with weights that represent the effect on interconnection complexity. This complexity is caused by sharing registers among different variables of the design [3]. The left-edge algorithm is applied on the storage allocation problem, and it allocates the minimum number of registers [8]. The left-edge algorithm has a polynomial complexity against the clique partitioning which is NP-complete. Nevertheless, the left-edge algorithm does not take into account the interdependence with the interconnect cost. This is considered in the weighted graph edges of the clique partitioning solution.

A weighted, bipartite-matching algorithm can be used to solve both the storage and functional unit allocation problems. First, a bipartite graph is generated which contains two disjoint sets, for example, one for variables and one for registers, or one for operations and one for functional units [9]. An edge between one node of the one of the sets and one node of the other represents an allocation of, for example, a variable to a register. The bipartite-matching algorithm has a polynomial complexity and it allocates the minimum number of registers. Moreover, this algorithm considers the effect of register allocation on the

design's interconnection elements because the edges of the two sets of the graph are weighted [9]. The datapaths that are generated by either constructive or decomposition allocation techniques can be further improved iteratively. This is done either by a simple assignment exchange, using the pairwise exchange of the simulated annealing, or by using a branch-and-bound approach. The latter reallocates groups of elements of different types in order to refine the datapath implementation [10].

2.3. Early High-Level Synthesis. HLS has been an active research field for more than two decades now. Early approaches of experimental synthesis tools that synthesized small subsets of programming constructs or proprietary modeling formats have emerged since the late 1980s. As an example, an early tool that generated hardware structures from algorithmic code, written in the PASCAL-like, digital system specification language (DSL) is reported in [11]. In this work, the three domains of integrated circuit designs were defined as the behavioral, structural, and geometrical. Behavioral synthesis is the transformation of behavioral descriptions (e.g., program code) into circuit structures. This can be done at different levels, for example, at the register-transfer, at the gate or logic level, at the transistor or electric level, and so forth. The geometrical domain involves the generation of the integrated circuit geometrical features such as the circuit layout on the silicon array. What the authors in [11] named as behavioral synthesis is of course defined in our days in much more detail, it is extended at the abstraction level of the specifications and it comes under the name high-level synthesis (HLS). The problem of HLS is extremely complex, but it is much more understood in our days than in the early days of the first synthesis systems. The main tasks that were identified in [11] were compilation, datapath, and control synthesis from imperative specifications (e.g., in DSL), optimization (area and speed), and circuit assembly. The circuit structure generated in [11] is coded in the structure description language (STRUDEL), and this in turn in ported to the Carlsruhe Digital System CADDY to generate the geometrical description of the circuit. Examples of other behavioral circuit specification languages of that time, apart from DSL, were DAISY [12], ISPS [13], and MIMOLA [14]. The synthesis system in [11] performs the circuit compilation in two steps: first step is datapath synthesis which is followed by control synthesis. The authors claimed the lack of need for verification of the generated circuit after synthesis, since it is correct by construction due to automated circuit synthesis methods.

The PARSIFAL DSP synthesis system from GE Corporate and Development division was one of the earliest synthesizers that targeted DSP applications [15]. The designed circuit is described with a combination of algorithmic and structural level and using PARSIFAL it is synthesized in a bit-serial DSP circuit implementation. PARSIFAL is part of a larger E-CAD system called FACE and which included the FACE design representation and design manager core. FACE includes interfaces to synthesis tools, analysis tools, physical assembly tools, libraries, and external tools such as parsers and formatters. The synthesis subsystem of FACE is interactive and it utilizes the FACE core functions. FACE focuses on design transformations and optimizations which are suitable for pipelined and nonpipelined architectures. The FACE synthesis process includes the following tasks: minimize the execution time of expressions, maximize hardware resource sharing, insert multiplexers, and schedule operations in pipeline stages. It is thus obvious that FACE and PARSIFAL were suitable for DSP-pipelined implementations, rather than they constitute a more general hardware synthesis system.

The synthesis optimization tasks such as scheduling of operations and allocation of registers and busses, considering timing and hardware resource-constraints, are analyzed in [16]. According to [16], scheduling consists of determining the propagation delay of each operation and then assigning all operations into control steps (states) of a finite-state machine. Different types of scheduling approaches are explained. Algorithms such as list-scheduling, attempt to minimize the total execution time of the state machine while obeying to resource constraints. List-scheduling uses a local priority function to postpone the assignment of operations into states, when resource constraints are violated. On the contrary, force-directed scheduling (FDS) tries to satisfy a global execution deadline (time constraint) while minimizing the utilized hardware resources (functional units, registers and busses). The way FDS does this is by positioning similar operations in different control states, so that the concurrency of operations is balanced without increasing the total execution time of the circuit. In this way, each structural unit retains a high utilization which results into reducing the total number of units that are required to implement the design. This is achieved in three basic steps: determine the time-frame of each operation, generate a distribution graph, and calculate the force associated with each operation assignment. In [16], minimizing the cost of storage units and interconnections is addressed as well. The force-directed list scheduling (FDLS) algorithm attempts to implement the fastest schedule while satisfying fixed hardware resource constraints. FDLS is similar to the list scheduling approach. However, in FDLS, the force is the priority function rather than the mobility of urgency of operations. Another implementation exploration approach is also outlined in [16] by combining FDS and FDLS. In this approach, first the FDS method is applied to find the near-optimal allocation by satisfying a fixed maximum time constraint. Then, the designer runs FDLS on the results of FDS in order to try and find an even faster implementation. After scheduling, the following problems are addressed: bind operations to functional units, bind storage actions to registers, and bind data-transfer operations to interconnections. Also merging registers, merging multiplexers, and good design partitioning are analyzed in [16]. However, there are no indications as to how fast the synthesis algorithms run using the publication's techniques.

The authors in [17] defined as the main problem in HLS the mapping of a behavioral description into a register-transfer level (RTL) circuit description which contains a datapath and a control unit. In our days, the latter can be implemented with a finite-state machine (RTL) which controls a datapath of operators, storage elements and a number of data-steering multiplexers. According to [17], the main tasks in HLS include allocation, scheduling, and binding. According to [18], scheduling is finding the sequence of which operations to execute in a specific order so as to produce a schedule of control steps with allocated operations in each step of the schedule; allocation is defining the required number of functional, storage, and interconnect units; binding is assigning operations to functional units, variables, and values to storage elements and forming the interconnections amongst them to form a complete working circuit that executes the functionality of the source behavioral model. First, the input behavioral description is transformed into a control/data-flow graph (CDFG). Then, various optimization algorithms run on this CDFG in order to drive the implementation of the final circuit implementation. The CDFG captures the algorithmic characteristics of the input behavioral program (e.g., in VHDL or Verilog) as well as the data and control dependency between the operations to be scheduled. Apparently, two operations that have a read-after-write dependency from one another, they cannot be scheduled in the same control step (or state). The authors in [18] introduce various problems that are encountered within various scheduling approaches: the unconstrained scheduling (UCS) problem, the time-constrained scheduling (TCS) problem, the resource-constrained scheduling (RCS) problem and mixed approaches such as the time- and resource-constrained scheduling (TRCS) problem. Also, advanced synthesis issues such as chaining (concatenating a different operations within the same control step in a chain) and multicycling (spreading the execution of an operation over more than one control step), handling in a special way control structures such as nested if-then-else and loop constructs, and various issues of constraining the global execution time and the latency of operations by the user of the synthesis tool, are addressed in [18]. Moreover, [18] defines and analyses the most common scheduling algorithms and approaches which include as-soon-as-possible (ASAP) scheduling, as-late-as-possible (ALAP) scheduling, list scheduling, force-directed scheduling, and integer linear programming (ILP).

The V compiler [19] translates sequential descriptions into RTL models using parsing, scheduling, and resource allocation. The source sequential descriptions are written in the V language which includes queues, asynchronous calls, and cycle blocks and it is tuned to a kind of parallel hardware RTL implementations. The utilized parser is built from a LALR grammar, and the parse tree includes leaves representing syntactic tokens and vertices (nodes) representing syntactic units of the source code. The V compiler marks the statements in the generated RTL and simulation code so that the user can trace the statements back in the V code by using and observing the token number. It also treats the hardware state machine as a directed, (possibly) cyclic control graph. Each vertex of the graph represents a state of the state machine and a set of operators to execute on the particular cycle. Each edge between vertices represents a state transition which can be guarded by a Boolean variable. Thus, if a vertex has multiple transitions to other vertices, then the conditions of these multiple edges must be mutually exclusive. The inputs and outputs of operations and the conditions on the state transitions and operators are initially treated all as variables. Later and during RTL implementation, these variables are implemented with wires or with registers. The V compiler utilizes percolation scheduling [20] to "compress" the state machine in time, and achieve the required degree of parallelism by meeting time constraints. Apart from the RTL models, the compiler generates also simulation code in PL/I so to simulate and verify the generated hardware implementation models.

A timing network is generated once from every different behavioral design in [21] and is annotated with parameters for every different scheduling approach. The produced timing network is based solely on the control and data graphs that are derived from the input specification, before scheduling and allocation. The scheduling optimization approach in [21] attempts to satisfy a given design cycle for a given set of resource constraints, using the timing model parameters. An integrated approach for scheduling, allocation, and binding in datapath synthesis is explained in [22]. Using highly generalized modules, this approach uses an integer linear program (ILP) which minimizes a weighted sum of area and execution time of the implementation. We can say that this implements a mixed time and resource-constrained scheduling. The above modules can execute an arbitrary number of different operations, using, for example, different numbers of control steps for different operations. Moreover, the same operation can be executed on a variety of modules possibly involving different number of control steps. The synthesis approach in [22] attempts to minimize the execution time and the hardware area of an initial data-flow graph (DFG) by using two types of constraints: the data dependency constraints (DD-constraints) and an operation ordering based on the sharing of functional units by the operations (UU-constraints). Also, this work [22] includes extensions of the ILP approach for pipelined functional units and for operation chaining. A prototype synthesizer called Symphony [22], in combination with three benchmarks that were executed through the Symphony system, namely, a fifth-order elliptical wave filter, a differential equation, and a bandpass filter. For these benchmarks and according to the authors of [22], the Symphony tool delivers better area and speed than ADPS [23]. It seems from the type of scheduling approach as well as the presented tests that the approach in [22] is rather suitable for data-flow-dominated designs such as DSP blocks and not for more general complex control flow designs.

The CALLAS synthesis framework [24] transforms algorithmic, behavioral VHDL models into VHDL RTL and gate netlists, under timing constraints. These netlists are then implemented into available technologies using available commercial logic synthesis tools. If the timing constraints are too tight for the scheduler, then CALLAS produces an ASAP schedule and issues a relevant error message. The EXPANDER tool is connected to the back-end of CALLAS in order to support low-level synthesis of the produced implementation using specific delay, area, and library components. CALLAS produces the final implementation via

a number of iterative high-level and RTL transformations upon an initial structure which is found in the algorithmic VHDL source code. The user of CALLAS can drive these transformations by using a synthesis script. Compilation of the algorithmic code (from a subset of the VHDL language) delivers initial data flow and control flow graphs, and an initial processing generates a starting ALAP schedule without resource constraints. Afterwards, the control flow graph is reduced so that the fixed I/O operation schedule is satisfied. The initial structure is optimized by a number of high-level and RTL refining transformations. Then, the produced structure is further going through a logic optimization and technology mapping by the EXPANDER tools, and thus a VHDL or EDIF [25, 26] netlist is generated. The generated circuit is implemented using a Moore-type finite-state machine (FSM), which is consistent with the semantics of the VHDL subset used for the specification code. The synthesis transformations in CALLAS include removal of superfluous edges in the control flow graph, removal of unnecessary data transfers between registers, and control flow graph reduction (scheduling) so as to meet the specified I/O-timing constraints. Other optimizations include lifetime analysis, register sharing, operator sharing, multiplexor optimization, arithmetic and logic transformations, optimizing of the datapath/controller interface, flattening of complex functional units, partitioning, and logic minimization. These optimizations utilize techniques such as clique partitioning, path analysis, and symbolic simulation. Formal verification techniques such as equivalence checking, which checks the equivalence between the original VHDL FSM and the synthesized FSM are used in the CALLAS framework by using the symbolic verifier of the circuit verification environment (CVE) system [27]. A number of benchmarks and industrial designs were executed within the CALLAS framework and confirmed its usability.

The Prolemy framework [28] allows for an integrated hardware-software codesign methodology from the specification through to synthesis of hardware and software components, simulation, and evaluation of the implementation. Prolemy is a tool-set that allows the simulation, and rapid prototyping of heterogeneous hardware + software systems. The block is the basic unit of modularity inside Prolemy. Blocks communicate with each other and with their computing environment through portholes. The tools of Prolemy can synthesize assembly code for a programmable DSP core (e.g., DSP processor), which is built for a synthesis-oriented application. A domain in Ptolemy consists of a set of blocks, targets, and associated schedulers that conform to the operational semantics. These semantics determine how blocks interact. Some of the simulation domains supported by Ptolemy include the synchronous dataflow (SDF), dynamic dataflow (DDF), and digital hardware modeling (Thor). For example, for every commercial DSP processor there are corresponding models and a simulator. This simulator is invoked when the user wants to verify a design that contains the corresponding processor. Mixed digital and analog components, for example, A/D and D/A converters and filters can be represented as components with their functional models in the SDF domain. The engineers of

Ptolemy have supported the generation of C and C++ code for a variety of processors. In Ptolemy, an initial model of the entire system is partitioned into the software and hardware parts which are synthesized in combination with their interface synthesis. Then, the hardware, software, and interface implementation models can be cosimulated and the overall system prototype can be evaluated. The unified representation of hardware and software components allows the migration of functions between the two implementations with their interfaces being automatically synthesized as well. This process is not fully automatic but the users of Ptolemy are benefited with interoperability of the tools.

The Cosyma framework [29] realizes an iterative partitioning process, based on hardware extraction algorithm which is driven by a cost function. The primary target in this work is to minimize customized hardware within microcontrollers but the same time to allow for space exploration of large designs. The Cosyma hardware-software cosynthesis targets a processor core, memory, and custom coprocessing engines. In the Cosyma flow, the implementation of the system focuses on the generation of machine code for the embedded microprocessor. Custom hardware replaces the equivalent software parts, only when timing constraints are violated by the generalized processor code, or when the completion of the embedded system requires basic, available, and cheap I/O peripherals. The specialized coprocessors of the embedded system can be synthesized using HLS tools. Hardware/software partitioning is automatic in the Cosyma flow. Initially, the whole system is implemented in a set of hardware components. Then, gradually as many as possible of these hardware components are transformed into software components, with the precondition that timing constraints and system synchronization are satisfied. The specification language is based on C and it contains the following extensions: timing (minimum and maximum delays), tasks, and task intercommunication. Partitioning occurs at different levels of system granularity: task, function, basic block, and single statement. Parallelism in the Cosyma C language is explicit and it is defined by the user (the programmer). The extended syntax (ES) graph is used as the internal representation of the design in Cosyma. ESG is extended by a symbol table as well as data and control dependencies. The ES graph is used for both partitioning and cost estimation as well as for software and hardware C generation. The hardware description is in turn ported to the HLS Olympus tool [30]. Cosyma utilizes its ES internal format to estimate possible speedups of the critical loops in the design and, therefore, aid towards the required software-hardware partitioning. Partitioning is based on a partitioning cost function to drive the hardware implementation of the system components that can be implemented well in hardware. Such a cost function includes knowledge about synthesis, compilers, and libraries. An example is a specific cost function for the extraction of coprocessors that implement computation-time-intensive parts of the application such as nested loops. The work in [29] included tests and experimental results based on a configuration of an embedded system, which is built around the Sparc microprocessor.

AMICAL is a VHDL-based behavioral synthesis tool of the early 1990s [31]. A number of constraints were imposed on the writing style of VHDL in order to use AMICAL for HLS compilation of hardware architectures. One strong application use of AMICAL was the synthesis of control-intensive communication protocols. In order to achieve this, AMICA utilizes control-flow graphs, dynamic loop scheduling, in order to represent and process constructs such as nested loops, unstructured control statements such as loop exits wait statements used for synchronization. Nevertheless, AMICAL is not strictly an HLS system with the meaning given to HLS in this paper, since instead of general purpose programming format, it accepts (and it is oriented to) descriptions in VHDL which requires the designer to think about hardware-specific features when modeling of the system is realized.

The work in [32] discusses a methodology for cosimulation and cosynthesis of mixed hardware-software specifications. During cosynthesis, hardware-software partitioning is executed in combination with control parallelism transformations. The hardware-software partition is defined by a set of application-level functions which are implemented with application-specific hardware. The control parallelism is defined by the interaction of the processes of the functional behavior of the specified system. Finding the appropriate control concurrency involves splitting of merging processes or moving functionality from one process to another. The cosimulation environment produces a mixed system model that is functionally correct but it may not meet design goals. The cosynthesis tools are then used to modify the hardware-software partition and the control concurrency so that design goals are satisfied. Afterwards, the software part is implemented with standard compilation into system memory and the hardware part is synthesized with HLS tools and implemented with reconfigurable Xilinx FPGAs and two field-programmable interconnect chips from Aptix. All of these modules are plugged in the backplane of the host computer, so that implementation measurements can be realized. There are three abstractions of hardware-software interactions: send/receive/wait transactions between application program and custom hardware, register read/write between the I/O driver running in the host computer and the bus interface of the custom hardware, and bus transactions between the two I/O bus sides. The system behavior is modeled using a set of communicating sequential processes [33]. Each process can be assigned either to hardware or to software implementation. The following types of interprocess communication primitives exist in the system: synchronized data transfer, unsynchronized (unbuffered) data transfer, synchronization without data transfer, and communication with a shared memory space. Cosimulation is implemented in [32] using a Verilog simulator and a Verilog PLI interface. Two example applications were used to evaluate the cosynthesis and cosimulation environment: the Sphinx speech phoneme recognition system and a data compression/encryption application.

Yet another hardware-software codesign methodology is presented in [34], which employs synthesis of heterogeneous systems. The synthesis process is driven by timing constraints which drive the mapping of tasks onto hardware or software parts so that the performance requirements of the intended system are met. This method is based on using modeling and synthesis of programs written in the HardwareC language. This enables the use of the Olympus chip synthesis system for prototyping of the designed application [30]. A set of interacting processes which are instantiated in design blocks using declarative semantics are included in the HardwareC model. When all tasks are completed, the hosting process restarts itself. All of the processes can execute concurrently in the system model. Hierarchically related sequencing graphs are produced from the input HardwareC specification. Within each graph, vertices represent input program operations and edges represent dependencies between operations. Two vertices, namely, the source (beginning) and sink (end) represent no operations. Operations in different graphs can pass messages to each other in the graph model, in the same manner as send and receive. This is a very important feature in modeling of heterogeneous systems because the processor (which implements the software part of specification) and the custom hardware (which implements the hardware part of specification) may run on different clocks and speeds. Timing constraints are used to select the specific system implementation so as to satisfy specific performance requirements. Timing constraints are of two types: min/max delay constraints and execution rate constraints. For example, minimum delay constraints are captured by providing weights at the edges of the graph, to indicate delay to the corresponding source operations of each edge. Performance measurement is done on the basis of operation delays. These delays are estimated separately for the hardware and software parts of the system based on the type of hardware technology which is used to implement the hardware part of the system, and the processor which is used to run the software. The assignment of an operation to software or hardware implementations affects the delay of the operation. Moreover, moving operations from the hardware to software parts and vise versa involve additional delays due to emerging intercommunication delays. All these delays are used to determine the hardware/software partitioning of the final system implementation. An example application which was used to test the methodology in [34] was an Ethernet-based network coprocessor. The authors concluded that the use of their proposed hardware-software codesign methodology can aid significantly the design and development of embedded real-time systems which have a simple configuration as compared to that of a general purpose computing system.

2.4. Next-Generation High-Level Synthesis Tools. More advanced methodologies and tools started appearing from the late 1990s and continue with more improved input programming code sets as well as scheduling and other optimization algorithms. Furthermore, system level synthesis matured in the last decade by using more (application-wise) specialized and platform-oriented methodologies. The CoWare hardware-software codesign environment [35] is based on a data model that allows the user to specify, simulate, and produce heterogeneous implementations from heterogeneous specification source models. The choice of implementing real-time telecommunications DSP transformations on programmable DSP processors or application-specific hardware is driven by tradeoffs between cost, power, performance, and flexibility. The synthesis approach in [35] focuses on designing telecommunication systems that contain DSP, control loops, and user interfaces. The synchronous dataflow (SDF) type of algorithms, found in a category of DSP applications, can easily be synthesized into hardware from languages such as SILAGE [36], DFL [37], and LUSTRE [38]. The advantage of this type of designs is that they can be scheduled at compile time and the execution of the compiled code can be two orders of magnitude faster than event-driven VHDL (e.g., RTL) simulations. In contrast to this, dynamic dataflow (DDF) algorithms consume and produce tokens that are data dependent, and thus they allow for complex if-then-else and while loop control constructs. One way to deal with the data-dependent DDF algorithms is to map them onto the worst case SDF and schedule them at compile time. Another way is to partition the DDF into partial SDFs that are triggered by internal or external Boolean conditions. Then, these partial SDFs need to be scheduled at run time using the I/O timing constraints of the DSP signals and other external events. CAD systems that allow for specifying both SDF and DDF algorithms and perform as much as possible static scheduling are the DSP station from Mentor Graphics [39], PTOLEMY [40], GRAPE-II [41], COSSAP from Synopsys, and SPW from the Alta group [42]. Processes are used to realize modularity in the specification models of the CoWare tool [35]. A behavioral interface with read/write ports implements the communication between processes. Process ports that communicate with each other are connected through a channel. The data model is hierarchical and allows for gradual refinement of channels, ports, and protocols into lower levels of objects, by continuously adding detail. The most abstract object is the primitive object. In contrast, a hierarchical object contains implementation detail. A thread is a single flow of control within a process. There are slave threads and autonomous threads [35]. Communication between threads in different processes is called interprocess communication. Shared variables or signals, that are declared within the context of a process, are used for intraprocess communication. Channels and ports can be refined via adding more detail onto them, through the CoWare's design flow. The CoWare data model is suitable for merging of processes and for design for reuse and reuse of designs. Software/hardware communication is implemented in CoWare by means of memory-mapped I/O, instruction-programmed I/O, and interrupt control modules. The CoWare methodology was evaluated in [35] using a design example, which is a pager, based on spread-spectrum techniques. One important conclusion in [35] was that there is a pressing need for bottom-up formal verification tools, which can evaluate both functionality and timing of the design before and after synthesis.

C models that include dynamic memory allocation, pointers, and the functions malloc and free are mapped onto hardware in [43]. The implementation method in [43] instantiates a custom (to the application) hardware memory allocator. The allocator is coupled with the specific memory architecture. Moreover, this work supports the resolution of pointers without any restriction on the underlying data structures. Many networking and multimedia applications are implemented in hardware or mixed hardware/software platforms and they feature heavy use of complex data structures which are sometimes stored in one or multiple memory banks. An immediate result of this is that some features of C/C++ which were originally designed for software development are now strong candidates for hardware design as well. The SpC tool which was developed in [43] resolves pointer variables at compile time and thus C functional models are synthesized into hardware efficiently. In a hardware implementation of pointers, memory allocation may be distributed onto multiple memories, and the data which are referenced by the pointers may be stored in memories, registers, or wires. Therefore, the synthesis tool needs to automatically generate the appropriate circuit to allocate, access (read/write) and deallocate data. The potential values of all pointers of an application program are identified by a compiler technique called pointer analysis. In order to implement dynamic memory allocation in hardware, there is a need to synthesize circuits to access, modify, or deallocate the location which is referenced by each pointer. For this purpose, the aliasing information [43] must be both safe and accurate. The authors in [43] assume that the computational complexity of flow-sensitive and context-sensitive analysis is not high because of the small size and simplicity of the programs and function calls which are used in hardware synthesis. This of course is not guaranteed since modern system descriptions could easily contain some thousands of lines of hierarchical code to describe complex hardware architectures. The subset of C which is accepted by the methodology in [43] includes malloc/free and all types of pointers and type casting. However, pointers that point to data outside the scope of a process (e.g., global variables) are not allowed. The synthesis of functions in C, and, therefore, the resolution of pointers and malloc/free inside of functions, is not included in this work. In order for the C code with the pointers to be efficiently mapped onto hardware, first the memory is partitioned into sets which can include memories, registers, or wires, and which can also represent pointers. Pointers are resolved by encoding their value and generating branching statements for loads and stores. Dynamic memory allocation and deallocation is executed by custom hardware memory allocators. The SpC tool [43] takes a C function with complex data structures and generates a Verilog model. The different techniques and optimizations described above have been implemented using the SUIF compiler environment [44]. The memory model consists of distinct location sets, and it is used to map memory locations onto variables and arrays in Verilog. Then, the generated Verilog module can be synthesized using commercial synthesis tools such as the behavioral compiler of synopsys. The case studies that evaluated and tested this methodology included a video algorithm and an asynchronous transfer mode (ATM) segmentation engine.

A heuristic for scheduling behavioral specifications that include a lot of conditional control flow is presented in [45]. This heuristic is based on a specific intermediate design representation which, apart from established techniques such as chaining and multicycling, enables more advanced techniques, such as conditional resource sharing and speculative execution, which are suitable for scheduling conditional behaviors. This work intends to bridge the gap in design implementation quality between HLS results from dataflow-dominated descriptions, and those from conditional control-flow-dominated source models. Generally, although HLS was accepted by the engineering community earlier for dataflow oriented applications, it took some time before it became adopted, and it is still not widely accepted for designs that contain complex conditional control flow, such as nested if-then-else and loop constructs. This intermediate design representation is called hierarchical conditional dependency graph (HCDG). The heuristics for HLS tasks that are invented for the HCDG have been developed to deal with complex control flow that involves a degree of control hierarchy. HCDGs introduced two new concepts: a hierarchical control representation and the explicit representation of both data and control dependencies in the design. This explicit representation of control dependencies is suitable for exploring maximum parallelism in the implementation, by rearranging these control dependencies. Because exploiting parallelism is easier for custom hardware designs than for software ones, being able to express maximum parallelism at the intermediate form level of a hardware design is essential. The HCDG can be successful in avoiding the negative effects of syntactic variance effects in the specification code of the designed system.

The hierarchical control representation of HCDG enables the HLS tasks such as scheduling, allocation, and binding. In [45], symbolic names are given to the Boolean conditions under which the various operations are executed and values are assigned to variables. Those symbolic names are called guards. In an HCDG, there are two types of nodes: guard nodes and operation nodes. Guard nodes represent the symbolic names of the various conditions under which operations are executed. Operation nodes represent I/Os, computations, data multiplexing, and storage elements. In an HCDG, there are two types of edges: data dependencies and control dependencies. Data dependencies are precedence constraints from one operation node to another. This defines the dataflow-dependent order of operation execution order. Control dependencies designate which conditions (guards) must evaluate to true so that the data values are computed and considered as valid. Each operation node has its control dependency edge from its guard. Guards can be also hierarchical, which results into a graphical representation of nested control constructs (e.g., and if-then-else nested inside another if-then-else, etc.). Therefore, there is a guard hierarchy graph for every design in [45]. Deriving HCDGs from conditional behaviors is being exercised in [45], but deriving them from loop constructs is reported in the particular work [45] as being the subject of future work. In order to schedule conditional behaviors efficiently, the mutual exclusiveness of the conditions must be exploited. This means being able to conditionally share resources and schedule operations effectively. In order to do this, complete lists of mutually exclusive guards have to be constructed. For large and complex designs, this means that a very large number of mutual exclusiveness tests have to be performed on potential pairs of guards. Nevertheless, this number of tests can be drastically reduced in [45] by using the inclusion relations represented by the guard hierarchy graph. Using the above techniques, the following HLS transformations are enabled: lazy execution, node duplication, speculative execution, false-path elimination, and conditional resource sharing. Moreover, operation chaining and multicycle operations are considered. A special priority function based on guard hierarchy and graph node mobility is utilized in order to obtain the node priorities when executing scheduling. Mutual exclusiveness information is very useful for applying register allocation and for other types of resource sharing such as the one applied to interconnects. The HLS techniques presented in [45] were implemented in a prototype graphical interactive tool called CODESIS which used HCDG as its internal design representation. The tool can generate VHDL or C code from the HCDG, but no reports about translating a standard programming language into HCDG are known so far.

The HLS approach presented in [46] utilizes a coordinated set of coarse-grain and fine-grain parallelizing transformations on the input design model. These transformations are executed in order to deliver synthesis results that do not suffer from the negative effects of complex control constructs in the specification code. These transformations are applied both during a presynthesis phase and during scheduling, in order to improve the quality of synthesis output. During presynthesis, the following transformations are applied: common subexpression elimination (CSE), copy propagation, dead code elimination, loop-invariant code motion, as well as restructuring transformations such as loop unrolling and loop fusion. Then, during scheduling, aggressive speculative code motions (transformations) are used to reorder, speculate, and sometimes duplicate operations in the design. In this way, maximum parallelizing is applied on the synthesis results. A technique called dynamic CSE, dynamically coordinates CSE, speculation, and conditional speculation during scheduling. During scheduling, specific code motions are enabled, which move operations through, beyond, and into conditional blocks with the purpose of maximizing parallelism and, therefore, increase design performance. The scheduling heuristic, the code motion heuristic, dynamic transformations, and loop pipelining are executed. All of these tasks use functions from a tool library, which includes percolation and trailblazing, speculative code motions, chaining across conditions, CSE, and copy propagation. Then, during the binding and control synthesis steps, the operation and variable binding as well as FSM generation and optimization are executed. All these techniques were implemented in the SPARK HLS tool, which transforms specifications in a small subset of C into RTL VHDL hardware models. A resource-constrained scheduler is used in SPARK and it is essentially a priority-based global list scheduling heuristic. The user provides SPARK with a library of resources, which include among other details the type and number of each resource. This user library is used

by the HLS tool, to allocate operations and registers onto library components. In terms of intermediate design representations, SPARK utilizes both control/data flow graphs (CDFGs) as well as an encapsulation of basic design blocks inside hierarchical task graphs (HTGs) [46]. HTGs allow for coarse-grain code restructuring such as loop transformations and an efficient way to move operations across large pieces of specification code. This is why the combination of CDFGs and HTGs in SPARK is so successful. Nevertheless, there are serious restrictions on the subset of the C language that SPARK accepts as input, and limitations such as inability to accept design hierarchy modules (e.g., subprograms) and of "while" type of loops. SPARK is validated in [46] by synthesizing three large examples: MPEG-1, MPEG-2, and the GIMP image processing tool.

Typical HLS tasks such as scheduling, resource allocation, module binding, module selection, register binding, and clock selection are executed simultaneously in [47] so as to achieve better optimization in design energy, power, and area. The scheduling algorithm utilized in [47] applies concurrent loop optimization and multicycling and it is driven by resource constraints. The state transition graph (STG) of the design is simulated in order to generate switched capacitance matrices. These matrices are then used to estimate power/energy consumption of the design's datapath. The initial schedule is optimized by multiple execution sequences of module selection, module sharing, and register sharing tasks. Nevertheless, the input to the HLS tool which was developed in [47] is not program code in a popular language but a proprietary format representing an enhanced control-data-flow graph (CDFG) as well as an RTL design library and resource constraints. In order to facilitate the capturing of control constructs such as if-then-else and loops, as well as memory access sequences, special nodes and edges were added to enhance this proprietary CDFG. The scheduler takes the CDFG and resource constraints as input and produces a result in the form of an optimized STG. In the synthesis algorithm, the cost function (for optimization) can be area, power, or energy. The synthesis process is iterative and it continuously improves the cost function until all constraints and data dependencies are met. The iterative improvement algorithm is executed by means of multiple passes until there is no potential improvement on the cost functions. In every pass, a sequence of the following moves is generated; the moves can be module selection, module sharing and register sharing. After each move, the behavior of the system is rescheduled and the cost is reestimated. If that move generates the best reduction of cost, then the move is saved, otherwise, different moves are selected. If the cost is reduced in the current pass, then a new pass is generated and the scheduling continues. This iterative process runs until there is no potential improvement in the cost functions. The tool generates RTL Verilog implementations. The developed HLS system is targeted at control-intensive applications, and it is also applicable to dataflow-dominated designs. The system was tested using a number of control-intensive benchmarks, such as for loop, concurrent loops, nested loops, greatest common divisor, a fifth-order Elliptic wave filter, and a popular dataflow-dominated benchmark. The synthesis results focused more on power reduction up to 70% rather than area or speed results. Most of the benchmarks took a number of minutes to execute on a conventional Pentium III PC.

An incremental floorplanner is described in [48] which is used in order to combine an incremental behavioral and physical optimization into HLS. These techniques were integrated into an existing interconnect-aware HLS tool called ISCALP [49]. The new combination was named IFP-HLS (incremental floorplanner high-level synthesis tool), and it attempts to concurrently improve the design's schedule, resource binding and floorplan, by integrating high-level and physical design algorithms. Moreover, the impact of interconnect on area and power consumption of integrated circuits was considered in this work. To define the problem this method is based on the following equation:

$$T_{\text{clock}} = \frac{T_s}{c_{\text{steps}}}, \qquad (1)$$

where T_{clock} is the system clock period, T_s is the constraint on the input data rate (sample period), and c_{steps} is the number of clock cycles required to process an input sample. Given c_{steps}, an ASAP schedule is generated for an initial solution to determine whether it meets timing. An iterative improvement algorithm is then applied on this initial solution, in order to reduce the switched capacitance while it still satisfies the sample period constraint. From the way the problem and the solution are defined in this HLS approach, it seems that the latter is suitable for dataflow-dominated designs and not for control-intensive applications. IFP-HLS generates one initial solution, at the maximum number of c_{steps} and then it applies incremental floorplanning and it eliminates redundant operations. In this way, the solution is improving as the c_{steps} decreases. If a solution meets its timing requirement after rescheduling, then rebinding is not necessary. In any other case, it rebinds some tasks and uses parallel execution to improve performance. Possible pairs of tasks that are initially assigned to the same functional unit are split onto separate functional units [48].

For a given c_{steps}, the floorplan is incrementally modified to see if this improves the solution quality. If it does, then this change is saved. Otherwise, the floorplan change is rejected and other modifications are attempted to determine whether they improve the solution, and so on [48]. In order to guide these changes, the tool extracts physical information from the current incrementally generated floorplan. IFP-HLS incrementally performs scheduling, allocation, and binding by modifying iteratively c_{steps}, and it determines which operations need to be rescheduled or rebound (split) in order to meet the timing constraints. In each step, the floorplanner is updated. An incremental simulated annealing floorplanner is embedded into the IFP-HLS tool which was designed for design quality and not for speed. The floorplanner handles blocks with different aspect ratios and generates nonslicing floorplans. Every synthesis move either removes a single module or it splits a module into two. Therefore, most of the modifications are small and their effects on the floorplan are local, rather than global. In this way, an existing floorplan can be used as the base for each new floorplan. In practice,

the authors found this approach to deliver quality-of-results and performance improvements, even compared with a very fast constructive floorplanner.

Fifteen different benchmarks were used to evaluate the utility of this approach in [48]. The average improvements of IFP-HLS over ISCALP, for implementations with nonunity aspect ratio functional units, are 14% in area, 4% in power consumption, 172% in reduction in the number of merge operations, and 369% in CPU time. The average improvements of IFP-HLS over ISCALP, for implementations with unity aspect ratio functional units, are 12% in area, 7% in power consumption, 100% in reduction in the number of merge operations, and for some benchmarks the IFP-HLS CPU run time was 6 times less than that of the ISCALP method.

The study in [50] discusses an HLS methodology which is suitable for the design of distributed logic and memory architectures. Beginning with a behavioral description of the system in C, the methodology starts with behavioral profiling in order to extract simulation statistics of computations and references of array data. This allows the generation of footprints which contain the accessed array locations and the frequency of their occurrence. Array data reference operations with similar access patterns are grouped together into a computation partition, using these footprints. A method to assign each such partition onto a different subsystem is used. In this way, a cost function is minimized that includes balancing the workloads, synchronization overheads, and locality of data accesses. Then, array data are distributed into different partitions. This is done so that the data accesses will be as much as possible local to each subsystem, based on the clustering of their reference operations. Synchronization code is inserted into the implementation's behavior, in order to implement correct communication between different partitions. This results into a distributed logic/memory microarchitecture RTL model, which is synthesizable with existing RTL synthesizers, and which consists of two or more partitions, depending on the clustering of operations that was applied earlier. These techniques are implemented into an industrial tool called Cyber [51]. Several benchmark applications were run on the tool to produce distributed logic/memory implementations. The results featured a performance increase of up to twice and reduction up to 2.7 times of the delay X energy product over single-memory and homogeneously partitioned designs.

Communicating processes which are part of a system specification are implemented in [52]. In contrast to the conventional HLS approach which synthesizes each concurrent process of the system individually, the impact of the operation scheduling is considered globally in [52], in the system critical path (as opposed to the individual process critical path). First, the system is scheduled by assuming that there are unlimited resources for each process. Then, the scheduled design is simulated, and using the simulation's execution traces, system performance is analyzed and the critical path(s) of the behavior is (are) extracted. Using this information about the design, the criticality of operations is calculated based upon whether they belong to the critical path(s) or the near-critical path(s). Then, the relative resource requirement of each process is calculated which depends on the type and number of critical operations that a process contains. With this information for each process, the resources for the overall system are budgeted. The resource budget is then used as a constraint to reschedule the whole design. The rescheduled design is simulated again and the critical paths are yet one more time extracted from the traces. If the critical path changes, then the above process is repeated again and again until the critical path remains the same after each resource reallocation. When the extracted critical paths become the same, and using the last resource budget, the behavior model is passed to the rest of the HLS tasks, such as resource sharing and generation of the controller and datapath. In this way, the RTL hardware implementation of the multiple processes is built. It is argued by the authors in [52] that this methodology allocates the resources where they are mostly needed in the system, which is in the critical paths, and in this way it improves the overall multiprocess designed system performance.

The work in [53] contributes towards incorporating memory access management within an HLS design flow. It mainly targets digital signal processing (DSP) applications but also more general streaming systems can be included along with specific performance constraints. A particular memory sequencer architecture is discussed in [53] and utilized by its methodology. This methodology can pipeline both static and dynamic memory access sequences. In order to take advantage of the memory sequencer, specific enhancements of the typical HLS flow are introduced. The targeted architecture template for the signal processors includes the processing unit (PU) which contains the datapath and a controller, the memory unit (MemU) which executes pipeline accesses to memories, and the communication unit (ComU) which handles communication from/to the rest of the design's computing environment. The synthesis process is performed on the extended data-flow graph (EDFG) which is based on the signal flow graph. The EDFG models both the access and data computations, the transfers of data, and the condition statements for addressing, computation, and data transfers, respectively. Mutually exclusive scheduling methods [54, 55] are implemented with the EDFG. This is achieved because EDFG allows for data and conditional semantics to be handled in the same way, and thus the exploitation of potential design parallelism can be maximized.

Special EDFG structure nodes are defined, so as to represent the arrays and their components access in the application. In order to handle memory access dependencies, the write after write, and read after write dependencies are taken into account and the structure nodes are renamed after for example, a write access. This is done in order to remove ambiguous dependency accesses for scalar load and store operations. Conditional nodes are also defined in EDFG. This is done so as to model conditioned operations and memory accesses. There are dependencies between the calculation of the condition's value and all the included conditioned operations (inside the conditional structure). The function $t(u)$, for operation u, annotates the EDFG edge, in order to capture the delay (time) that operation takes from the change of its inputs to propagate the result at the outputs (see the following paragraphs for HLS internal format descriptions). This delay is essentially the transfer time from the predecessor of the operation, to its successor. In a first annotation step, all operations, including the dynamic address calculations, are assumed to be implemented in the datapath unit of PU. Moreover, using the available memory mapping data, the data nodes are also annotated. In order to transform an annotated graph into a coherent graph [53], the location of the graph nodes is checked. If the location of all the predecessors and successors of a node is not the same, then a transfer node is inserted. Based on a set of criteria [53], dynamic address computation operations are moved from the datapath unit onto the sequencer, which is called address computation balancing. This is done so as to increase the overall system performance. The processed by these annotations and improvements graph is then given to the GAUT HLS tool [56] to perform operator selection and allocation, scheduling, and binding. GAUT implements a static list scheduling algorithm so as to maximally parallelize the initial schedule. This methodology is suitable for dataflow-dominated applications such as video streaming and linear DSP algorithms.

A combined execution of decomposition and pattern-matching techniques is applied on HLS problems, in order to reduce the total circuit area in [57]. The datapath area is reduced by decomposing multicycle operations, so that they are executed on monocycle functional units (FUs that take one clock cycle to execute and deliver their results). Furthermore, when other techniques used to guide operator, decompositions such as regularity exploitation can deliver high-quality circuits. In this way, operations extract their most common operation pattern, usually repeated in many clock cycles. Thus, the circuit that is needed to execute the selected operation pattern is shared among many operations in many cycles, and, therefore, the total hardware area is drastically reduced. The algorithm presented in [57] takes as input a behavioral design description and time constraints, and it selectively decomposes complex operations into smaller ones, in order to schedule in every clock cycle a similar number of decomposed fragments of operators, with the same pattern. This method considers only operation decompositions that meet the time constraints. Also, some of the decompositions reduce the length of the clock cycle. This results into increasing the system's performance. The HLS output is a complete datapath with FUs, multiplexers, registers and some glue logic, as well as a controller. The number, type, and width of the resources used in the produced datapath are generally independent from the input behavioral hardware description. This is due to the operation decompositions which are applied through the synthesis process.

A simple formal model that relies on an FSM-based formalism for describing and synthesizing on-chip communication protocols and protocol converters between different bus-based protocols is discussed in [58]. The discussed formalism enables the detailed modeling of existing commercial protocols, and the analysis of protocol compatibility. Furthermore, the most important is that it facilitates the automated and correct-by-construction synthesis of protocol converters between existing popular communication protocols. The utilized FSM-based format is at an abstraction level which is low enough for its automatic translation into HDL descriptions. The generated HDL models are synthesizable with commercial tools. Typically a system-on-a-chip (SoC) includes intellectual property (IP) blocks that are connected together either directly on a bus or via specialized wrappers. The wrappers play the role of converters from the IP's interface into the bus protocol, so that all the SoC parts collaborate with each other. Usually engineers build these wrappers manually, and this is done, based on a nonformal knowledge about the bus protocol. Up to the publishing of this work, there were no automated converter synthesis techniques employed in industrial or academic practice. The work in [58] contributes towards three aspects of protocol converter synthesis: a formal, FSM-based model for protocol definition, a precise definition of protocol compatibility, and a definition of converters and converter correctness (for a given pair of existing and known protocols).

Synchronous FSMs with bounded counters that communicate via channels are used in [58] to model communication protocols. Protocol channels are attributed with a type and a direction. A channel type can be either control or data, and direction can be either input or output. A channel action can be write, read, or a value test on a channel. The bounded counters are used in the model so as to keep a data item valid on a channel, for a number of clock cycles. Between two changes in the counter value, any read or write action indicates repetition of data values. Bounded counters facilitate smaller and precise models of data bursts on channels. Protocols which execute concurrently are described by the parallel composition of the protocols. The parallel composition of two protocols describes all the possible control states that the protocols may be in, when they run concurrently. The following constraints must be satisfied, in order to make sure that data flows between these protocols: data is read by one protocol only when it is written by the other; a specific data item can be read as distinct exactly once; no deadlocks can occur and livelocks can always be avoided. The last condition makes sure that every data transfer can terminate in a finite number of steps. In order to satisfy the second constraint of correct data flow, the data actions, along a path between two protocols, need to be correct. This means that every written data item is read as new before it is read as a repeated item. Also, a new data item can be written only if the previous one has been read. Furthermore, there should be no read repetition between a new write and a new read action. The utilized formal model allows for analyzing and checking compatibility between two existing protocols. The model devised in [58] is validated with an example of communication protocol pairs which included AMBA APB and ASB. These protocols are checked regarding their compatibility, by using the formal model.

The following constraints have to be checked by the formal techniques, so as to make sure that correct data flow is happening through a protocol converter in [58]: data is read by a protocol(/converter) only when the data is written by the converter(/a protocol); a data item can be read as distinct exactly once; no deadlocks and livelocks can occur; every data that is sent (written) from P1 (P2) to the converter will be sent (written) by the converter to P2 (P1); every data written to the converter was previously written by a protocol. A converter itself is an FSM with bounded counters and a finite buffer for each output data channel. A pair of protocols, data channel mapping, and buffer sizes is given as input to the converter synthesizer. The converter synthesizer generates the most general (correct) protocol converter. Protocol converter testcases that were used to evaluate the work in [58] inclued an ASB to APB converter and a set of converters between the open core protocol (OCP) and the AMBA family of bus protocols. The existing synthesis framework is limited to protocols that can be defined by a single FSM, and for more than one FSM per protocol description capabilities, future work on this is envisaged by the authors.

The methodology of SystemCoDesigner [59] uses an actor-oriented approach so as to integrate HLS into electronic system level (ESL) design space exploration tools. Its main aim is to automate the design and building of correct-by-construction system on a chip (SoC) implementations from a behavioral model. The design starts with an executable SystemC system model. Then, commercial synthesizers such as Forte's Cynthesizer are used in order to generate hardware implementations of actors from the behavioral model. The produced actor implementations are characterized based on their area (number of lookup tables, and block memories) and their latency. This enables the design space exploration in finding the best candidate architectures (mixtures of hardware and software modules). After deciding on the chosen solution, the suitable target platform is then synthesized with the implementations of the hardware and software parts.

Modules or processes are modeled in [59] as actors which communicate with other actors via a number of communication channels. This is the starting point for modeling a system in [59]. The specification language of an actor is a subset of SystemC which is defined in SysteMoC library [60]. SystemC actors communicate via SystemC FIFO channels, and their functionality is implemented in a single SystemC thread. Each SysteMoC actor is specified by a finite state machine (FSM), which defines the communication methods that the FSM controls. Each such actor can be transformed into hardware (using Cynthesizer) or software implementations. Moreover, the use of a commercial tool for hardware synthesis allows for arriving at design solution evaluations, so as to decide about the most suited solution, in terms of hardware resources and system throughput. The performance information, the executable actor system specification, and an architecture template are the inputs for design space exploration. The architecture template is represented by a graph, which represents all the possible hardware modules, the processors, and the communication infrastructure. The designer can select from within this graph the solutions that satisfy the user requirements and which produce tradeoffs between hardware size and performance.

The final step of this methodology is to generate the FPGA-based SoC implementation from the chosen hardware/software solution. This is done by connecting existing IP blocks and processor cores with the communication elements from an appropriate library. Moreover, the program code for each processor is generated, in order to achieve rapid prototyping. The final FPGA bitstream is generated in [59] using the Xilinx EDK (Embedded Development Kit) tools. A motion-JPEG test application was used to validate the proposed methodology in [59]. The architecture template used an embedded Microblaze processor core, 224 FIFOs, and 19 modules generated by the HLS tool. The complete system specification used 319 actor mapping edges and the design space exploration produced 5×10^{33} different alternative solutions. An instance of the Microblaze core including memory and bus resources was instantiated during platform synthesis and for each processor used. The rest of the hardware modules were inserted in the form of Verilog netlists which were generated by Cynthesizer (HLS) and Synplify by Synplicity (RTL synthesis) tools. Moreover, FIFO primitives were instantiated for communication between the system's blocks. For the particular testcase (JPEG), the objectives taken into account during design space exploration, included throughput, latency, number of flip-flops, number of lookup tables, block-RAMS, and multipliers. Based on the proposed methodology, the formal underlying mechanisms and the used examples, it was concluded that SystemCoDesigner method is suitable for stream-based applications, found in areas such as DSP, image filtering, and communications. Up to now, there are no indications on how well this methodology would perform in applications with complex control flow.

A formal approach is followed in [61] so as to prove that every HLS translation of a source code model produces a RTL model that is functionally equivalent to the one in the behavioral input to the HLS tools. This technique is called translation validation and it has been maturing via its use in the optimizing software compilers. In [61], HLS is seen as a sequence of refinements of the original specification (behavioral) code down to the final RTL implementation model. It is argued in [61] that if it is formally proved that these refinement steps maintain the behavioral properties of the original design, then it reduces the need to reverify (e.g., with simulations) the correctness of the produced RTL. The validating system in [61] is called SURYA and it uses the Simplify theorem prover to implement the validation algorithms. SURYA was used to validate the SPARK HLS tool [46], and SURYA managed to find two bugs in the SPARK compilations, which were unknown before.

The translation validation methodology [61] consists of two algorithm components: the checking algorithm and the inference algorithm. Given a simulation relation, the checking algorithm determines whether or not this relation is a correct refinement simulation relation. The inference algorithm uses the specification and the implementation programs to infer a correct simulation relation between them. The inference algorithm establishes a simulation relation that defines which points in the specification program are related to the corresponding points in the implementation program. First the inference algorithm is applied to infer a simulation relation and then the checking algorithm is used to verify that the produced relation is the required one, in order to check that a program is a relation of another program. The translation validation algorithm models the environment of the design as a set of processes, which are executed in parallel with the processes of the specification and the implementation. The simulation relation includes a set of entries of the form gl1, gl2, $\varnothing$, where gl1 and gl2 are locations in the specification and implementation programs, respectively, and $\varnothing$ is a predicate over variables in the specification and the implementation. The pair gl1, gl2 captures how control flow points (control states) relate in the specification and implementation programs, and $\varnothing$ captures how data are related between the two programs. The checking algorithm establishes correctness of a relation, if having an entry (gl1, gl2, $\varnothing$), and if the specification and implementation programs start executing in parallel from states gl1 and gl2, respectively, where $\varnothing$ holds, and they reach another pair of states gl1$'$ and gl2$'$, then in the resulting simulation relation entry (gl1$'$, gl2$'$, $\varnothing'$), $\varnothing'$ holds in the resulting states. If there are multiple paths from an entry, the checking algorithm in [61] checks all of them.

In [61], the inference algorithm begins with finding the points in the specification and simulation programs that need to be related in the simulation. Then, it moves further down in the control flow, in both the specification and implementation programs until it finds a branch or a read/write operation on a visible channel. Furthermore, the algorithm corelates the branches in the specification and the implementation, and it finds the local conditions which must hold in order for the visible instructions to match. When instructions write to visible output channels, the written values must be the same. When instructions read from externally visible input channels, the local conditions state that the specification and implementation programs read from the same point in the conceptual stream of input values. Once the related pairs of locations gl1, gl2 are all collected, a constraint variable is defined to represent the state-relating formula that will be used in the relation for this pair. Then, a set of constraints are applied on these constraint variables to make sure that the relation is indeed a simulation. The first kind of constraints makes sure that the computed simulation relation is strong enough, so that the visible instructions have the same behavior in the specification and the implementation programs. A second kind of constraints is used to state the relationship between a pair of related locations and other pairs of related locations. When all the constraints are generated, then an algorithm sets all the constraint variables to true and strengthens the constraint variables until a theorem prover can show that all constraints are satisfied.

An assumption is made by the formal model of refinement in [61], that the specification and the implementation are single entry and single exit programs. A transition diagram represents every process in these programs. This diagram uses generalized program locations and program transitions. A program location represents a point in the control flow of the program and it is either a node identifier, or a pair of two locations which refer to the state of two processes that are running in parallel. A program transition is represented by instructions and it defines how the program state changes from one location to another. Within this concept of models, two execution sequences of programs are equivalent if the two sequences contain visible instructions that are pairwise equivalent. In case that the inference algorithm cannot find an appropriate relation, then the user can provide the simulation relation by hand, and use the checking algorithm in order to verify that the relation is a correct one. The SURYA validation system was applied on SPARK HLS compilations to evaluate the equivalence between the intermediate representation (IR) of SPARK and the scheduled IR of the same translation process.

The replacement of flip-flop registers with latches is proposed in [62] in order to yield better timing in the implemented designs. The justification for this is that latches are inherently more tolerant to process variations than flip-flops. The latch replacement in [62] is executed not only during the register allocation task, but in all steps of HLS, including scheduling, allocation, and control synthesis. A prerequisite for correct latch replacement is to avoid having latches being read and written at the same time. The concept of the p-step is introduced in [62]. The p-step is the period during which the clock is high or low. Using the p-step as the elementary time unit instead of the conventional clock-cycle makes scheduling more flexible and it becomes easier to reduce the latency. In [62], the list scheduling algorithm is enhanced with the p-step concept, and a method is used to reduce the latency by determining the duty cycle of the clock, and therefore the p-step. In order to control the p-step schedule, dual-edge-triggered flip-flops are used in controller synthesis, since both clock edges are used to define the boundaries of the p-steps. These techniques were integrated into a tool called HLS-1. HLS-1 translates behavioral VHDL code into a synthesized netlist. The method was evaluated with a number of behavioral benchmarks as well as an industrial H.264 video coding application.

The execution time of operators (e.g., multipliers and adders) is formulated mathematically in [62]. This is realized using the clock period, the maximum delay of a functional unit (FU) executing the specific operator, the clock-to-Q delay, the setup time for the utilized flip-flops, and the delay of multiplexers. The transparent phase is the period of time that the clock is high, and the nontransparent phase is the remainder of the clock period. The mathematical analysis of timing using latches is formulated in [62] using the clock period, the time of the transparent phase, and the residual delay. The latter is the remainder of the delay time from modulo-dividing with the clock period. Using these mathematical models, and assuming a 30% duty cycle, it is shown in [62] that an example multiplier will need four p-steps, if it is scheduled to start at the first transparent phase, and will need three p-steps if it is scheduled to start at the second (nontransparent) phase. When flip-flops are used instead, the same multiplier will need two clock steps (equivalent to four p-steps) to execute which is longer than in the case of latches. The whole schedule can be optimized

by using the p-step as the basic scheduling unit and by modifying the duty cycle of the clock. Tighter schedules can be produced since p-steps allow scheduling at both edges of the clock. Moreover, register allocation is facilitated since operations can complete in a nontransparent p-step, and, therefore, read/write conflicts that are inherent in latch registers can be resolved. This method assumes that the delay of the controller is negligible, as compared to the transparent and nontransparent phase times. Nevertheless, implementing registers with latches instead of edge-triggered flip-flops is generally considered to be cumbersome due to the complicated timing behavior of latches.

2.5. Considering Interconnect Area and Delay. Usually, HLS tools estimate design area and timing using an aggregate sum of area and timing models of their functional unit, storage, and interconnect elements taken from the component libraries that they use. However, when moving into the deep submicron technologies, the area and timing of the chip's wires become significant compared to those of the implementation logic. Thus, new models and optimization approaches are needed in order to take into account the effect of the interconnections. In this direction, mature HLS tools consider more accurate models of the impact of interconnect on area and timing of the implementation. Given a DFG, performance estimation tools use a set of resources and resource delays, as well as the clock cycle to calculate a lower-bound completion delay for nonpipelined, resource constrained scheduling problems [63]. The work in [64] presents an algorithm which computes lower bounds on the number of functional units of each type. These functional units are required to schedule a DFG in a given number of control steps [64]. The lower bounds are found by relaxing either the precedence constraints or the integrity constraints, and the method estimates functional-unit area in order to generate resource constraints and thus reduce the search space, or in combination with an exact formulation for design space exploration.

In [65], a high-level approach to estimate the area is proposed. This approach focuses on predicting the interconnect area and it is suitable for standard cell implementations. The work in [66] proposes simultaneous functional unit binding and floorplanning during synthesis. An analytical technique, which includes the placement and binding problems in a single, mixed, ILP model, is discussed in [67] for a linear, bit-slice architecture. This model is able to minimize the overall interconnections of the resulting datapath. In [68] synthesis for datapath is discussed which is based on multiple-width shared bus architecture. This technique utilizes models of circuit area, delay, power consumption, and output noise which are related to functional unit grouping, binding, allocation, and different word-lengths. Functional unit grouping and multiple-width bus partitioning are executed during allocation but before scheduling. According to the authors, this increases the synthesis flexibility and the possibility for better synthesis results. The aim is to reduce the delay, as well as the interconnection cost and power consumption of the implementation.

2.6. Synthesis for Testability. HLS for testability can be achieved by reducing the number of self-looped registers, while considering the tradeoff between testability improvement and area increase. In [69], the switching property of multiplexors and buses is used to reduce the area and test generation costs. This is achieved by analyzing the location of switches during the selection of partial test registers, and by using these switches to transfer test data through them. In [70], the testability of the design is analyzed at the behavioral level, by considering loops and other control structures. This is done so as to improve the testability by including test constraints, during allocation of registers and production of interconnections. Simultaneous scheduling and allocation of testable functional units and registers under testability, area and performance constraints, are performed in [71] using a problem-space genetic algorithm. Binding for testability is implemented in two stages in [72]. First, a binder with test cost function generates a design almost without any loops. Then, the remaining register self-loops are broken by alternating the module and register binding.

A two-stage objective function is used in [73] so that synthesis of the behavioral code requires less area and test cost, by estimating the area and testability as well as the effects of every synthesis transformation. Next, a randomized branch-and-bound decent algorithm is used to identify that particular sequence of transformations. This achieves the best results in terms of area and test cost. A high-level synthesis-for-testability approach was followed in [74] where the testability of the hardware was increased by improving the controllability of the circuit's controller. This is a testability increase via improving the circuit's controller design.

2.7. Synthesis for Low Power. A number of portable and embedded computing systems and applications such as mobile (smart) phones, PDAs, and so forth, require low power consumption, therefore, synthesis for low energy is becoming very important in the whole area of VLSI and embedded system design. During the last decade industry and academia invested on significant part of research regarding VLSI techniques and HLS for low power design. In order to achieve low energy in the results of HLS and system design, new techniques that help to estimate power consumption at the high-level description level are needed. In [75], switching activity and power consumption are estimated at the RTL description taking also into account the glitching activity on a number of signals of the datapath and the controller. Important algorithmic properties in the behavioral description are identified in [76] such as the spatial locality, the regularity, the operation count, and the ratio of critical path to available time. All of these aim to reduce the power consumption of the interconnections. The HLS scheduling, allocation, and binding tasks consider such algorithmic statistics and properties in order to reduce the fanins and fanouts of the interconnect wires. This will result into reducing the complexity and the power consumed on the capacitance of the interconnection buses [77].

The effect of the controller on the power consumption of the datapath is considered in [78]. The authors suggest a special datapath allocation technique that achieves low power. Pipelining and module selection was proposed in [79] for low power consumption. The activity of the functional units was reduced in [80] by minimizing the transitions of the functional unit's inputs. This was utilized in a scheduling and resource binding algorithm, in order to reduce power consumption. In [81], the DFG is simulated with profiling stimuli, provided by the user, in order to measure the activity of operations and data carriers. Then, the switching activity is reduced, by selecting a special module set and schedule. Reducing supply voltage, disabling the clock of idle elements, and architectural tradeoffs were utilized in [82] in order to minimize power consumption within an HLS environment.

Estimating the power consumption of a system, chip of SoC (system-on-a-chip), often requires a lot of design detail to be taken into account. This, in turn, leads to very slow simulations, although these are accurate, and thus results into very long design times, when low energy is considered throughout the development flow. In order to achieve faster simulation times for energy consumption, than RTL simulations, the cycle-accurate, bit-accurate (CABA) level is utilized in [83], in order to produce fast and more effective power estimates. Bit-accurate means that the communication protocols between design components are implemented at a bit level in the CABA model. Moreover, the CABA level simulation is realized cycle-by-cycle which achieves the required detail of the power estimates. In order to increase the efficiency and productivity in designing complex SoCs, the Model-Driven Engineering methodology (MDE) is adopted in [83]. MDE enables the automatic generation of system simulation components from models described in a diagrammatic UML format. For this, a UML profile is used (for more details about UML in designing systems, please refer to following paragraphs/sections). Using low level characterization, accurate power models are constructed which contain energy information for the different activities of system components. Then, these power models are simulated to add the power cost of the specific activity of the component to the overall power consumption estimate. The MDE module generation approach in [83] utilizes activity counters of white-box IP blocks and the connectivity of estimate modules for black-box IP blocks, which are used to calculate the energy consumption of complex SoCs. The simulations are realized at the SystemC level which achieves the intended estimation accuracy and simulation speed for the whole SoC.

The energy consumption of memory subsystem and the communication lines within a multiprocessor system-on-a-chip (MPSoC) is addressed in [84]. This work targets streaming applications such as image and video processing that have regular memory access patterns. These patterns can be statically analyzed and predicted at compile time. This enables the replacement of conventional cache memories with scratch-pad memories (SPMs), which are more efficient than cache, since they do not use tagged memory blocks. The way to realize optimal solutions for MPSoCs is to execute the memory architecture definition and the connectivity synthesis in the same step. In [84], memory and communication are cosynthesized, based on multiprocessor data reuse analysis.

The data reuse analysis determines a number of buffers which contain the frequently used data in the main memory. Then, the buffer mapping onto physical memory blocks is done simultaneously with communication synthesis, for minimal energy, while satisfying delay constraints.

2.8. Controller versus Datapath Tradeoffs. With the conventional synthesis approaches, the controller is implemented after the datapath is completed. Nevertheless, there are tradeoffs between datapath and controller in terms of area and performance. In this direction, excessive loop unrolling, particularly on many levels of nested loops in the behavioral model, can produce hundreds of states which generate a very large state encoder. This will reduce the achievable clock speed, which will definitely reduce the performance of the implementation. On the other hand, a very simple controller with straight command wires towards the datapath, will end up in heavy use of multiplexers (used for data routing through the functional units) which will have again a negative impact on the minimum clock cycle which can be achieved. In [85], the controller overhead is taken into account at every level of the hierarchy before the datapath is fully implemented. This approach is suitable for regular behavioral model algorithms. The system clock period is minimized during allocation in [86], by an allocation technique which considers the effect of the controller on the critical path delay.

2.9. Internal and Intermediate Design Formats Used in Synthesis. One of the most important aspects of compilers and therefore HLS synthesizers is the internal representation of the algorithmic information that they use. The internal format used in [1] consists of three graphs which all share the same vertices. If P is a program in DSL, after decomposing complex expressions into simple, three address operations, W is the set of variables and V the set of operations then the internal form S of the program contains the three directed graphs as follows:

$$S = (G_S, G_D, G_C), \tag{2}$$

where

$$\begin{aligned} G_S &= (V, E_S), \\ G_D &= (V \cup W, E_D), \tag{3} \\ G_C &= (V, E_C), \end{aligned}$$

and where the edges E correspond to E_S = sequence, E_D = dataflow, and E_C = constraints. The sequences set of edges are related to the dependencies from one operation to the other. The dataflow edges represent the data processing structure. These edges connect inputs and output of every operation inside the specified circuit. The constraints edges represent timing deadlines from each operation.

The HCDG [45] consists of operation nodes and guard nodes. The HCDG also contains edges which are precedence constraints for data which determine the order of operations, and for control (guards), which determine which Boolean expressions must evaluate to true, in order for the dependent

operations to execute. Guards are a special type of node and they represent Boolean conditions that guard the execution of nodes which operate on data. If there are multiple but mutually exclusive assignments to the same variable which happens as an example within different if-then-else true/false branches, then this is represented in HCDG with a static single assignment. This assignment receives the results of the mutually exclusive operations through a multiplexing logic block (operation node in HCDG). The HCDG itself and the mutual exclusiveness of pairs of guards are utilized in [45] to aid the efficient HLS scheduling transformations of the synthesis method developed there.

The hierarchical task graph (HTG) is a hierarchical intermediate representation for control-intensive designs and it is used by the SPARK HLS tools [46]. An HTG is a hierarchy of directed acyclic graphs, that are defined by $G_{HTG}(V_{HTG}, E_{HTG})$, where the vertices V_{HTG} are nodes of one of the three following types.

(1) Single nodes that have no subnodes and they capture basic blocks. A basic block is a sequence of operations that have no control flow branches between them.

(2) (Hierarchical) Compound nodes that are HTGs which contain other HTG nodes. They capture if-then-else or switch case blocks or a series of other HTGs.

(3) Loop nodes that capture loops. Loop nodes contain the loop head and loop tail. The latter are simple nodes. Also, loop nodes contain the loop body which is a compound node.

The set of edges E_{HTG} indicate flow of control between HTG nodes. An edge (htg_i, htg_j) in E_{HTG}, where $htg_i, htg_j \in V_{HTG}$, where htg_i is the start node and htg_i is the end node of the edge, denotes that htg_j executes after htg_i has finished its execution. Each node htg_i in V_{HTG} has two special nodes, $htg_{Start}(i)$ and $htg_{Stop}(i)$, which also belong to V_{HTG}. The htg_{Start} and htg_{Stop} nodes for all compound and loop HTG nodes are always single nodes. The htg_{Start} and htg_{Stop} nodes of a loop HTG node are the loop head and loop tail, respectively. The htg_{Start} and htg_{Stop} of a single node represent the node itself [46]. HTGs are providing the means for coarse-grain parallelizing transformations in HLS, since they allow the movement of operations through and across large chunks of structured high-level code blocks. These blocks are complex conditional structures in the C language. In this way, the HTGs are very useful for the optimizing transformations of the HLS scheduler. Their drawback though is their high complexity in translating from regular programming languages' code into a combination of CDFGs and HTGs, such as it happens in the SPARK HLS tool [46].

A special version of CDFG is developed in [47], which serves two purposes: to be the input design format for their HLS tool, and to facilitate HLS optimizations. In particular, its purpose is to preserve and exploit further the parallelism inherent in control-dominated designs. In order to achieve this, the following special nodes were introduced in the CDFG.

(1) The SLP node represents the start of a loop and it selects between the initial value of the loop variable and the value, which is calculated from the last iteration of the executed loop.

(2) The EIF node represents the end of an if-then-else branch and it is used to select the correct value from the if-and-else branches. Both SLP and EIF nodes are implemented with multiplexers in the corresponding datapath.

(3) The BLP node sends the values of the variables which are computed by the current iteration of a loop, back to the SLP node which will select the value for the next loop iteration.

(4) The ELP represents the end of the loop. All the loop variables have to be passed through the ELP node, before they are fed to operations which use them, outside of the loop.

In this way, the synthesizer can identify easily the beginning, the end and the range of a loop using the SLP, BLP, and ELP nodes of the graph. The CDFG model in [47] includes support for memory operations such as load and store. Memory access sequences are defined with a special edge of the CDFG between the corresponding load and store nodes.

The extended data-flow graph (EDFG) which is used in [53] is a finite, directed, and weighted graph:

$$G = (V, E, t), \qquad (4)$$

where V is the set of vertices (nodes) of computation and memory access, E is the set of edges representing precedence rules between the nodes, and the function $f(u)$ is the computation delay of node u. A path in G is a connected sequence of nodes and edges of the graph G. A synthesis system which includes optimizations on the computing part and the sequencer part of a custom DSP subsystem utilizes the above EDFG [53].

2.10. Diagrammatic Input Formats and Embedded Systems.

The Unified Modeling Language or UML is a general purpose language for modeling in a diagrammatic way, systems which are encountered in object-oriented software engineering. In 1997, the Object Management Group (OMG) has added UML in its list of adopted technologies, and since then, UML has become the industry standard for modeling software-intensive systems [87]. Although UML is widely known for its diagrammatic ways to model systems, these models contain more information than just system diagrams. These diagrams are usually formed by experienced system architects. UML diagrams belong to two general categories: static or structural diagrams and dynamic or behavioral diagrams. UML models contain also information about what drives and checks the diagrammatic and other elements (such as the use cases). Structural diagrams include the class, component, composite structure, deployment, object, package, and profile diagram. Dynamic diagrams include the activity, communication, sequence, state, interaction overview, timing, and use case diagram [87].

OMG has defined a standard set of languages for model transformation called QVT (query/view/transformation). The set of QVT-like implementations of UML include the Tefkat language, the ALT transformation language which is a component of the Eclipse project, and the Model Transformation Framework (MTF) which was the outcome of the IBM project alphaworks [88]. Using QVT-like transformation languages, UML models can be translated to other languages, for example, programming language formats. UML can be extended with various ways for customization: tag definitions, constraints, and stereotypes, which are applied to elements of the model. UML Profiles are collections of such UML extensions that collectively customize UML for a particular design/application area (e.g., banking, aerospace, healthcare, financial) or platform (e.g. .NET). A stereotype is rendered as a name enclosed by guillemets ($\ll\gg$ or $\langle\!\langle\,\rangle\!\rangle$) and placed above the name of another element.

The area of real-time and embedded systems is a domain that UML can be extended so that it provides more detail, in modeling events and features of such systems, for example, mutual exclusion techniques, concurrency, and deadline specifications. After the standard of UML2 was adopted by OMG the earlier "UML Profile for Schedulability, Performance and Time" (SPT) for embedded systems was found problematic in terms of flexibility and expression capabilities, and consequently OMG issued a new request for proposals (RFPs) for a profile of this specific domain. The result of this effort was a UML profile called MARTE (Modeling and Analysis of Real-Time and Embedded systems) [89]. The primary goal of MARTE was to enable the formal specification of real-time constraints and the embedded system characteristics such as memory size/capacity and power consumption, modeling of component-based architectures, and the adaptability to different computational paradigms such as synchronous, asynchronous and timed.

In order to support modeling of embedded and real-time systems, the MARTE architecture offers the following four modeling capabilities.

(i) *QoS-aware modeling* with the following formats: HLAM: for modeling high-level RT QoS (Real-Time Quality of Service). NFP: for declaring, qualifying, and applying semantically well-formed nonfunctional issues. Time: for defining and manipulating time. VSL: the Value Specification Language is a textual language for specifying algebraic expressions.

(ii) *Architecture modeling* with the following features: GCM: for architecture modeling based on interacting components. Alloc: for specifying allocation of functionalities to entities that realize these functionalities.

(iii) *Platform-based modeling* with the following capabilities: GRM: for modeling and specifying the usage of common platform resources at system-level. SRM: for modeling multitask-based designs. HRM: for modeling hardware platforms.

(iv) *Model-based QoS analysis* with the following features: GQAM: for annotating models subject to quantitative analysis. SAM: for annotating models subject of scheduling analysis. PAM: for annotating models subject of performance analysis.

For more details on the above acronyms and UML MARTE features, the reader can refer to [89, 90].

Gaspard2 is an Integrated Development Environment (IDE) for SoC (system-on-chip) visual comodeling. It allows or will allow modeling, simulation, testing, and code generation of SoC applications and hardware architectures. Gaspard2 is an autonomous application based on Eclipse [91]. Specification of the Gaspard UML profile can be found in [92]. This profile is an extension of UML semantics to enable the modeling of a SoC, and it is based on MARTE. According to the Gaspard methodology, this is done in three steps: the application, the hardware architecture, and the association of the application to the hardware architecture. The application includes the behavior of the SoC, and it is implemented with a data-flow model, but control flows are allowed via additional mechanisms. The Gaspard profile allows also the modeling of massively parallel and repetitive systems. Gaspard achieves the generation of system components by using model transformations, and it targets VHDL and SystemC code.

Among others, the Gaspard UML profile includes the hardware architecture package, which allows modeling of hardware at a system level. This is of particular interest to the subject of this review paper. For this purpose, the Gaspard UML profile uses the *Hardware Component*. The Hardware Component can be refined using stereotypes to a Processor, a Communication, or a Memory. The Gaspard2 profile enables the modeling of the parallelism and the data dependencies, which are inherent in the application to be designed every time. Application control concepts are modeled in the profile, by allowing the description of synchronous reactive systems [92]. Among the applications which were experimentally designed with the Gaspard2 tool and reported, there is a correlation algorithm and its transformation to the VHDL model, and a radar application, which was implemented as an SoC including 8 PowerPC cores. Moreover, experiments with automatic generation and compilation of SystemC code are reported.

3. The Intermediate Predicate Format

The Intermediate Predicate Format (IPF) (The Intermediate Predicate Format is patented with patent number: 1006354, 15/4/2009, from the Greek Industrial Property Organization.) was invented and designed by the author of this paper as a tool and media for the design encapsulation and the HLS transformations in the CCC (Custom Co-processor Compilation) hardware compilation tool (this hardware compiler method is patented with patent number: 1005308, 5/10/2006, from the Greek Industrial Property Organization). A near-complete analysis of IPF syntax and semantics can be found in [93]. Here, the basic features and declarative semantics of IPF are discussed along with some example IPF data. The IPF file consists of a number of tables (lists) of homogeneous Prolog predicate facts. These facts are

logic relations between a number of objects that are sited as a list of positional symbols or reference numbers of other facts of the same, or other tables inside the IPF database. Therefore, the IPF style allows for both declarative (Prolog) and sequential (list-based) processing of the logic facts of IPF by the CCC (Custom Co-processor Compilation) HLS tool transformations in a formal way.

The formal methodology discussed here is motivated by the benefits of using predicate logic to describe the intermediate representations of compilation steps. Another way to use the logic predicate facts of IPF is to use the resolution of a set of transformation Horn clauses [94], as the building blocks of an HLS compiler with formal transformations and a state machine optimization engine. This logic inference engine constitutes the most critical (HLS-oriented back-end) phase of the CCC hardware compiler. The inference engine allows for an efficient implementation of the hardware compilation tasks, such as the mapping of complex data and control structures into equivalent hardware architectures in an optimal way, as well as scheduling and grouping the abstract data operations of the source programs into hardware machine (FSM) control states. The choice of logic predicates turns the HLS process into a formal one. Moreover, there have been a number of other successful uses of the Prolog language in critical areas, for example, in solving the scheduling problem of air-flight control and aircraft landing, expert decision systems, and so forth.

The IPF database is produced by the front-end phase of the CCC (Custom Co-processor Compilation) compiler (see following paragraphs), and it captures the complete algorithmic, structural, and data typing information of the source programs. The source programs model the system's behavior in a number of ADA subroutines. The IPF facts are formal relations between values, types, objects and other programming entities of the source program, as well as other IPF facts. The general syntax of the IPF facts follows the following format:

$$\text{fact\_id}(object1, object2, \ldots, objectN) \qquad (5)$$

The predicate name fact_id relates in this fact the objects object1 to objectN in a logical way. IPF facts represent an algorithmic feature such as a program operation, a data object description, a data type, an operator, and a subprogram call. An example of a plus (+) operation which is an addition is described by the following, program table fact:

$$\text{prog\_stmt}(\text{``subprogram2''}, 3,0,63,3,9,10,5) \qquad (6)$$

The predicate fact prog_stmt of (6) describes an addition (operator reference = 63), which is the 3rd operation of the ADA subprogram subprogram2. This operation adds two operands with reference numbers 3 and 9 and produces a result on a variable with reference number 10. These operands and result data descriptions are part of the data table and for this example they are given in the following examples ((7), (8), and (9)):

$$\text{data\_stmt}(\text{“subprogram2”, “}dx\text{”}, 3, 2, \text{“var”}, \text{sym}(\text{“node”})) \tag{7}$$

...

$$\text{data\_stmt}(\text{“subprogram2”, “}dy\text{”}, 9, 2, \text{“var”}, \text{sym}(\text{“node”})) \tag{8}$$

$$\text{data\_stmt}(\text{“subprogram2”, “}xc\text{”}, 10, 2, \text{“var”}, \text{sym}(\text{“node”})). \tag{9}$$

In the above data table facts, we see their reference numbers 3, 9, and 10 which are used in the program table fact of (6), and their names (variable ids) are dx, dy, and xc, respectively. Apart from their host subprogram, these facts describe variables (see the "var" object) and they are of type 2 (integer). This type is described in the type table of the same IPF database with the type fact as it is written bellow:

$$\text{type\_def}(2, \text{“integer”}, 32, \text{“standard”}, 0, \text{“single\_t”}, 0, 0, 0) \tag{10}$$

The type definition of the integer type is given in (10), and there are various objects related under this type fact such as the kind of this type ("single_t" which means with no components or with a single component), the name ("integer") of the type and its size in bits (32). A complete description of the IPF fact objects and structure is not the purpose of this work. Nevertheless, a near-complete description can be found in [93].

From the above, it can be concluded that the IPF facts are logical relations of objects, and this formal description is used by the back-end phase of the CCC compiler in order to implement the HLS transformations of the tool. The CCC HLS transformations use the IPF facts of the source design, along with other logical rules in order to "conclude" and generate the RTL hardware models at the output of the CCC compiler. The generated RTL models (coded in VHDL) can be synthesized, in turn, by commercial and research RTL synthesizers, into technology gate-netlists, along with other, technology-specific and EDA vendor-specific ECAD back-end tools, in order to produce the final implementations of the described system.

It can be derived from the above forms (IPF excerpts) that IPF is suitable for declarative processing which is done by Prolog code, as well as linear, sequential processing. The latter is enabled from the way that some IPF facts (e.g., data table facts) are referenced with their linear entry numbers in other IPF facts (e.g., program table facts). In this way, lists can be built and processed by prolog predicates that utilize list editing and with recursive processing so as to easily implement the generation and processing of lists, for example, the initial schedule (state list) which includes the FSM states and their components (e.g., operations and conditions-guards). Also, both these types of processing in Prolog as well as the nature of the IPF predicate facts are formal, which makes the whole transformation from the source

code down to the generated FSM-controlled hardware, a provably correct one. This eliminates the need to reverify the functionality of the generated hardware with traditional and lengthy RTL simulations, since due to the formal nature of the transformations the generated hardware is correct-by-construction. Therefore, valuable development time is saved in order to take important decisions about the high-level architecture template options such as the positioning of large data objects such as arrays on embedded scratch pad or external shared memories.

4. Hardware Compilation Flow

The front-end compiler translates the algorithmic data of the source programs into the IPF's logic statements (logic facts). The inference logic rules of the back-end compiler transform the IPF facts into the hardware implementations. There is a one-to-one correspondence between the source specification's subroutines and the generated hardware implementations. The source code subroutines can be hierarchical, and this hierarchy is maintained in the generated hardware implementation. Each generated hardware model is a FSM-controlled custom processor (or coprocessor, or accelerator), that executes a specific task, described in the source program code. This hardware synthesis flow is depicted in Figure 1.

Essentially, the front-end compilation resembles software compilation and the back-end compilation executes formal transformation tasks that are normally found in HLS tools. This whole compilation flow is a formal transformation process, which converts the source code programs into implementable RTL (Register-Transfer Level) VHDL hardware accelerator models. If there are function calls in the specification code, then each subprogram call is transformed into an interface event in the generated hardware FSM. The interface event is used so that the "calling" accelerator uses the "services" of the "called" accelerator, as it can be thought in the source code hierarchy.

5. Back-End Compiler Inference Logic Rules

The back-end compiler consists of a very large number of logic rules. The back-end compiler logic rules are coded with logic programming techniques, which are used to implement the HLS algorithms of the back-end compilation phase. As an example, one of the latter algorithms reads and incorporates the IPF tables' facts into the compiler's internal inference engine of logic predicates and rules [94]. The back-end compiler rules are given as a great number of definite clauses of the following form:

$$A_0 \leftarrow A_1 \wedge \cdots \wedge A_n \text{ (where } n \geq 0), \tag{11}$$

where $\leftarrow$ is the logical implication symbol ($A \leftarrow B$ means that if B applies then A applies), and $A_0, \ldots, A_n$ are atomic formulas (logic facts) of the form:

$$\text{predicate\_symbol}(\text{Var\_1}, \text{Var\_2}, \ldots, \text{Var\_N}), \tag{12}$$

where the positional parameters Var_1,..., Var_N of the above predicate "predicate_symbol" are either variable names (in the case of the back-end compiler inference rules), or constants (in the case of the IPF table statements) [93, 94]. The predicate syntax in (12) is typical of the way of the IPF facts and other facts interact with each other, they are organized and they are used internally in the inference engine. Thus, the hardware descriptions are generated as "conclusions" of the inference engine and in a formal way from the input programs by the back-end phase, which turns the overall transformation into a provably correct compilation process. In essence, the IPF file consists of a number of such atomic formulas, which are grouped in the IPF tables. Each such table contains a list of homogeneous facts which describe a certain aspect of the compiled program. For example all prog_stmt facts for a given subprogram are grouped together in the listing of the program statements table.

6. Inference Logic and Back-End Transformations

The inference engine of the back-end compiler consists of a great number of logic rules (like the one in (11)) which conclude on a number of input logic predicate facts and produce another set of logic facts and so on. Eventually, the inference logic rules produce the logic predicates that encapsulate the writing of RTL VHDL hardware coprocessor models. These hardware models are directly implementable to any hardware (e.g., ASIC or FPGA) technology, since they are technology and platform independent. For example, generated RTL models produced in this way from the prototype compiler were synthesized successfully into hardware implementations using the Synopsys DC Ultra, the Xilinx ISE, and the Mentor Graphics Precision software without the need of any manual alterations of the produced RTL VHDL code. In what follows, an example of such an inference rule is shown:

$$\text{dont\_schedule(Operation1, Operation2)}$$
$$\longleftarrow \text{examine(Operation1, Operation2)}, \qquad (13)$$
$$\text{predecessor(Operation1, Operation2)}$$

The meaning of this rule that combines two input logic predicate facts to produce another logic relation (dont_schedule), is that when two operations (Operation1 and Operation2) are examined and the first is a predecessor of the second (in terms of data and control dependencies), then do not schedule them in the same control step. This rule is part of a parallelizing optimizer which is embedded in the inference engine and it aggressively "compresses" the execution time of the generated coprocessor by making a number of operations parallel in the same control step, as soon as of course the data and control dependencies are still satisfied. This parallelizing optimizer is called "PARCS" (meaning: Parallel, Abstract Resource-Constrained Scheduler).

The way that the inference engine rules (predicates relations-productions) work is depicted in Figure 2. The last produced (from its rule) predicate fact is the VHDL RTL writing predicate at the top of the diagram. Right bellow level 0 of predicate production rule there is a rule at the level-1, then level-2 and so on. The first predicates that are fed into

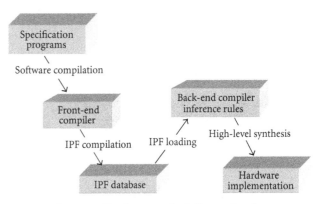

FIGURE 1: Hardware synthesis flow and tools.

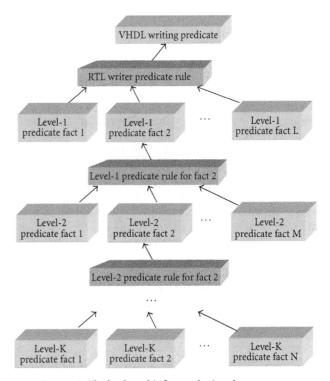

FIGURE 2: The back-end inference logic rules structure.

this engine of production rules belong to level-K, as shown in this figure. Level-K predicate facts include of course the IPF facts that are loaded into the inference engine along with the other predicates of this level. It is clear from all this that the back-end compiler works with inference logic on the basis of predicate relation rules and, therefore, this process is a formal transformation of the IPF source program definitions into the hardware accelerator (implementable) models. There is no traditional (imperative) software programming involved in this compilation phase, and the whole implementation of the back-end compiler is done using logic programming techniques. Of course in the case of the prototype compiler, there is a very large number of predicates and their relation rules that are defined inside the implementation code of the back-end compiler, but the whole concept of implementing this phase is as shown in Figure 2.

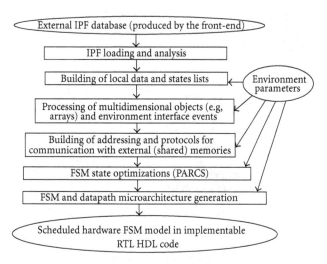

FIGURE 3: The processing stages of the back-end compiler.

The above fact production rules include the loading of IPF, the generation of list of data objects (virtual registers) and operators (including the special operators of communication with memories and the external computing environment), the initial and the processed list of states, the list of predecessor relations between operations, the PARCS optimizer, the datapath and FSM architecture generators, and so forth. The user of the back-end compiler can select certain environment command list options as well as build an external memory port parameter file as well as drive the compiler's optimizer with specific resource constraints of the available hardware operators.

The above predicate rules implement the various stages of the back-end compiler. The most important of these stages can be seen in Figure 3. The compilation process starts with the loading of the IPF facts into the inference rule engine. After the IPF database is analyzed, the local data object and operation and initial state lists are built. Then, the environment options are read and the temporary lists are updated with the special (communication) operations as well as the predecessor and successor dependency relation lists. After the complete initial schedule is built and concluded, the PARCS optimizer is run and the optimized schedule is delivered to the microarchitecture generator. The transformation is concluded with the formation of the FSM and datapath implementation and the writing of the RTL VHDL model for each accelerator that is defined in each subprogram of the source code program.

As already mentioned, from each subprogram which is coded in the specification program, a separate hardware accelerator model is generated. All these hardware models are directly implementable into hardware using commercial CAD tools, such as the Synopsys DC-ultra, the Xilinx ISE, and the Mentor Graphics Precision RTL synthesizers. Also, the hierarchy of the source program modules (subprograms) is maintained and the generated accelerators may be hierarchical. This means that an accelerator can invoke the services of another accelerator from within its processing states, and that other accelerator may use the services of yet another

accelerator, and so on. In this way, a subprogram call in the source code is translated into an external coprocessor interface event of the corresponding hardware accelerator.

7. The PARCS Optimizer

The various source program operations are scheduled using the optimizing algorithm PARCS. PARCS always attempts to schedule as many as possible operations in the same control step, satisfying of the data and control dependencies and the specific resource (operator) constraints if any, provided by the user.

The pseudocode for the main procedures of the PARCS scheduler is shown in Algorithm 1. The PARCS scheduler consists of a great number of predicate rules. All these are part of the inference engine of the back-end compiler. The utilized predicates are produced with formal logic rules such as the one in (11). A new design to be synthesized is loaded via its IPF into the back-end compiler's inference engine. Hence, the IPF's facts as well as the newly created predicate facts from the so far logic processing, "drive" the logic rules of the back-end compiler which generate provably correct hardware architectures. For example, the following PARCS scheduler rule:

$$\text{process\_state\_ops}(\text{Current\_state}, \text{Current\_list\_of\_operations},$$
$$\text{New\_states\_list\_of\_operations})$$
$$\longleftarrow \text{no\_dependencies}(\text{Current\_list\_of\_operations},$$
$$\text{New\_states\_list\_of\_operations}),$$
$$\text{absorb}(\text{Current\_state}, \text{New\_states\_list\_of\_operations})$$
$$(14)$$

is a logic production between three predicates. The meaning is that if predicate no_dependencies is true (in other words if there are not any dependencies between the list of the current state operations and those of the next—under examination—state), then predicate absorb is examined. If in turn absorb is true, which applies when it is executed to absorb the new list of operations into the current state, then process_state_ops is produced, which in turn means that the production rule is executed successfully. For the inference engine execution, this means that another fact of predicate process_state_ops is produced and the PARCS algorithm can continue with another state (if there are any left). The desirable side-effect of this production is that the list of operations of the newly examined state are absorbed into the current PARCS state, and PARCS processing can continue with the remaining states (of the initial schedule).

It is worthy to mention that although the HLS transformations are implemented with logic predicate rules, the PARCS optimizer is very efficient and fast. In most of benchmark cases that were run through the prototype hardware compiler flow, compilation did not exceed 1–10 minutes and the results of the compilation were very efficient as it will be explained bellow in the paragraph of experimental results. This cause and result/effect relation between these two predicates is characteristic of the way the back-end compiler's inference engine rules work. By

(1) start with the initial schedule (including the special external port operations)
(2) Current PARCS state < −1
(3) Get the 1st state and make it the current state
(4) Get the next state
(5) Examine the next state's operations to find out if there are any dependencies with the current state
(6) If there are no dependencies then absorb the next state's operations into the current PARCS state; If there are dependencies then finalize the so far absorbed operations into the current PARCS state, store the current PARCS state, PARCS state < −PARCS state +1; make next state the current state; store the new state's operations into the current PARCS state
(7) If next state is of conditional type (it is enabled by guarding conditions) then call the conditional (true/false branch) processing predicates, else continue
(8) If there are more states to process then go to step 4, otherwise finalize the so far operations of the current PARCS state and terminate

ALGORITHM 1: Pseudocode of the PARCS scheduling algorithm.

using this type of logic rules the back-end compiler achieves provably correct transformations on the source programs.

8. Generated Hardware Architectures

As mentioned already the hardware architectures that are generated by the back-end synthesizer are platform and RTL tool-independent. This means that generalized micro-architectures are produced, and they can be synthesized into hardware implementations by using any commercial RTL synthesizer without the slightest manual modifications of the generated RTL VHDL code. Furthermore, the generated accelerator architecture models are not dependent to any hardware implementation technology. Therefore, they can be, for example, synthesized into any ASIC or FPGA technology. When they need to be implemented by RTL synthesizers targeting FPGAs, with restricted functional unit and register on-chip resources, then the user of the tools can run the back-end compiler with a resource constraint file. Thus, PARCS will parallelize operations only to the extent that the resource constraints are not violated.

As already mentioned, the back-end stage of microarchitecture generation can be driven by command-line options. One of the options, for example, is to generate massively parallel architectures. The results of this option are shown in Figure 4. This option generates a single process-FSM VHDL description with all the data operations being dependent on different machine states. This means that every operator is enabled by single wire activation commands that are driven by different state register values. This in turn means that there is a redundancy in the generated hardware, in a way that during part of execution time, a number of state-dedicated operators remain idle. However, this redundancy is balanced by the fact that this option achieves the fastest clock cycle, since the state command encoder, as well as the data multiplexers are replaced by single wire commands which do not exhibit any additional delay.

Another microarchitecture option is the generation of traditional FSM + datapath-based VHDL models. The results

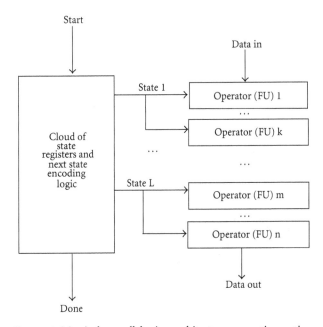

FIGURE 4: Massively-parallel microarchitecture generation option.

of this option are shown in Figure 5. With this option activated, the generated VHDL models of the hardware accelerators include a next state process as well as signal assignments with multiplexing which correspond to the input data multiplexers of the activated operators. Although this option produces smaller hardware structures (than the massively parallel option), it can exceed the target clock period due to larger delays through the data multiplexers that are used in the datapath of the accelerator.

Using the above microarchitecture options, the user of the inference-based hardware compiler can select various solutions between the fastest and larger massively parallel microarchitecture, which may be suitable for richer technologies in terms of operators such as large ASICs, and smaller and more economic (in terms of available resources) technologies such as smaller FPGAs.

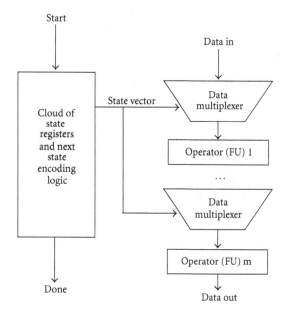

FIGURE 5: The traditional FSM + datapath generated microarchitecture option.

As it can be seen in Figures 4 and 5, the produced coprocessors (accelerators) are initiated with the input command signal START. Upon receiving this command the coprocessors respond to the controlling environment with the handshake output signal BUSY and right after they start processing the input data in order to produce the results. This process may take a number of clock cycles and it is controlled by a set of states (discrete control steps). When the coprocessors complete their processing, they notify their environment with the output signal DONE. In order to conclude the handshake, the controlling environment (e.g., a controlling central processing unit) responds with the handshake input RESULTS_READ, to notify the accelerator that the processed result data have been read by the environment. This handshake protocol is also followed when one (higher-level) coprocessor calls the services of another (lower-level) coprocessor. The handshake is implemented between any number of accelerators (in pairs) using the START/BUSY and DONE/RESULTS_READ signals. Therefore, the set of executing coprocessors can be also hierarchical in this way.

Other environment options, passed to the back-end compiler, control the way that the data object resources are used, such as registers and memories. Using a memory port configuration file, the user can determine that certain multidimensional data objects, such as arrays and array aggregates, are implemented in external (e.g., central, shared) memories (e.g., system RAM). Otherwise, the default option remains that all data objects are allocated to hardware (e.g., on-chip) registers. Of course the external memory option is more economic in terms of accelerator compilation time and register use, but it causes a longer processing time, due to the communication protocols that are generated, every time that a datum is accessed from/to the external shared memory. Nevertheless, all such memory communication

protocols and hardware ports/signals are automatically generated by the back-end synthesizer, and without the need for any manual editing of the RTL code by the user. Both synchronous and asynchronous memory communication protocol generation are supported in the memory port options file.

9. Coprocessor-Based, Hardware/Software Codesign and Coexecution Approach

The generated accelerators can be placed inside the computing environment that they accelerate or can be executed standalone. For every subprogram in the source specification code one coprocessor is generated to speed up (accelerate) the particular system task. The whole system can be modeled in the ADA software code to implement both the software and hardware models of the system. The whole ADA code set can be compiled and executed with the host compiler and linker to run and verify the operation of the whole system at the program code level. This high-level verification is done by compiling the synthesizable ADA along with the system's testbench code and linking it with the host compiler and linker. Then the test vectors can be fed to the system-under-test and the results can be stored in test files, by simply executing the ADA code. In this way, extremely fast verification can be achieved at the algorithmic level. It is evident that such behavioral (high-level) compilation and execution is orders of magnitude faster than conventional RTL simulations. In this way, the hardware/software codesign flow is enabled and mixed systems can be modeled, verified and prototyped in a fraction of the time needed with more conventional approaches.

It is worthy to mention that the whole codesign flow is free of any target architecture templates, platforms or IP-based design formats, which makes it portable, and adaptable to the target system updates and continuous architecture evolution. This is due to the fact that the generated coprocessors as well as their hardware-to-hardware and hardware-to-software interfaces are of generic type and so they can be easily enhanced to plug in the most demanding computing environments, with a minimal level of effort. This is not the case with IP-based design approaches, since the predesigned, and preconfigured IPs are most of the times difficult to adapt to existing target architectures, and their interfaces are often the most constraining obstacles for the integration with the rest of the developed system. Moreover, this paper's codesign approach is free of any target architecture templates and, therefore, free of any core or interface constraints for the integration of the generated custom hardware modules. Therefore, using the general I/O handshake of this approach, extremely complex systems can be delivered in a fraction of time which is needed when using platform or IP based approaches.

After the required coprocessors are specified, coded in ADA, generated with the prototype hardware compiler, and implemented with commercial back-end tools, they can be downloaded into the target computing system (if the target technology consists of FPGAs) and executed to

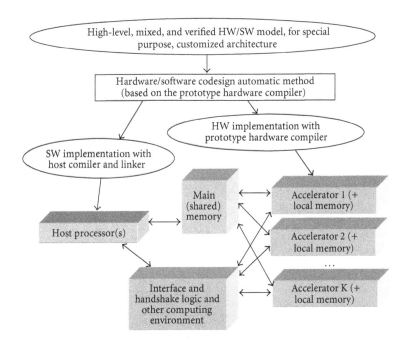

FIGURE 6: Host computing environment for hardware/software co-design and co-execution.

10. Experimental Results and Evaluation of the Method

In order to evaluate the efficiency of the presented HLS and ESL method, five benchmarks from the area of hardware compilation and high-level synthesis were run through the front-end and the back-end compilers. The programs were executed on a Pentium-4 platform running the MS-Windows-XP-SP2 operating system. The five design benchmarks include a DSP FIR filter, a second-order differential equation iterative solver which has long been a well-known high-level synthesis benchmark, an RSA crypto-processor from cryptography applications, a synthetic benchmark that uses two level nested for-loops, and a large MPEG video compression engine. The fourth benchmark includes subroutines with two-dimensional data arrays stored in external memories. These data arrays are processed within the bodies of 2-level nested loops.

All of the above-generated accelerators were simulated and the RTL models matched the input source program's functionality. The state number reduction after applying the PARCS optimizer, on the various modules of the five

benchmarks is shown in Table 1. State reduction rate of up to 35% was achieved with the back-end compiler flow. Also, the number of lines of RTL code is orders of magnitude more compared with the lines of the source code model for each submodule. This indicates the gain in engineering performance when the prototype ESL tools are used to automatically implement the computing products. This is due to the time gained by building and verifying (by program execution) fast executable specifications in high-level programs, as opposed to run the system verification only when all the hardware details are fixed and then perform time-consuming detailed (RTL or structural) hardware design and simulations. It is well accepted in the engineering community that the verification time at the algorithmic program level is only a small fraction of the time required for verifying designs at the RTL or the gate-netlist level. This gain is invaluable for developing complex computing systems. It can also be used to eliminate the need for design cycle iterations, later on in the design flow. Such design iterations would be caused by functional errors and specification mismatches, which are very frequent when using conventional implementation methodologies, such as RTL coding or schematic design.

The relative reduction of the number of states in the largest design module (subroutine) of the application, before and after the PARCS parallelizing optimizer, is shown graphically in Figure 7. The reduction of states reaches up to 30 to 40% at some cases which is a significant improvement. Such optimizations are usually very difficult to be done manually, even by experienced ASIC, HDL designers when the number of states exceeds a couple of dozens in the designed application. Noticeably, there were more than 400 states in the initial schedule of the MPEG benchmark. In addition to this, manual coding is extremely prone to errors

TABLE 1: State reduction statistics from the IKBS PARCS optimizer for the five benchmarks.

Module name	Initial schedule states	PARCS parallelized states	State reduction rate
FIR filter main routine	17	10	41%
Differential equation solver	20	13	35%
RSA main routine	16	11	31%
Nested loops 1st subroutine	28	20	29%
Nested loops 2nd subroutine (with embedded mem)	36	26	28%
Nested loops 2nd subroutine (with external mem)	96	79	18%
Nested loops 3rd subroutine	15	10	33%
Nested loops 4th subroutine	18	12	33%
Nested loops 5th subroutine	17	13	24%
MPEG 1st subroutine	88	56	36%
MPEG 2nd subroutine	88	56	36%
MPEG 3rd subroutine	37	25	32%
MPEG top subroutine (with embeded mem)	326	223	32%
MPEG top subroutine (with external mem)	462	343	26%

TABLE 2: Area and timing statistics from UMC 65 nm technology implementation.

Area/time statistic	Massively parallel, initial schedule	Massively parallel, PARCS schedule	FSM + datapath, initial schedule	FSM + datapath, PARCS schedule
Area in square nm	117486	114579	111025	107242
Equivalent number of NAND2 gates	91876	89515	86738	83783
Achievable clock period	2 ns	2 ns	2 ns	2 ns
Achievable clock frequency	500 MHz	500 MHz	500 MHz	500 MHz

which are very cumbersome and time consuming to correct with (traditional) RTL simulations and debugging.

The specification (source code) model of the various benchmarks, and all of the designs using the prototype compilation flow, contains unaltered regular ADA program code, without additional semantics, and compilation directives which are usual in other synthesis tools which compile code in SystemC, HandelC, or any other modified program code with additional object class and TLM primitive libraries. This advantage of the presented methodology eliminates the need for the system designers to learn a new language, a new set of program constructs or a new set of custom libraries.

Moreover, the programming constructs and semantics, that the prototype HLS compiler utilizes are the subset which is common to almost all of the imperative and procedural programming languages such as ANSI C, Pascal, Modula, and Basic. Therefore, it is very easy for a user that is familiar with these other imperative languages, to get also familiar with the rich subset of ADA that the prototype hardware compiler processes. It is estimated that this familiarization does not exceed a few days, if not hours for the very experienced software/system programmer/modeler.

Table 2 contains the area and timing statistics of the main module of the MPEG application synthesis runs. Synthesis was executed on a Ubuntu 10.04 LTS linux server with Synopsys DC-Ultra synthesizer and the 65 nm UMC technology libraries. From this table, a reduction in terms of area can be observed for the FSM + datapath implementation

against the massively parallel one. Nevertheless, due to the quality of the technology libraries the speed target of 2 ns clock period was achieved in all 4 cases.

Moreover, the area reduction for the FSM + datapath implementations of both the initial schedule and the optimized (by PARCS) one is not dramatic and it reaches to about 6%. This happens because the overhead of massively-parallel operators is balanced by the large amount of data and control multiplexing in the case of the FSM + datapath option.

11. Conclusions and Future Work

This paper includes a discussion and survey of past and present existing ESL HLS tools and related synthesis methodologies. Formal and heuristic techniques for the HLS tasks are discussed and more specific synthesis issues are analyzed. The conclusion from this survey is that the author's prototype ESL behavioral synthesizer is unique in terms of generality of input code constructs, the formal methodologies employed, and the speed and utility of the developed hardware compiler.

The main contribution of this paper is a provably correct, ESL, and high-level hardware synthesis method and a unified prototype tool-chain, which is based on compiler-compiler and logic inference techniques. The prototype tools transform a number of arbitrary input subprograms (at the moment coded in the ADA language) into an equivalent

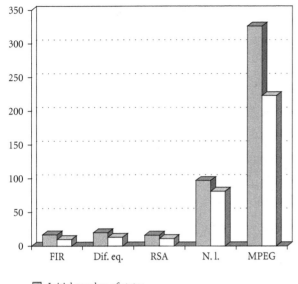

Initial number of states
Optimised states

FIGURE 7: Optimization (reduction) of number of states.

number of functionally equivalent RTL VHDL hardware accelerator descriptions. A very large number of input program applications were run through the hardware compiler, five of which were evaluated in this paper. In all cases, the functionality of the produced hardware implementations matched that of the input subprograms. This was expected due to the formal definition/implementation of the transformations of the hardware compiler, including the intermediate IPF form and the inference rules of the back-end phase. Encouraging state-reduction rates of the PARCS scheduler optimizer were observed for five benchmarks in this paper, which exceed 30% in some cases. Using its formal flow, the prototype hardware compiler can be used to develop complex systems in orders of magnitude shorter time and lower engineering effort, than that which are usually required using conventional design approaches such as RTL coding or IP encapsulation and schematic entry using custom libraries.

Existing HLS tools compile usually a small subset of the programming language, and sometimes with severe restrictions in the type of constructs they accept (some of them do not accept while-loops for example). Also, most of them produce better results on linear, data-flow-oriented specifications. However, a large number of applications found in embedded and telecommunication systems, mobile, and other portable computing platforms involve a great deal of complex control flow with nesting and hierarchy levels. For this kind of applications, a lot of HLS tools produce low level of quality results. The prototype ESL tool developed by the author has proved that it can deliver a better quality of results in applications with complex control such as image compression and processing standards. Moreover, a more general class of input code constructs are accepted by the front-end compiler and, therefore, a wider range of applications can be prototyped using the CCC HLS tool.

Moreover, using the executable ADA (and soon ANSI-C) models (executable specifications) for the designed system, the user of this hardware/software codesign methodology, can easily evolve the formally verified and synthesized, mixed architecture of the product or application that he intends to develop, and in a fraction of time that this is done with platform or IP based, or other conventional design methodologies. This is due to the core functionality and interface constraints that are introduced when predesigned architecture templates or IP blocks are involved. Moreover, due to the latter problem, large gaps in the intended-to-resulted system performance are usually observed, which often constitutes even a development halt for commercial (e.g., embedded) and other computing products.

Future extensions of this work include undergoing work to upgrade the front-end phase to accommodate more input programming languages (e.g., ANSI-C, C++) and the back-end HDL writer to include more back-end RTL languages (e.g., Verilog HDL), which are currently under development. Another extension could be the inclusion of more than 2 operand operations as well as multicycle arithmetic unit modules, such as multicycle operators, to be used in datapath pipelining. Moreover, there is ongoing work to extend the IPF's semantics so that it can accommodate embedding of IP blocks (such as floating-point units) into the compilation flow and enhance further the schedule optimizer algorithm for even more reduced schedules. Also, other compiler phase validation techniques based on formal semantic such as RDF and XML flows are investigated and are currently under development. Furthermore, connection flows from the front-end compiler to even more front-end diagrammatic system modeling formats such as the UML formulation are currently investigated.

References

[1] B. M. Pangrle and D. D. Gajski, "Design tools for intelligent silicon compilation," *IEEE Transactions on Computer-Aided Design of Integrated Circuits and Systems*, vol. 6, no. 6, pp. 1098–1112, 1986.

[2] E. F. Girczyc, R. J. A. Buhr, and J. P. Knight, "Applicability of a subset of Ada as an algorithmic hardware description language for graph-based hardware compilation," *IEEE Transactions on Computer-Aided Design of Integrated Circuits and Systems*, vol. 4, no. 2, pp. 134–142, 1985.

[3] P. G. Paulin and J. P. Knight, "Force-directed scheduling for the behavioral synthesis of ASIC's," *IEEE Transactions on Computer-Aided Design of Integrated Circuits and Systems*, vol. 8, no. 6, pp. 661–679, 1989.

[4] I. C. Park and C. M. Kyung, "Fast and near optimal scheduling in automatic data path synthesis," in *Proceedings of the 28th ACM/IEEE Design Automation Conference*, pp. 680–685, June 1991.

[5] N. Park and A. C. Parker, "Sehwa: a software package for synthesis of pipelined data path from behavioral specification," *IEEE Transactions on Computer-Aided Design of Integrated Circuits and Systems*, vol. 7, no. 3, pp. 356–370, 1988.

[6] E. F. Girczyc, "Loop winding—a data flow approach to functional pipelining," in *Proceedings of the IEEE International Symposium on Circuits and Systems*, pp. 382–385, 1987.

[7] C. J. Tseng and D. P. Siewiorek, "Automatic synthesis of data path on digital systems," *IEEE Transactions on Computer-Aided Design of Integrated Circuits and Systems*, vol. 5, no. 3, pp. 379–395, 1986.

[8] F. J. Kurdahi and A. C. Parker, "REAL: a program for register allocation," in *Proceedings of Design Automation Conference (DAC '87)*, pp. 210–215, Miami Beach, Fla, USA, 1987.

[9] C. Y. Huang, Y. S. Chen, Y. L. Lin, and Y. C. Hsu, "Data path allocation based on bipartite weighted matching," in *Proceedings of the 27th ACM/IEEE Design Automation Conference*, pp. 499–504, June 1990.

[10] F. S. Tsay and Y. C. Hsu, "Data path construction and refinement. Digest of Technical papers," in *Proceedings of the The International Conference on Computer-Aided Design (ICCAD '90)*, pp. 308–311, Santa Clara, Calif, USA, 1990.

[11] R. Camposano and W. Rosenstiel, "Synthesizing circuits from behavioral descriptions," *IEEE Transactions on Computer-Aided Design of Integrated Circuits and Systems*, vol. 8, no. 2, pp. 171–180, 1989.

[12] S. D. Johnson, *Synthesis of Digital Designs from Recursion Equations*, MIT Press, Cambridge, Mass, USA, 1984.

[13] M. R. Barbacci, G. E. Barnes, R. G. Cattell, and D. P. Siewiorek, "The ISPS computer description language," Tech. Rep. CMU-CS-79-137, School of Computer Science, Carnegie Mellon University, 1979.

[14] P. Marwedel, "The MIMOLA design system: tools for the design of digital processors," in *Proceedings of the 21st Design Automation Conference*, pp. 587–593, 1984.

[15] A. E. Casavant, M. A. d'Abreu, M. Dragomirecky et al., "Synthesis environment for designing DSP systems," *IEEE Design and Test of Computers*, vol. 6, no. 2, pp. 35–44, 1989.

[16] P. G. Paulin and J. P. Knight, "Algorithms for high-level synthesis," *IEEE Design and Test of Computers*, vol. 6, no. 6, pp. 18–31, 1989.

[17] D. D. Gajski and L. Ramachandran, "Introduction to high-level synthesis," *IEEE Design and Test of Computers*, vol. 11, no. 4, pp. 44–54, 1994.

[18] R. A. Walker and S. Chaudhuri, "Introduction to the scheduling problem," *IEEE Design and Test of Computers*, vol. 12, no. 2, pp. 60–69, 1995.

[19] V. Berstis, "V compiler: automating hardware design," *IEEE Design and Test of Computers*, vol. 6, no. 2, pp. 8–17, 1989.

[20] J. A. Fisher, "Trace Scheduling: a technique for global microcode compaction," *IEEE Transactions on Computers*, vol. 30, no. 7, pp. 478–490, 1981.

[21] A. Kuehlmann and R. A. Bergamaschi, "Timing analysis in high-level synthesis," in *Proceedings of the IEEE/ACM International Conference on Computer-Aided Design (ICCAD '92)*, pp. 349–354, November 1992.

[22] T. C. Wilson, N. Mukherjee, M. K. Garg, and D. K. Banerji, "ILP solution for optimum scheduling, module and register allocation, and operation binding in datapath synthesis," *VLSI Design*, vol. 3, no. 1, pp. 21–36, 1995.

[23] C. A. Papachristou and H. Konuk, "A linear program driven scheduling and allocation method followed by an interconnect optimization algorithm," in *Proceedings of the 27th ACM/IEEE Design Automation Conference*, pp. 77–83, June 1990.

[24] J. Biesenack, M. Koster, A. Langmaier et al., "Siemens high-level synthesis system CALLAS," *IEEE Transactions on Very Large Scale Integration (VLSI) Systems*, vol. 1, no. 3, pp. 244–252, 1993.

[25] The Electronic Design Interchange Format, Wikipedia, the free encyclopedia, 2011, http://en.wikipedia.org/wiki/EDIF.

[26] M. S. Rubin, "Computer Aids for VLSI Design. Appendix D: Electronic Design Interchange Format," 2011, http://www.rulabinsky.com/cavd/text/chapd.html.

[27] T. Filkorn, "A method for symbolic verification of synchronous circuits," in *Proceedings of the Computer Hardware Description Languages and their Applications (CHDL '91)*, pp. 229–239, Marseille, France, 1991.

[28] A. Kalavade and E. A. Lee, "A hardware-software codesign methodology for DSP applications," *IEEE Design and Test of Computers*, vol. 10, no. 3, pp. 16–28, 1993.

[29] R. Ernst, J. Henkel, and T. Benner, "Hardware-software cosynthesis for microcontrollers," *IEEE Design and Test of Computers*, vol. 10, no. 4, pp. 64–75, 1993.

[30] G. De Micheli, D. Ku, F. Mailhot, and T. Truong, "The Olympus synthesis system," *IEEE Design and Test of Computers*, vol. 7, no. 5, pp. 37–53, 1990.

[31] A. Jerraya, I. Park, and K. O'Brien, "AMICAL: an interactive high level synthesis environment," in *Proceedings of the 4th European Conference on Design Automation with the European Event in ASIC*, pp. 58–62, 1993.

[32] D. E. Thomas, J. K. Adams, and H. Schmit, "A model and methodology for hardware-software codesign," *IEEE Design and Test of Computers*, vol. 10, no. 3, pp. 6–15, 1993.

[33] C. A. R. Hoare, *Communicating Sequential Processes*, Prentice-Hall, Englewood Cliffs, NJ, USA, 1985.

[34] R. K. Gupta and G. De Micheli, "Hardware-software cosynthesis for digital systems," *IEEE Design and Test of Computers*, vol. 10, no. 3, pp. 29–41, 1993.

[35] I. Bolsens, H. J. De Man, B. Lin, K. Van Rompaey, S. Vercauteren, and D. Verkest, "Hardware/software co-design of digital telecommunication systems," *Proceedings of the IEEE*, vol. 85, no. 3, pp. 391–417, 1997.

[36] D. Genin, P. Hilfinger, J. Rabaey, C. Scheers, and H. De Man, "DSP specification using the Silage language," in *Proceedings of the International Conference on Acoustics, Speech, and Signal Processing*, pp. 1057–1060, April 1990.

[37] P. Willekens, "Algorithm specification in DSP station using data flow language," *DSP Applications*, vol. 3, no. 1, pp. 8–16, 1994.

[38] N. Halbwachs, P. Caspi, P. Raymond, and D. Pilaud, "The synchronous data flow programming language LUSTRE," *Proceedings of the IEEE*, vol. 79, no. 9, pp. 1305–1320, 1991.

[39] M. Van Canneyt, "Specification, simulation and implementation of a GSM speech codec with DSP station," *DSP and Multimedia Technology*, vol. 3, no. 5, pp. 6–15, 1994.

[40] J. T. Buck, "PTOLEMY: a framework for simulating and prototyping heterogeneous systems," *International Journal in Computer Simulation*, pp. 1–34, 1992.

[41] R. Lauwereins, M. Engels, M. Ade, and J. A. Peperstraete, "Grape-II: a system-level prototyping environment for DSP applications," *Computer*, vol. 28, no. 2, pp. 35–43, 1995.

[42] M. S. Rafie, "Rapid design and prototyping of a direct sequence spread-spectrum ASIC over a wireless link," *DSP and Multimedia Technology*, vol. 3, no. 6, pp. 6–12, 1994.

[43] L. Séméria, K. Sato, and G. De Micheli, "Synthesis of hardware models in C with pointers and complex data structures," *IEEE Transactions on Very Large Scale Integration (VLSI) Systems*, vol. 9, no. 6, pp. 743–756, 2001.

[44] R. P. Wilson, "Suif: an infrastructure for research on parallelizing and optimizing compilers," *ACM SIPLAN Notices*, vol. 28, no. 9, pp. 67–70, 1994.

[45] A. A. Kountouris and C. Wolinski, "Efficient scheduling of conditional behaviors for high-level synthesis," *ACM Transactions on Design Automation of Electronic Systems*, vol. 7, no. 3, pp. 380–412, 2002.

[46] S. Gupta, R. K. Gupta, N. D. Dutt, and A. Nicolau, "Coordinated parallelizing compiler optimizations and high-level synthesis," *ACM Transactions on Design Automation of Electronic Systems*, vol. 9, no. 4, pp. 441–470, 2004.

[47] W. Wang and T. K. Tan, "A comprehensive high-level synthesis system for control-flow intensive behaviors," in *Proceedings of the 13th ACM Great Lakes symppsium on VLSI (GLSVLSI '03)*, pp. 11–14, 2003.

[48] Z. P. Gu, J. Wang, R. P. Dick, and H. Zhou, "Incremental exploration of the combined physical and behavioral design space," in *Proceedings of the 42nd Design Automation Conference (DAC '05)*, pp. 208–213, 2005.

[49] L. Zhong and N. K. Jha, "Interconnect-aware high-level synthesis for low power," in *Proceedings of the IEEE/ACM International Conference on Computer Aided Design (ICCAD '02)*, pp. 110–117, November 2002.

[50] C. Huang, S. Ravi, A. Raghunathan, and N. K. Jha, "Generation of heterogeneous distributed architectures for memory-intensive applications through high-level synthesis," *IEEE Transactions on Very Large Scale Integration (VLSI) Systems*, vol. 15, no. 11, pp. 1191–1203, 2007.

[51] K. Wakabayashi, "C-based synthesis experiences with a behavior synthesizer, "Cyber"," in *Proceedings of the Design, Automation and Test in Europe*, pp. 390–393, 1999.

[52] W. Wang, A. Raghunathan, N. K. Jha, and S. Dey, "High-level synthesis of multi-process behavioral descriptions," in *Proceedings of the 16th IEEE International Conference on VLSI Design (VLSI '03)*, pp. 467–473, 2003.

[53] B. Le Gal, E. Casseau, and S. Huet, "Dynamic memory access management for high-performance DSP applications using high-level synthesis," *IEEE Transactions on Very Large Scale Integration (VLSI) Systems*, vol. 16, no. 11, pp. 1454–1464, 2008.

[54] K. Wakabayashi and H. Tanaka, "Global scheduling independent of control dependencies based on condition vectors," in *Proceedings of the 29th ACM/IEEE Design Automation Conference*, pp. 112–115, June 1992.

[55] S. Gupta, N. Dutt, R. Gupta, and A. Nicolau, "Dynamically increasing the scope of code motions during the high-level synthesis of digital circuits," *IEE Proceedings*, vol. 150, no. 5, pp. 330–337, 2003.

[56] E. Martin, O. Santieys, and J. Philippe, "GAUT, an architecture synthesis tool for dedicated signal processors," in *Proceedings of the IEEE International European Design Automation Conference (Euro-DAC '93)*, pp. 14–19, Hamburg, Germany, 1993.

[57] M. C. Molina, R. Ruiz-Sautua, P. García-Repetto, and R. Hermida, "Frequent-pattern-guided multilevel decomposition of behavioral specifications," *IEEE Transactions on Computer-Aided Design of Integrated Circuits and Systems*, vol. 28, no. 1, pp. 60–73, 2009.

[58] K. Avnit, V. D'Silva, A. Sowmya, S. Ramesh, and S. Parameswaran, "Provably correct on-chip communication: a formal approach to automatic protocol converter synthesis," *ACM Transactions on Design Automation of Electronic Systems*, vol. 14, no. 2, article 19, 2009.

[59] J. Keinert, M. Streubuhr, T. Schlichter et al., "SystemCoDesigneran—automatic ESL synthesis approach by design space exploration and behavioral synthesis for streaming applications," *ACM Transactions on Design Automation of Electronic Systems*, vol. 14, no. 1, article 1, 2009.

[60] J. Falk, C. Haubelt, and J. Teich, "Efficient representation and simulation of model-based designs in SystemC," in *Proceedings of the Forum on Design Languages*, pp. 129–134, Darmstadt, Germany, 2006.

[61] S. Kundu, S. Lerner, and R. K. Gupta, "Translation validation of high-level synthesis," *IEEE Transactions on Computer-Aided Design of Integrated Circuits and Systems*, vol. 29, no. 4, pp. 566–579, 2010.

[62] S. Paik, I. Shin, T. Kim, and Y. Shin, "HLS-1: a high-level synthesis framework for latch-based architectures," *IEEE Transactions on Computer-Aided Design of Integrated Circuits and Systems*, vol. 29, no. 5, pp. 657–670, 2010.

[63] M. Rim and R. Jain, "Lower-bound performance estimation for high-level synthesis scheduling problem," *IEEE Transactions on Computer-Aided Design of Integrated Circuits and Systems*, vol. 13, no. 4, pp. 451–458, 1994.

[64] S. Chaudhuri and R. A. Walker, "Computing lower bounds on functional units before scheduling," *IEEE Transactions on Very Large Scale Integration (VLSI) Systems*, vol. 4, no. 2, pp. 273–279, 1996.

[65] H. Mecha, M. Fernandez, F. Tirado, J. Septien, D. Mozos, and K. Olcoz, "Method for area estimation of data-path in high level synthesis," *IEEE Transactions on Computer-Aided Design of Integrated Circuits and Systems*, vol. 15, no. 2, pp. 258–265, 1996.

[66] Y. M. Fang and D. F. Wong, "Simultaneous functional-unit binding and floorplanning. Digest of Technical Papers," in *Proceedings of the International Conference on Computer-Aided Design (ICCAD '94)*, pp. 317–321, Santa Clara, Calif, USA, 1994.

[67] M. Munch, N. Wehn, and M. Glesner, "Optimum simultaneous placement and binding for bit-slice architectures," in *Proceedings of the Asia and South Pacific Design Automation Conference (ASP-DAC '95)*, pp. 735–742, September 1995.

[68] A. Ahmadi and M. Zwolinski, "Multiple-width bus partitioning approach to datapath synthesis," in *Proceedings of the IEEE International Symposium on Circuits and Systems (ISCAS '07)*, pp. 2994–2997, May 2007.

[69] R. Gupta and M. A. Breuer, "Partial scan design of register-transfer level circuits," *Journal of Electronic Testing*, vol. 7, no. 1-2, pp. 25–46, 1995.

[70] M. L. Flottes, D. Hammad, and B. Rouzeyre, "High level synthesis for easy testability," in *Proceedings of the European Design and Test Conference*, pp. 198–206, Paris, France, 1995.

[71] M. K. Dhodhi, F. H. Hielscher, R. H. Storer, and J. Bhasker, "Datapath synthesis using a problem-space genetic algorithm," *IEEE Transactions on Computer-Aided Design of Integrated Circuits and Systems*, vol. 14, no. 8, pp. 934–944, 1995.

[72] A. Mujumdar, R. Jain, and K. Saluja, "Incorporating testability considerations in high-level synthesis," *Journal of Electronic Testing*, vol. 5, no. 1, pp. 43–55, 1994.

[73] M. Potkonjak, S. Dey, and R. K. Roy, "Synthesis-for-testability using transformations," in *Proceedings of the Asia and South Pacific Design Automation Conference (ASP-DAC '95)*, pp. 485–490, September 1995.

[74] F. F. Hsu, E. M. Rudnick, and J. H. Patel, "Enhancing high-level control-flow for improved testability. Digest of Technical Papers," in *Proceedings of the International Conference on Computer-Aided Design (ICCAD '96)*, pp. 322–328, San Jose, Calif, USA, 1996.

[75] A. Raghunathan, S. Dey, and N. K. Jha, "Register-transfer level estimation techniques for switching activity and power consumption," in *Proceedings of the IEEE/ACM International*

Conference on Computer-Aided Design, pp. 158–165, November 1996.

[76] J. Rabaey, L. Guerra, and R. Mehra, "Design guidance in the power dimension," in *Proceedings of the 1995 20th International Conference on Acoustics, Speech, and Signal Processing*, pp. 2837–2840, May 1995.

[77] R. Mehra and J. Rabaey, "Exploiting regularity for low-power design," in *Proceedings of the IEEE/ACM International Conference on Computer-Aided Design*, pp. 166–172, November 1996.

[78] A. Raghunathan and N. K. Jha, "Behavioral synthesis for low power," in *Proceedings of the IEEE International Conference on Computer Design*, pp. 318–322, October 1994.

[79] L. Goodby, A. Orailoglu, and P. M. Chau, "Microarchitectural synthesis of performance-constrained, low-power VLSI designs," in *Proceedings of the IEEE International Conference on Computer Design*, pp. 323–326, October 1994.

[80] E. Musoll and J. Cortadella, "Scheduling and resource binding for low power," in *Proceedings of the 8th International Symposium on System Synthesis*, pp. 104–109, September 1995.

[81] N. Kumar, S. Katkoori, L. Rader, and R. Vemuri, "Profile-driven behavioral synthesis for low-power VLSI systems," *IEEE Design and Test of Computers*, vol. 12, no. 3, pp. 70–84, 1995.

[82] R. San Martin and J. P. Knight, "Power-profiler: optimizing ASICs power consumption at the behavioral level," in *Proceedings of the 32nd Design Automation Conference*, pp. 42–47, June 1995.

[83] C. Trabelsi, R. Ben Atitallah, S. Meftali, J. L. Dekeyser, and A. Jemai, "A model-driven approach for hybrid power estimation in embedded systems design," *Eurasip Journal on Embedded Systems*, vol. 2011, Article ID 569031, 2011.

[84] I. Issenin, E. Brockmeyer, B. Durinck, and N. D. Dutt, "Data-reuse-driven energy-aware cosynthesis of scratch pad memory and hierarchical bus-based communication architecture for multiprocessor streaming applications," *IEEE Transactions on Computer-Aided Design of Integrated Circuits and Systems*, vol. 27, no. 8, pp. 1439–1452, 2008.

[85] D. S. Rao and F. J. Kurdahi, "Controller and datapath trade-offs in hierarchical RT-level synthesis," in *Proceedings of the 7th International Symposium on High-Level Synthesis*, pp. 152–157, May 1994.

[86] S. C. Y. Huang and W. H. Wolf, "How datapath allocation affects controller delay," in *Proceedings of the 7th International Symposium on High-Level Synthesis*, pp. 158–163, May 1994.

[87] UML 2.0, 2012, http://www.omg.org/spec/UML/2.0/.

[88] Model Transformation Framework, 2012, http://www.alphaworks.ibm.com/tech/mtf.

[89] UML MARTE, 2012, http://www.omgwiki.org/marte/.

[90] MARTE specification version 1.0., 2012, http://www.omg.org/spec/MARTE/1.0/PDF/.

[91] The Eclipse Software, 2012, http://en.wikipedia.org/wiki/Eclipse_(software).

[92] Gaspard2 UML profile documentation, 2012, http://www.lifl.fr/west/gaspard/gaspard-profile.pdf.

[93] M. Dossis, "Intermediate predicate format for design automation tools," *Journal of Next Generation Information Technology*, vol. 1, no. 1, pp. 100–117, 2010.

[94] U. Nilsson and J. Maluszynski, *Logic Programming and Prolog*, John Wiley & Sons, 2nd edition, 1995.

Towards Self-Adaptive KPN Applications on NoC-Based MPSoCs

Onur Derin,[1] Prasanth Kuncheerath Ramankutty,[1] Paolo Meloni,[2] and Emanuele Cannella[3]

[1] ALaRI, Faculty of Informatics, University of Lugano, 6904 Lugano, Switzerland
[2] Department of Electrical and Electronic Engineering, Faculty of Engineering, University of Cagliari, 09123 Cagliari, Italy
[3] LIACS, Leiden University, 2333 CA Leiden, The Netherlands

Correspondence should be addressed to Onur Derin, derino@alari.ch

Academic Editor: Phillip A. Laplante

Self-adaptivity is the ability of a system to adapt itself dynamically to internal and external changes. Such a capability helps systems to meet the performance and quality goals, while judiciously using available resources. In this paper, we propose a framework to implement application level self-adaptation capabilities in KPN applications running on NoC-based MPSoCs. The monitor-controller-adapter mechanism is used at the application level. The monitor measures various parameters to check whether the system meets the assigned goals. The controller takes decisions to steer the system towards the goal, which are applied by the adapters. The proposed framework requires minimal modifications to the application code and offers ease of integration. It incorporates a generic adaptation controller based on fuzzy logic. We present the MJPEG encoder as a case study to demonstrate the effectiveness of the approach. Our results show that even if the parameters of the fuzzy controller are not tuned optimally, the adaptation convergence is achieved within reasonable time and error limits. Moreover, the incurred steady-state overhead due to the framework is 4% for average frame-rate, 3.5% for average bit-rate, and 0.5% for additional control data introduced in the network.

1. Introduction

Recent trends in microprocessor design have witnessed a paradigm shift from single core architectures towards Multi-processor-System-on-Chips (MPSoCs) due to unsustainable increases in power dissipation while running a single processor at very high frequencies. As the number of cores in the system increases, on-chip communication becomes a bottleneck. To address the scalability issues of MPSoCs, Networks-on-chips (NoCs) [1] have emerged as a new communication paradigm. However, even in the case of NoC-based systems, if shared memory access is employed, memory coherence protocols induce an overhead in the communication network rendering the gain from additional cores useless. No Remote Memory Access (NORMA) [2] model addresses this problem by assigning a private local memory for each NoC tile. This solution is especially suited for programming models based on message passing.

Embedded systems are often subject to stringent non-functional goals such as high computational performance and dependability, low power consumption, memory usage, and chip area. Satisfying such requirements imposed by the application designer on systems with increasing complexity of the underlying architectures is a fundamental challenge. To deal with this problem, designers often resort to self-adaptation-based techniques [3]. Self-adaptive systems are able to react when the actual operating conditions of the system such as the workload, the internal/external conditions, and the quality-of-service goals differ from the design-time assumptions.

The techniques to be developed for implementing self-adaptive applications depend heavily on the adopted model of computation. In this paper, we adopt Kahn Process Networks (KPN) [4] model due to its suitability for NORMA-based NoC multiprocessors. KPN represents a stream-oriented computation model, where an application is organized as streams and computational blocks; streams represent the flow of data, while computational blocks represent operations on a stream of data, making it a suitable computation model to represent most of the signal processing and multimedia applications of the embedded systems world.

There are certain challenges to be tackled when designing self-adaptive systems. A general concern is the overhead introduced in making the system monitorable and adaptable. A large overhead can easily compensate the benefits of adaptation. There are two types of overhead. The first type, which can be called *steady state overhead*, is the overhead experienced simply due to the additional hardware or software for enabling monitoring and adaptation capabilities. It is present even when there are no ongoing adaptations. This overhead should be minimized because it has to be afforded at all times. The second type, which can be called *transient overhead*, is the overhead experienced while an adaptation is taking place. The major sources of this overhead are the adaptation control logic and the realization of an adaptation. If the system is expected to have frequent adaptations, then care must be taken to minimize this type of overhead.

Separation of concerns is a key feature for self-adaptive systems. However, the realization of this principle is quite challenging for several reasons. It emphasizes that the application programmer should be involved as minimally as possible in making the system self-adaptive. Although it may be possible to realize this for adaptations at the run-time environment and hardware levels because of the clear interface between the application and the execution platform, it is a more difficult task for application level adaptations. Intrinsic application knowledge by the application programmer is required in order to expose the feasible adaptations in the application. Automatic inference of such adaptations would be very difficult, if possible at all. Depending on the adaptation goal, another difficulty is in the inference of what to monitor and how to monitor it without involving the programmer. There is a semantic gap to be bridged between the given goal and the application. Monitoring involves choosing the correct program variables and operating on them in order to calculate the actual metric that corresponds to the goal. Another issue with the separation of concerns principle is that it is likely to conflict with the low overhead goal mentioned previously. The less the programmer has to do would lead to the more the self-adaptation logic has to do, thus yielding to more overhead due its complexity. Last but not least, the behavior of the adaptation controller is application-dependent. Machine learning algorithms can be used to obtain the application knowledge, particularly the relation between the goal and the adaptations, but it would result in a complex control logic with a bigger overhead which may not be acceptable for embedded systems. Alternatively, the required application knowledge can be provided to the controller by the application programmer.

Another fundamental challenge for system-wide self-adaptivity is presented by the management of the adaptations. The systems are usually faced with multiple goals to satisfy at run-time such as a desired throughput, low power consumption, and high dependability. Satisfying all the goals by controlling various possible adaptation options is a difficult task. Changing the set of goal types would require a complete or partial redesign of the controller. Possible solutions to this problem are automated controller synthesis or designing generic controllers.

In this paper, we are addressing the application level self-adaptation challenges mentioned above in the context of streaming applications based on the KPN model and running on NORMA-based NoC multiprocessors. The main contribution of this work is the investigation of fuzzy control as a generic adaptation management mechanism for self-adaptive systems. In doing so, methods for adding adaptation and monitoring capabilities to KPN applications are proposed. Results are presented showing the generality and quality of control. The overhead of the proposed self-adaptive framework is also reported with a case study.

The remaining part of the paper is organized as follows. An overview of the related work is provided in Section 2. Section 3 introduces our framework with implementation details of monitoring, controlling, and adaptive tasks. Section 4 discusses adaptive-MJPEG as a case study, which is built using the proposed M-C-A framework. The results of the case study are provided in Section 5. Section 6 discusses the main design principles and generality of the proposed framework, while Section 7 concludes our work.

2. Related Work

In [5], authors presented a monitor-controller-adapter-based framework to enable self-adaptivity for streaming applications. The paper introduces a framework based on the KPN computation model. However, implementation details of monitors and adaptation controllers are not provided. Even though a case study is provided, no results are available to evaluate the framework in terms of its effectiveness and performance (timing, convergence, etc.).

A standardized way to manage self-adaptivity at application level is provided in [6], which proposes *separation of concerns* between adaptation management and system functionalities. Self-adaptivity is obtained by applying a set of *adaptation policies* on software components, while these policies are triggered by certain configurable system events. Possible adaptations for component behavior and application parameters are also discussed. Unfortunately, they do not discuss if and how a general goal is achieved.

In [7], the authors present the results of project MADAM that has delivered a comprehensive solution for the development and operation of context-aware, self-adaptive applications. The main contributions of this work are (a) a sophisticated middleware that supports the dynamic adaptation of component-based applications, and (b) an innovative model-driven development methodology based on abstract adaptation models and corresponding model-to-code transformations.

A generic model of a self-adaptive system is presented in [8], in which a proposal to manage self-adaptivity at hardware and software levels by means of a decentralized control algorithm is provided. A goal management methodology, a goal specification interface, along with a decentralized and coordinated control mechanism is proposed as part of this work.

In [9–11], several techniques for fine-grained QoS control of multimedia applications are presented. The proposed methods generate a controlled application that meets given

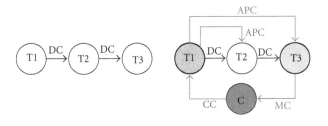

DC: data channel   CC: control channel

MC: monitor channel   APC: adaptation propagation channel

T1: adaptive task

C: adaptation controller

(a) KPN application   (b) Self-adaptive KPN application

FIGURE 1: A self-adaptive KPN application based on M-C-A framework.

QoS requirements from an input application software. The controller monitors the progress of the computation in a cycle and chooses the next action to run and its quality level, guided by safety and optimality constraints for the system. Our work differs from these methods in two aspects: (1) we target applications running on MPSoCs in a distributed manner, whereas these works consider single threaded applications for which it is possible to estimate by using timing analysis and profiling techniques, worst-case execution times and average execution times, for different levels of quality. (2) Our controller is generic and requires minimal knowledge of application characteristics as compared to these methods which require deep knowledge of the data-flow structure of the application.

A middleware-based approach to enable run-time migration of processes among tiles of a NoC is presented in [12]. Such a technique helps in achieving application-independent adaptivity support such as fault tolerance. On the other hand, our work deals with application-dependent parameter adaptations using a M-C-A based approach.

3. Self-Adaptive KPN Applications Using Distributed M-C-A Framework

This section presents our framework to build self-adaptive component-based applications by incorporating a distributed monitor-controller-adapter (M-C-A) mechanism in the KPN application pipeline (as proposed in [5]). Monitoring involves measurements of various parameters to check whether the system meets the assigned goals. The controller is capable of driving adaptations when goals are not met, whereas adapters are in charge of performing adaptations. In case of KPN applications running on MPSoCs, various tasks of the application will be mapped onto different tiles of the platform. Hence it is quite possible that the parameter to be monitored is present in one tile, whereas the task to be adapted may exist on a different tile. This forces the

monitor, controller, and adapters to be implemented on different tiles in a distributed manner. For example, in case of a video encoder application, bit-rate monitoring should be done on the tile where sink task is present whereas the frame-size adapter logic has to be present on the tile where source task is located. Our framework represents a self-adaptive application in terms of the following entities: adaptive tasks implementing adapter functions, monitoring tasks calling monitoring functions, adaptation controller(s), and adaptation propagation channels alongside the original task graph. Figure 1 depicts a simple KPN application and its self-adaptive version based on our framework.

3.1. Adaptive Task. In order to implement application specific adaptations, each task should expose its adaptation space (set of adaptable parameters) to the external world. Adaptive tasks will have *control channels* and multiple optional *adaptation propagation channels* in addition to nominal input/output data channels. Control channels carry the control commands from the controller to adaptive tasks whereas adaptation propagation channels carry new parameter values from adaptive tasks to other tasks which require these updated values. For example, in case of an adaptive source task (which supports frame-size adaptation) in a video encoding application, control channel will carry the frame-size control command from the controller, whereas the adaptation propagation channels will carry the new frame-size to any other relevant tasks. The frequency at which these channels will be read/written by the task depends on the application as well as the granularity required for the control. In order to perform the adaptation, the task should read the control command from the control channel and call the adapter functions, with control command as the argument. It should also send the modified values of the adapted parameter to other tasks which need these updated parameters. Figure 2 shows the modifications required (shown in blue) to transform a KPN task into an adaptive KPN task.

```
adaptiveTask()
{
  for(i=0; i<M; i++) {

      read(CTRL_CH, &ctrlSignal);
      adaptParam(ctrlSignal);
      write(ADAPT_PROP_CH, newParam);

      for(j=0; j<N ; j++) {
          read(DATA_IN_CH, &inData)
          outData = process(inData);
          write(DATA_OUT_CH, outData);
      }
  }
}
```

FIGURE 2: An adaptive task.

```
monitoringTask()
{
  for(i=0; i<M; i++) {

      int dataCounter = 0;
      for(j=0; j<N ; j++) {
          read(DATA_IN_CH, &inData);
          dataCounter += sizeof(inData);
          outData = process(inData);
          write(DATA_OUT_CH, outData);
      }

      timeStamp t = getCurrentTime();
      alignSlidingWindow(dataCounter, t);
      br = calculateBitrate();
      tr = calculateTokenrate();
      write(MONITOR_CH_BR, br);
      write(MONITOR_CH_TR, tr);
  }
}
```

FIGURE 3: A monitoring task.

3.1.1. Adapter Functions. Adapter functions perform the actions needed to perform the adaptations. The implementation of adapter functions is parameter dependent. An adapter function for adapting "param1" has the following signature: void adaptParam1(CtrlCommand c); where control command argument can take one of the following values: (a) −2: modify the adaptable parameter so as to aggressively reduce the monitored parameter, (b) −1: modify the adaptable parameter so as to mildly reduce the monitored parameter, (c) 0: maintain same value for the parameter, (d) +1: modify the adaptable parameter so as to mildly increase the monitored parameter, (e) +2: modify the adaptable parameter so as to aggressively increase the monitored parameter. The adapter functions need to be implemented by the application programmer with appropriate interpretation of the mild/aggressive changes to the parameter.

3.2. Monitoring Task. Monitoring refers to the measurement of a parameter in the system, that is, of interest. The accuracy and timing of these measurements are critical, since it impacts the overall quality of adaptation. A normal KPN task is converted to a monitoring task by calling monitoring functions provided by the framework. Figure 3 shows a simple monitoring task obtained by modifying a typical KPN task by adding calls to the monitoring functions (shown in blue). Our framework supports two types of throughput monitoring: bit-rate and token-rate. The granularity of monitoring is application-dependent and it is the application programmers responsibility to insert calls to the monitoring functions at an appropriate place in the code. Furthermore, the framework assumes support from the platform to measure the current time. Monitoring task should also send the monitored parameter values to the adaptation controller using monitor channels.

3.2.1. Monitoring Functions. The following are the monitoring functions provided.

AlignSlidingWindow. We propose sliding-window monitoring, which is triggered by a call to the alignSlidingWindow function. Sliding window method is deployed to find the average of last few instantaneous values of a monitored parameter. It is realized using two circular arrays of size equal to *monitor-width*, which is configurable in the implementation. These arrays are used to hold the parameter values and the timestamp of their measurements. When alignSliding-Window is called (with the newly captured parameter value and its timestamp as arguments), the windows are adjusted so that the arrays contain the most recent parameter values.

CalculateTokenRate. Token rate is the number of tokens received per unit time by the monitoring task. It is calculated using the number of entries in the sliding window and the difference in timestamps between the latest and oldest entries.

CalculateBitRate. This function calculates the throughput of the generated data. Throughput (bit-rate) is calculated by dividing the sum of all entries in the monitoring window by the difference in timestamps between the latest and oldest entries.

The width of the sliding window can be specified by the application programmer using the monitor-width parameter. This parameter decides the sensitivity of the control mechanism (i.e., how fast the variations in the monitored variables are perceived). If the monitor-width is too large, the sensitivity will be low, that is, the effect of a particular adaptation strategy will be reflected in the average value only after many values got generated under that strategy. On the other hand, a very small monitor window helps in detecting changes in the parameter very fast. However, this may cause large ripples in the output since any adaptation strategy needs some settling time before its effects are visible. Hence it is very important to keep monitor-width at an optimum value to obtain a good quality of adaptation.

3.3. Controller. The most important entity of any adaptation scheme is the controller, because it takes decisions to steer the monitored parameters towards their target values. The correctness and speed of the decisions taken by the controller influence the effectiveness of the adaptation mechanism. Hence controller is the most critical entity in the design of self-adaptive systems. In order to free the application developer from self-adaptivity concerns, our framework provides a generic *fuzzy logic* [13] based adaptation controller that should work for any application being run on the platform.

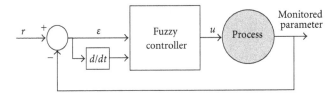

FIGURE 4: A simple fuzzy control-based system.

Fuzzy logic is a form of multivalued logic that deals with reasoning in an approximate way rather than precise. It is derived from the fuzzy set theory which is based on the understanding that every fact is present or not up to a certain degree. Fuzzy control represents formal methodology for presentation, manipulation, and implementation of human heuristic knowledge about how certain processes should be controlled by using a simple, rule-based "*if X and Y then Z*" approach rather than attempting to model a system mathematically. For example, instead of dealing with temperature control in precise terms, fuzzy controller uses linguistic terms such as "*if (process is too cool) and (process is getting colder) then (heat the process)*" or "*if (process is too hot) and (process is heating) then (cool the process quickly).*" These terms are imprecise yet very descriptive of what must actually happen. We chose to use fuzzy logic control since the mathematical models of most application processes are unknown and would be very difficult to build, yet it can easily be described linguistically such as if process is very hot and the temperature is increasing, it is clear that the process has to be cooled quickly.

Figure 4 depicts a simple fuzzy logic controlled system. Here some parameter of interest within the system is monitored. The error signal (ϵ) is the difference between the reference value (r) of the parameter and its monitored value. The fuzzy control logic takes this error signal and its rate of change as inputs and generates the control signal (u) as the output, which will be fed to the adapter logic.

We propose to implement a separate fuzzy controller for each specified goal of the system, thus offering scalability in terms of adding new goals. This also allows controller tasks to be placed in tiles which are at optimum distances from the corresponding adaptive and monitoring tasks, hence reducing the latency and the amount of network traffic introduced by control data. The frequency at which the controller should be run is application-dependent. For example, in case of a frame-rate control in a video encoder, the algorithm can be run for every third video frame.

Our design of the fuzzy controller is based on the following parameters.

Error (ϵ). The difference between the monitored value of a parameter and its target value.

Delta Error ($\Delta\epsilon$). The difference between current error and previous error.

Control Settling Width. The duration for which the controller should wait for a control decision to take its effect on

TABLE 1: Error ranges for the fuzzy controller.

Error range	Range name
(Error threshold high) $< \epsilon$	Positive huge
(Error threshold low) $< \epsilon \leq$ (error threshold high)	Positive large
$0 \leq \epsilon \leq$ (error threshold low)	Positive small
$-$(Error threshold low) $\leq \epsilon < 0$	Negative small
$-$(Error threshold high) $\leq \epsilon < -$ (error threshold low)	Negative large
$\epsilon < -$(error threshold high)	Negative huge

TABLE 2: Delta-error ranges for the fuzzy controller.

Delta-error range	Range name
(Delta error threshold) $< \Delta\epsilon$	Positive large
$0 \leq \Delta\epsilon \leq$ (delta error threshold)	Positive small
$-$(delta error threshold) $\leq \Delta\epsilon < 0$	Negative small
$\Delta\epsilon < -$(delta error threshold)	Negative large

TABLE 3: Control levels and their meanings.

Control levels	Meaning
-2	Aggressively reduce the monitored parameter
-1	Mildly reduce the monitored parameter
0	Maintain same value for the monitored parameter
$+1$	Mildly increase the monitored parameter
$+2$	Aggressively increase the monitored parameter

the monitored parameter before taking the next decision. In other words, settling width represents the duration between two consecutive control decisions. For example, in the case of frame-rate control, the settling width can be represented in terms of the number of frames between two consecutive control decisions.

Error Threshold Low and Error Threshold High. Threshold values divide the error axis into distinct intervals (i.e., error ranges). The decision taken by the controller depends on which interval in the error axis the current error value belongs to.

Delta Error Threshold. Similar to the error thresholds, delta-error threshold divides the delta-error axis into sub intervals (i.e., delta-error ranges). The interval in which delta-error falls also influences the decision of the controller.

Depending on which interval the value of error/delta-error falls, they are assigned a range value. Tables 1 and 2 give all the possible range values and the corresponding range names for errors and delta-errors, respectively.

Our controller implements five discrete levels of control as detailed in Table 3. For example, to reduce the monitored parameter aggressively, controller generates -2 as the control command. Similarly $+1$ at the controller output seeks for mild increase in the parameter. The interpretation of these discrete outputs is parameter dependent and has to be done by the adapter functions.

The decision making algorithm of the controller is summarized as follows.

(i) If error range is *positive huge* then control command is -2 (i.e., if the current value of the parameter is very much greater than the target value then seek to decrease it aggressively).

(ii) If error range is *positive large* and delta-error range is *negative large* then control command is 0 (i.e., if the current value of the parameter is greater than the target value and the error is decreasing at a very fast pace then seek to maintain previous situation. This means that the decision taken at the previous step was correct, so do not change anything).

(iii) If error range is *positive large* and delta-error range is not *negative large* then control command is -1 (i.e., if the current value of the parameter is greater than the target value and the error is not decreasing at a very fast pace then reduce the parameter mildly. This means that the decision taken at the previous step was not enough and further reduction of parameter value is needed).

(iv) If error range is *positive small* and delta-error range is *positive large* then control command is -1 (i.e., if the current value of the parameter is slightly greater than the target value and the error is increasing at a very fast pace then reduce the parameter mildly. This means that even though error is within the tolerance band it is deviating in the positive direction very fast, so try reducing the parameter value mildly).

(v) If error range is *positive small* and delta-error range is not *positive large* then control command is 0 (i.e., if the current value of the parameter is slightly greater than the target value and the error is not increasing at a very fast pace then seek to maintain previous situation. This means that error is smoothly maintaining its value within the tolerance limits, so no action needed).

(vi) If error range is *negative small* and delta-error range is *negative large* then control command is $+1$ (i.e., if the current value of the parameter is slightly lesser than the target value and the error is decreasing at an abrupt pace then increase the parameter mildly. This means that even though error is within the tolerance band it is deviating in the negative direction very fast, so try increasing the parameter value mildly).

(vii) If error range is *negative small* and delta-error range is not *negative large* then control command is 0 (i.e., if the current value of the parameter is slightly lesser than the target value and the error is not decreasing fast then nothing needs to be changed. This means that error is smoothly maintaining its value within the tolerance limits, so no action needed).

(viii) If error range is *negative large* and delta-error range is *positive large* then control command is 0 (i.e., if the current value of the parameter is much smaller than the target value and the error is increasing at a very

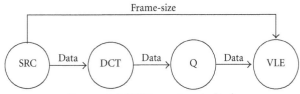

FIGURE 5: MJPEG encoder pipeline.

TABLE 4: Adaptation control algorithm.

Control command		Delta-error			
		POS_large	POS_small	NEG_small	NEG_large
Error	POS_huge	−2	−2	−2	−2
	POS_large	−1	−1	−1	0
	POS_small	−1	0	0	0
	NEG_small	0	0	0	1
	NEG_large	0	1	1	1
	NEG_huge	2	2	2	2

fast pace then seek to maintain previous situation. This means that the decision taken at the previous step was correct, so no action required).

(ix) If error range is *negative large* and delta-error range is not *positive large* then control command is +1 (i.e., if the current value of the parameter is much smaller than the target value and the error is not increasing at a very fast pace then seek to increase the parameter mildly. This means that the decision taken at the previous step was not enough and further increase of parameter is needed).

(x) If error range is *negative huge* then control command is +2 (i.e., if the current value of the parameter is very much smaller than the target value then seek to increase it aggressively).

Table 4 captures the behavior of the algorithm for all possible situations.

The functioning of the controller can be summarized as below. For every new received value of the monitored parameter, the controller decides whether to take a new control decision depending on the settling-width. If this input has to be ignored for a parameter then the corresponding adaptive task will be asked to maintain its previous situation (by sending 0 as the control command). On the other hand, if this input has to be considered for a parameter then following actions are performed. Error and delta-error for that parameter are calculated first. Then control algorithm will be run using these values to decide the control command. The generated command will be communicated to the respective adaptive task through the control channel.

4. Case Study: Motion JPEG (MJPEG)

This section presents MJPEG [14], a popular video compression standard, as a case study to demonstrate our framework. This algorithm is selected because its processes are coarse grained with high computation/communication ratio, a characteristic of an application suited for NoC-based MPSoCs. A typical MJPEG encoder pipeline is shown in Figure 5, where all the components can be modeled as KPN tasks.

Video Source (SRC). This component captures the input video frame-by-frame and feeds it to the succeeding components in the pipeline one block (8 × 8 pixels) at a time.

Discrete Cosine Transform (DCT). This component performs discrete cosine transform on each video block received from the SRC component and sends it to the Quantizer for further

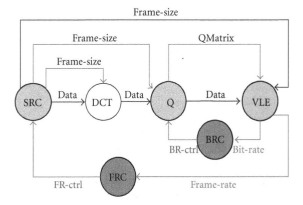

FIGURE 6: Adaptive-MJPEG encoder pipeline (see the color legend of Figure 1).

processing. DCT is widely used for multimedia compression algorithms such as MP3, JPEG, and MPEG, where high frequency components of less amplitude can be discarded without compromising quality.

Quantization (Q). Quantization refers to reducing the amplitude of a signal to achieve compression. In MJPEG, an 8 × 8 matrix of coefficients (QMatrix) is used for this purpose and the resultant data is rounded off to the nearest integer. The Quantizer also performs a 2D to 1D conversion of the quantized blocks by doing a zig-zag scan.

Variable Length Encoding (VLE). VLE is the last stage of MJPEG pipeline, where entropy (Huffman) encoding is done on the received video blocks. VLE also acts as the sink component, generating the final MJPEG stream by inserting headers/markers to indicate the start/end of each frame.

4.1. Self-Adaptive MJPEG. In this section, we present the implementation of the self-adaptive MJPEG encoder on our NoC-based platform using our M-C-A framework. This implementation supports autonomous control of bit-rate (BR) and frame-rate (FR) to match the target values set by the user. Bit-rate adaptation is achieved by controlling the quality of encoding (by scaling the QMatrix accordingly), whereas frame-size scaling is used to control the frame-rate.

$$CTRL\_SETTLE\_WIDTH\_BR = CTRL\_SWF\_BR \times MONITOR\_WIDTH$$
$$CTRL\_SETTLE\_WIDTH\_FR = CTRL\_SWF\_FR \times MONITOR\_WIDTH$$

$$ERR\_THRESHOLD\_BR = ERR\_TF\_BR \times TARGET\_BR$$
$$ERR\_THRESHOLD\_HIGH\_BR = ERR\_THF\_BR \times TARGET\_BR$$

$$ERR\_THRESHOLD\_FR = ERR\_TF\_FR \times TARGET\_FR$$
$$ERR\_THRESHOLD\_HIGH\_FR = ERR\_THF\_FR \times TARGET\_FR$$

$$DERR\_THRESHOLD\_BR = DERR\_TF\_BR \times TARGET\_BR$$
$$DERR\_THRESHOLD\_FR = DERR\_TF\_FR \times TARGET\_FR$$

CTRL_SWF_BR: Control Settling Width Factor for Bit-rate
CTRL_SWF_FR: Control Settling Width Factor for Frame-rate
ERR_TF_BR: Error Threshold factor for Bit-rate
ERR_THF_BR: Error Threshold High factor for Bit-rate
ERR_TF_FR: Error Threshold factor for Frame-rate
ERR_THF_FR: Error Threshold High factor for Frame-rate
DERR_TF_BR: Delta-error Threshold factor for Bit-rate
DERR_TF_FR: Delta-error Threshold factor for Frame-rate

FIGURE 7: Settling widths and error thresholds for controller.

The modifications done on the MJPEG pipeline to make it self-adaptive are shown in Figure 6 and are as follows.

4.1.1. Monitoring VLE.
The VLE task is equipped with monitoring capabilities (for bit-rate and frame-rate) by adding calls to the monitoring functions. Monitoring is done at the frame-level, hence these function calls are made after the task has accumulated all the blocks corresponding to one frame. Timestamp of a frame is measured by reading the hardware timer register of the NoC platform. Every time a new frame is generated, *alignMonitorWindow()* function is called with the frame-size and timestamp as arguments. Average values of the bit-rate and frame-rate are obtained by calling *calculateBitRate()* and *calculateTokenRate()* functions, respectively.

4.1.2. Controllers.
We decided to implement two independent controllers, one for bit-rate and the other for frame-rate. The design principles are as detailed in the previous section. In our implementation, the settling-widths are specified as a fraction of the monitor-width whereas the threshold values of error and delta-error signals are taken as a percentage of the target parameter values. These fraction parameters are exposed such that they can be fine tuned by the user. Calculation of settling-widths and threshold values used in our implementation are shown in Figure 7. For every newly generated frame, the controllers receive the monitored values of bit-rate and frame-rate. Depending on the settling-width, they decide whether to take a new control decision. If a new control decision is needed, the fuzzy control algorithm will be run using the error and delta-error values for the input. The generated control-command for bit-rate is sent to the adaptive Quantizer task, whereas the frame-rate control-command is sent to the adaptive Source task.

4.1.3. Adaptive Quantizer.
The quantization of the data has a direct impact on the generated bit-rate of the encoder. The output bit-rate can be adapted to the required level by scaling the QMatrix. For example, when the quantization coefficients are small, the output of the quantizer has more

nonzero values and hence the VLE component will produce more bits per frame. On the other hand, when the input data is quantized using large quantization coefficients, fewer bits will be generated per frame. Figure 8 shows the output bit-rates for various scaling factors of QMatrix in case of a slow, 128×128 pixel present the results of running our self-adaptive MJPEG encoder onel video.

To make the quantizer adaptive, adaptBitrate() function is implemented, which takes the control command from the bit-rate controller as input. The implemented bit-rate adapter logic supports two levels of scaling for the QMatrix-aggressive and mild. The algorithm maintains three parameters (configurable by the user), namely QuantScaleCoeff, AggrQScaleFactor, and MildQScaleFactor to perform the adaptations.

QuantScaleCoeff (Quantization Scaling Coefficient). The coefficient by which all Q-Matrix coefficients will be multiplied to produce its scaled version.

AggrQScaleFactor (Aggressive Quantization Scaling Factor). The constant by which previous value of QuantScaleCoeff will be multiplied/divided to obtain its current value in case of aggressive scaling.

MildQScaleFactor (Mild Quantization Scaling Factor). The constant by which the previous value of QuantScaleCoeff will be multiplied/divided to obtain its current value in case of mild scaling.

The bit-rate adapter works as follows. Before reading the data for a new frame, the quantizer task reads the bit-rate control command from the controller and calls adaptBitrate() function with this value. If the decision by the controller is to aggressively decrease the bit-rate, the current value of the *QuantScaleCoeff* will be multiplied by AggrQScaleFactor to obtain its new value. On the other hand, if the adapter is asked to mildly increase the bit-rate, previous value of *QuantScaleCoeff* will be divided by *MildQScaleFactor* to get its new value. The value of *QuantScaleCoeff* will be left unchanged to keep the bit-rate at

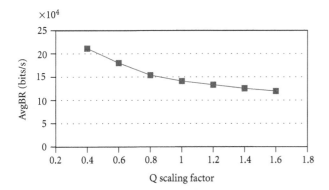

FIGURE 8: Bit-rate variation with respect to QMatrix scaling.

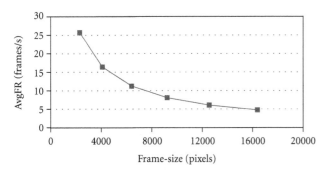

FIGURE 9: Frame-rate variation with respect to frame-size scaling.

the current level. Once the new value for the *QuantScaleCoeff* is decided, the scaled version of the QMatrix is calculated by multiplying all its elements by this new *QuantScaleCoeff*. For all the blocks of the frame, this scaled version of the QMatrix will be used. The quantizer task also sends the newly generated QMatrix to the VLE through a dedicated adaptation propagation channel so that it can be inserted in the frame header of the generated frame.

4.1.4. Adaptive Source. The output frame-rate is decided by how fast the encoder can complete the processing of one frame. Since the processing time for a frame is proportional to the amount of data contained in it, frame-rate can be controlled by scaling the dimensions of the input video. Even though this will produce smaller images at the output, target frame-rate can be easily achieved by using this method. Figure 9 shows the impact of the frame-size parameter on the output frame-rate.

The source task is made adaptive by providing the adaptFramerate() function, which takes care of scaling the input frame size. The implementation of frame-size scaling logic is based on the following configurable parameters.

CurFrameNumVBlocks. The number of vertical blocks in the current frame.

CurFrameNumHBlocks. The number of horizontal blocks in the current frame.

AggrFsScaleFactor (Aggressive Frame-Size Scaling Factor). The constant by which current value of frame-size (number

of vertical and horizontal blocks) will be multiplied/divided to obtain its new value in case of aggressive scaling.

MildFsScaleFactor (Mild Frame-Size Scaling Factor). The constant by which current value of frame-size (number of vertical and horizontal blocks) will be multiplied/divided to obtain its new value in case of mild scaling.

The algorithm functions as follows. Similar to the bit-rate adaptation, the Source task reads the frame-rate control command from the controller and passes this value to the adaptFrameSize() function. If the decision by the controller is to aggressively decrease the frame-rate, the previous values of the *curFrameNumVBlocks* and *curFrameNumHBlocks* will be multiplied by *AggrFsScaleFactor* to obtain their new values. Similarly, if the adapter is asked to mildly increase the frame-rate, these parameters will be divided by *MildFsScaleFactor* to calculate their new values. To keep frame-rate at the current level, the number of blocks in the frame will be left unchanged. The frame-rate adapter also sends the new value of the frame-size to DCT, Q, and VLE tasks using separate adaptation propagation channels so that they know exactly how many blocks to be processed for the next frame.

4.1.5. Adaptation Propagation Channels. Some additional channels need to be added to the pipeline to communicate the changes done by the adaptive tasks to other tasks. A channel to send the scaled version of the QMatrix from Quantizer to VLE is added. This is necessary because the QMatrix used for a particular frame needs to be inserted in its header so that the decoder can use the correct value while decoding the frame. Channels to propagate new frame-size values are also added between Source-DCT and Source-Q tasks. Quantizer and DCT should know the frame-size to calculate the number of blocks to be processed for each frame. To send the frame-size values from Source to VLE, we use the existing channel in the original task graph.

5. Results

In this section, we present the results of running our self-adaptive MJPEG encoder on a 2×2 NoC-based FPGA platform. The platform is generated by the SHMPI builder tool [15] and it is a mesh-based 2×2 NoC consisting of Microblaze processors emulated on a Xilinx Virtex6 FPGA. The software stack enabling the execution of KPN applications on this platform is based on the request-driven middleware explained in [12].

5.1. Design Space Exploration for Adaptation Control. As evident from the design of M-C-A framework, the quality of the adaptation control is influenced by various parameters used inside the monitors, controllers, and adapters. In order to achieve smooth and fast adaptation, a careful selection of these parameters is needed. To find such a combination, a design space exploration (DSE) is performed. The first step in DSE is to determine the design space for the configurable parameters. The design space tends to be enormous due to the large number of parameters and the different values each can assume. To carry out the DSE within a reasonable time,

TABLE 5: Design space for the M-C-A framework.

Parameter	Values
Monitor width	6, 12, 20
Settling width factor (BR)	0.1, 0.2
Settling width factor (FR)	0.1, 0.2
Error threshold factor (BR)	0.05, 0.1
Error threshold factor high (BR)	0.15, 0.2
Delta-error threshold factor (BR)	0.03
Error threshold factor (FR)	0.1, 0.2
Error threshold factor high (FR)	0.2, 0.3
Delta-error threshold factor (FR)	0.05
Mild Q scaling factor	1.1, 1.2
Aggressive Q scaling factor	1.4, 1.6
Mild frame-size scaling factor	1.1, 1.2
Aggressive frame-size scaling factor	1.25, 1.4

TABLE 6: Two step DSE for adaptation control.

Parameter	After step 1	After step 2
Monitor width	—	12
Settling width factor (BR)	—	0.2
Settling width factor (FR)	0.2	0.2
Error threshold factor (BR)	—	0.05
Error threshold factor high (BR)	—	0.2
Delta-error threshold factor (BR)	—	0.03
Error threshold factor (FR)	0.2	0.2
Error threshold factor high (FR)	0.3	0.3
Delta-error threshold factor (FR)	0.05	0.05
Mild Q scaling factor	—	1.1
Aggressive Q scaling factor	—	1.6
Mild frame-size scaling factor	1.1	1.1
Aggressive frame-size scaling factor	1.25	1.25

we chose only a few values for each parameter. The design space used is captured in Table 5.

The evaluation of a design point is based on the following two metrics speed of adaptation (quantified by rise/fall time) and convergence of adaptation (quantified by mean absolute error).

Rise/Fall Time. It is the time (in number of frames) taken by the system to move from an initial state to the target state.

Mean Absolute Error. It is the mean of absolute error values for a monitored parameter over several consecutive frames.

To calculate these two metrics for a monitored parameter, the encoder is run for a fixed number of frames of a test video with an initial value of the parameter. Then its value is changed to the target value and the system is allowed to adapt. The number of frames taken for the parameter to reach within a tolerance band ($\pm 5\%$) about its target value is the rise/fall time. The absolute error value for the parameter is calculated for all frames starting from where it reached the tolerance band till the last frame. The mean of these absolute error values gives the mean absolute error. We have used the following sets of goals for the DSE experiments: initial BR = 200000 bits/sec, initial FR = 8 frames/sec, final BR = 300000 bits/sec, and final FR = 16 frames/sec.

Since both bit-rate and frame-rate control are considered in the case study, the DSE is a four-dimensional minimization problem consisting of rise-times and mean-absolute-errors for BR and FR control as objectives. In order to simplify the procedure, the following facts are taken into account. Bit-rate adaptation has no impact on the frame-rate, since it only scales the QMatrix (i.e., data to be processed per frame does not change). On the other hand, frame-rate adaptation affects also the bit-rate, since it changes the amount of data generated per frame. So, initially the DSE is done by varying only those parameters that affect the frame-rate. The bit-rate controller is turned off during this step to obtain the optimum frame-rate control parameters. This step is a two-dimensional optimization

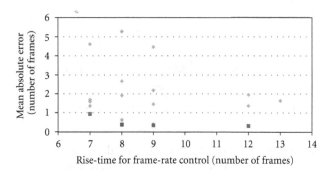

■ Pareto point

■ Selected Pareto point

FIGURE 10: DSE for frame-rate control (step 1).

problem over a smaller design space. The results of the first DSE stage are presented in Figure 10. The Pareto points are represented with rectangular markers, whereas the selected Pareto point is colored in red. In the second step, only bit-rate control parameters are varied while using the values of the selected Pareto point from the first step for frame-rate control parameters. Both bit-rate and frame-rate control are enabled in this step. Pareto points are obtained with respect to the four optimization objectives. The selected parameter values after each DSE step is shown in Table 6.

In order to assess the sensitivity of the control quality to the design parameters, we calculated the distribution of all the points in the design space. The cumulative distributions of error and rise-time for bit-rate are shown in Figure 11. It can be seen that 95% of the design points have less than 5% bit-rate error, whereas the rise-time of 90% of them are below 8 frames. Similar plots for frame-rate are shown in Figure 12. Here 80% of the design points have less than 12% frame-rate error, whereas the rise-time of 84% of them are below 9 frames. This shows the generality of the proposed solution, because even for nonoptimal parameter configurations, the system is able to adapt fast while keeping the error within tolerable limits.

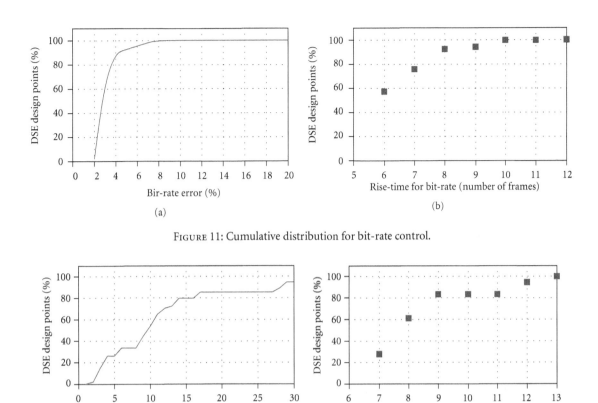

FIGURE 11: Cumulative distribution for bit-rate control.

FIGURE 12: Cumulative distribution for frame-rate control.

5.2. Bit-Rate and Frame-Rate Adaptation Tests. To demonstrate the effectiveness of our adaptation scheme, we conducted various experiments by setting different goals for bit-rate and frame-rate. All these tests are carried out using 128×128 video (for 200 frames) stored in the memory. The selected Pareto point (shown in Table 6) obtained from the DSE is used to configure the controller. Figure 13 shows the results when the encoder is run with initial BR = 200000 bits/sec, initial FR = 8 frames/sec, final BR = 300000 bits/sec and final FR = 16 frames/sec. The adaptation in terms of quantization scaling coefficient and frame-size is also shown. It can be seen that the scaling coefficient is reduced from its initial value of 1 to a value of 0.5 to meet the initial bit-rate. But after frame 60, its value is further reduced to 0.35 to increase the bit-rate to its final value. Similarly, the frame-size is reduced from its initial value of 16000 pixels to 9000 pixels in order to achieve the initial frame-rate of 8 fps. But after frame 60, it is further reduced to about 4000 pixels to increase the frame-rate to 16 fps. The rise time and mean absolute errors for this scenario are: rise time (BR) = 6 frames, mean absolute error (BR) = 7684 bits (2.56%), rise time (FR) = 9 frames, mean absolute error (FR) = 0.33 frames (2.06%).

5.3. Fast Video versus Slow Video. Figure 14 shows the results of evaluating the framework using slow and fast video inputs. Figure 14(a) characterizes the two videos in terms of the number of bytes generated by the encoder per frame (for 128 $\times$ 128 video), when there is no bit-rate/frame-rate control. From Figures 14(b) and 14(c), it can be seen that for both videos, the targets are achieved with the following metrics.

Slow Video. Rise time (BR) = 6 frames, mean absolute error (BR) = 7790 bits (2.59%), rise time (FR) = 9 frames, mean absolute error (FR) = 0.36 frames (2.25%).

Fast Video. Rise time (BR) = 5 frames, mean absolute error (BR) = 10440 bits (3.48%), rise time (FR) = 9 frames, mean absolute error (FR) = 0.24 frames (1.5%).

The results reveal that for slow video the bit-rate control converges fast whereas for fast video, a lot of ripples are observed at the output, resulting in a higher mean absolute error. In case of frame-rate control the fastness or slowness of the input does not have much impact and the frame-size converges to the same value in both cases without ripples.

5.4. Cost of Adaptation. To measure the steady-state overhead due to the introduction of the M-C-A feedback loop in the application pipeline, the following procedure is used. First, the encoder is run without the feedback loop as well as the adaptation propagation channels to obtain the average value of frame-rate without the framework. The experiment is repeated after introducing the M-C-A loop

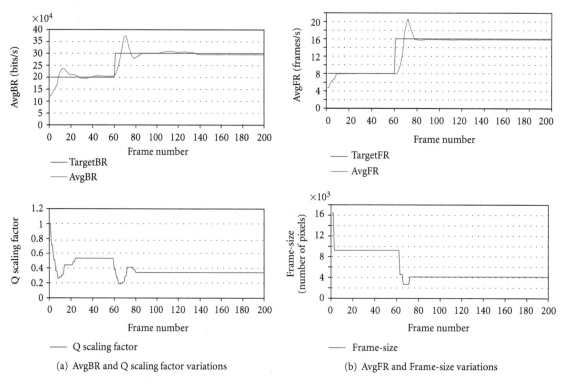

(a) AvgBR and Q scaling factor variations

(b) AvgFR and Frame-size variations

FIGURE 13: Results for initial BR = 200000 bps, initial FR = 8 fps, and final BR = 300000 bps, final FR = 16 fps.

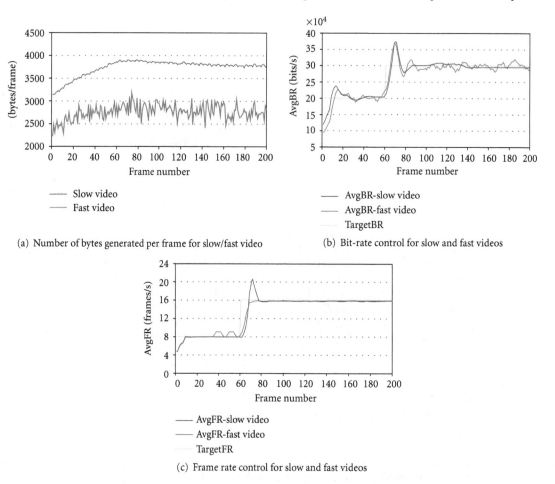

(a) Number of bytes generated per frame for slow/fast video

(b) Bit-rate control for slow and fast videos

(c) Frame rate control for slow and fast videos

FIGURE 14: Results for bit-rate/frame-rate control for slow and fast videos.

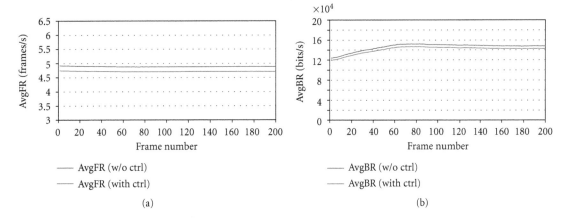

Figure 15: Cost of adaptation in terms of reduction in BR/FR.

and the additional channels to obtain the reduced frame-rate. In this case, both bit-rate and frame-rate control are turned off inside the controller, since only the overhead due to the framework needs to be measured. Figure 15 depicts the outcome of this test for a 128×128 test video. It is observed that the introduction of the framework results in a frame-rate reduction of only 4%. Similarly, the reduction in bit-rate is about 3.5%. The reduction in the bit-rate and frame-rate is due to the increase in the inter-arrival time between frames.

The overhead in terms of the additional control data introduced by our M-C-A mechanism is minimal. For every video frame, it sends a total of 72 additional tokens over the network. This includes one token from monitoring task to bit-rate controller, one token from monitoring task to frame-rate controller, one token from bit-rate controller to Quantizer task, one token from frame-rate controller to Source task, 64 tokens from Quantizer to VLE (to send the QMatrix), two tokens from Source to DCT (to send the height and width of the frame), and two tokens from Source to Quantizer (to send the height and width of the frame). This is equivalent to 288 bytes of data since a token is represented as integer type by the middleware. For a 128×128 frame the total video data to be sent over the NoC is 49152 bytes. This includes the pixel data sent from Source to DCT, DCT to Quantizer, and Quantizer to VLE. So the framework introduces approximately 0.5% of additional control data.

5.5. Effect of Parameter Variations. This section presents the experimental results regarding the effect of varying various design parameters on the quality of adaptation control.

5.5.1. Monitor-Width. Figure 16 shows the impact of varying the monitor-width on the four quality metrics of the controller. Monitor-width plays an important role in deciding the sensitivity of the control mechanism. If the monitor-width is too large the sensitivity will be low, because the effect of a particular adaptation decision will be reflected in the average value only after many frames are generated with that decision, resulting in an increase in rise/fall time. On the other hand, very small monitor windows will help in

detecting changes in the monitored parameter at a very early stage. However, this may cause large ripples in the output since any adaptation strategy needs some time for its effect to be visible at the output, resulting in large errors in the monitored parameter. Similarly, when the monitor-width is large, the error will increase due to slow response of the controller. Hence it is very important to keep the monitor-width at an optimum value.

5.5.2. Q Scaling Factors. Figure 17 shows the effect of variations in Q scaling factors on the quality of control. Adapters deploy aggressive scaling when the monitored value of the parameter deviates too much from the target, whereas mild scaling is used otherwise. A high value of aggressive scaling factor will help to reduce the rise/fall time, but it may cause large overshoots in the output and hence may increase the average error. Similarly, a small value for mild scale factor will help in reducing the ripples after the output converges. From the results, it can be deduced that large values for Q scaling factors will cause larger average errors in the output, in spite of the reduction in rise/fall time.

5.5.3. Error Thresholds. Figure 18 shows the effect of variations in error thresholds on the bit-rate control. The x-axis represents bit-rate error thresholds in the format (error-threshold-low, error-threshold-high, delta-error-threshold). From the results, it can be seen that when *error-threshold-low* is increased keeping *error-threshold-high* as constant, the mean-error increases. This is due to the possibility of the monitored parameter settling at a value which is far from its target, thus increasing the error. On the other hand, when *error-threshold-high* is increased keeping *error-threshold-low* as constant, the rise-time increases. This can be explained as follows: when *error-threshold-high* is large, aggressive scaling is used less often, causing an increase in the rise-time.

5.6. Reusing the Adaptation Controller. The results presented in Section 5.1 use the MJPEG encoder case study and are performed with the aim of minimizing both rise-time and mean-error. The framework requires fine tuning in order to be used for a different application. The effect of parameter

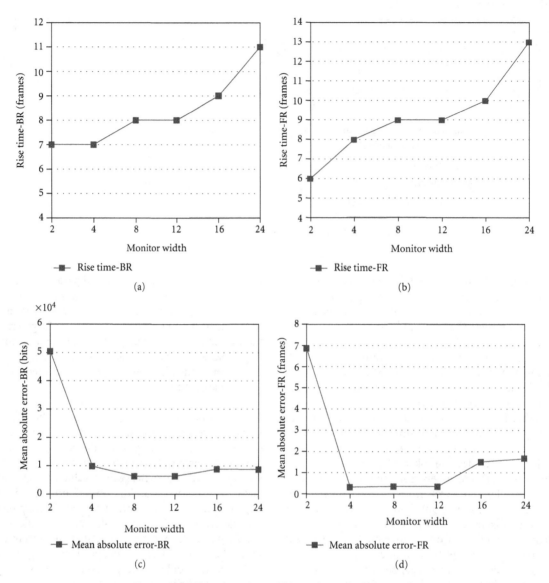

FIGURE 16: Effect of monitor-width on the quality of control.

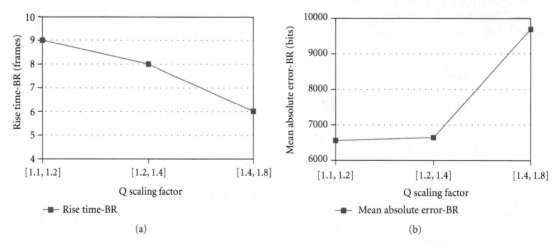

FIGURE 17: Effect of Q scaling factors on quality of control.

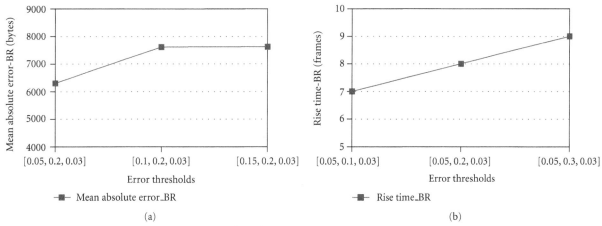

FIGURE 18: Effect of error thresholds on quality of control.

variations studied in Section 5.5 can be used as a guideline while configuring the adaptation controller for a new set of application requirements. For example, to increase the responsiveness of the control, either the *aggressive scaling factor* can be increased or the *error-threshold-high* can be reduced. Similarly, if the application demands a closer convergence of a parameter to the target value while tolerating slow response, the user can tighten the *error-threshold-low* and lessen the *aggressive scaling factor*.

6. Discussion on the Framework

The self-adaptivity mechanism proposed in this work relies on monitoring, controlling and adaptation capabilities. For the monitoring and adaptation support, despite the fact that some general mechanisms such as monitoring and adaptive functions are used, the methods are based on some advantages that come with the KPN computation model. In this work, we are particularly interested in throughput monitoring and parametric adaptations. The KPN model facilitates implementation of such monitoring and adaptation capabilities. For the former, since KPN is composed of computational blocks and their explicit communication with tokens over channels, monitoring the throughput (e.g., the rate at which tokens are produced as well as the bit-rate on a channel) can be achieved in an application independent manner. For the latter, the reconfiguration of the application to work with a new value of an application parameter requires that the relevant parts of the application to be updated consistently. Consistency implies that a token is processed by tasks throughout the application pipeline with the right parameter value. KPN helps in achieving this by synchronizing the updating of tasks via blocking channels. These properties of the KPN model address the aforementioned *separation of concerns* challenge.

On the other hand, the fuzzy control approach is not specific to KPN and can be used for controlling any self-adaptive system. The control is event-based rather than time-based. Unlike the widely practiced periodic monitoring and control, this approach involves monitoring in an event-based manner (e.g., at the end of processing of a frame). Such an approach is suited better for networked systems as it is less sensitive to possible delays in the network and incurs less overhead on the amount of data transferred on the network. Comparison of these approaches is left as a future work.

7. Conclusion

In this paper, we proposed an approach to implement application level self-adaptation capabilities for KPN applications running on networks-on-chip based MPSoCs. The proposed framework is based on introducing a monitor-controller-adapter mechanism in the application pipeline. Techniques to add monitoring and adaptation capabilities to normal KPN tasks are discussed along with the design of a generic fuzzy logic-based adaptation controller. Finally, we presented an adaptive MJPEG case study on a FPGA based 2×2 NoC platform. Our results show that even if the parameters of the fuzzy control are not tuned optimally, the adaptation convergence is achieved within reasonable time and error limits for most of the designed controllers. Moreover, the steady-state overhead introduced due to the framework is low (4%) in terms of frame-rate reduction. Since the controller is a generic one, this framework can be easily integrated to other applications also, requiring minimal modifications to the code.

Acknowledgments

This work was funded by the European Commission under the project MADNESS (no. FP7-ICT-2009-4-248424). The paper reflects only the authors' view; the European Commission is not liable for any use that may be made of the information contained herein.

References

[1] G. De Micheli and L. Benini, *Networks on Chips: Technology and Tools*, Morgan Kaufmann, 2006.

[2] E. Carara, A. Mello, and F. Moraes, "Communication models in networks-on-chip," in *Proceedings of the 18th IEEE/IFIP International Workshop on Rapid System Prototyping (RSP '07)*, pp. 57–60, IEEE Computer Society Press, May 2007.

[3] J. Kramer and J. Magee, "Self-managed systems: an architectural challenge," in *Proceedings of the Future of Software Engineering (FoSE '07)*, pp. 259–268, Washington, DC, USA, May 2007.

[4] G. Kahn, "The semantics of a simple language for parallel programming," in *Proceedings of the IFIP Congress on Information Processing*, J. L. Rosenfeld, Ed., pp. 471–475, North-Holland, New York, NY, 1974.

[5] O. Derin and A. Ferrante, "Enabling self-adaptivity in component based streaming applications," in *SIGBED Review, Special Issue on the 2nd International Workshop on Adaptive and Reconfigurable Embedded Systems (APRES '09)*, vol. 6, 2009.

[6] P. Charles David and T. Ledoux, "Towards a framework for self-adaptive component-based applications," in *Proceedings of Distributed Applications and Interoperable Systems*, vol. 2893 of *Lecture Notes in Computer Science*, pp. 1–14, Springer, 2003.

[7] K. Geihs, P. Barone, F. Eliassen et al., "A comprehensive solution for application-level adaptation," *Software - Practice and Experience*, vol. 39, no. 4, pp. 385–422, 2009.

[8] O. Derin, A. Ferrante, and A. V. Taddeo, "Coordinated management of hardware and software self-adaptivity," *Journal of Systems Architecture*, vol. 55, no. 3, pp. 170–179, 2009.

[9] J. Combaz, J. C. Fernandez, T. Lepley, and J. Sifakis, "Fine grain QoS control for multimedia application software," in *Proceedings of the Design, Automation and Test in Europe (DATE '05)*, vol. 2, pp. 1038–1043, March 2005.

[10] J. Combaz, J. C. Fernandez, J. Sifakis, and L. Strus, "Using speed diagrams for symbolic quality management," in *Proceedings of the 21st International Parallel and Distributed Processing Symposium (IPDPS '07)*, pp. 1–8, March 2007.

[11] M. Jaber, J. Combaz, L. Stras, and J. C. Fernandez, "Using neural networks for quality management," in *Proceedings of the 13th IEEE International Conference on Emerging Technologies and Factory Automation (ETFA '08)*, pp. 1441–1448, September 2008.

[12] E. Cannella, O. Derin, P. Meloni, G. Tuveri, and T. Stefanov, "Adaptivity support for mpsocs based on process migration in polyhedral process networks," *VLSI Design*, vol. 2012, Article ID 987209, 17 pages, 2012.

[13] L. A. Zadeh, "Fuzzy sets," *Information and Control*, vol. 8, no. 3, pp. 338–353, 1965.

[14] P. Lieverse, T. Stefanov, P. Van der Wolf, and E. Deprettere, "System level design with spade: an M-JPEG case study," in *Proceedings of the International Conference on Computer-Aided Design (ICCAD '01)*, pp. 31–38, November 2001.

[15] P. Meloni, S. Secchi, and L. Raffo, "An FPGA-based framework for technology-aware prototyping of multicore embedded architectures," *IEEE Embedded Systems Letters*, vol. 2, no. 1, pp. 5–9, 2010.

4

An SOA-Based Model for the Integrated Provisioning of Cloud and Grid Resources

Andrea Bosin[1, 2]

[1] Dipartimento di Fisica, Università degli Studi di Cagliari, Complesso Universitario di Monserrato, 09042 Monserrato, Italy
[2] Istituto Nazionale di Fisica Nucleare (INFN), Complesso Universitario di Monserrato, Sezione di Cagliari, 09042 Monserrato, Italy

Correspondence should be addressed to Andrea Bosin, andrea.bosin@dsf.unica.it

Academic Editor: Guoquan Wu

In the last years, the availability and models of use of networked computing resources within reach of e-Science are rapidly changing and see the coexistence of many disparate paradigms: high-performance computing, grid, and recently cloud. Unfortunately, none of these paradigms is recognized as the ultimate solution, and a convergence of them all should be pursued. At the same time, recent works have proposed a number of models and tools to address the growing needs and expectations in the field of e-Science. In particular, they have shown the advantages and the feasibility of modeling e-Science environments and infrastructures according to the service-oriented architecture. In this paper, we suggest a model to promote the convergence and the integration of the different computing paradigms and infrastructures for the dynamic on-demand provisioning of resources from multiple providers as a cohesive aggregate, leveraging the service-oriented architecture. In addition, we propose a design aimed at endorsing a flexible, modular, workflow-based computing model for e-Science. The model is supplemented by a working prototype implementation together with a case study in the applicative domain of bioinformatics, which is used to validate the presented approach and to carry out some performance and scalability measurements.

1. Introduction

In the last years, the availability and models of use of networked computing resources within reach of e-Science are rapidly changing and see the coexistence of many disparate paradigms, featuring their own characteristics, advantages, and limitations. Among the main paradigms, we find high-performance computing (HPC), grid, and cloud. In all cases, the objective is to best provide hardware and software resources to user applications with the help of schedulers, reservation systems, control interfaces, authentication mechanisms, and so on.

At the same time, a number of works [1–4] have proposed a number of models and tools to address the growing needs and expectations in the field of e-Science. In particular, the works in [4, 5] have shown the advantages and the feasibility, but also the problems, of modeling e-Science environments and infrastructures according to the service-oriented architecture (SOA) and its enabling technologies such as web services (WS). Among the main advantages of such approach, we find interoperability, open standards, modularity, dynamic publish-find-bind, and programmatic access.

A detailed comparison of the characteristics of HPC, grid, and cloud paradigms is presented in [6], where it is observed that none of these paradigms is the ultimate solution, and a convergence of them all should be pursued. Even if many computing paradigms show some kind of SOA awareness, heterogeneous resource provisioning still remains an open problem because of the many integration issues, such as usage model, life-cycle management, authentication, application programming interfaces (APIs), adopted standards (or no standard at all), services (e.g., storage, authentication), network segmentation or isolation between different resources, monitoring, workflow languages, and engines.

In this paper, we suggest a model to promote the convergence and the integration of the different computing paradigms and infrastructures for the dynamic on-demand provisioning of the resources needed by e-Science environments. Promoting the integration, cooperation, and interoperation of heterogeneous resources has the advantage of allowing users to exploit the best of each paradigm. In addition, the availability of cloud resources, capable of instantiating standard or custom virtual machines (VMs) on a per-user basis, gives a number of value-added enhancements:

(i) allowing the execution of platform-dependent applications which may be bound to specific operating system flavors or libraries not generally available;

(ii) permiting dynamic provisioning of different workflow engines;

(iii) giving the additional flexibility to run web service applications and enact workflows where and when the user wishes (e.g., users may well decide to take advantage of pay-per-use commercial providers such as Amazon or Rackspace).

Our model is not meant to replace existing HPC, grid, and cloud paradigms, rather it is an attempt aimed at complementing, integrating, and building on them by playing the role of a dynamic resource aggregator exposing a technology agnostic abstraction layer.

At the same time, we aim at endorsing a flexible, modular, workflow-based computing model for e-Science. Our proposal borrows many SOA concepts and standards from the business domain, including the adoption of the *Business Process Execution Language (BPEL)* for workflow design and execution. A motivation of our approach is almost evident: the SOA paradigms, and in particular web services and BPEL, are based on widely accepted standards and supported by many software tools, both open source and commercial.

In addition, we describe a working proof-of-concept implementation together with a case study in the bioinformatics domain, which is used to validate the proposed approach and to address issues such as performance and scalability, shortcomings, and open problems.

Though we are not presenting a revolutionary approach or completely new ideas, we believe that the exploration, exploitation, and integration of existing technologies and tools, especially those based on open standards, in new and different ways can contribute with added value to the field and may be of interest to readers. In particular, with respect to previous work, we have the following:

(i) BPEL has been used unmodified, while other works have added custom extensions;

(ii) the model is open to the integration of both new computing infrastructures and workflow systems;

(iii) the model is meant to work with the widest spectrum of resources (in most works, resources are limited to just one type, e.g., grid);

(iv) open standards have been adopted to the maximum extent (in many other works, nonstandard ad hoc solutions have been adopted);

(v) we are not (yet) proposing a production implementation; instead, we have chosen to explore and verify in practice the possibility of employing tools and technologies based on open standards in new and different ways, strongly believing that this may give a valuable contribution to tackle the problem of heterogeneous resource provisioning;

(vi) we are not focusing on directly improving existing works and systems, rather we investigated a different direction that might be promising, being mainly based on open standards;

(vii) the model is open not only to incorporate previous work (and indeed it does), but also to be incorporated.

The paper is organized as follows. Section 2 reviews some related work, while Section 3 provides a summary of resources and provisioning systems. Section 4 presents a model promoting the convergence and the integration of such systems for the dynamic on-demand provisioning of resources from multiple providers. Section 5 describes a working implementation of the model, Section 6 covers a case study in the bioinformatics domain, and Section 7 presents some of the results and discusses issues and open problems. Conclusions are then drawn in Section 8.

2. Related Work

Software applications have been built to address a wide spectrum of scientific workflows, ranging from basic tools that are designed to handle "desktop" tasks such as simple data analysis and visualization to complex workflow systems that are designed to run large-scale e-Science applications on remote grid resources. These systems need to support multiple concurrent users, deal with security requirements, and run workflows that may require the use of a sophisticated layer of services [7].

In [3], authors identify desiderata for scientific workflow systems—namely, clarity, predictability, reportability, and reusability. Moreover, ease of composition and editing, the ability to automatically log and record workflow enactments, and the flexibility to incorporate new tools are all important features [7]. The interoperability aspects of scientific workflow systems are addressed in [2], which investigates the differences in execution environments for local workflows and those executing on remote grid resources. A complete overview of features and capabilities of scientific workflow systems is presented in [1].

There is a number of widely recognized grid workflow projects like Triana [8, 9], Kepler [10], Pegasus [11], and ASKALON [12]. Many of these began their life in the "desktop" workflow space and have evolved over time to address the large-scale e-Science applications. Specifically designed for the life sciences, Taverna [13, 14] was the first system to recognize the importance of data provenance and semantic grid issues.

While developed for the business domain, technologies like BPEL are recognized suitable to address the requirements of e-Science applications [4], supporting the composition of large computational and data analysis tasks that must be executed on supercomputing resources. BPEL is recognized by [1] as the de facto standard for web-service-based workflows. An architecture for the dynamic scheduling of workflow service calls is presented in [15], where control mechanisms of BPEL are combined with an adaptive runtime environment that integrates dedicated resources and on-demand resources provided by infrastructures like Amazon Elastic Compute Cloud. Reference [16] presents the design and implementation of a workflow management system based on BPEL in a grid environment. Based on BPEL, QoWL [17] and GPEL [18] are significant examples of workflow systems designed for dynamic, adaptive large-scale e-Science applications.

The use of BPEL for grid service orchestration is proposed as foundation in [19] since it fulfills many requirements of the WSRF standard. The appropriateness of BPEL is also examined and confirmed in [20–22]. These works mainly focus on scientific workflows and rely on extending or adapting BPEL, thus creating dialects.

Many authors consider the problem of resource provisioning from the perspective of conventional grid applications. Following this approach, grid and cloud convergence is achieved in such a way to expand a fixed pool of physical grid resources, usually managed by a workload and resource management system (WRMS), by providing new virtual grid resources on-demand and dynamically leasing them from one or more dynamic infrastructure management systems (DIMSs).

Reference [6] presents a hybrid computing model which is aimed at executing scientific applications in such a way to satisfy the given timing requirements. Applications are represented by workflows, that is, a set of jobs with precedence constraints. The basic building block is the elastic cluster, characterized by (1) dynamic infrastructure management services; (2) cluster-level services such as workload management; (3) intelligent modules that bridge the gap between cluster-level services and dynamic infrastructure management services. An infrastructure for the management and execution of workflows across multiple resources is then built by using multiple elastic clusters coordinated by a workflow management system.

Reference [15] explores on-demand provisioning of cloud resources directly at the workflow level, using BPEL as the workflow language. When, during workflow enactment, a service is invoked, the request is routed to the service instance running on the best-matching host (e.g., lowest load); if no best-matching host is available, a new VM is provisioned from a cloud to run a new instance of the required service.

The idea of virtual clusters on a physical grid is explored in [23], where virtual organization clusters provide customized, homogeneous execution environments on a per-virtual organization basis. The authors describe a clustering overlay for individual grid resources, which permits virtual organizations of federated grid users to create custom computational clouds with private scheduling and resource control policies.

The feasibility of using one or more cloud providers for deploying a grid infrastructure or parts of it has been studied in [24]; such an approach permits the elastic growth of the given grid infrastructure in such a way to satisfy peak demands or other requirements.

The approach presented in this work has been previously pursued [5, 25], with particular emphasis on SOA and BPEL adequacy for e-Science environments and less attention to the general problem of resource provisioning.

3. Resources and Provisioning Systems

We start this section with a brief description of the most common resource types available to e-Science environments and then discuss the main features of the existing management systems.

High-performance computing (HPC) resources are tightly-coupled (e.g., by a high-performance communication device such as an InfiniBand switch) sets of computing equipment with (usually) a high degree of hardware and software homogeneity. HPC resources are in most cases managed by legacy schedulers which represent a big issue for interoperability. HPC infrastructures typically provide the following:

(i) high-performance hardware enabling strongly coupled parallelism,

(ii) resource scheduling/reservation,

(iii) homogeneous hardware and software environments.

Grid resources are loosely coupled sets of computing equipment with (usually) a local (e.g., per site) high degree of hardware and software homogeneity. Physical separation is not an issue and resources are managed through the abstraction, of virtual organizations (VOs) with the possibility of federating many different VOs. The open grid services architecture [26], or OGSA, is a framework for developing grid management services according to the service-oriented architecture, thus enabling ease of integration and interoperability between sites, even if grids have limited interoperability between different grid software stacks [6]. Grid infrastructures may offer the following:

(i) large sets of computing resources,

(ii) resource scheduling/reservation,

(iii) advanced storage services,

(iv) specialized workflow systems,

(v) advanced monitoring services,

(vi) homogeneous operating system and software environments.

Cloud resources are based on loosely coupled sets of computing equipment with no need or guarantee of hardware and software homogeneity and in many cases distributed at different physical locations. In this paradigm, the physical machine (PM) hardware and software are almost completely hidden, and a virtual machine (VM) abstraction is exposed to the user. Most cloud management systems are designed according to SOA concepts and expose their functionality through Soap-based or RESTful interfaces, thus improving ease of access, integration, and interoperability. One interesting characteristic of clouds is the ability to provide resources with certain characteristics, that is, specific software libraries or configurations, dynamically on demand and on a per-user basis [24]. Cloud infrastructures present the following:

(i) extremely flexible/customizable operating system and software environments,

(ii) API based on open standards (e.g., Soap, REST),

(iii) on-demand provisioning,

(iv) increasing the number of resources offered by commercial providers.

Specialized resources are "unique" nodes on the network where a very specific activity can take place (e.g., data acquisition from an attached physical device), but sharing such resources on the network may not be straightforward, since in many cases they expose custom APIs.

At last, *personal resources*, such as desktops or laptops, provide users with the maximum ease of use in terms of flexibility and customization, often at the expense of limiting the interoperability with other resources. A personal resource usually is the main door for accessing the network, and it is both the starting and end point for user interaction with e-Science environments (e.g., start an experiment, monitor its execution, collect results, and write reports).

HPC and grid resources are usually controlled by *workload and resource management systems (WRMSs)* which support (1) resource management; (2) job management; (3) job scheduling. The term job refers to the set of instructions needed to run an application or part of it on a batch system, written according to some Job Description Language (JDL). A WRMS can be built on top of another WRMS, as it is usually the case with grid middleware which relies upon an underlying batch system referred to as a local resource management system (LRMS).

Users are granted access to a WRMS in a number of ways: (1) interactively from a front-end machine using a command line interface (CLI); (2) programmatically by means of specialized API; (3) in some cases, programmatically by means of technology agnostic API, for example, Open Grid Forum Distributed Resource Management Application API (DRMAA) [27]. Authentication mechanisms may range from simple credentials such as user/password to sophisticated X.509 certificates based on a public key infrastructure, both for users and software services.

An example of grid WRMSs is gLite computing resource execution and management (CREAM) [28] for which job submission and execution can be summarized as follows: (1) a grid user, using his/her X.509 credentials, obtains an authentication proxy from the VO membership service (VOMS), prepares the job, and submits both the JDL file and proxy to CREAM service; (2) user authentication and authorization (by Local Centre Authorization Service, LCAS) is performed; (3) user request is mapped to a CREAM command and queued; (4) the CREAM command

is processed and mapped to a specific LRMS request, and grid user is mapped to an LRMS user (by Local Credential Mapping Service, LCMAPS); (5) the request is submitted to the LRMS.

Cloud resources are typically supervised by *dynamic infrastructure management systems (DIMSs)*, which offer two kinds of functionality: (1) physical resource management; (2) service management, where provisioned services are implemented using virtual resources. We are mainly interested in the *infrastructure as a service (IaaS)* model, which offers the maximum flexibility by providing virtual machines and the management interface, as well as storage. User access is performed: (1) interactively from a client application; (2) through a browser by means of suitable plug-ins; (3) programmatically by means of specialized API; (4) programmatically by means of technology agnostic API such as Amazon Elastic Compute Cloud (EC2) and Simple Storage Service (S3) [29, 30], or Open Cloud Computing Interface (OCCI) [31]. Authentication mechanisms may vary as in the case of WRMS.

OCCI is an open protocol and API originally created for all kinds of management tasks of (cloud) infrastructures such as deployment, autonomic scaling, and monitoring. It has evolved into a flexible API with a strong focus on interoperability while still offering a high degree of flexibility. OCCI makes an ideal interoperable boundary interface between the web and the internal resource management system of infrastructure (cloud) providers.

At the heart of OCCI model, we find the *resource* which is an abstraction of a physical or virtual resource, that is, a VM, a job in a job submission system, a user, and so forth. The API allows for the creation and management of typical IaaS resources such as *compute, network,* and *sorage.*

OCCI is being implemented only in the latest releases of many cloud DIMSs we have tested (mainly Eucalyptus, OpenNebula, and OpenStack), and as such we were not able to test it extensively, yet we believe it is a first important and promising step towards cross-cloud integration.

An example of a cloud DIMS is Eucalyptus Community Cloud [32] where VM deployment follows a number of steps: (1) a user requests a new VM to the cloud controller (CLC) specifying disk image and characteristics (or flavor), (2) the CLC authorizes the request and forwards it to the cluster controller (CC), (3) the CC performs resource matching and virtual network setup (hardware, IP addresses, and firewall rules) and schedules the request to a node controller (NC), (4) the NC retrieves disk image files from Walrus repository service, (5) the NC powers up the VM through the configured hypervisor, and (6) the user logs into the VM.

Quite interestingly, in [6], it is recognized that both WRMS and DIMS can be well described by the managed computation factory model introduced in [33] and shown in Figure 1. In this model, clients of computational resources do not directly interact with the bare resources, rather they work with the *managed computation* abstraction. A managed computation can be (1) started, (2) stopped, (3) terminated, (4) monitored, and/or (5) controlled by interfacing with a *managed computation factory*. The factory is in charge

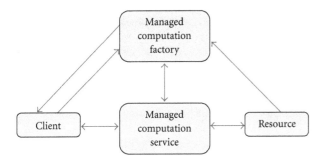

FIGURE 1: Managed computation factory model.

of creating the managed computation, which is assigned to one or more computational resources. The managed computation often operates as a service, hence the name *managed computation service* in Figure 1.

4. Integrated Provisioning of Resources

To address the needs of a wide community of users wishing to exploit at best the resources they have access to (e.g., those granted to them at no charge), we propose to design an abstraction layer between applications and resources, in such a way that resources can be requested, provisioned, used, monitored, and disposed without worrying about the underlying technological infrastructure. Promoting the integration, cooperation, and interoperation of heterogeneous resources has the advantage of allowing users to exploit the best of each paradigm.

In a scenario based on "smart" resource aggregation, new applications may enjoy many benefits; it is possible to imagine a distributed application orchestrated by a workflow where (1) a VM on a cloud runs the workflow engine, (2) the bulk computation is performed in parallel on an HPC infrastructure, (3) data postprocessing is executed on a grid (or cloud), (4) results are viewed on a personal resource, and optionally (5) steps 2–4 are part of an iterative computation.

At a first sight, there may be no benefits for existing applications, unless they are modified, but cloud flexibility may nevertheless help. Indeed, a user application developed for a grid, or other resources may become unusable if (1) the user has no (or no longer) access to the grid, or (2) an update in grid operating system/middleware requires modifications to the application. A possible solution is then to deploy the desired flavor of grid on top of a cloud, as explored in [24], and run the unmodified application.

In this section, we describe a model to promote the convergence, integration, cooperation, and interoperation of different computing paradigms and infrastructures, for the dynamic on-demand provisioning of the resources from multiple providers as a cohesive aggregate. The model, depicted in Figure 2, builds upon HPC, grid, and cloud systems leveraging existing WRMS and DIMS and connecting the different components through SOA interfaces whenever possible, directly or by means of suitable wrappers/adapters.

At the same time, the proposed design aims at endorsing a flexible, modular, workflow-based collaborative environment for e-Science. The latter sees the integration and interoperation of a number of software components, such as

(i) workflows or processes, to define and coordinate complex scientific application or experiments;

(ii) service interfaces, to expose the logic of scientific applications;

(iii) components, to implement rules and perform tasks related to a specific scientific domain.

At the implementation level, the choice of SOA as the enabling technology for a common integration and interoperation framework sounds realistic due to the:

(i) availability of SOA standards for workflow systems (i.e., BPEL);

(ii) availability of web service libraries to build new applications and to wrap existing ones;

(iii) existence of SOA standards covering areas like data access, security, reliability, and so forth;

(iv) access to a number of computing infrastructures (e.g., grid) is, at least partially, SOA aware.

In the envisioned collaborative environment, resources are needed both for running scientific (web) services and processes, and we distinguish two kinds of resource requests:

(i) scientific service (SS) requests for the execution of scientific application modules; scientific services, possibly exposed as web services, have the responsibility of the computation on the assigned resources;

(ii) scientific process requests for the execution of scientific workflows; scientific workflows or processes, enacted by a workflow engine, orchestrate one or more scientific services and are in charge of (1) obtaining the resources needed for each computation represented by a service and (2) managing their life cycle; scientific processes may as well expose workflow instances through a web service interface.

Scientific service and process requests, conforming to SOA, are described by XML documents (see Figure 4 for an example).

Resources, which can be physical (PM) or virtual (VM), are classified accordingly: *worker nodes* run scientific applications modules, while *workflow engine nodes* are dedicated to the execution of workflow engines (WfEs). The distinction between workflow engine and worker nodes is mainly logical; a WfE node is a VM (or PM) resource allocated for the execution of a workflow engine, while a worker node is a PM or VM allocated to run a module of a scientific application in the form of a web service or other type of software component. However, it should be noted that, at different times, a resource may act as a worker node or as a workflow engine node, depending on the managed computation assigned to it. In addition, all the resources

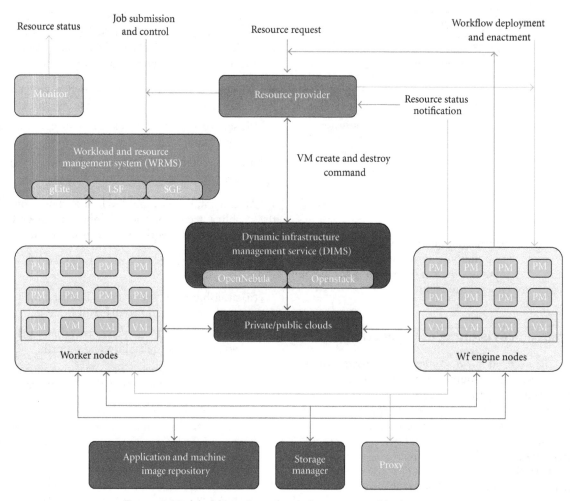

FIGURE 2: Model of dynamic on-demand resource provisioning system.

belong to one or more WRMSs and/or DIMSs, with the possible exception of some personal and specialized resource.

Figure 3 shows a diagram synthesizing the dependencies and interactions between users and the main components of the model and its subsequent implementation, which we are going to describe in greater detail in this and the next sections.

4.1. Resource Provider. At the core of the model, we find the *resource provider* service which acts as a high-level managed computation factory exposing a web service interface:

(i) it accepts requests for resources from clients;

(ii) it translates and forwards requests to the underlying WRMS and DIMS;

(iii) it receives resource heartbeats and notifications;

(iv) it notifies asynchronous clients of resource endpoint, availability, and status changes.

All resource requests are submitted to the resource provider, which takes the appropriate actions based on the request type, as we are going to describe in the following subsections together with the other components

of the model. A successful resource request will start the desired managed computation and provide the user with the computation service network end point and identifier: due to the nature of the resources and of their management systems, this may not immediately happen, leaving users waiting for a variable amount of time. Consequently, the resource provider offers different strategies to inform users when their managed computation is at last started; in particular, clients may submit their resource requests in a number of ways:

(i) a synchronous request returns successfully within a given timeout only if the computation starts before the timeout expires;

(ii) an asynchronous request without notification returns immediately: clients may periodically poll the resource provider to know if the computation has started;

(iii) an asynchronous request with notification returns immediately but allows clients to be notified as soon as the computation starts (clients must be able to receive notifications).

The resource provider is also responsible for disposing resources (canceling jobs in a WRMS or terminating VMs in

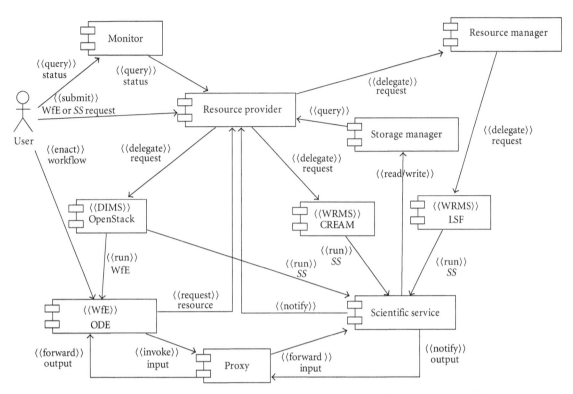

FIGURE 3: Component diagram with basic dependencies.

a DIMS) upon explicit request, resource lifetime expiration, or in case of problems. The associated scientific service or workflow engine is informed of the imminent disposal, is explicitly in charge of its own clean-up (and should be implemented accordingly), and is required to notify the resource provider immediately before exiting.

4.2. Scientific Process Requests. A scientific workflow or process is a high-level description of the process used to carry out computational and analytical experiments, modeled as a directed graph consisting of task nodes and data-flow or control-flow edges denoting execution dependencies among tasks. A process instance is executed by a workflow engine, an application which needs a computing resource to run on. During workflow execution or enactment, workflow engines generally schedule tasks to be invoked according to the data-flow and control-flow edges. A request for a resource dedicated to the execution of a workflow engine, workflow deployment, and the subsequent enactment of a workflow instance is satisfied by materializing an appropriate VM, that is, an operating system embedding the desired workflow engine. The request specifies the following:

(i) the cloud type (e.g., Eucalyptus Community Cloud) that determines the API to use when connecting to the cloud-specific *DIMS*;

(ii) the DIMS interface endpoint, typically a URL;

(iii) the user authentication credentials;

(iv) the VM characteristics or flavor, for example, number of CPUs, RAM size, and so forth;

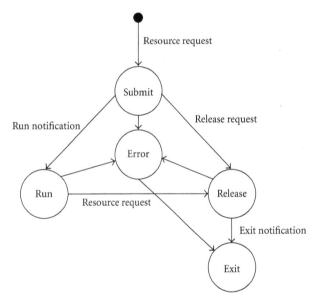

FIGURE 4: State diagram for an abstract resource.

(v) a custom VM image embedding the desired workflow engine;

(vi) the workflow image, that is, the URL of the archive containing the BPEL documents and related files.

When the resource provider processes the request, a VM creation command is submitted to the cloud-specific DIMS. The latter schedules the instantiation of a new VM with the given characteristics on the corresponding cloud (pool of resources) and returns a VM identifier or an error. As soon as the VM is up and running, the embedded workflow engine is started and the workflow image is downloaded and deployed; the resource provider is then notified of the WfE interface end point.

A workflow is an abstract representation of a scientific application and is made of a set of tasks or jobs with precedence constraints between them [6]. Each job needs a resource to run on, and the workflow places the corresponding scientific service requests on the resource provider.

4.3. Scientific Service Requests. A request for a resource needed to run a job, that is, a module of a scientific application in the form of a scientific service, specifies the following:

(i) the resource type, either a resource managed by a WRMS (e.g., CREAM) or a cloud resource made available through a DIMS;

(ii) the WRMS or DIMS interface endpoint (URL);

(iii) the user authentication credentials;

(iv) the resource requirements, for example, RAM size;

(v) the web service (application) image, that is, the URL of the archive containing the web service executable and related files.

The resource provider forwards the request to the specified DIMS or WRMS. A conventional job submitted to an HPC or grid batch system contains the instructions needed to start the computation, written according to some Job Description Language (JDL). In our case, the job responsibility is to start the web service and wait until it stops, while the real computation is orchestrated by a workflow through one or more invocations of the web service. The resource provider is in charge of preparing the job submitted to the WRMS by translating the specifications contained in the resource request (an XML document) into the corresponding JDL. Job submission to a WRMS returns a job identifier or an error. If the job is to be executed by a dedicated VM allocated on a cloud, the VM is created as described in the previous section, except that a standard machine image is used unless a custom image is specified; the VM is instructed to execute the job after booting the operating system.

As soon as the job is started on a worker node, be it a PM or VM, it notifies the workflow (via the resource provider) of the endpoint of the web service, which is ready and listening for incoming messages. When all the resources requested by the workflow are available, the execution can proceed with the invocation of all the required web services in the specified order.

Algorithm 1 shows a fragment of the XML document representing a scientific service request for a cloud resource, where the cloud interface is Amazon EC2, the WS image can be download from the URL http://ws-cyb.dsf.unica.it/ws/jar/WekaDataMining.jar, and the cloud provider is OpenStack [34] with its own set of requirements

(endpoint, region, VM image, and flavor) and user credentials (username/password).

4.4. External Resources. In the foreseen environment, specific activities (e.g., data acquisition from an attached physical device) can take place on specialized nodes on the network; these activities may be exposed by dedicated static services which can be invoked from within a workflow.

In addition, an interesting degree of interactivity may be added to plain workflow execution by invoking a visualization service, for example, at the end of each iteration in an iterative simulation. Such visualization service may be well executed on a personal resource, such as the user desktop, to give a real-time visual feedback of the state of the simulation.

If the service is static, its endpoint is "immutable," and it can simply be hard-coded into the workflow description, but the visualization service presents a problem. Hard-coding a user-specific endpoint (the desktop network address) makes the workflow unusable by different users. We explicitly handle resource requests that refer to external resources and for which creation is not needed. This allows workflows to manage all jobs exactly in the same way, delegating to the resource provider the responsibility for provisioning a new resource only if needed. The latter is directly notified by resources of their endpoint on the network, and in turn, it can notify workflows in such a way to allow dynamic endpoint injection.

4.5. Proxy. In general, worker nodes and workflow engine nodes live on different private networks which are not directly connected to one another (the only assumption we do is that they can open network connections towards the Internet through some kind of Network Address Translation or NAT service), so a *proxy* service is essential in routing messages from scientific processes (workflows) to scientific services (web services) and vice versa.

4.6. Other Services. The other components that complete the model are briefly described here, leaving some details to the next section. The *storage manager* provides temporary storage to data-intensive scientific services; multiple storage managers can coexist in such a way to ensure optimal performance and scalability when needed. The *monitor* is a simple service that can be queried for resource status information. The *application and machine image repository (AMIR)* hosts the applications (e.g., scientific service and process images) and virtual machine disk images that will be executed on the provisioned resources.

5. Implementation

In this section, we describe a working prototype implementation of the model outlined before. We have tried to give a high-level schematic description of the implementation in such a way to avoid overwhelming the reader with unnecessary and less interesting details. We have privileged

```
<BSRequest>
  <BSScheduler>EC2</BSScheduler>
  http://ws-cyb.dsf.unica.it/ws/jar/WekaDataMining.jar
  <BSJavaOptions>-Xmx2048m</BSJavaOptions>
  <BSRequirements>
    <EC2Params>
      <ec2Provider>nova-ec2</ec2Provider>
      <ec2Endpoint>http://172.16.3.3:8773/services/Cloud</ec2Endpoint>
      <ec2Region>nova</ec2Region>
      <ec2Image>ami-lennyws</ec2Image>
      <ec2Flavor>m1.small</ec2Flavor>
    </EC2Params>
  <BSRequirements>
  <BSCredentials>
    <CryptedPWAuth>
      <username>...</username>
      <cryptedPW>...</cryptedPW>
    </CryptedPWAuth>
  <BSCredentials>
</BSRequest>
```

ALGORITHM 1: XML fragment of the document representing a scientific service request.

the description of the idea and of the issues of the single components in the context of the presented model.

According to the general philosophy of an SOA-based framework, we have developed a number of infrastructure (web) services corresponding to various components of the model—using the Java programming language—and reused open-source tools and systems whenever possible, operating the necessary integration. Figure 3 shows the component diagram of the presented implementation with the basic dependencies between components, as better described in the following subsections.

Integrating WRMS and DIMS requires (1) that they expose a network-enabled public interface, possibly based on SOA standards and (2) embedding the necessary logic into a module of the resource provider. Such integration is usually performed for entire classes of WRMS or DIMS: a specific instance may then provide its resources at any time as soon as a resource request refers to it. This allows, for example, drawing resources from two or more Eucalyptus Community Cloud infrastructures at the same time.

In this work, we have developed modules to interact with the following WRMSs:

(i) gLite v3.2 compute element (CE) [35];

(ii) gLite v3.2 computing resource execution and management (CREAM) [28];

(iii) platform load sharing facility v6.2 (LSF) [36];

(iv) oracle grid engine v6.2 (SGE) [37].

CE and CREAM expose OGSA-compliant interfaces and, in addition, it is possible to resort to existing Java API such as jLite [38]. On the contrary, LSF does not offer a similar functionality, so we have developed a simple but effective web-service wrapper, the *resource manager*, and

deployed it to one of the submission hosts, on top of the LSF command line interface. We have followed the same strategy for SGE, too, even if the latter supports the Open Grid Forum Distributed Resource Management Application API (DRMAA) [27].

On the cloud side, we have integrated the following:

(i) Open Nebula [39] defined by its developers is as an "industry standard open source cloud computing tool";

(ii) Open Stack [34] is an open-source porting of Rackspace's DIMS;

(iii) Eucalyptus Community Cloud [32] is presented as "a framework that uses computational and storage infrastructure commonly available to academic research groups to provide a platform that is modular and open to experimental instrumentation and study."

According to their documentation, all these systems expose a RESTful interface compatible with Amazon Elastic Compute Cloud (EC2) [29] and Simple Storage Service (S3) API [30], which are becoming a de facto standard. In practice, the compatibility is not full, but for OpenStack and Eucalyptus, we have successfully employed such interface with the help of the jclouds library [40]. OpenNebula needs additional components to expose the EC2 interface, so we have decided to use its native interface, which is anyway satisfactory.

The above DIMS can cope with different virtualization systems (hypervisors): *Xen* and *Kernel-based virtual machine (KVM)* are the most commonly used. Even if we find KVM more straightforward to use on computers that support hardware-assisted virtualization (both Intel VT-x and AMD-V), the specific hypervisor is almost completely hidden to the user by the same abstraction layer, that is, the *libvirt* virtualization API [41].

5.1. Resource Provider. In the prototype implementation, the *resource provider* functionality is mapped onto a hierarchy of Java classes and is exposed through a web service interface. It would be impossible to describe all classes in detail here, so we only list their key responsibilities:

(i) process all resource requests and make up the corresponding jobs;

(ii) interact with WRMS and DIMS for job and VM scheduling, execution, and control;

(iii) receive status notifications from resources and deliver them to the interested entities (e.g., workflows or monitoring applications);

(iv) dispose resources;

(v) manage resource context and status;

(vi) register proxies, storage managers, and monitoring applications;

(vii) trace message flow and inform registered monitoring applications;

(viii) enforce elementary security practices: authentication credentials containing plain text passwords must be encrypted with the resource provider public key before transmission; if necessary, the use of one-time security tokens can be enabled;

(ix) assign registered proxies and storage managers to scientific services.

5.2. Abstract Resources. The Java classes implementing the resource provider functionality work with an abstract representation of scientific process and service resources, embodied by the class SSResource, which does not depend on the resource type. The dynamic behavior of an abstract resource is captured by the state diagram shown in Figure 4.

If a resource request is permissible, a new instance of the specific SSResource subclass is created with status set to Submit and the corresponding physical or virtual resource creation advances as described in Section 4. As soon as the resource becomes ready, the associated scientific process or service sends a (resource status) notification message to the resource provider, and such event triggers a change of status from Sumbit to Run. Only at this point, the resource can be used, and the resource provider notifies all the interested entities. Once the resource is no longer needed, it may be disposed; its status is then set to Release and the disposal of the corresponding physical or virtual resource proceeds according to the previous section. The scientific process or service sends another (resource status) notification message that causes the status to change from Release to Exit.

All the other state transitions are triggered by error conditions.

5.3. Scientific Services. *Scientific services* implement the logic of scientific applications, usually in a modular form where the whole logic is partitioned into reusable, loosely coupled, cohesive software modules. In an SOA-based framework, scientific services expose their functionality through a web service interface formally described by a WSDL document. To be best integrated in our model, scientific services, in addition to the core scientific functionality just described, must implement some housekeeping operations, too:

(i) immediately after start-up, they must notify the resource provider of their status (RUN);

(ii) immediately before exiting, they must notify the resource provider of their status (EXIT);

(iii) they must retrieve from the resource provider the assigned proxy and storage manager service end points;

(iv) they should expose some standard operations such as version(), load(), and exit(),

(v) they should provide asynchronous operations for long-running computations.

To ease the realization of new scientific services, or for wrapping existing applications into a web service container, we have developed a small housekeeping Java library implementing the above common tasks. As a simple example, consider the *MyScientificService* web service class, implementing the *MyScientificServicePortType* interface (defined by the corresponding WSDL port type) and exposing a *myOperation* operation. The simplified class diagram that illustrates how the scientific service can be implemented in Java, taking advantage of the housekeeping library, is shown in Figure 5. The responsibilities of each class in the diagram are the following:

(i) *SS*: common functionality useful to all scientific services;

(ii) *SSPublisher*: entry-point class which publishes the scientific service and initializes the network channel toward the proxy;

(iii) *SSConnectionClient*: it manages network channel and receives input messages from proxy;

(iv) *SSNotify*: it manages notification messages;

(v) *SSThread*: common functionality useful to all implementations of scientific service synchronous/asynchronous operations;

(vi) *MyScientificService*: scientific service implementation;

(vii) *MyScientificServicePortType*: scientific service interface with the list of all exposed operations;

(viii) *MyOperationThread*: implementation of the scientific service operation *myOperation* which may be executed asynchronously in a separate thread (useful for long-running computations).

Scientific service images are uploaded to the AMIR to be retrieved and deployed by scientific resource requests.

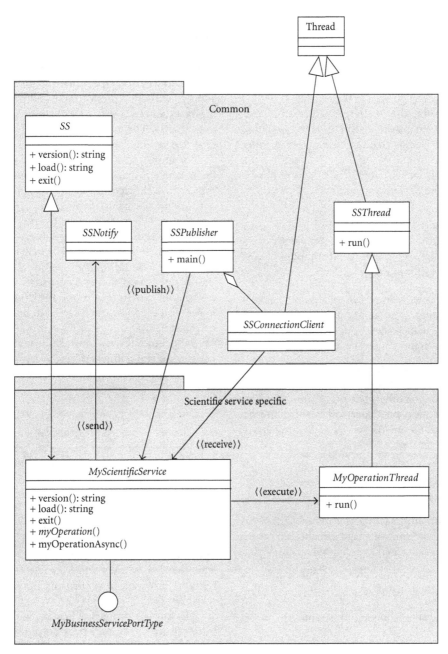

FIGURE 5: Scientific service class hierarchy.

5.4. Scientific Processes and Workflow Engines. As suggested in [5, 15], the choice of a workflow language naturally leads to the Business Process Execution Language [42] which belongs to the family of SOA standards. BPEL is complementary to the web service definition language (WSDL) [43], and in fact, BPEL instances are themselves web services. Both languages are XML based, and both make use of the XML schema definition language (XSD). A number of BPEL engines were considered:

(i) sun BPEL engine for Glassfish server (no longer maintained);

(ii) Oracle BPEL Process Manager in the Oracle SOA Suite 11g (commercial) [44];

(iii) ActiveVOS BPEL execution engine (commercial) [45];

(iv) Orchestra (open source) [46];

(v) Apache Orchestration Director Engine or ODE in brief (open source) [47].

Due to our preference for open-source software and self-contained tools, in the current implementation, we have chosen to work with ODE v1.3.5. This requires (1) a module in the resource provider to manage WfE requests, (2) a simple SOA wrapper to interface ODE with the resource provider and clients, and (3) a VM image embedding ODE. The WfE node component is then a VM image which provides the guest operating system preinstalled with some ready-to-run workflow engine such as ODE.

It is worth mentioning that the implementation is open to the integration of all standalone self-contained workflow engines, based on BPEL or not, that can be remotely executed on a nongraphical resource.

The VM disk image embedding ODE is deployed to the AMIR together with the workflow images.

5.5. Network Connectivity. One important practical issue not immediately evident from the model is the complexity of the network connections between the different components. We start from some basic assumptions.

(i) The resource provider must live on a public network so that every other component can contact it, including all the users of the system which, in a collaborative distributed environment, can be located anywhere.

(ii) Worker and WfE nodes, as already observed, may live on different private networks which are not directly connected to one another, but we assume that they can open network connections towards the Internet through some kind of NAT service. The same is true for personal resources.

(iii) WRMS and DIMS, if not living on a public network, must be accessible from the resource provider (e.g., via a virtual private network or VPN).

(iv) The application and machine image repository may be on a public network or may be replicated on the private networks attached to each pool of PM/VM.

(v) The storage manager must live on a public network to allow for the sharing of data.

In addition, we have the following constraints:

(1) the resource provider (public network) is required to notify a WfE (private network) when a requested scientific service resource is ready;

(2) a WfE needs to send request-response or one-way messages to scientific services running on WN or personal resources and living on different private networks;

(3) a scientific service running on a WN may need to send (notify) one-way messages to a WfE which is not on the same private network.

The first constraint can be satisfied by setting up a VPN between the WfE node and the resource provider: the VM that executes the WfE can be instructed to initialize the VPN during start-up; the other two by implementing a proxy service as described in the next subsection. The resulting network connectivity is synthesized in Figure 6.

5.6. Proxy. The *proxy* service acts as an intermediary for routing (Soap) messages from WfE to scientific services and vice versa. When the resource provider needs to notify a WfE about the endpoint (URL) of a newly started scientific service, it replaces the scientific service private network address with the proxy public address. In this way, the messages sent by a WfE to a scientific service are in fact sent to the proxy, which performs a sort of message routing to its final destination, based on a special message tag.

For improved scalability, many proxies can register with the resource provider. The latter assigns one of the available proxies to each scientific service. Each proxy is then in charge of routing messages to its own pool of scientific services that may live on different private networks. In principle, we could link the proxy and its pool of services with a VPN, but setting it up requires privileges usually not granted to a job in a WRMS. In practice, every scientific service, upon start-up, simply opens and shares a persistent bidirectional network connection with its own proxy; the latter will use this channel to route all the messages directed to the service.

The *scientific service proxy* component manages request-response and one-way messages from WfE to scientific services, while the notification proxy component is responsible for managing one-way messages from scientific services to WfE.

5.7. Other Services. As previously discussed, *storage managers* provide temporary storage to data-intensive scientific services. When the output from a scientific service serves as input for a subsequent service invocation during workflow execution, it would be ineffective to transfer the data back to the workflow and forth again to the next service. The storage manager handles plain and efficient HTTP uploads and downloads, assigning a unique public URL to the uploaded data so that they can be easily retrieved later when needed. many storage managers can register with the resource provider, thus ensuring optimal performance and scalability.

Monitor is a simple application with a web service client interface on the resource provider side and an HTTP/HTML interface on the user side, which can be queried for resource status. Monitor shows information, in XHMTL format, about the resource context related to scientific services, such as resource identifier, status, WSDL port type, last operation invoked, and the related time stamp.

The *application and machine image repository* is distributed over a number of components: a simple HTTP server hosts all the scientific service and process images, while every DIMS manages its own dedicated virtual machine image repository.

6. Case Study

The case study focuses on a specific bioinformatics domain: the application of machine learning techniques to molecular biology. In particular, microarray data analysis [48] is a challenging area since it has to face with datasets composed by

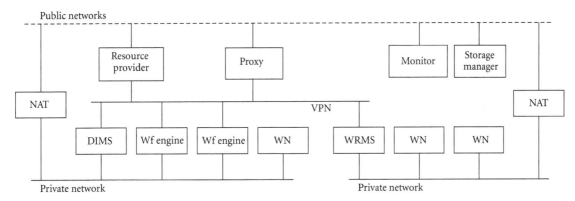

FIGURE 6: Schema of network connectivity.

a relatively low number of records (samples) characterized by an extremely high dimensionality (gene expression values).

6.1. Scientific Context and Background. Microarray experiments generate datasets in the form of $M \times N$ matrices, where M is the number of samples (typically $M \sim 100$), and N is the number of genes ($N > 10,000$). Such gene expression data can be used to classify the biologic samples based on the pattern of expression of all or a subset of genes. Reference datasets, needed by machine learning techniques, are generated from the experimental data by assigning a class label to all the samples (this is usually done manually by a domain expert). The construction of a classifier proceeds by (1) selecting an informative set of genes (features or attributes) that can distinguish between the various classes, (2) choosing an appropriate mathematical model for the classifier, (3) estimating the parameters of the model from the data in the *training set*, that is, a properly chosen subset of the reference dataset, and (4) calculating the accuracy of the classifier using the *test set*, that is, the remaining independent subset not used in training the classifier. With the help of the resulting classifier, class labels can then be automatically assigned to new unclassified microarray samples with an error margin which depends on the accuracy of the classifier.

Due to the huge number of genes probed in a microarray measure, the possibility of training a classifier using the expression values of a smaller but significant subset of all the genes is of particular interest. Many mathematical and statistical methods (e.g., chi-square) exist for selecting a group of genes of a given size and, after filtering out from the dataset all the other genes, a classifier can be trained and its accuracy tested. The subset of significant genes is then iteratively expanded or collapsed, and the previous procedure is repeated; in this way, it is possible to compare the accuracy of the classifier as a function of the size of the subset (i.e., number of attributes) and try to determine the "optimal" group of genes (Figure 7).

The reference dataset used in our experiment covers microarray measures related to the acute lymphoblastic leukemia [49], with 215 samples in the training set and 112 samples in the test set characterized by 12557 gene expression values and 7 class labels.

6.2. User Interaction. User interaction should be kept as much as possible (1) well-defined, (2) simple, and (3) independent of the WRMS/DIMS used, that is, technology agnostic; conforming to SOA, user interaction is based on the exchange of XML documents.

Users wishing to run a workflow-based application should provide the following information:

(i) URL of the image of the workflow to be deployed and enacted on demand (from a public repository or user provided, e.g., AMIR);

(ii) URL of the images of all scientific services to be started on demand and used by the workflow (from a public repository or user provided);

(iii) endpoint and authentication credentials of the WRMS/DIMS required to provide the resources to run the on-demand workflow engine and scientific services.

Based on the above information, users (1) prepare and send to the resource provider the workflow engine request document, (2) when the engine becomes ready, enact one or more workflow instances by preparing and sending the corresponding input documents, and (3) when finished, send to the resource provider the release request for the engine.

According to the information specified in the input document, the workflow is in charge of (1) composing and sending to the resource provider the scientific service request documents for all on-demand services, (2) when all scientific services are ready, invoking them in the specified order with the required input, and (3) in the end, sending to the resource provider the release request for all scientific services.

The SoapUI [50] application provides a GUI that can be of valuable help; after reading the WSDL document associated to a web service, it automatically lays out the structure of the XML input document leaving the user with the simpler task of filling in the data. SoapUI can also send the document to the given web service or workflow.

6.3. Scientific Services. The core of the scientific application is a modular web service, *Weka Data Mining*, which exposes

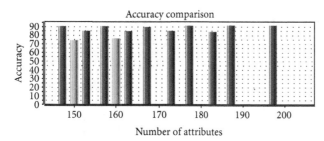

FIGURE 7: Snapshot of the bar chart generated by the visualization service.

a number of operations implementing basic data mining algorithms such as the following:

(i) feature (attribute) selection and ranking, for example, sort features according to some criteria;

(ii) dataset filtering, for example, remove all but the top-ranked features from a dataset;

(iii) model building, for example, train a classifier using a reference training set;

(iv) model testing, for example, calculate model accuracy using an independent test set.

The web service is built on top of the powerful open-source Weka library [51]. Data mining tasks may be long running, and the service exposes each operation both in synchronous (request-response) and asynchronous (one-way request and notify) form. The service is capable of retrieving input data, which may be large, via HTTP from a given URL, that is, from web server or storage manager; at the same time output data can be saved via HTTP to a given URL, that is, again to a storage manager. The service supports the processing of concurrent requests thus allowing for parallel flows of execution in the invoking workflow.

In addition, we have developed a visualization web service, *Chart*, which is a simple bar chart viewer based on the open-source JFreeChart library [52]; special attention has been paid to properly manage concurrent invocations resulting from parallel workflow execution as described in the next subsection. Figure 7 shows an example of chart generated by the service.

The scientific service images are available from the AMIR.

6.4. Workflows. The workflow developed for this case study is, in fact, a nested workflow. According to its definition, a BPEL process is also a web service, and it is perfectly legal to invoke a process from within another one. The invoked process, or *core process*, orchestrates a single iterative computation which trains a classifier and calculates its accuracy for an increasing number of attributes, as described before. The invoking process, or *wrapper process*, manages the concurrent

execution of a variable number of core processes and links to an external visualization service, running on the user desktop, for monitoring the real-time execution of these processes. In particular, the wrapper process waits for the user to launch the visualization service before invoking the core processes. The core process iteratively invokes the different operations exposed by the Weka Data Mining service to build the classification model and to evaluate its accuracy and invokes the visualization service with the accuracy result; the latter accordingly updates the cumulative accuracy bar chart. A snapshot of the bar chart taken during execution, and shown in Figure 7, illustrates some points:

(i) colored bars represent accuracy; bars of the same color are associated to the same type of data mining model and are calculated by the same core workflow;

(ii) groups of contiguous bars of different colors represent the same iteration, that is, the same number of attributes, and are calculated by different core workflows;

(iii) missing bars witness that the execution of core workflows is asynchronous, that different data mining models have different build times, and/or that underlying resources have different speed.

In addition, missing bars may also show that a problem has occurred with one of the core workflows.

Workflow images are available from the AMIR.

6.5. Running Experiments. The general scenario for running an experiment can be synthesized by the following list of user activities:

(1) choose an experiment, that is, the workflow that describes it (an URL pointing to the workflow archive); in case of a new experiment, prepare the workflow image and upload it to the AMIR;

(2) prepare the experiment inputs, that is, make data files available as URLs;

(3) prepare and submit to the resource provider the XML document describing the workflow engine request;

(4) wait for the system to provision the workflow engine and to deploy the workflow;

(5) prepare and submit the workflow input document to the workflow engine;

(6) start the external helper services, if any, as needed, for example, the visualization service;

(7) wait for workflow execution: this typically involves the provisioning of the resources needed by the scientific services and their execution as orchestrated by the workflow.

If the workflow is linked to a visualization service, its progress can be followed graphically (Figure 7). Alternatively, the monitor service can be queried for resource and scientific service status. In addition, a monitoring application can be

```
<classification>
  <trainingDataset>http://www.dsf.unica.it/~andrea/train.arff</trainingDataset>
  <testDataset>http://www.dsf.unica.it/~andrea/test.arff</testDataset>
  <applyDataset>http://www.dsf.unica.it/~andrea/test.arff</applyDataset>
  <classifierName>weka.classifiers.functions.MultilayerPerceptron</classifierName>
  <attributeNumberMin>10</attributeNumberMin>
  <attributeNumberMax>200</attributeNumberMax>
  <attributeNumberInc>10</attributeNumberInc>
  <rankerName>none</rankerName>
  <seriesLabel>MultilayerPerceptron</seriesLabel>
</classification>
```

ALGORITHM 2: XML fragment of the workflow input document (classification input).

registered with the resource provider to receive and view all resource status notifications and message flows.

Algorithm 2 shows a fragment of the workflow input document which describes the input to the Weka Data Mining service (datasets, classifier, and number of attributes), needed by the core process. In addition, the XML fragment shown in Algorithm 1 represents the scientific service request needed by the wrapper process to obtain a resource to run the Weka Data Mining service. Both XML fragments are part of the same workflow input document.

In the experiment related to Figure 7, the wrapper process enacts three core processes working with different classifiers: nearest neighbors (IB1), neural network (multilayer Perceptron), and rule based (PART); the datasets, the chi-square attribute selection algorithm, and the iterations over an increasing number of attributes are the same. Three different VMs delivered by a private OpenStack cloud run the Weka Data Mining services (one per classifier).

7. Results and Discussion

The extensive tests performed and the results obtained for the case study presented in the previous section help us to address in some detail the following aspects in the next subsections: (1) performance and scalability, (2) shortcomings, and (3) open problems. The performance evaluation presented is by no means exhaustive: extensive comparison with existing and much more mature production systems is left for the future, after all the many tunings and modifications that the proposed prototype system implementation requires.

7.1. Performance and Scalability. To measure the time needed to start a managed computation, we have considered three main phases: (1) the request processing time is small compared to other times; (2) the resource setup time depends on WRMS/DIMS and is similar for the employed HPC and grid systems (on average about 1 minute) and higher for cloud systems, unless special tuning is performed [53] (on average 5–10 minutes which can be reduced to 1 minute); (3) workflow engine and scientific service startup times are comparable to the previous phase but depend on network speed for downloading images. VM performance might be an issue, so we have compared execution times using PM and VM both for workflow engines and scientific services and found no substantial differences; our tests require relevant CPU and network I/O activities and no heavy local disk I/O which may be one of the slowness reasons with VM [53].

The test workflow described above has been enacted with the following parameters: the wrapper process starts 10 concurrent instances of the core process, each invoking its own scientific service during 20 iterations; scientific services have been executed both on homogeneous resources and on a mix of geographically distributed heterogeneous infrastructures such as Cybersar [54] and FutureGrid [55]. The generated data flow is the following: 2000 Soap messages exchanged through the proxy service, 600 data files downloaded from web repositories (approximately 4.5 GB of data), 800 write operations and 1000 read operations to/from storage manage service. The execution time varies with the resource hardware but also with the available network bandwidth between scientific services, data repositories, and storage manager.

Many concurrent enactments of the test workflow can be used to assess system scalability: with the available resources, 10 concurrent workflows were enacted (i.e., 10 workflow engines on cloud and 100 scientific services half on cloud and half on HPC/grid) without any particular problem except for some transient failures in providing the requested resources occurred with some WRMS/DIMS (mostly Eucalyptus). From the tests performed, we expect that the system can manage a number of concurrent scientific services up to 1000 or more if the proxy service is replicated as discussed later on.

A key point in workflow engine and overall system scalability and performance is the management of the data flow for data intensive computations. Many workflow engines (including BPEL) act as brokers for all message exchanges between the scientific services participating in the workflow, but embedding large datasets into such messages is not efficient and can lead to a collapse of both the engine and the proxy service. Rather, web repositories and the storage manager, can be used, and datasets can be indirectly passed to scientific services as URL references; in this way, each scientific service can directly and efficiently read/write data from/to repositories and the storage manager, thus minimizing transfers and improving scalability and performance.

7.2. Shortcomings. A number of problems are related to the BPEL language and the engine implementations. The BPEL specifications [42] do not allow multiple receive activities in the same scope with the same port type and operation. This is an annoying limitation which may be overcome by duplicating the operations with different names. Different BPEL engines miss some of the functionality dictated by the standard or implement nonstandard features. An example is variable initialization, required by some engines and automatically performed by others; another is *partnerLink* assignment whose syntax can be different depending on the engine. In ODE, web service functionality is built on top of Apache Axis2 [56], the older Apache WS framework, and many advanced features are missing, for example, WS-Security.

Another point that deserves some attention is the disposal of resources when they are no longer needed. In principle, the resource life cycle, that is, provisioning, usage, and disposal, can be managed through the workflow if the correct support is provided at the scientific service level. If no error occurs, things go as expected, but if only the workflow fails before disposal, a bunch of resources may be left around reserved, unused, and in some cases charged for. In addition, a failure with a resource or scientific service may leave a workflow indefinitely waiting for it; the list of possible errors is long. BPEL fault and compensation handlers may help in designing better error resilience but can do nothing if the workflow engine or its VM crashes. The infrastructure services (resource provider, DIMSS, and WRMS) must then be charged of the extra responsibility of resource disposal when something goes wrong, for example, by periodically checking resource status for failures or long inactivity periods or other abnormal behavior.

7.3. Open Problems. The model presented in this work represents an attempt aimed at experimenting possible ways to cope with the general and complex problem of the integration of heterogeneous resources from multiple providers as a cohesive aggregate and unavoidably has a number of limitations and aspects not (adequately) covered; among others we have the following.

(i) Scalability with the number of workflow instances and scientific services can be an issue for the proxy service since it mediates most message exchanges; to account for this, more than one proxy can register with the resource provider, which assigns one of the available proxies to each scientific process and service, thus ensuring proper load balancing. Resource provider scalability has not been assessed except for the consideration that resource provider and all related services can be replicated allowing for static load balancing (the same WRMS/DIMS can be shared by different resource providers). The storage manager service can be replicated, too, but

assignment to a scientific process or service should be based on some kind of network distance metric.

(ii) Redundancy of the resource provider service could be arguably obtained by means of standard high-availability techniques [57] if persistent data is stored into independent and replicated DBMS; in addition, the use of multiple proxy and storage manager services, as suggested above, should also help to guarantee the necessary redundancy.

(iii) Application recovery in case of network or other failures has not been taken into consideration; the simple solution of automatically reenacting failed workflows may work in case of transient failures but will not work in case of structural failures (e.g., when a computation exceeds the memory limit of a resource).

(iv) The need for a meta-scheduler has not been investigated, since WRMS and DIMS provide their own schedulers; if needed, such a meta-scheduler should be able to manage resource requests with very different requirements and resource pools (WRMS and DIMS) that change over time and over users.

Another important point concerns existing applications, domain-specific and resource-specific tools; many VOs have developed their own domain-specific, workflow scheduling systems which provide extensive monitoring, scheduling, data access and replication, and user priority management capabilities. We expect that users may be concerned by the problems/efforts required to use or even reimplement such applications and tools in a new environment [58]. According to what we said in the introduction, however, our proposal is not meant to "replace" but rather to "complement," so we must be pragmatic: it makes no sense to bother users which are happy with their applications, tools, and resources. Many "conventional" users will simply have no benefits from dynamic on-demand provisioning of resources, but many others may be attracted by this on one hand and by the advantages offered by the SOA approach on the other hand and may be interested in creating new or better applications using existing ones as building blocks; in most cases, it will not be necessary to reimplement applications and tools but simply wrap them with an SOA interface.

8. Conclusion

In this paper, we have presented a unified model for the dynamic on-demand provisioning of computational resources from multiple providers, based on the convergence and integration of different computing paradigms and infrastructures, and leveraging SOA technologies. Heterogeneous distributed resources are presented to their users with the illusion of a cohesive aggregate of resources, accessible through a well-defined standards-based software interface.

In addition, we have explored the adoption of standard unmodified BPEL language and existing engines for workflow description and enactment. Indeed, BPEL is not extremely popular in the workflow community, so we were interested in evaluating (also in practice) its advantages/limitations given its big merit of being an open standard (with special emphasis in relation to SOA) unlike most of the other languages employed in existing workflow systems and also to rouse new interest about it in the workflow community. At the same time, the presented model is intentionally flexible enough to allow us to employ other workflow systems such as Pegasus, Kepler, or Taverna; in particular, we plan to explore Taverna, thanks to the standalone "Taverna Server" component released by the Taverna team and which should be easily integrated with our proposed system.

In our opinion, the model benefits from a number of qualifying and distinctive features; it (1) is founded on firm SOA principles; (2) integrates different computing paradigms, systems, and infrastructures; (3) is open to further integrations and extensions both in terms of new resource management systems (WRMS and DIMS) and workflow management systems; (4) takes advantage from the integration and reuse of open-source tools and systems; (5) includes built-in scalability for some of the components; (6) promotes the porting and the development of new applications exposed as web services.

The effectiveness of the model has been assessed through a working implementation, which has shown its capabilities but also a number of open problems. In addition, the discussion of a case study in the bioinformatics field has hopefully given some hints on the practical possibilities of the proposed approach.

As discussed in Section 7, workflow management poses a number of problems. As well, another consideration is worth mentioning here, that is, the fact that BPEL workflow design is not straightforward even using the available graphical editors. Peeking at the business domain, the potential of the business process model and notation (BPMN) probably deserves some investigation in the future, given the capability of generating BPEL workflows directly from BPMN models.

In addition, we plan to extend the presented implementation (1) with the inclusion of new WRMS/DIMS and (2) with the integration of workflow engines to include both BPEL-based tools like Orchestra and tools like Taverna, which is not using BPEL.

Acknowledgments

The author acknowledges the Cybersar Consortium for the use of its computing facilities. This material is based upon work supported in part by the National Science Foundation under Grant no. 0910812 to Indiana University for "Future-Grid: An Experimental, High-Performance Grid Test-bed." Partners in the FutureGrid Project include University of Chicago, University of Florida, San Diego Supercomputer Center-UC San Diego, University of Southern California, University of Texas at Austin, University of Tennessee at Knoxville, University of Virginia, Purdue University, and Technische University Dresden.

References

[1] E. Deelman, D. Gannon, M. Shields, and I. Taylor, "Workflows and e-Science: an overview of workflow system features and capabilities," *Future Generation Computer Systems*, vol. 25, no. 5, pp. 528–540, 2009.

[2] E. Elmroth, F. Hernández, and J. Tordsson, "Three fundamental dimensions of scientific workflow interoperability: model of computation, language, and execution environment," *Future Generation Computer Systems*, vol. 26, no. 2, pp. 245–256, 2010.

[3] T. McPhillips, S. Bowers, D. Zinn, and B. Ludäscher, "Scientific workflow design for mere mortals," *Future Generation Computer Systems*, vol. 25, no. 5, pp. 541–551, 2009.

[4] A. Akram, D. Meredith, and R. Allan, "Evaluation of BPEL to scientific workflows," in *Proceedings of the 6th IEEE International Symposium on Cluster Computing and the Grid (CCGRID '06)*, pp. 269–272, IEEE Computer Society, May 2006.

[5] A. Bosin, N. Dessì, and B. Pes, "Extending the SOA paradigm to e-Science environments," *Future Generation Computer Systems*, vol. 27, no. 1, pp. 20–31, 2011.

[6] G. Mateescu, W. Gentzsch, and C. J. Ribbens, "Hybrid Computing-Where HPC meets grid and Cloud Computing," *Future Generation Computer Systems*, vol. 27, no. 5, pp. 440–453, 2011.

[7] G. Fox and D. Gannon, "A survey of the role and use of web services and service oriented architectures in scientific/technical Grids," Tech. Rep. 08/2006, Indiana University, Bloomington, Ind, USA, 2006.

[8] I. Taylor, M. Shields, I. Wang, and A. Harrison, "Visual Grid workflow in Triana," *Journal of Grid Computing*, vol. 3, no. 3-4, pp. 153–169, 2005.

[9] D. Churches, G. Gombas, A. Harrison et al., "Programming scientific and distributed workflow with Triana services," *Concurrency Computation Practice and Experience*, vol. 18, no. 10, pp. 1021–1037, 2006.

[10] D. D. Pennington, D. Higgins, A. Townsend Peterson, M. B. Jones, B. Ludäscher, and S. Bowers, "Ecological Niche modeling using the Kepler workflow system," in *Workflows for eScience: Scientific Workflow for Grids*, I. Taylor, E. Deelman, D. Gannon, and M. Shields, Eds., pp. 91–108, Springer, Berlin, Germany, 2007.

[11] E. Deelman, G. Singh, M. H. Su et al., "Pegasus: a framework for mapping complex scientific workflows onto distributed systems," *Scientific Programming*, vol. 13, no. 3, pp. 219–237, 2005.

[12] T. Fahringer, R. Prodan, and R. Duan, "ASKALON: a development and Grid computing environment for scientific workflows," in *Workflows for eScience: Scientific Workflow for Grids*, I. Taylor, E. Deelman, D. Gannon, and M. Shields, Eds., pp. 450–471, Springer, Berlin, Germany, 2007.

[13] T. Oinn, M. Addis, J. Ferris et al., "Taverna: a tool for the composition and enactment of bioinformatics workflows," *Bioinformatics*, vol. 20, no. 17, pp. 3045–3054, 2004.

[14] T. Oinn, P. Li, D. Kell et al., "Taverna/myGrid: aligning a workflow system with the life sciences community," in *Workflows for eScience: Scientific Workflow for Grids*, I. Taylor, E. Deelman, D. Gannon, and M. Shields, Eds., pp. 300–319, Springer, Berlin, Germany, 2007.

[15] T. Dörnemann, E. Juhnke, and B. Freisleben, "On-demand resource provisioning for BPEL workflows using amazon's elastic compute cloud," in *Proceedings of the 9th IEEE/ACM International Symposium on Cluster Computing and the Grid*

(CCGRID '09), pp. 140–147, IEEE Computer Society, May 2009.

[16] R. Y. Ma, Y. W. Wu, X. X. Meng, S. J. Liu, and L. Pan, "Grid-enabled workflow management system based on Bpel," *International Journal of High Performance Computing Applications*, vol. 22, no. 3, pp. 238–249, 2008.

[17] I. Brandic, S. Pllana, and S. Benkner, "High-level composition of QoS-aware grid workflows: an approach that considers location affinity," in *Proceedings of the Workshop on Workflows in Support of Large-Scale Science (WORKS '06)*, pp. 1–10, Paris, France, June 2006.

[18] A. Slominski, "Adapting BPEL to scientific workflows," in *Workflows for eScience: Scientific Workflow for Grids*, I. Taylor, E. Deelman, D. Gannon, and M. Shields, Eds., pp. 208–226, Springer, Berlin, Germany, 2007.

[19] F. Leymann, "Choreography for the Grid: towards fitting BPEL to the resource framework," *Concurrency Computation Practice and Experience*, vol. 18, no. 10, pp. 1201–1217, 2006.

[20] K. M. Chao, M. Younas, N. Griffiths, I. Awan, R. Anane, and C. F. Tsai, "Analysis of grid service composition with BPEL4WS," in *Proceedings of the18th International Conference on Advanced Information Networking and Applications (AINA '04)*, pp. 284–289, March 2004.

[21] T. Dörnemann, T. Friese, S. Herdt, E. Juhnke, and B. Freisleben, "Grid workflow modeling using Grid-specific BPEL extensions," in *Proceedings of German e-Science Conference*, Baden-Baden, Germany, 2007.

[22] W. Emmerich, B. Butchart, L. Chen, B. Wassermann, and S. L. Price, "Grid service orchestration using the Business Process Execution Language (BPEL)," *Journal of Grid Computing*, vol. 3, no. 3-4, pp. 283–304, 2005.

[23] M. A. Murphy and S. Goasguen, "Virtual Organization Clusters: self-provisioned clouds on the grid," *Future Generation Computer Systems*, vol. 26, no. 8, pp. 1271–1281, 2010.

[24] C. Vázquez, E. Huedo, R. S. Montero, and I. M. Llorente, "On the use of clouds for grid resource provisioning," *Future Generation Computer Systems*, vol. 27, no. 5, pp. 600–605, 2011.

[25] A. Bosin, N. Dessì, M. Bairappan, and B. Pes, "A SOA-based environment supporting collaborative experiments in E-science," *International Journal of Web Portals*, vol. 3, no. 3, pp. 12–26, 2011.

[26] I. Foster, K. Kesselman, J. M. Nick, and S. Tuecke, "The physiology of the grid—an open grid services architecture for distributed systems integration globus alliance," 2002, http://www.globus.org/alliance/publications/papers/ogsa.pdf.

[27] P. Tröger, "DRMAAv2—An Introduction," 2011, http://www.drmaa.org/drmaav2-ogf33.pdf.

[28] C. Aiftimiei, P. Andreetto, S. Bertocco et al., "Design and implementation of the gLite CREAM job management service," *Future Generation Computer Systems*, vol. 26, no. 4, pp. 654–667, 2010.

[29] AWS, "Amazon Web Services: Amazon Elastic Compute Cloud—API Reference," 2011, http://awsdocs.s3.amazonaws.com/EC2/latest/ec2-api.pdf.

[30] AWS, "Amazon Web Services: Amazon Simple Storage Service—API Reference," 2006, http://awsdocs.s3.amazonaws.com/S3/latest/s3-api.pdf.

[31] R. Nyren, A. Edmonds, A. Papaspyrou, and T. Metsch, "Open Cloud Computing Interface—Core," 2011, http://ogf.org/documents/GFD.183.pdf.

[32] D. Nurmi, R. Wolski, C. Grzegorczyk et al., "The eucalyptus open-source cloud-computing system," in *Proceedings of the 9th IEEE/ACM International Symposium on Cluster Computing and the Grid (CCGRID '09)*, pp. 124–131, IEEE Computer Society, May 2009.

[33] I. Foster, K. Keahey, C. Kesselman et al., "Embedding community-specific resource managers in general-purpose grid infrastructure," Tech. Rep. ANL/MCS-P1318-0106, Argonne National Laboratory, Lemont, Ill, USA, 2006.

[34] K. Pepple, *Deploying OpenStack*, O'Reilly Media, Sebastopol, Calif, USA, 2011.

[35] E. Laure, S. M. Fisher, A. Frohner et al., "Programming the Grid with gLite," *Computational Methods in Science and Technology*, vol. 12, no. 1, pp. 33–45, 2006.

[36] LSF, "Platform Load Sharing Facility," 2005, http://www.platform.com/workload-management/high-performance-computing.

[37] SGE, "Oracle Grid Engine," 2009, http://www.oracle.com/us/products/tools/oracle-grid-engine-075549.html.

[38] O. V. Sukhoroslov, "JLite: a lightweight Java API for gLite," 2009, http://jlite.googlecode.com/files/jLite.pdf.

[39] B. Sotomayor, R. S. Montero, I. M. Llorente, and I. Foster, "Virtual infrastructure management in private and hybrid clouds," *IEEE Internet Computing*, vol. 13, no. 5, pp. 14–22, 2009.

[40] JCLOUDS, "Jclouds multi-cloud library," 2011, http://code.google.com/p/jclouds.

[41] Libvirt, "The virtualization API," 2011, http://libvirt.org.

[42] OASIS, "Web Services Business Process Execution Language Version 2.0," 2007, http://docs.oasis-open.org/wsbpel/2.0/wsbpel-v2.0.html.

[43] W3C, "Web Services Description Language 1.1," 2001, http://www.w3.org/TR/wsd.

[44] ORACLE, "Oracle BPEL Process Manager," 2011, http://www.oracle.com/technetwork/middleware/bpel/overview/index.html.

[45] AVOS, "ActiveVOS platform," 2011, http://www.activevos.com.

[46] OW2, "Orchestra User Guide," 2011, http://download.forge.objectweb.org/orchestra/Orchestra-4.9.0-UserGuide.pdf.

[47] ODE, "Apache Orchestration Director Engine," 2011, http://ode.apache.org.

[48] A. Bosin, N. Dessì, and B. Pes, "A cost-sensitive approach to feature selection in micro-array data classification," in *Proceedings of the 7th international workshop on Fuzzy Logic and Applications: Applications of Fuzzy Sets Theory (WILF '07)*, vol. 4578 of *Lecture Notes in Computer Science*, pp. 571–579, Springer, 2007.

[49] E.-J. Yeoh, M. E. Ross, S. A. Shurtleff et al., "Classification, subtype discovery, and prediction of outcome in pediatric acute lymphoblastic leukemia by gene expression profiling," *Cancer Cell*, vol. 1, no. 2, pp. 133–143, 2002.

[50] SOAPUI, "Eviware SoapUI," 2011, http://www.soapui.org.

[51] M. Hall, E. Frank, G. Holmes, B. Pfahringer, P. Reutemann, and I. H. Witten, "The WEKA data mining software: an update," *SIGKDD Explorations*, vol. 11, no. 1, pp. 10–18, 2009.

[52] D. Gilbert, "JFreeChart Java chart library," 2011, http://www.jfree.org/jfreechart.

[53] A. Bosin, M. Dessalvi, G. M. Mereu, and G. Serra, "Enhancing eucalyptus community cloud," *Intelligent Information Management*, vol. 3, no. 4, pp. 52–59, 2012.

[54] Cybersar, "Cybersar consortium for supercomputing, computational modeling and management of large databases," 2006, http://www.cybersar.com.

[55] FutureGrid, "FutureGrid: a distributed testbed for Clouds, Grids, and HPC," 2009, https://portal.futuregrid.org.

[56] AXIS2, "Apache Axis2," 2011, http://axis.apache.org/axis2/java/core/.

[57] LHA, "Linux-HA," 2011, http://www.linux-ha.org/wiki/Main_Page.

[58] W. Gentzsch, "Porting applications to grids and clouds," *International Journal of Grid and High Performance Computing*, vol. 1, no. 1, pp. 55–77, 2009.

5

Assessing the Open Source Development Processes Using OMM

Etiel Petrinja and Giancarlo Succi

Center for Applied Software Engineering, Free University of Bozen/Bolzano, 39100 Bolzano/Bozen, Italy

Correspondence should be addressed to Etiel Petrinja, etiel.petrinja@unibz.it

Academic Editor: Gerardo Canfora

The assessment of development practices in Free Libre Open Source Software (FLOSS) projects can contribute to the improvement of the development process by identifying poor practices and providing a list of necessary practices. Available assessment methods (e.g., Capability Maturity Model Integration (CMMI)) do not address sufficiently FLOSS-specific aspects (e.g., geographically distributed development, importance of the contributions, reputation of the project, etc.). We present a FLOSS-focused, CMMI-like assessment/improvement model: the QualiPSo Open Source Maturity Model (OMM). OMM focuses on the development process. This makes it different from existing assessment models that are focused on the assessment of the product. We have assessed six FLOSS projects using OMM. Three projects were started and led by a software company, and three are developed by three different FLOSS communities. We identified poorly addressed development activities as the number of commit/bug reports, the external contributions, and the risk management. The results showed that FLOSS projects led by companies adopt standard project management approaches as product planning, design definition, and testing, that are less often addressed by community led FLOSS projects. The OMM is valuable for both the FLOSS community, by identifying critical development activities necessary to be improved, and for potential users that can better decide which product to adopt.

1. Introduction

Free/Libre Open Source Software (FLOSS) development approaches differ from the traditional software development approaches [1] such as the waterfall or the spiral. The FLOSS approaches have specific characteristics as the geographical distribution of the development team [1]. The developers usually do not know personally each other, there are no budget constraints, and so forth. However, some traditional software development issues as [2]: faults insertion, continuous change of requirements, and growing complexity, are present also in agile and FLOSS projects with additional critical aspects that have to be addressed. Some of these, are for example, issues related to a strongly distributed development process, and absence of formal responsibility of developers for meeting deadlines.

The software development process is increasingly being defined and standardized [3]. Assessment models have been defined for evaluating the quality of the software development process. Only by assessing it, it is possible to identify poorly implemented practices, identify missing practices, and improve the development process. Only by assessing the quality of the development process it might be possible to optimise the use of resources and reduce the development time. For successfully assessing the process, it is possible to use an assessment approach that addresses key aspects of the development process. For this reason, it is important to modify an assessment approach or use different approaches when assessing different types of software processes. One standardized approach to assess the quality of the software development process is the Capability Maturity Model Integration (CMM/CMMI) [4]. It is both an assessment and an improvement model for software development. CMMI is increasingly being adopted by the software industry and the number of experts that are knowledgeable in its structure and usage is already large.

This paper presents a FLOSS-development-process assessment and improvement model and shows its application on three case studies. The Open Source Maturity Model (OMM) [5, 6] was designed with the aim of increasing the perceived quality of the FLOSS development process [7]. The trustworthiness of FLOSS is an important criteria when potential users decide to download and try to use the FLOSS product [8]. A study conducted on a large group of stakeholders, both from the software industry, and members of FLOSS communities [8], unveiled this. Specially stakeholders from the software industry stressed the importance of quantitative measurements of the quality of FLOSS. Without quality metrics potential users have problems when selecting and adopting FLOSS products. The main beneficiaries of the OMM are potential users of FLOSS products, especially integrators of FLOSS products. For example, software companies that adopt FLOSS products and integrate them into composed software products that can be either FLOSS or proprietary. FLOSS communities can also benefit from a large number of users attracted by a good OMM assessment, especially integrators from the software industry that can contribute new code to the project. The results of the conducted stakeholders survey was an important source of information for the design of a new assessment model. The large majority of metrics listed in OMM are addressing quantitative measurements of the FLOSS development process suggested by the stakeholders included in the study.

The existent FLOSS assessment models have not yet been largely adopted. However, when they are used, they provide indications about the quality of FLOSS projects. The OMM maintains some similarities with existent models. However the advantages of OMM, if we compare it with other FLOSS-oriented assessment models, is its particular focus on the development process. The OMM prescribes practices as: time-related implementation and management of the testing process; support of good maintenance practices; measure response time of the community to improvement suggestions from the community, the performing of configuration audits; inclusion of the plan for process quality; and so forth. Available FLOSS models sometimes address similar aspects, however at a coarser level of details. Aspects that distinguish the OMM from other models are often related to the management and the improvement of adopted software development practices.

The assessment of the development process can bring benefits not just to the further improvement of the process itself but also to an increase of the quality of the FLOSS product. By omitting the analysis of process characteristics as: the quality of the testing plan, the project, and the process-planning characteristics, and others, we could miss aspects related to the survivability [9] and the quality of the development process. These aspects are useful indicators, not just of the current quality of the project but also, of its potential future evolution. The OMM helps when deciding to adopt a FLOSS product, specially if the product will be integrated in a composed product created by a software integrator. Compared to CMMI, OMM addresses FLOSS-specific aspects that are not addressed by CMMI. A CMMI assessment is usually an extensive process that is not used for assessing small software companies or single-software projects. On contrary, OMM was designed specifically for assessing single FLOSS projects, and the assessment process is considerably shorter than the CMMI assessment. The OMM should cover all key aspects of the FLOSS, however it should be flexible and allow the assessment of just some parts of the development process.

Despite OMM diverges in several aspects from CMMI, there are similarities. The structure, the content of the model, and the assessment process share common elements. Part of the motivation for designing a similar model was based on the fact that CMMI is currently the largely used software development process assessment methodology. Although there are still several problems adopting CMMI in the software industry, there is already a considerable expertise in the software industry that we wanted to benefit from. Experts from the software industry that know CMMI can easily become users of the OMM model.

Three key contributions of this paper are:

(1) A description of the QualiPSo OMM, a FLOSS-oriented development process assessment model.

(2) A report of the application of the QualiPSo OMM on six-case studies; assessing FLOSS projects started and led by a software company (two SMEs and one large software integrator company) and projects developed by FLOSS communities.

(3) The presentation of improvement opportunities for the assessed FLOSS projects.

Section 2 presents the related work. The third section describes key characteristics of the used assessment model. In section four, we present how the OMM model should be used. In section five, we present six case studies. We present the results of the assessment of the FLOSS projects in the sixth section. The seventh section contains the discussion of the most important results. In the section eight, we present the threats to validity and finally we draw the conclusions and propose the future work.

2. Related Work

The adoption of software assessment methodologies has been studied extensively in the last decade [10–13]. Roberts et al. [12] studied factors influencing the adoption of software methodologies. They identified factors as: the organisational system development methodology (SDM) transition, the functional management involvement/support the use of models, and the external support. The study provided useful indications to researches by identifying a list of measures to be checked, and to developers by providing a guide to aspects that should be considered when implementing a system. The study conducted by Misra et al. [14] provides a list of best practices and factors that influence the quality of Agile software development. Most of those factors are also part of the OMM model. Khalifa and Verner considered human behaviour when analysing the adoption of the waterfall and the prototyping methodologies [10]. By studying the behaviour of developers and other stakeholders they identified two factors that influence the perceived quality of the development method: the facilitating conditions, and the process quality. The product quality was not identified as a statistically significant factor for explaining the usage. Their work sheds some light on the perceived quality of the development process and the impact of the methodology. Their results show the importance of the development process adopted by software developers which was one of our motivation factors when designing OMM. Matook and Indulska conducted a study of the development and measurement of the quality of process models by using the quality function deployment approach and proposed a tool that can be used for evaluating process models [11].

The quality of reference models can influence the final quality of the developed software and reduce development costs and development time. von Wangeheim et al. conducted a study on the methodological support of creation and modification of the software process capability/maturity models (SPCMM) [13]. An important aspect they have identified is that "SPCMM elements are not explicitly and systematically related to quality and performance goals." We adopted some of the approaches proposed by the presented studies. Several results are aligned with findings described in the cited literature. The key difference is our focus on the FLOSS development process.

The CMMI model has been increasingly adopted by software companies [4]. The research of the applications of CMMI showed that after a decade of the availability of the CMM half of the companies involved in the SEI study were classified in its lower maturity level [4]. Other studies reported an even higher level of companies classified as CMM level 1 [15]. Recently, discording studies of the adoption of CMMI had been published; some studies found a growth and improvement of the quality of assessed companies [16], on contrary Staples et al. [17] report that the adoption of CMMI is still difficult for several reasons. For example, one reason is the cost and the complexity of the CMMI assessment process. Companies might not be interested to adopt the CMMI model due to its complexity or because they use other assessment and improvement models.

There are several studies presenting modifications or extensions of reference models. Many of them analyse the adoption of CMMI in small and medium enterprises (SMEs). Staples et al. [17] and Guerrero and Eterovic reported that the adoption of CMM is difficult in small enterprises [18]. Methodologies are often adapted to specific assessment needs or simplified methodologies are used [17]. Assessment methodologies have been proposed also for the agile software development approach [19]. Paulk studied the issues related to the use of agile approaches and the CMM assessment methodology [20]. He concluded that both methodologies can benefit from each other. von Wangeheim et al. [21] have studied the adoption of ISO/IEC 15504 in SMEs and found that the adoption level of Reference models is much lower in SMEs than in large companies. Dybå [22] presented the adoption of process improvement methodologies in the Scandinavian Context focusing on the quality management aspects which we considered important when we designed OMM. Contrary to other studies, he found that SMEs implement process improvement elements efficiently as large companies. Our paper describes the use of a reference model dedicated to FLOSS projects. During the study we have encountered many issues identified by the cited studies that were all conducted on non-FLOSS software projects. Their findings were important for understanding the issues that we found during our research.

The Open Source Maturity Model (OSMM) assessment methodology for FLOSS projects was presented by Cap Gemini in year 2003 [23]. Afterwards several new methodologies were proposed, some of them are: the Open Source Maturity Model (OSMM) from Navica Inc. [24], the Methodology of Qualification and Selection of Open Source software (QSOS) [25], the Open Business Readiness Rating (OpenBRR) [26], the Open Business Quality Rating (Open BQR) [27], the Qualoss methodology [28], and the SQO-OSS quality model [29]. To our knowledge there are only few studies analysing and validating previously listed FLOSS assessment models. A comparison study of OpenBRR and QSOS was performed by Deprez and Alexandre [30]. Their study identified positive and negative aspects of both models. A similar approach was done by Petrinja et al. [6]. The authors of the study compared the use of OpenBRR, QSOS, and OMM to assess two FLOSS projects: Firefox and Chromium. Most of these models have a repository available on the web where users can see examples of assessments of popular FLOSS projects; there are, for example, 101 available assessment results obtained using the QSOS model.

Some of these methodologies were proposed by private entities as, for example, the OSMM methodology. More often they were proposed by research centres, universities, or individuals. They share common aspects, the most important is the set of software characteristics they measure. We analysed those characteristics and reused some of them while designing OMM. The reuse of characteristics included in other methodologies was dictated by the aim of providing an as possible complete measurement of the FLOSS process.

3. Characteristics of OMM

The OMM is a FLOSS assessment and improvement model that was designed with the aim of being able to support the assessment of the quality of the FLOSS development process. FLOSS adoption is susceptible to the lack of trust in its quality, both of the development process and of the software product. The quality of the software product is related to the quality of the development process that is adopted to produce the software product. Our aim was not just to improve the stakeholders perception of the quality of FLOSS, by providing a detailed set of metrics characterising the development process, but also of its quantitatively measurable quality. The lack of trust in FLOSS is often unjustified, and therefore, it is important to understand what are the issues that hinder the trust.

3.1. The Inputs for Building the Model. The information gathered for the design of the model was based on different types of users, development approaches, and on previous studies. We have conducted personal interviews with 52 individuals in the first iteration of the research [8]. The interviewees were experts from the software industry (Siemens, Engineering Ingegneria Informatica, Bull, Atos, IBM, Mandriva, Thales, etc.) and members of FLOSS communities (Apache HTTP Server, Eclipse, Emacs, Linux Kernel, Mozilla project, GNOME, Debian, etc.). The two groups were equally represented. The majority of participants covered managerial and development roles. Some of them were working in the industry and at the same time participating in FLOSS communities. Following a predefined questionnaire, we collected opinions and the practices interviewees use when developing, using, or adopting FLOSS. During the interviews we focused on: the quality, the FLOSS stakeholders, the technology used, and the business aspects. However, the whole questionnaire covered sixteen topics and contained 53 questions. Interviews were usually face to face and the meetings lasted between one and two hours. There were always at least two researchers participating to the meeting and annotating the answers. After the meeting, the draft of the answers collected during the interview was sent to interviewees that had to confirm its correctness. We conducted a second iteration of the information collection in the form of a survey that we conducted with the help of a web questionnaire. After analysing the results of interviews and surveys we identified the areas of the FLOSS development process that participants consider important for improving the quality of FLOSS.

Other sources of information for the design of the model were [7]: the literature review, and the study of existent FLOSS assessment methodologies and standards as: OpenBRR, QSOS, CMMI, ISO/IEC 15504, and so forth. These sources were used when the answers from the experts were lacking sufficient details about the development process they mentioned.

Interviews and surveys were the main source for topics that are important for FLOSS stakeholders. These topics are measured on different granularity levels inside OMM. The CMMI principles influenced the design of the OMM structure and the assessment process. From the literature review we gathered additional details about FLOSS practices and the whole development process. These elements were inserted into the OMM as questions on different levels of the model.

3.2. High-Level Components of OMM. The key components of OMM are elements focusing on important aspects of the FLOSS development process. We identified a list of elements that influence the perceived quality of the FLOSS development process by a large group of stakeholders in FLOSS projects. We name these components TrustWorthy Elements (TWEs). From interviews and surveys, we obtained a list of TWEs that were mentioned by a large percentage of experts. We were able to compose a ranked list of topics where some of the TWEs were considered important by a large percentage of experts. The addressing of the needs of software users and integrators, that are the first potential users of OMM, influenced the type of elements inserted into OMM. Some questions as for example: "check the availability of the requirements specification" can be considered not important for simple FLOSS projects. However, the majority of successful FLOSS projects that have many users and contributions, sometimes contributed by the software industry, take in consideration aspects related to requirements specification and other aspects important for a (FLOSS) software project. Several elements in the structure of the proposed model resemble elements in CMMI; OMM is

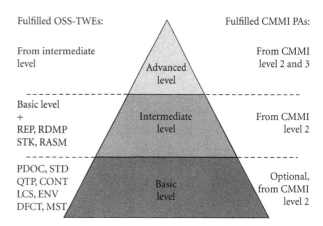

FIGURE 1: Three OMM maturity levels.

structured in levels, practices are important building blocks of the model, they focus on elements that are assessed also in the CMMI, and so forth. Both models aim to be usable for assessment but also for improvement of the development process. Similarly as in the CMMI model, we have proposed a level structure for the OMM model. We limit the number of maturity levels to three (in CMMI there are 5 maturity levels) (see Figure 1):

(1) the basic level with 11 TWEs,

(2) the intermediate level with 7 TWEs,

(3) the advanced level with 7 TWEs.

When we talk about maturity we used a simple definition (Dictionary.com) that says that a software product or a software process is mature when it has reached a high (or full) development. The full development in OMM is when all practices that are expected by stakeholders, quality standards, and the technological process are fulfilled.

The TWEs were distributed into three maturity levels according to their importance for interviewed and surveyed stakeholders in FLOSS projects. TWEs considered important for improving the perceived quality of the FLOSS development process were inserted into lower OMM levels. For example, license management was considered important for a large percentage of participants to the initial research, therefore we have decide to put the TWE LCS into the Basic OMM level; the level that should be first implemented. We based our classification of TWEs also on the complexity of its implementation. Reputation of a FLOSS project has also an important influence on the perceived quality of the assessed FLOSS project, however, we decided to put the REP TWE into the Advanced OMM level because it is not easy to build the reputation of a FLOSS project. Our initial distribution of TWEs in the three levels was tested during the validation of the model. After collecting the results of the assessments we identified few TWEs that had to be moved between levels.

The information about the maturity level reached by a FLOSS project provides a single figure about its maturity. Somebody can argue that the collection of TWEs and their distribution into the three maturity levels is not the only possible interpretation of the maturity of a FLOSS project.

We think that a better source of information about the quality and maturity of a FLOSS development process is the whole set of assessment values for each TWE. These values represent quantitatively measured characteristics of the FLOSS project. We identified a set of 25 key TWEs:

(i) PDOC—Project documentation.

(ii) STD—Use of established and widespread standards.

(iii) QTP—Quality of the testing process.

(iv) LCS—Licenses management.

(v) ENV—Environment.

(vi) DFCT—Number of commits and bug reports.

(vii) MST—Maintainability and stability.

(viii) CM—Configuration Management.

(ix) PP1 and PP2—Product planning, project planning.

(x) REQM—Requirements management.

(xi) RDMP and RDMP2—roadmap.

(xii) STK—Stakeholders.

(xiii) PPQA—Process and product quality assurance.

(xiv) PMC—Project monitoring and control.

(xv) TST1 and TST2—Test.

(xvi) DSN1 and DSN2—Design.

(xvii) CONT—Contributions.

(xviii) RASM—Results of third-party assessment.

(xix) REP—Reputation.

(xx) PI—Product integration.

(xxi) RSKM—Risk management.

Twelve TWEs address generic software development practices, for example project management (PM) and risk management (RSKM), the others address FLOSS specific aspects as the contribution level (CONT) and the Licenses management (LCS). The TWEs are high-level elements that we specialized into smaller components that can be assessed easier and increase the granularity level of the assessment. The identification of components that address a small aspect of the software development process limit the subjectivity of the assessment. The smaller are the assessed components of the development process, the more precise is the assessment.

Questions as: "Check the availability of FAQ documents" can be simply answered by searching through the web pages of the FLOSS project. The experience of an OMM assessment team, gained with the assessment of several FLOSS projects, help to precisely assign an assessment value to each practice. Based on experiments conducted during the validation of OMM [6] we identified that distinct assessors assign similar grades for measured characteristic. The variability of assessment values, based on the subjective perception of questions and documents evaluated, is small.

3.3. Low-Level Components of OMM. We used the Goal Question Metric approach (GQM) [31] to derive the components of the OMM model that are part of the TWE elements. In the GQM we have to identify the Goals that we wish to achieve; the Questions to which we will have to answer to be able to know if the Goal has been reached; and the lower level is composed by metrics that have to be measured to answer to the questions. The number of the goals specified varies between one and five and depends on the complexity of the TWE to which they belong. Some TWE (e.g., Design 2 (DSN2) have 5 goals and addresses aspects as requirements, components solutions, and design decisions) have several goals, others (as Roadmap 2) have just one goal. The elements were extracted by the interviews and surveys conducted, from the literature study, from other models, and from the experience of the team that designed the OMM. Questions were written in a structured form and they were circulated inside the team. A common agreement had to be reached inside the team on the elements inserted into OMM.

We have designed the create, the manage, and the improve set of questions and most TWEs contain a goal that is addressing each of these three aspects. A similar design is used in the CMMI. Goals first address aspects related to the "creation" of: the documentation (e.g., the PDOC TWE has a goal: "Create product documentation."), software components, processes, and so forth. The "manage" type of goals address the management of already created elements. The last type of goals addresses the activities related to the "improvement" of the development practices adopted, the software components created, the documentation, and so forth. It was not always possible to include the three types of goals for all TWEs but we followed this structure wherever it was possible. Each goal is composed by one or more practices. They specialize goals and characterize activities that are usually conducted inside the FLOSS project. OMM contains 122 practices for the complete assessment process. The GQM approach requires the definition of "questions" that inside the OMM are called "practices" for maintaining the similarity with the CMMI naming convention. An example of a practice from the PDOC TWE is:

Practice PDOC.3.2—"Improve the support for several natural languages."

Metrics are the lowest level of the OMM model. In the current version of the model there are 630 metrics. The metrics are used to measure if a practice is fulfilled completely, partially, or not at all.

The number of metrics is large and it may be perceived as too large for a FLOSS assessment. However, the granularity level of metrics in OMM is optional; assessors can decide to assess just the practices and not consider metrics in details. An assessment without metrics will be of smaller precision and with less value for people reading the results, but it will still give a usable OMM assessment result. The 122 questions representing practices are comparable to the level of details of methodologies as QSOS and OpenBRR and it can be assessed in a time frame ranging from two to four hours depending on the size of the assessed project.

3.4. The Rating Mechanism. In the OMM model each assessed value can reach a specific threshold value. These should be defined uniformly for the whole model to limit the bias. We have decided to use a uniform threshold value for the whole model; there are four possible assessment values ranging from 1 to 4 with the possibility to assign a 0 for metrics that do not apply in specific domains. For example Practice ENV.1.3 (Select integrated management and communication tools used in the project) in the TWE assessing the Environment aspects contains several metrics that should be searched and measured, for example: Eclipse, BlueFish, Kdevelop, and others. A FLOSS project will probably adopt just one of the development environments and not all of them. During the assessment we have to measure the diffusion of the use of the adopted environment; all others will be considered not applicable (assessed with 0). The threshold value of 4 means that the implementation of the requested elements is fulfilled more than 75%, value 3 means that it is fulfilled between 50% and 75%, value 2 between 25% and 50%, and value 1 that its implementation is lower than 25% of what requested by the practice.

We have decided not to prescribe a complete list of elements that have to be implemented in a project to reach a specific threshold level as it is done in OpenBRR and QSOS. The first version of the OMM model contained the exact definition of threshold values, however the elements present in each level were quite arbitrary and based on the results of the first validations we decided to insert this information as subprocess elements that have to be considered but are not strictly prescribed for reaching a threshold level. Therefore, the decision to assign a 1, 2, 3, or 4 value depends on the decision of the assessment team based on the information available. The assessor proposes an assessment value (1, 2, 3, or 4) based on his previous domain knowledge and the assessment team can agree with the value or propose new documents that support a different assessment value. The documents showing the activity of the FLOSS project used during the assessment should be collected and archived by the assessors and made available as proof of the assessment result.

A detailed description of all 25 TWEs will not be provided in this paper (for details see the document: http://www.qualipso.org/sites/default/files/Open Maturity Model .pdf). We present here just part of the structure described in previous sections that is schematically presented in Table 1. We can see all four granularity levels of the OMM model related to documentation aspects inside the FLOSS project:

(i) the TWE: PDOC: Project Documentation;

(ii) description of the purpose of the PDOC TWE: Develop and maintain project documentation, making it readily accessible to the community;

(iii) the first goal PDOC.1: Provide high quality documentation;

(iv) the goal is specialised into three practices, the first one is PDOC.1.1: Create development documentation;

(v) the lowest granularity level (LookFors) contains the set of documents we have to search in the assessed project (for example: Check the availability of requirements specification).

We can see in the example questions related to the software product (check the availability of a user's guide) and questions related to the development process (check the availability of work flow guidelines). The assessment team must decide what is the quality and completeness of the requirements specification documentation available in the project based on the available documents and previous experience of the team.

The OMM model divides the development process into small activities that can be assessed quantitatively. The experience of the assessor and the adoption of assessment best practice guidelines guarantees a good precision of the whole assessment process. Case studies and experiments conducted [6] demonstrate that the value assessed by more individuals does not vary strongly. Therefore, in general we can be confident in the objectivity of the assessment result.

The rating (R) mechanism defines how to aggregate the assessment values for the FLOSS development process by aggregating the assessments on different granularity levels: the OMM maturity level $R(\text{ML}_i)$, the TWE level $R(\text{TWE}_i)$, the goal level $R(G_i)$, and the Practice $R(P_i)$ level. The rating is performed by calculating the average value of the elements aggregating the elements from the lower level (see (1) for Practice rating, (2) for Goal rating, and (3) for TWE rating).

Calculation of the Rating of a Practice

$$R(P_i) = \frac{\sum_{\text{All Metrices}} \text{Metric}_i}{\text{number of Metrices}}. \tag{1}$$

Calculation of the Rating of a Goal

$$R(G_i) = \frac{\sum_{\text{All Practices}} \text{Practice}_i}{\text{number of Practices}}. \tag{2}$$

Calculation of the Rating of a TWE

$$R(\text{TWE}_i) = \frac{\sum_{\text{All Goals}} \text{Goal}_i}{\text{number of Goals}}. \tag{3}$$

The weighting of metrics (assigning different importance to some metrics) is subjected to several potential risks [32] that can distort the assessment result. We decided to do just a simple averaging of metrics. Offering to readers of the assessment results a preferred level of granularity provides a more informative source of details about the assessed FLOSS project. We are considering also additional weighting mechanisms, but for an empirically supported mechanism we need a large set of assessment data which will be collected with a larger usage of the model.

The overall rating can be calculated to:

(i) identify the OMM maturity level of the FLOSS project,

TABLE 1: Mobile OS project assessment results for the project documentation (PDOC) Trustworthy element.

PDOC: Project documentation Purpose: Develop and maintain project documentation, making it readily accessible to the community.		2.11
Goal/practice	Goal/practice description	
Goal PDOC 1	Provide high quality documentation	2.67
Practice PDOC-1.1	Create development documentation	3
LookFor	Check the availability of requirements specification	3
	Check the availability of high level design/product architecture	4
	Check the availability of detailed design	3
	Check the availability of technical documentation (e.g., for use in debugging)	2
	Check the availability of workflow guidelines (for checking, testing...)	4
Practice PDOC-1.2	Create user documentation	3
LookFor	Check the availability of a user's guide	3
	Check the availability of FAQ documents	3

(ii) to identify the percentage of implementation of specific TWEs or goals.

The calculation of the maturity level is not performed by aggregating the values of TWEs in that maturity level but by using (4):

Calculation of the OMM Maturity Levels

$$R(\text{ML}) = \frac{\sum_{\text{All practices}} P_i}{\max \sum_{\text{All practices}} P_i}. \quad (4)$$

There are two possible outcomes:

(1) OMM Level fulfilled: $R(\text{ML}) \geq 90\%$,

(2) OMM Level not fulfilled: $R(\text{ML}) < 90\%$.

There can be differences between FLOSS development processes, therefore the assignment of the OMM maturity level allows flexibility. For specific FLOSS projects some practices can be of limited importance and the project is not implementing them. The project can be otherwise of high quality but because of just few not important practices it would not reach a specific maturity level. By assigning a maturity when fulfilling 90% of practices, the approach provides some flexibility. The OMM model can be used for assessing different FLOSS projects, therefore it is not convenient to have a rigid set of practices that have to be fulfilled in all types of FLOSS projects. By using (4), a FLOSS project can fulfil an OMM maturity level if it implements more than 90% of practices required for the specific level.

4. The OMM Assessment Process

There are two possible assessment approaches envisioned by OMM:

(1) a complete (internal) OMM assessment where in the assessment process participate individuals who have access to all documents of the assessed project, and

(2) a partial (external) OMM assessment where the assessors assess only documents available: on the web, in mailing lists, in forums, in the source code, and so forth.

The first approach is intended for companies or organizations that want to integrate the assessed FLOSS tool with their software products or they want to start contributing to the FLOSS project. The first approach is also appropriate for companies that have started a software project and they wish to monitor its development. The second approach is more common for individuals who are interested just in the overall quality or in few specific quality aspects of the assessed software project.

FLOSS projects usually publish their documents on the web, however it is still not always possible to find information about the project development process, as for example some architectural decisions. This is especially the case for FLOSS projects that are strongly supported by a software company. Many decisions and activities, in this type of projects, are taken according to companies' rules and these information are often not publicly available on the web.

The OMM assessment is done by using the assessment questionnaire covering all TWEs. Each element has to be assessed or identified as not applicable (for few cases). It is not necessary to rate all metrics, however they should be taken in consideration when assessing practices to which they belong. All practices have to be assessed for obtaining a complete OMM assessment.

The assessment team reviews relevant documents and the information related to the assessed practice and has to meet an agreed assessment value. After reviewing the available documents and listening to the descriptions of the representatives of the FLOSS project, the assessor proposes the assessment value based on assessment rules and assessment best practices. If the project representatives do not agree with the assessment value they can object and present missing documents or explanations. The last assessment should be agreed between assessors. All the documents used during the assessment should be collected and archived as source of information for the assessment. Documents reviewed during the OMM assessment are numerous, ranging from: the documentation available on the web, to bug/issue reports, the concurrent versioning system logs, the mailing list archives, the forum archives, the software code itself, and so forth. Most of the information needed for assessing a FLOSS project are available online. In FLOSS projects led by companies few documents can be restricted and they cannot be published, however for a complete assessment the assessment team should be able to evaluate them.

5. Case Studies Design

We present the results of six case studies performed on six FLOSS projects. We will use the following names to refer to the projects: the Mobile OS Project, the Network Monitoring Project, the Business Intelligence Project, the Apache community Project, the SourceForge community project, and the Mozilla community Project. The first three projects were started by three software companies that still have a leading role in the assessed FLOSS projects. Their developments have been strongly influenced by decisions taken by the three companies. The contributions from the FLOSS community have grown slowly. The second three projects are typical examples of community grown projects hold in three different FLOSS projects web available repositories. The studies presented are not proper "Yin" case studies but detailed inspections of software products and software development processes. The assessments were conducted by the designers of OMM together with people who are involved in the assessed projects. The three companies might use recognised assessment schemes such as ISO9001, ISO15504, or CMMI for their development, however none of these addresses FLOSS specific characteristics. The OMM assessment of the three community grown projects were conducted by the OMM designers with the help of master students.

For the studies, we used two slightly different assessment scales; for assessing the Business Intelligence and the Network Monitoring projects we used a three-levels scale (1–3), while when assessing the other projects we decided to extend the scale to four levels (1–4). We have to take in consideration this difference when comparing the results of the six assessments. The comparisons we do between the projects are limited to a simple observation of which project obtained better grades for specific characteristics. The difference of scales prevents us to do detailed comparisons, however, this was not the purpose of this study. We just assessed the projects for demonstrating the use of OMM, and we present the results in common tables. We decided to change the scale from three levels to four to study the precision of the assessment results. The only difference is in the middle value 2 that was split with the new scale into two values: 2 and 3. In the new scale (1–4) value 1 is still 1 and value 3 became 4. By splitting the middle threshold value into two thresholds assessors can specify if a metric is above (obtaining a 3) or bellow (obtaining a 2) the average implementation of the assessed metric. For a direct comparison of assessed values from all projects we have to

normalize the values. The normalized assessment values are presented in Table 2.

The OMM assessment process usually lasts from 5 to 12 hours for larger FLOSS projects. In our case, the shortest assessment time was needed for the Mobile OS project that was finished in 5 hours, and the longest time was necessary to assess the Business Intelligence project that was finished in 10 hours. The time necessary for the assessment is shortened if the participants of the assessment team coming from the assessed FLOSS project prepare for the assessment by reading the OMM questions and preparing the documents and figures required during the assessment.

During the assessment of industry based projects there were participants from the team that built OMM and one or more participants from the assessed FLOSS project. During the assessment the OMM questionnaire was used. The creators of OMM were reading the questions and the members of the FLOSS project provided answers and when available showed documents and data to confirm their answers. Based on the previous experience of assessors with the assessment of other FLOSS projects and the documentation presented, a grade was assigned for each characteristic measured by OMM. The final grade was agreed inside the assessment team. At the end of the assessment the values were aggregated and the figures on different levels of granularity were calculated. The assessment team prepared a consolidated report with analysis of the assessments and improvement suggestions for the FLOSS project. The members of the assessed industry started FLOSS project had to review the final assessment and to confirm the results.

5.1. The Mobile OS Project. The company developing the Mobile OS Project was founded in 2002. The company has grown to be an important mobile open source market player with millions of downloads. It offers solutions based on a dual license; the commercial software is used by companies in the mobile industry, including software firms, device manufacturers, service providers, system integrators, and others. Currently it employees 85 professionals.

The Mobile OS project was started in the same year as the company and it represents its key product.

5.2. The Network Monitoring Project. The company developing the Network Monitoring Project was founded in 1993. From the beginning it was focused on the integration and development of the information infrastructure for science. It is implementing innovative technologies for the national scientific network of a large European country. Currently it employees 250 specialists.

The Network Monitoring project was started in 2006 and it is one of several projects run by the company.

5.3. The Business Intelligence Project. The company developing the Business Intelligence Project was founded in 1980. It is a multinational software integrator with 6300 employees distributed in several countries worldwide. Its core business is innovation in the ICT sector specialised in activities as applied software research. The company is an international

TABLE 2: Normalized assessment results of OMM trustworthy elements for all six projects.

	OMM trustworthy element	Mobile OS project	Network monitoring/inventory project	Business intelligence suite project	Apache community project	SourceForge community project	Mozilla community project
Basic OMM level	PDOC	2.11	2	1.89	1.89	2.89	2.89
	STD	3.38	1.5	2.25	3	2.83	2.17
	QTP	2.6	1.9	1.3	1.8	1.6	2
	LCS	3.78	1.22	2.67	3.86	2.86	2.43
	ENV	2.83	2.42	2.33	2.67	2.33	3
	DFCT	2	1.8	1.8	1.78	3	2.22
	MST	3.17	2.17	1.5	1.8	3.4	2
	CM	3.43	2.43	2.57	2.43	3	2.14
	PP1	3.22	2.33	2.11	1.67	2.11	1.44
	REQM	3.5	2.25	1.75	1.25	2.75	1.75
	RDMP	3.33	2.67	1.67	1	3	2.67
Intermediate OMM level	RDMP2	1.33	2	1	1	4	1
	STK	3	1.4	1.3	1.7	2.4	1.6
	PPQA	2.67	1.67	1	1.5	1.67	1.5
	PMC	3.63	2	1.63	1.5	2.13	1.75
	TST 1	3	2.25	1.38	1.25	2.38	1.38
	DSN 1	3.25	1.75	2.25	1.5	2.25	2
	PP2	3.6	1.4	1.2	1.4	2	1.6
Advanced OMM level	CONT	1.67	1	1.5	1.67	2.17	1.83
	RASM	2.22	1.11	1.67	1.11	2	1.44
	REP	3.2	1.6	1.6	2	2	2.6
	PI	3.56	2.22	1.67	1.78	1.89	2.33
	DSN 2	2.86	2.14	1.71	1.43	2.21	1.79
	RSKM	1	1.29	1.57	1	1.29	1.14
	TST2	3.6	2.4	2	1.2	2.6	2

player and the third IT operator in a large European country. Its work is focused on the software value chain.

The Business Intelligence project was started in 2005 and it represents only a small segment of the work performed by the company.

5.4. The Apache Community Project. The Apache community is part of the Apache Software Foundation (ASF) that was established in 1999. The community has grown to be an important supporter of the FLOSS development and it holds currently more than 100 FLOSS projects. Some of them are key building blocks of the FLOSS software suites as the Apache http web server.

The assessed FLOSS project was started in the year 2000 and is an important component for software developers. In the last years it has reached maturity and its development is mostly dedicated to maintenance activities.

5.5. The SourceForge Community Project. The SourceForge was for several years the largest web available repository of FLOSS projects. It offers several tools for FLOSS development

and it holds at the moment more than 400.000 FLOSS projects. There is not a unique SourceForge community; there are thousands of small communities that form around single projects. However, they usually use the available tools and some developers participate in more than one project. The service was established in the year 1999 and it soon attracted thousands of participants.

The assessed project is a free and open source instant messaging application. The project was started in the year 2005 and it is still evolving.

5.6. The Mozilla Community Project. Mozilla is a global nonprofit organization connecting users, contributors, and developers contributing to more than 240 projects. Some of them popular as the Firefox web browser or the Thunderbird mail client. The Mozilla was created in the year 1998 with the release of the Netscape browser source code.

The assessed project was first released in the year 1998 and since than it is a popular tool for bug/issue management used by software developers.

TABLE 3: Number of OMM practices reaching a specific threshold level.

	OMM trustworthy element	Mobile OS project				Network monitoring/ inventory project				Business intelligence suite project				Apache community project				SourceForge community project				Mozilla community project			
	Treshold value	1	2	3	4	1	2	3	4*	1	2	3	4*	1	2	3	4	1	2	3	4	1	2	3	4
Basic OMM level	PDOC	2	4	3	0	2	5	2	0	2	6	1	0	4	2	3	0	2	0	4	3	0	2	6	1
	STD	0	2	1	5	4	4	0	0	2	2	4	0	1	1	1	3	0	3	1	2	1	3	2	0
	QTP	0	6	2	2	2	4	3	0	7	3	0	0	3	6	1	0	6	2	2	0	1	8	1	0
	LCS	0	1	0	8	7	2	0	0	0	3	6	0	0	0	1	6	1	2	1	3	2	2	1	2
	ENV	0	1	5	0	0	3	2	0	0	4	2	0	0	3	2	1	1	3	1	1	0	1	4	1
	DFCT	0	5	0	0	2	2	1	0	2	2	1	0	4	3	2	0	0	3	3	3	1	5	3	0
	MST	0	1	3	2	1	3	2	0	3	3	0	0	1	4	0	0	0	1	1	3	0	5	0	0
	CM	0	0	4	3	1	2	4	0	1	1	5	0	1	3	2	1	1	2	0	4	1	4	2	0
	PP1	0	2	3	4	0	6	3	0	1	6	2	0	4	4	1	0	4	1	3	1	5	4	0	0
	REQM	0	0	2	2	0	3	1	0	1	3	0	0	3	1	0	0	0	2	1	1	1	3	0	0
	RDMP	0	0	2	1	0	1	2	0	1	2	0	0	3	0	0	0	1	0	0	2	0	1	2	0
Intermediate OMM level	RDMP2	2	1	0	0	0	3	0	0	3	0	0	0	3	0	0	0	0	0	0	3	3	0	0	0
	STK	0	2	6	2	4	2	2	0	7	3	0	0	4	5	1	0	1	3	3	2	4	6	0	0
	PPQA	0	1	2	0	1	2	0	0	3	0	0	0	3	3	0	0	2	4	0	0	3	3	0	0
	PMC	0	1	1	6	0	8	0	0	3	5	0	0	5	2	1	0	2	3	3	0	3	4	1	0
	TST 1	1	2	1	4	0	6	2	0	5	3	0	0	6	2	0	0	0	5	3	0	6	1	1	0
	DSN 1	0	0	3	1	1	3	0	0	1	1	2	0	2	2	0	0	1	2	0	1	0	4	0	0
	PP2	0	0	2	3	3	2	0	0	4	1	0	0	3	2	0	0	2	1	2	0	2	3	0	0
Advanced OMM level	CONT	2	4	0	0	6	0	0	0	4	1	1	0	2	2	0	1	2	1	3	0	2	3	1	0
	RASM	3	1	5	0	8	1	0	0	3	6	0	0	8	1	0	0	3	4	1	1	5	4	0	0
	REP	0	0	4	1	3	1	1	0	2	3	0	0	1	3	1	0	0	2	2	0	0	2	3	0
	PI	0	0	4	5	2	3	4	0	4	4	1	0	3	5	1	0	4	3	1	1	0	6	3	0
	DSN 2	0	4	8	2	2	8	4	0	6	6	2	0	9	4	1	0	2	7	5	0	4	9	1	0
	RSKM	7	0	0	0	5	2	0	0	3	4	0	0	7	0	0	0	5	2	0	0	6	1	0	0
	TST2	0	0	2	3	0	3	2	0	1	3	1	0	4	1	0	0	0	3	1	1	0	5	0	0

6. Results

Table 1 presents the assessment results of the first Goal (PDOC 1: Provide High-Quality documentation) of the Project documentation TWE for the Mobile OS project. We present the complete results for one TWE. We have assessed the metrics ("LookFors") and the practices and calculated the goals and the TWEs. The OMM allows both a staged and a continuous assessment approach. We used the second approach where all OMM elements are assessed. We decided to assess elements from all three maturity levels to have a good understanding of basic and advanced practices. The final value for the Project documentation (PDOC) TWE of the Mobile OS project is 2,11 which means that the aspects related to product documentation are averagely addressed by the project and improvements are possible. We see that some aspects related to the project documentation are appropriately addressed by the Mobile OS project, others needs improvement. Table 2 shows the normalized assessment results for all six projects. In Table 3 we see the assessment results of practices for the assessed projects. The threshold value 4 is valid for the Mobile OS project and for the three community based projects. The Networking Monitoring and the Business Intelligence projects have a 0 for all practices in the last column (4*). Table 3 is the aggregation of the assessment results for the six projects. Since we are validating the OMM, we grouped results of all projects to be able to compare them. Figures 5, 6, and 7, and Table 3 provides an overview of which practices have to be improved in each FLOSS project. We present detailed results for each project separately in the following sections. We describe just the elements that obtained good and bad assessments for each of the six projects.

6.1. The Mobile OS Project. Figures 2, 3, and 4 present the basic, intermediate, and advanced OMM levels for the Mobile OS project. Figures 5, 6, and 7 present the percentage of practices reaching a specific-threshold assessment value (1–4). The TWEs that have a large percentage of practices assessed with a value 3 or 4 represent good coverage of TWEs by the FLOSS project. The TWEs with a large percentage

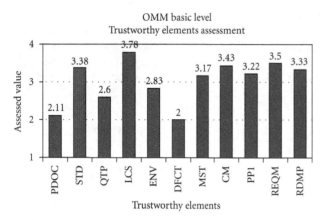

FIGURE 2: Mobile OS project OMM Basic level results.

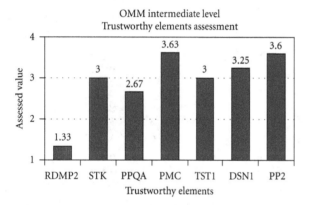

FIGURE 3: Mobile OS project OMM Intermediate level results.

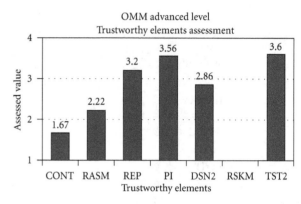

FIGURE 4: Mobile OS project OMM Advanced level results.

From Figures 5, 6, and 6 we see how many *practices* obtained good or poor assessments. The assessment value of a trustworthy element displayed in Table 2, and the percentage of practices obtaining a specific assessment value are related. For the Mobile OS project we see that in the:

Basic Level. There are 2 practices assessed with the value 1 only in the product documentation trustworthy element (PDOC). 6 practices in the quality of the testing plan (QTP) and 5 practices in the number of commits and bug reports (DFCT) TWE were assessed with the value 2. The highest grades were obtained for the adoption and management of aspects related to licenses (LCS) where 8/9 (8 out of 9 practices assessed in LCS) obtained the highest assessment value 4.

6.2. The Network Monitoring Project. We present the results for the other five Projects in the compact form of a table, nevertheless the graphical representation is easier to be interpreted.

In Table 2, we see the normalized results of the assessment of *trustworthy elements*. In this section, we describe the raw assessment data before the normalization.

Basic Level. Good results were obtained by: the roadmap (RDMP 2,67), the configuration management (CM 2,43), and the environment adopted (ENV 2,42). Poor results were obtained by: the standards implemented (STD 1,5) and the adoption and management of license aspects (LCS 1,22).

Intermediate Level. Only the testing trustworthy element obtained a good result (TST1 2,25) but there are three poor results: the stakeholders involvement (STK 1,4), the project planning (PP2 1,4), and the product and process quality assurance (PPQA 1,67).

Advanced Level. The advanced testing aspects were addressed appropriately (TST2 2,4) and partially also the project integration (PI 2,22). There are several aspects that are almost not addressed by the project, as: the external contributions to the project (CONT 1,0), the assessment of the project by external entities (RASM 1,11), and the risk management aspects (RSKM 1,29).

of practices assessed with values 2 or 1 represent FLOSS development processes that should be additionally improved by the FLOSS project.

In the second column of Table 2 we see the assessment results for the mobile OS project trustworthy elements.

Basic Level. The project obtained high grades for: the aspects related to the consistent adoption and management of licenses (LCS 3,78), the management of requirements (REQM 3,5), and the configuration management (CM 3,43). Low values were obtained by: the TWEs related to commits and bug reports (DFCT 2,0), and the documentation (PDOC 2,11).

Intermediate Level. Three best assessed trustworthy elements were: the project monitoring and control (PMC 3,63), the project planing (PP2 3,6), and the design of the product (DSN1 3,25). A low value was obtained by the advanced elements of the roadmap (RDMP2 1,33).

Advanced Level. The project obtained good assessments for: the advanced testing (TST2 3,6), the product integration (PI 3,56), and the reputation of the project (REP 3,2). Poor results obtained two TWEs: the risk management (RSKM 1,0) and the contributions from external developers (CONT 1,67).

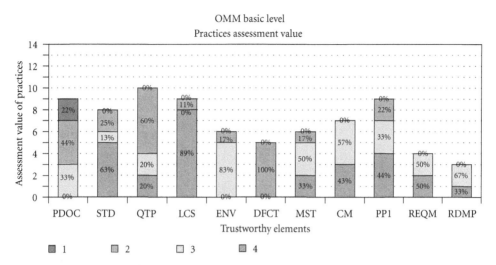

FIGURE 5: Mobile OS project OMM Basic level single practices threshold values.

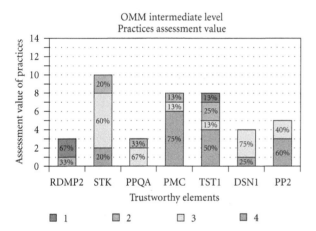

FIGURE 6: Mobile OS project OMM Intermediate level single practices threshold values.

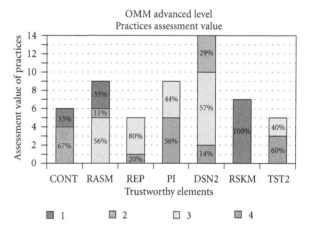

FIGURE 7: Mobile OS project OMM Advanced level single practices threshold values.

In Table 3, we see results related to good- and poor-assessed *practices*.

Basic Level. Configuration management (CM) with 4/7 (four out of seven) practices, and the roadmap (RDMP) with 2/3 practices obtained the highest possible value (3). There are many poor values as: the standards implemented by the project (STD) with 4/8 practices and the management of licenses (LCS) with 7/9 practices that obtained the value 1.

Intermediate Level. There is only the testing TWE (TST1) with all practices assessed with the values 2 and 3. Poor values were obtained by: the stakeholders involvement (STK) with 4/8 practices assessed with 1, the product and process quality assurance with all three practices assessed with either value 1 or 2, and the product plan TWE (PP1) with 3/5 assessed with 1.

Advanced Level. There is only the testing TWE (TST2) that fulfilled the majority of available practices. There are four

TWEs that have to be improved: the contribution (CONT) practices were not addressed at all by the project 6/6 obtained 1, external assessments of the project (RASM) 8/9 practices obtained 1, for the reputation of the project (REP) 3/5 practices obtained 1, and the risk management (RSKM) was addressed only marginally with 5/7 practices with 1.

6.3. The Business Intelligence Project. Some interesting results for the Business Intelligence project are presented in the following paragraphs. First we present the results for *trustworthy elements*.

Basic Level. Aspects as management of licenses (LCS 2,67), configuration management (CM 2,57), and development environment used (ENV 2,33) obtained relatively good results. Two TWEs with low assessment values were: the quality of the testing plan defined (QTP 1,3) and maintainability and stability (MST 1,5).

Intermediate Level. The Business Intelligence project obtained only one good assessment result; the design TWE

(DSN1 2,25). Other TWEs obtained poor results; the lowest were: the advanced roadmap (RDMP2 1,0), the Product and Process quality assurance (PPQA 1,0), and the process planing (PP2 1,2).

Advanced Level. The assessment values for most of the TWEs were similar; Advanced testing (TST2 2,0) obtained the highest value, and the contribution level (CONT 1,5) obtained the lowest value.

From Table 3, we see that the Business Intelligence project reached a good fulfilment of *practices* mainly in the basic level.

Basic Level. Standards implemented (STD) 4/8 obtained the value 3, management of licenses (LCS) 6/9 with the value 3, and configuration management (CM) 5/7 with value 3. The TWEs that can be still improved are: the quality of the testing plan (QTP) 7/10 practices obtained 1, the number of commits and bug reports (DFCT) with the 4/5 values with the value 1 or 2, and the maintainability and stability (MST) with 3/6 practices assessed with 1.

Intermediate Level. Only design (DSN1) obtained a larger part 2/4 of practices assessed with 3. Other TWEs obtained poor values; 3/3 for the advanced roadmap (RDMP2), 7/10 for the stakeholders involvement (STK), and 3/3 for the product and process quality assurance (PPQA), practices were assessed with 1.

Advanced Level. Only the testing TWE (TST2) has a relatively large percentage of practices 4/5 assessed with values 2 or 3. The majority of the practices were assessed with value 1.

6.4. The Apache Community Project. The results for the Apache community project are presented in the following paragraphs. The results for *trustworthy elements* are the following:

Basic Level. The management of licenses (LCS 3,86) is almost optimal, the configuration management (CM 2,43), the development environment used (ENV 2,67), and the standards implemented (STD 3,0) obtained good results. Two TWEs with low-fourassessment values were: the requirements management (REQM 1,25) and the roadmap availability (RDMP 1,0).

Intermediate level. The project obtained only intermediate results in the second OMM level. Only the stakeholders involvement (STK 1,7) obtained some positive practices assessments. Other TWEs obtained poor results; the lowest were: the advanced roadmap (RDMP2 1,0), and the basic testing aspects (TST1 1,25).

Advanced Level. The assessment values for most of the TWEs were similar; The project's reputation obtained the best value (REP 2,0). Advanced testing (TST2 1,2), the results of third-party assessment (RASM 1,11), and the risk management (RSKM 1,0) obtained low assessment results.

From Table 3 we see that the Apache community project reached a good fulfilment of practices only in the basic level.

Basic Level. Standards implemented (STD) 3/6 obtained the value 4, and the management of licenses (LCS) 6/7 with the value 4. The TWEs that can be still improved are: the number of commits and bug reports (DFCT) with the 4/9 values with the value 1, the product documentation (PDOC) with 4/9 with the value 1, and the project planning 1 (PP 1) with 4/9 obtaining the value 1. Several other practices can be addressed to increase the basic OMM quality of the Apache community project.

Intermediate Level. Only the stakeholders involvement (STK) and the project monitoring and control have obtained a 3 for one practice. The rest of practices have been assessed either with a 1 or 2. This means that the project should still work on the improvement of the intermediate level practices.

Advanced Level. The contributions TWE (CONT) have obtained one practice assessed with the highest grade. The rest of the practices obtained poor assessments.

6.5. The SourceForge Community Project. The results for the SourceForge community project are.

Basic Level. Four TWEs obtained good results in the basic level; the number of commits and bug reports (DFCT 3,0), the maintainability and stability (MST 3,4), the configuration management (CM 3,0), and the basic roadmap (RDMP 3,0). Several other TWEs obtained relatively good assessments. A problematic aspect was only the quality of the testing process (QTP 1,6) that was not addressed sufficiently inside the assessed SourceForge project.

Intermediate Level. The advanced aspects of the roadmap (RDMP2 4,0) obtained an excellent result. A problematic aspect of the intermediate OMM level was the process and product quality assurance (PPQA 1,67).

Advanced Level. The advanced testing aspects (TST2 2,6) obtained the highest grade in the advanced level. The worst result was obtained by practices of the risk management TWE (RSKM 1,29).

From Table 3, we see that the SourceForge community project reached a good fulfilment of *practices* in the basic level and just few in the intermediate level.

Basic Level. Many practices obtained the highest grade in the basic OMM level; the Project Documentation (PDOC) 3/9, the Licenses management (LCS) 3/7, the Number of commits and bug reports (DFCT) 3/9, the Maintainability and Stability (MST) 3/5, and the Configuration Management (CM) 4/7 aspects were addressed optimally by the assessed SourceForge project. More than half of the practices of the Quality of the testing plan (QTE) 6/10 TWE obtained, on contrary, the lowest grade and should be better addressed by the project's community.

Intermediate Level. The advanced aspects of the roadmap (RDMP2) 3/3 were optimally addressed. Apart the Stakeholders involvement (STK) all other TWEs have a below-the-average assessment value of the practices and can therefore be additionally improved.

Advanced Level. In the advanced level the practices obtained poor assessment results. Just the Contributions (CONT) 3/6 obtained the assessment value of 3, and the Reputation (REP) 2/4 practices obtained the assessment value of 3 were assessed with average assessment values. The other TWEs were assessed below the average and should be further improved.

6.6. The Mozilla Community Project. Some significant results for the Mozilla community project are presented in the following paragraphs.

Basic Level. Only the Product documentation (PDOC 2,89), the environment (ENV 3,0) and the basic roadmap TWE (RDMP 2,67) obtained an above-the-average grade. All the other TWEs were not well addressed by the project. The basic aspects of product planning, project planning (PP1 1,44) obtained the lowest assessment result.

Intermediate Level. The intermediate level TWEs obtained poor assessment result. The worst assessed TWEs were the advanced roadmap aspects (RDMP2 1,0), and the basic testing (TST1 1,38).

Advanced Level. The advanced TWEs were assessed just slightly better than the intermediate TWEs. The best result was achieved by the reputation TWE (REP 2,6). Two TWEs that should be improved by the project are the third-party assessment results available on the web (RASM 1,44) and the risk management (RSKM 1,14) by the community developing the project.

From Table 3, we see that the Mozilla community project reached an above-average fulfilment of *practices* just in the basic level.

Basic Level. The product documentation (PDOC) 6/9 obtained the value 3, the Environment (ENV) 4/6 obtained the value 3, and the basic Roadmap practices (RDMP) 2/3 obtained the value 3, were assessed above the average. The other practices obtained the assessment value 1 or 2. The basic aspects of Product Planning, Project Planning (PP1) can be still much improved since 5/9 practices obtained the assessment value 1.

Intermediate Level. Just two practices of all assessed in the intermediate level obtained the value 3 and none obtained a 4. The advanced roadmap (RDMP2) 3/3 obtained the value 1, and the basic-testing practices (TST1) 6/8 obtained the value 1, should be improved by the developers.

Advanced Level. Three practices of the reputation (REP) and the Product Integration (PI) TWEs were assessed with the value 3. No practice of the advanced OMM level was assessed

with a 4. The community should focus on the third-party assessment (RASM) practices where 5/9 obtained the lowest assessment value and the risk management (RSKM) TWE's practices where 6/7 obtained the assessment value 1.

7. Discussion

Based on the results we can identify aspects of the FLOSS development process that were not addressed sufficiently by the assessed projects. By aggregating all practices values for each project using (4); the Mobile OS project obtained the total value 2,88 (72%), the Networking Monitoring project obtained 1,88 (63%), the Business Intelligence project obtained 1,73 (58%), the Apache community project obtained 1,73 (43%), the SourceForge community project obtained 2,43 (61%), and the Mozilla community project obtained the aggregated assessment value of 1,95 (49%). The values in brackets present the percentage of the reached assessment value normalized by the highest possible assessment value; the percentages normalize the results for the assessments removing the differences related to the two-assessment scales used.

Critical TWEs in the Mobile OS project are the product documentation (2,11), the development environment (2,83), the number of commits and bug reports (2,00), and the testing (2,60). Those TWEs should be first improved since they are part of the Basic OMM level and as described in Section 2 they are perceived as important by a large percentage of potential FLOSS stakeholders. There are other aspects that the Mobile OS project should improve, but, since they are not part of the Basic OMM level, their improvement can be done after the Basic-level TWEs are addressed.

Comparing the six assessments we see that the Mobile OS project obtained the highest overall rating; the assessment results (taking in consideration different scale levels) are considerably higher than for the other industry led projects started later (2005 and 2006) but also higher than for the three community led projects that have started few years before the Mobile OS project. An explanation can be the importance of the assessed FLOSS project for the company. While the Mobile OS project is the key product of the first company and the main source of revenues, the other two company-led projects are just one of many projects developed by the two companies and are not critical for their business. This argument holds also for the community-led projects. The communities dedicate effort for the project but they are usually not constrained by strict deadlines and quality controls as an industry-led FLOSS project. Another reason is that the company involved in the Mobile OS project is more aware of FLOSS aspects addressed in OMM (as the reputation and the use of open standards) than the other two companies.

In all six cases there are several TWEs that obtained low grades. The lowest assessment values were obtained by the following TWEs (in brackets are the values for all the projects): External contributions to the project (1,67; 1,0; 1,5; 1,67; 2,17; 1,83), the advanced Roadmap (1,33; 2,0; 1,0; 1,0; 4,0; 1,0), and the Risk management (1,0; 1,29; 1,57; 1,0; 1,29; 1,14), and so forth. The only exception is the advanced roadmap that was optimally addressed by the assessed SourceForge community project. Some trustworthy elements were graded better in the Mobile OS project and partially in the three community-led projects than in the other two industry projects; as for example the reputation of the project (3,2; 1,6; 1,6; 2,0; 2,0; 2,6). This result does not surprise since the reputation usually grows with a longer existence of a FLOSS project.

Differently from FLOSS focused TWEs, all three industry projects cover well aspects addressed by traditional software development TWEs as: the configuration management (3,43; 2,43; 2,57; 2,43, 3,0; 2,14), the Product Planing (3,22; 2,33; 2,11; 1,67; 2,11; 1,44), and the testing (3,6; 2,4; 2,0; 1,2; 2,6; 2,0). We can see that the community-led projects obtained lower assessment values for these TWEs. Other TWEs obtained also high values in one or two projects as: the licenses management that is appropriately addressed by the Mobile OS (3,78) and the Business intelligence (2,25) projects, and obtained a low value in the Networking Monitoring project (1,22).

It is evident from the results that standard software development process aspects regularly used in the software industry are addressed appropriately by the three industry-led FLOSS projects. These software aspects are characterized by the following TWEs: the configuration management (CM), the product plan (PP1), the basic testing (TST1), the basic design (DSN1), the advanced testing (TST2), and the advanced design (DSN2). The software development processes used in the three companies leading a FLOSS project are used also in this kind of projects. Some FLOSS specific aspects as: the external contributions to the project (CONT), the reputation of the project (REP), and the stake-holders involvement (STK) on contrary are not addressed sufficiently by the industry-led projects but are in general better addressed by the three community-led projects.

Table 3 presents the level of fulfilment of all practices for each Trustworthy element. One result of the OMM assessment process conducted is a set of improvement suggestions for the assessed projects. If we mention just the TWEs that have to be improved first by each project we can say that:

(i) the Mobile OS project should focus first on the quality of the documentation (PDOC);

(ii) the Networking Monitoring project on the manage-ment of Licenses (LCS); the Business intelligence project on the quality of the testing plan (QTP);

(iii) the Apache community project on the practices of the basic roadmap (RDMP);

(iv) the SourceForge community project on the quality of the testing plan (QTP);

(v) the Mozilla community project on the basic Product Planning, Project Planning (PP1).

According to OMM only after improving the basic level practices the projects should focus on higher level practices.

8. Threats to Validity

The main type of threats faced in our research are internal. The OMM model itself is subjected to construct validity threats: are we really measuring what the metrics in the OMM are supposed to measure. The threats described in this section are of these two types. Due to the limitation of our research, to three industry-led and to three community initiated FLOSS projects, we cannot generalize the results to all FLOSS projects, therefore we did not consider particularly the external threats to validity.

An important threat to validity of our study is the subjectivity of the assessment process. Different assessors can interpret questions in a slightly different way and therefore provide a different assessment result. This problem is intrinsic to other software assessment methodologies as the OpenBRR, the QSOS, but also to the CMMI. There are however a series of measures adopted to minimise the subjectivity of the assessment process. The most important are: the standard and homogeneous formulation of questions throughout the whole model; the extent of the development process or documentation material that have to be analysed to evaluate each question (questions are precise and limited to one or few information sources); in the assessment process participate two or more experts that should meet a common assessment result. These are three elements mitigating the subjectivity of the assessment. From experiments conducted by comparing assessment results of several individuals assessing the same process activities, it is evident that the variability of assessment results is small [6].

An additional approach to mitigate the threat to validity related to subjectivity of the assessment is the expertise of assessors. The OMM model is new and therefore none of the participating assessors have a vast experience with its usage, however they were knowledgeable with CMMI assessments that inspired many design decisions related to the OMM model. Participants of the assessments were also people involved in the development of the assessed FLOSS project. They provided support when searching the needed documentation and indicating sources of information.

The time constraints of the assessment may have limited the precise assessment of few practices that would benefit from a tool support. The OMM model is improved once per year; the major improvement efforts are focused on the creation of tools that can automatically extract information as for example: the number of license files, the number of contributors, the type and the number of documentation, and so forth. At the time of assessment of the six projects we did not use assessment tools and we assessed all metrics manually, this could present a threat to the completeness of some metrics that require a tedious measurement process. However the number of these metrics is limited and it does not considerably influence the final assessment result.

9. Conclusions

The OMM assessment results can bring benefits to FLOSS users and to FLOSS communities. The assessments can be beneficial also to potential software integrators when they are deciding to use a FLOSS product. The final goal of the OMM is an improved quality of the FLOSS development process and therefore also the quality of the FLOSS products.

In this paper we present the results of six development process assessments of FLOSS projects that are led by three different software companies and by three different FLOSS communities. The study was performed using the OMM model analysing 25 process characteristics. The result of the assessment is the collection of values related to the FLOSS development process. The assessment results were aggregated on four levels of granularity; in this paper we present only two of them: the level of OMM Trustworthy elements presented in Table 2, and the level of OMM Practices presented in Table 3, visualizing the number of practices that were fulfilled in each threshold level.

The main result of the OMM assessment is the creation of a detailed picture of 25 aspects of the FLOSS development process. Tables and figures present a clear overview on aspects that have to be improved to arise the quality of the development process and subsequently the quality of the FLOSS product. From the figures we see which TWEs were insufficiently addressed by the assessed projects. Those TWEs were:

(i) the number of commits and bug reports (DFCT),

(ii) the external contribution to the project (CONT),

(iii) the risk management (RSKM).

Based on the results, the assessed FLOSS projects should check which practices, or more specifically, which documents are not available inside the project (in the Mobile OS project for example, a road map document should be created, and the technical documentation must be improved—see Table 1).

From the comparison of the results for the assessed projects we observed that specific FLOSS aspects obtained lower assessment results than standard software development practices. We can also see that the project that exists longer, both the industry-led and the FLOSS communities led, obtained better results related to the aspect of reputation. The Mobile OS project generically obtained better results from the other assessed projects; it appropriately implemented 72% of the 122 practices.

The results for the six studies demonstrate the applicability of the OMM and describe the benefits that FLOSS projects can have from the assessment. The validity of the research results is limited to the six studies; however the assessment process of a FLOSS project, either industry or pure FLOSS communities supported, would be conducted following a similar approach. The results of the study will bring concrete benefits to the quality of the three industry-led FLOSS development processes and it can suggest improvement activities necessary for the three community-led projects. The results of the first assessment are good indicators of which practices should be improved.

We plan to conduct a second set of assessments of the six projects after one year from the first assessment and compare the improvements of the development process. In the following months we plan to perform other assessments

of well-known FLOSS projects. Our aim is to use the model to assess a larger number of FLOSS projects where the leading role is maintained by the FLOSS community. We plan to compare those results with the one presented in this paper and further confirm the validity of the OMM model.

Acknowledgments

The research was conducted in the scope of the QualiPSo project (FP-IST-034763). The authors are grateful to all QualiPSo partners that contributed to the creation of the assessment model and the participants from the assessed FLOSS projects.

References

[1] E. S. Raymond, *The Cathedral and the Bazaar: Musings on Linux and Open Source by an Accidental Revolutionary*, O'Reilly & Associates, 2001.

[2] T. Dybå and T. Dingsøyr, "Empirical studies of agile software development: a systematic review," *Information and Software Technology*, vol. 50, no. 9-10, pp. 833–859, 2008.

[3] A. Fuggetta, "Software process: a roadmap," in *Proceedings of the Conference on the Future of Software Engineering (ICSE '00)*, pp. 25–34, ACM, Limerick, Ireland, June 2000.

[4] *Process Maturity Profile of the Software Community 1999 Year End Update*, Software Engineering Institute, 2000.

[5] E. Petrinja, R. Nambakam, and A. Sillitti, "Introducing the opensource maturity model," in *Proceedings of the ICSE Workshop on Emerging Trends in Free/Libre/Open Source Software Research and Development (FLOSS '09) collocated with 31st International Conference on Software Engineering*, pp. 37–41, Vancouver, Canada, May 2009.

[6] E. Petrinja, A. Sillitti, and G. Succi, "Comparing OpenBRR, QSOS, and OMM assessment models," in *Proceedings of the 6th International Conference on Open Source Systems (OSS '10)*, pp. 224–238, Notre Dame, Ind, USA, May 2010.

[7] Qualipso Consortium: QualiPSo—Quality Platform for Open Source Software, http://www.qualipso.org/index.php.

[8] E. Petrinja, A. Sillitti, and G. Succi, "Overview on trust in large FLOSS communities," in *Proceedings of the 4th International Conference on Open Source Systems (OSS '08)*, pp. 47–56, Milan, Italy, 2008.

[9] U. Raja and M. J. Tretter, "Defining and evaluating a measure of open source project survivability," *IEEE Transactions on Software Engineering*, vol. 38, no. 1, pp. 163–174, 2012.

[10] M. Khalifa and J. M. Verner, "Drivers for software development method usage," *IEEE Transactions on Engineering Management*, vol. 47, no. 3, pp. 360–369, 2000.

[11] S. Matook and M. Indulska, "Improving the quality of process reference models: a quality function deployment-based approach," *Decision Support Systems*, vol. 47, no. 1, pp. 60–71, 2009.

[12] T. L. Roberts, M. L. Gibson, K. T. Fields, and R. Kelly Rainer, "Factors that impact implementing a system development methodology," *IEEE Transactions on Software Engineering*, vol. 24, no. 8, pp. 640–649, 1998.

[13] C. G. Von Wangenheim, J. C. R. Hauck, A. Zoucas, C. F. Salviano, F. McCaffery, and F. Shull, "Creating software process capability/maturity models," *IEEE Software*, vol. 27, no. 4, pp. 92–94, 2010.

[14] S. C. Misra, V. Kumar, and U. Kumar, "Identifying some important success factors in adopting agile software development practices," *Journal of Systems and Software*, vol. 82, no. 11, pp. 1869–1890, 2009.

[15] E. Yourdon, "Where's the basis for year 2000 optimism?" *Computerworld*, vol. 32, no. 7, p. 68, 1998.

[16] M. Agrawal and K. Chari, "Software effort, quality, and cycle time: a study of CMM level 5 projects," *IEEE Transactions on Software Engineering*, vol. 33, no. 3, pp. 145–156, 2007.

[17] M. Staples, M. Niazi, R. Jeffery, A. Abrahams, P. Byatt, and R. Murphy, "An exploratory study of why organizations do not adopt CMMI," *Journal of Systems and Software*, vol. 80, no. 6, pp. 883–895, 2007.

[18] F. Guerrero and Y. Eterovic, "Adopting the SW-CMM in a small IT organization," *IEEE Software*, vol. 21, no. 4, pp. 29–35, 2004.

[19] A. Qumer and B. Henderson-Sellers, "A framework to support the evaluation, adoption and improvement of agile methods in practice," *Journal of Systems and Software*, vol. 81, no. 11, pp. 1899–1919, 2008.

[20] M. C. Paulk, "Extreme programming from a CMM perspective," *IEEE Software*, vol. 18, no. 6, pp. 19–26, 2001.

[21] C. G. von Wangeheim, A. Anacleto, and C. F. Salviano, "Helping small companies assess software processes," *IEEE Software*, vol. 23, no. 1, pp. 91–98, 2006.

[22] T. Dybå, "Factors of software process improvement success in small and large organizations: An empirical study in the scandinavian context," in *Proceedings of the 9th European Software Engineering Conference Held Jointly with 11th ACM SIGSOFT International Symposium on Foundations of Software Engineering*, pp. 148–157, ACM Press, September 2003.

[23] G. B. Dietrich, D. B. Walz, and J. L. Wynekoop, "The failure of SDT diffusion: a case for mass customization," *IEEE Transactions on Engineering Management*, vol. 44, no. 4, pp. 390–398, 1997.

[24] Navica Inc., The Open Source Maturity Model is a vital tool for planning open source success, http://www.oss-watch.ac.uk/resources/osmm.xml#body.1_div.2.

[25] Atos Origin, Method for Qualification and Selection of Open Source Software (QSOS), 2009, http://www.qsos.org/.

[26] A. Wasserman, M. Pal, and C. Chan, *Business Readiness Rating Project*, BRR Whitepaper 2005 RFC1, http://www.openbrr.org/.

[27] D. Taibi, L. Lavazza, and S. Morasca, *OpenBQR: A Framework for the Assessment of OSS*, Open Source Software 2007, Limerick, Ireland, 2007.

[28] D. Izquierdo-Cortazar, G. Robles, J. M. González-Barahona, and J.-C. Deprez, "Assessing FLOSS communities: an experience report from the QualOSS project," *Open Source Ecosystems: Diverse Communities Interacting*, vol. 299, p. 364, 2009.

[29] I. Samoladas, G. Gousios, D. Spinellis, and I. Stamelos, "The SQO-OSS quality model: Measurement based open source software evaluation," *IFIP International Federation for Information Processing*, vol. 275, pp. 237–248, 2008.

[30] J.-C. Deprez and S. Alexandre, *Comparing Assessment Methodologies for Free/Open Source Software: OpenBRR and QSOS*, Book chapter in Lecture Notes in Computer Science, Springer, Berlin, Germany, 2008.

[31] V. R. Basili, "Software modelling and measurement: the Goal/Question/Metric paradigm," Computer Science Technical Report Series CS-TR-2956 (UMIACS-TR-92-96), University of Maryland, College Park, Md, USA, 1992.

[32] S. Morasca, "On the use of weighted sums in the definition of measures," in *Proceedings of the 2010 ICSE Workshop on Emerging Trends in Software Metrics (WETSoM '10)*, pp. 8–15, ACM Press, May 2010.

6

Metadata for Approximate Query Answering Systems

Francesco Di Tria, Ezio Lefons, and Filippo Tangorra

Dipartimento di Informatica, Università degli Studi di Bari Aldo Moro, Via Orabona 4, 70125 Bari, Italy

Correspondence should be addressed to Francesco Di Tria, francescoditria@di.uniba.it

Academic Editor: Gerardo Canfora

In business intelligence systems, data warehouse metadata management and representation are getting more and more attention by vendors and designers. The standard language for the data warehouse metadata representation is the Common Warehouse Metamodel. However, business intelligence systems include also approximate query answering systems, since these software tools provide fast responses for decision making on the basis of approximate query processing. Currently, the standard meta-model does not allow to represent the metadata needed by approximate query answering systems. In this paper, we propose an extension of the standard metamodel, in order to define the metadata to be used in online approximate analytical processing. These metadata have been successfully adopted in ADAP, a web-based approximate query answering system that creates and uses statistical data profiles.

1. Introduction

The concept of metadata—born in the transactional systems literature—has gained the greatest attention in data warehousing environments, where two classes of metadata are distinguishable: back-room and front-room metadata. The first class aims to describe, among other things, the several heterogeneous data sources, the data transformation that must be performed to feed the data warehouse, and the refresh status of the stored data. The front-room metadata aim to represent the conceptual data model of the data warehouse and they are commonly used by the so-called business intelligence platforms in order to automatically generate the analytical queries.

According to [1], the business intelligence can be represented as an information supply chain, to highlight that the information comes from a set of data sources and goes through transformation processes, in order to become useful for decision making. However, this chain is composed of different steps, each of them being both producer and consumer of data and metadata. It is unlikely that a single vendor provides a complete system able to covers all the steps of the chain. For this reason, each step is usually managed by specific software tools, produced by different vendors. Of course, their integration is quite difficult, since each tool aims to improve its own effectiveness and efficiency. It follows that the metadata are commonly stored according to a proprietary format.

In order to overcome this limit, a central management of metadata is always a benefit for enterprises that are divided into departmental areas not directly linked among them. In this case, the most effective choice consists of using a central metadata repository [2] that must be *generic*, as it must allow to store metadata according to topics areas but not to specific tools; *integrated*, for it has to store metadata describing heterogeneous business assets (such as processes, documents, products, software tools, databases, and so on); *updated*, in order to be consistent with the business reality; *historical*, for all the insert-update-delete operations on the repository must be traced for data recovery and rollback.

Moreover, the central repository must rely on standard representations of metadata, since standard metadata allow different business intelligence ence tools to effectively communicate with each other (*i.e.*, tools integration) and provide a uniform management of data of various type and format (*i.e.*, data integration).

The current standard for data warehouse metadata definition is the Common Warehouse Metamodel (CWM), that provides a common model of metadata for both tools and data integration [3].

The OMG has also defined the XML Metadata Interchange (XMI) [4] as the XML-based physical layer to best allow the interoperability and the portability of metadata among the single components involved in business intelligence.

However, data warehouses are widely used also as data sources for specific analytical tools based on approximate query processing [5]. Such tools, or the so-called approximate query answering systems [6], are decision support systems that help decision makers by providing them with fast answers.

These software tools usually integrate traditional OLAP systems in order to return both approximate and/or exact answers, according to the user settings. Whereas the exact answers can be obtained by accessing real data, the approximate answers are obtainable only if preelaborated data are available. Therefore, the role and importance of metadata for approximate query answering systems relate to the need of tracing whether and which data have been transformed and prepared for the approximate query processing. In other words, based on these metadata, users are allowed (a) to know which data are available for approximate query processing and (b) to define queries that return (approximate) answers very quickly.

Currently, the CWM does not include a metamodel able to represent the metadata used by these systems and the aim of this paper is to extend the existing standard metamodel in order to define a novel metamodel that covers the issues related to approximate query processing in the scope of business intelligence.

This paper has the following structure. Section 2 presents the architecture of approximate query answering systems. Section 3 provides an overview of the CWM. Section 4 contains our proposal for the representation of metadata for approximate query answering systems, while Section 5 introduces our system and reports a case study. At last, Section 6 concludes the paper reporting final remarks.

2. Approximate Query Answering System

At the present time, approximate query answering systems are used in decision support systems, since they allow business users to obtain fast responses to queries whenever they do not need total precision or exact values [7]. Accuracy estimation is also provided along with the approximate answer.

Figure 1 depicts the high-level architecture of the approximate query answering system. Datasets stored in data sources (viz., the data warehouse DW) are preelaborated by a data reduction process in order to compute synopses of the data (DS). Data reduction is a process that reduces the cardinality of the DW and stores a small set of data solely. Data synopses are then used in the approximate query processing, whose aim is to perform traditional OLAP based on approximate answers. Approximate processing is able to provide fast answers to complex (and usually aggregate) queries that would normally require high computational time to produce the exact answers.

There are several consolidated methodologies that can be implemented in approximate query answering systems.

If the system adopts *summary tables*, the DS consists of materialized tables representing precomputed aggregate queries [8]. Of course, the creation of tables corresponding to all the possible user queries is an impracticable solution due to the explorative nature of analytical elaborations.

When using *wavelet-based* methodologies, the system computes a set of values, called *wavelet coefficients*, to be used in SQL instructions based on redefined SQL operators [9]. In monodimensional Haar wavelet decomposition, the DS is given by storing the average between a pair of values along with their difference. This computation is recursively repeated and, at each recursion, data with a lower resolution are obtained. So, given the vector $V_0 = \langle 2,2,4,6 \rangle$, $V_1 = \langle 2,5 \rangle$ is the vector with resolution 1, while $V_2 = \langle 3.5 \rangle$ is the vector with resolution 0. The differences are used to reconstruct original data and they are, respectively, $\langle 0, -1 \rangle$ for V_1 and $\langle -1.5 \rangle$ for V_2.

In *histogram-based* methodologies, the DS is represented by a set of histograms. The queries are translated into equivalent queries on these histograms, allowing the same expressivity of SQL operators [10]. Histograms store the frequency of data falling into a set of intervals, the so-called buckets, used to split the domain. The higher the number of buckets, the higher the accuracy of the approximate answers.

Sampling consists in collecting random samples of large volumes of data and in executing queries on these samples, in order to derive information on the original set of DW data. In this case, the size of the sample must be decided *a priori* and it depends on the DW cardinality [11]. So, in many cases, also querying the sample may require a high answering time. As an example, if the table cardinality is 100,000,000 of rows and the sample size is only 1% of the original data, then the sample cardinality is 1,000,000 of rows.

In *orthonormal series*, the probability density function of multidimensional relations is approximated by orthonormal polynomials. As a result, a set of coefficients are computed and stored in the DS database [12]. The number of the coefficients depends on the polynomial approximation degree and not on the DW relation cardinality. Therefore, a constant response time is observed in these systems. As a counterpart, the approximation degree affects the accuracy of the approximate answers.

Since the advantages of approximate query processing have been widely accepted, further methodologies have been defined in last years. Emerging methodologies are based on graphs [13], genetic algorithms [14], and probabilistic models [15].

Once the data reduction has been performed, it is important to trace which fields and relations have been actually reduced, as some data stored in the database can be ignored for decision making based on approximate answers. Therefore, tracing which data have been reduced provides decision makers with the knowledge about which data are effectively available for approximate query processing. This

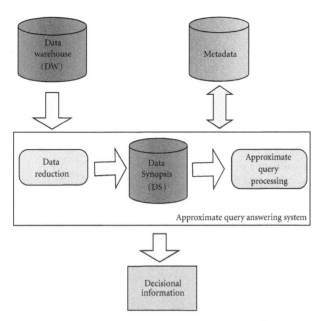

FIGURE 1: Approximate query answering system architecture.

knowledge is usually managed by metadata, that is, data providing a semantic level.

Currently, the metadata are stored in a central repository in standard format, in order to be shared and used by the several business intelligence tools produced by various vendors. As an example, these metadata are used by the business intelligence platforms to represent the multidimensional model of the data warehouse and to generate SQL instructions automatically without writing lines of code [2]. Moreover, the standard metadata are usually exported in XMI [4], as this XML-based layer provides interoperability among business intelligence tools.

However, the CWM does not include a metamodel that covers approximate query processing. So, there is no standard representation of metadata useful for approximate query answering systems. As already stated, these systems need to compute synopses of the data stored in a data warehouse. Then, the synopsis is used for the computation of the analytical queries. Therefore, this kind of systems need to know which data have been effectively reduced and, consequently, usable in the approximate query processing. Of course, this information must be provided by metadata. For this reason, a central research topic related to approximate query processing is strictly related to the representation of metadata.

2.1. Towards Metadata Identification. Here we focus on approximate query answering systems which adopt methodologies performing a data reduction and whose general architecture accords with the one depicted in Figure 1. For these methodologies, we present the metadata to be generated and used in approximate query processing in order to satisfy both user needs and system requirements.

In general, we distinguish between user-oriented metadata and system-oriented metadata. User-oriented metadata

are those corresponding to the user choices, for example, as previously seen, which tables and columns have been selected for the data reduction. However, some of these strongly depend on the adopted methodology for the data reduction and, therefore, they are *specific* to the context or system implementation.

System-oriented metadata are those generated by the system on the basis of the user choices. These metadata provide further and immediate information about the compressed data, such as the refresh date. Nonetheless, some of these metadata—the column domain, for example—may be used by the algorithms performing the approximate query processing.

Table 1 reports the metadata identification for each methodology.

2.2. Metadata Requirements. From Table 1, we observe that the metadata are mainly used to know which elements of a relational database have been selected by the user for the approximate query processing. These elements are effectively reduced and stored in another database (viz. the DS database). Therefore, the Metadata database (cf. Figure 1) stores the following items:

(i) the name of the data warehouse along with the connection information,

(ii) the names of the reduced tables of a given data warehouse,

(iii) the names of the reduced columns, for each selected table.

In reference to the underlying system methodology, users perform usually further choices, which can affect the accuracy of approximate answers. Using orthonormal series, the approximation degree must be chosen, for example.

TABLE 1: Metadata identification.

| Methodology | User-oriented metadata | | System-oriented metadata |
	Common	Specific	
Summary table			Refresh date
Wavelet		Resolution level	Table cardinality Column domain Refresh date
Histogram	Data warehouse name Reduced table name Reduced column name	Bucket width	Table cardinality Column domain Number of buckets Refresh date
Sampling		Sample size	Table cardinality Refresh date
Orthonormal series		Approximation degree	Table cardinality Column domain Refresh date

Also these values must be preserved as metadata. However, since these parameters are specific, a general solution is provided by using an opportune descriptor—consisting of the pair (*name*, *value*)—to represent data whose semantics depends on the context. This solution can be also adopted for system-oriented metadata.

Then, using metadata, users are allowed to formulate queries that will be automatically traduced into SQL statements, in the case they are exact queries, or into *ad hoc* plans for accessing data in the DS database, whenever they are approximate queries. In fact, the latter must be suitably transformed in order to define a data access plan whose features strongly depend on the adopted methodology.

As an example, in orthonormal series, a *sum* aggregate query is traduced into a call to the function *sum* (*d*, *tableStruct*, *columnsStruct*, *intervalsStruct*) where:

(i) *d* is the approximation degree set by the user;

(ii) *tableStruct* is the data structure storing several information—the cardinality, for example—about the reduced table involved in the query;

(iii) *columnsStruct* is the data structure storing information about the reduced columns involved in the query;

(iv) *intervalsStruct* is the data structure storing information about the query intervals set by the user.

These parameters are used to load the coefficients up to degree *d* relative to the reduction of the required columns of the table.

3. Overview of the Standard Metamodel

The current standard for the definition of the metadata to be used in business intelligence and data warehousing is the CWM [3].

The CWM is composed of a set of modular metamodels, structured in layers, where each metamodel depends only on the metamodels of the underlying layers.

Since the CWM is based on the object model, a metamodel is logically represented by a set of classes (the so-called package) that are related to each other via associations. The classes and associations are specified according to the Meta Object Facility (MOF) [16], which is an extension of the object model based on the Unified Modelling Language (UML). In this context, the MOF acts as a meta-metamodel able to represent CWM metamodels. Therefore, every instance of a class of the CWM metamodel is a metaobject, representing an element of the target model.

As an example, the relational metamodel (see Section 3.1) allows to describe the metadata of relational databases and each class instance represents an element of the relational database being modelled (*i.e.*, a table, column, constraint, or data type, and so on).

The layers and related metamodels are as follows.

Object Model. The layer that groups all the metamodels that provide the basic constructs for creating and describing the other metamodels.

(i) *Core* is the metamodel containing basic classes and associations used by all other packages.

(ii) *Behavioural* is the metamodel collecting together classes and associations that describe the behaviour of objects, such as operations and methods.

(iii) *Relationships* is the metamodel collecting together classes and associations that describe the relationships between objects, each one being an association (*i.e.*, is-part-of relationship) or a generalization (*i.e.*, is-type-of relationship).

(iv) *Instance* is the metamodel that allows the inclusion of data instances in the metadata.

Foundation. The layer that groups all the metamodels that are devoted to represent the concepts and structures shared by overlaying metamodels.

(i) *Business Information* is the metamodel supporting business-oriented services, such as name and description of the elements of the target model.

(ii) *Data Types* is the metamodel supporting the definition of constructs useful to create specific data types in the target model.

(iii) *Expressions* is the metamodel that provides basic support for defining expression trees, in order to allow objects to record shared expressions in common form.

(iv) *Key Index* is the metamodel used for specifying instances and for identifying alternate keys of instance sortings, such that they can be shared among the various data models that employ them.

(v) *Type Mapping* is the metamodel that supports the mapping of data types between different systems.

(vi) *Software Development* is the metamodel containing classes devoted to record how the software is used in the data warehouse.

Resource. The layer that groups all the metamodels that allow to represent different resource types.

(i) *Object* metamodel contains classes and associations that allow to represent metadata of objects (*i.e.,* the object model itself).

(ii) *Relational* contains classes and associations that allow to represent metadata of relational databases.

(iii) *Record* contains classes and associations that allow to represent metadata of record data resources.

(iv) *Multidimensional* contains classes and associations that allow to represent metadata of multidimensional databases.

(v) *XML* contains classes and associations that allow to represent metadata of XML documents.

Analysis. The layer that groups all the metamodels that must be implemented by business intelligence tools.

(i) *Transformation* contains classes and associations that represent metadata used by data transformation tools.

(ii) *OLAP* contains classes and associations that represent metadata used by OLAP tools.

(iii) *Data Mining* contains classes and associations that represent metadata used by data mining tools.

(iv) *Information Visualization* contains classes and associations that represent metadata used by tools devoted to support the graphical visualization of information.

(v) *Business Nomenclature* contains classes and associations that represent metadata about business taxonomy and glossary.

Management. The layer that groups all the metamodels that represent high-level tasks.

(i) *Warehouse process* is the metamodel that documents the process flows used to execute transformations.

(ii) *Warehouse operation* is the metamodel that contains classes recording the day-to-day operations of the warehouse processes.

In the next sections, we briefly discuss the Relational, Transformation, and OLAP metamodels, in order to show the context of data warehousing, and we consider only the relational metamodel in order to define an extension of the CWM. This extension enables representing the standard metadata for approximate query answering systems that perform reductions of the data stored in data warehouses [17]. These systems are usually built on the relational model (*i.e.,* they are ROLAP systems).

3.1. Relational Metamodel. Figure 2 depicts a simplified but essential version of the relational metamodel, that states that each schema of a relational database is composed of a set of tables, whereas each table is composed of a set of columns. In fact, the main classes of this metamodel (viz. Schema, Table, and Columns) inherit from the basic classes of the Core metamodel (viz. Package, Class, Attribute, Namespace, Classifier, and Feature).

On the basis of the associations defined in the Core metamodel, it is possible to state that a table owns a set of columns, in the same way as a class owns a set of attributes, whereas both Table and Class classes are specialization of the Classifier class.

Finally, a table is owned by a relational schema. A further class, named Catalog, represents a physical database that includes one or more relational schemas, each of them representing an independent logical database.

This metamodel allows representing also the usual constraints that must be defined in relational databases, such as primary key and foreign key constraints. According to this metamodel, it is possible to create a set of metaobjects (instances of classes of this metamodel), in order to represent the several elements of a relational database.

3.2. Transformation Metamodel. This metamodel includes classes and associations useful to represent metadata related to the data transformation occurring in a business intelligence system.

The transformations are thought as a set of rules to change data format. Each rule is composed of (a) a transformation function, (b) a data source, and (c) a data target.

3.3. OLAP Metamodel. The data warehouse conceptual schema is designed according to the multidimensional model [18, 19], that can be graphically represented using the metaphor of the cube. According to this metaphor, a fact related to an occurring event of interest can be represented as a cube. Moreover, a fact can be described by numeric attributes that provide quantitative information. These

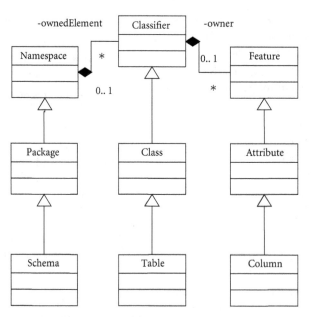

FIGURE 2: Part of the relational metamodel.

Management	Warehouse Process			Warehouse Operation		
Analysis	Transformation	OLAP	Data Mining	Information Visualization	Business Nomenclature	OL2AP
Resource	Object	Relational		Record	Multidimensional	XML
Foundation	Business Information	Data Types	Expressions	Key Index	Type Mapping	Software Development
Object Model	Core	Behavioral		Relationships		Instance

FIGURE 3: Extended CWM block diagram.

numeric attributes are the so-called measures. Therefore, each cell of the cube stores a single numeric value, pointed out by a set of dimensions representing levels of analysis. The first-level dimensions define the minimum granularity of the data stored in the cube. The set of the first-level dimensions forms the primary aggregation pattern. Further levels define how the data can be aggregated. The levels, which are in one-to-many relationship among themselves, form a hierarchy that represents an aggregation path.

The logical models to describe a data warehouse conceptual schema are MOLAP and ROLAP. In MOLAP, data warehouses are built on multidimensional databases, whose metadata are defined by the Multidimensional metamodel. On the other hand, in ROLAP, data warehouses are built on relational databases, whose metadata are defined by the relational metamodel.

The OLAP metamodel allows to define metadata used by OLAP tools, in order to represent the metadata of a data warehouse, built on both the ROLAP and the MOLAP technologies.

For the sake of simplicity, Relational and Multidimensional metamodels represent the data warehouse metadata at the logical level, while the OLAP metamodel describes the data warehouse metadata at the conceptual level.

4. Extension of the Standard Metamodel

As widely explained in [20, 21], the importance of metadata derives from the fact that they represent the only way to provide further knowledge about a business process or a component of an information system. In our context, the metadata are used to describe data reduction processes for supporting approximate query answering systems in multidimensional analyses. Since the CWM does not include a metamodel to define metadata for approximate query answering systems, we extended the CWM with a further metamodel, namely OL2AP, which stands for OnLine Approximate Analytical Processing.

We included the OL2AP metamodel in the Analysis layer of the CWM (cf. Figure 3) that groups all the metamodels that must be implemented by business intelligence tools performing approximate query processing.

The aim of this metamodel consists of tracing:

(i) which fact tables have been chosen for data reduction among all the tables of a data warehouse;

(ii) which dimension tables have been involved in the data reduction;

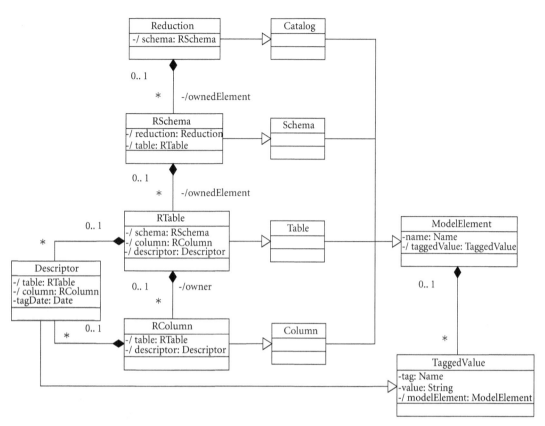

FIGURE 4: *OL2AP* Metamodel.

(iii) which attributes of the selected tables have been reduced;

(iv) the possible parameters of the data reduction.

The dimensions and measures of cubes that have been reduced are effectively available for the approximate query processing. Therefore, the decision maker is able to express analytical queries involving the reduced attributes in order to obtain fast responses.

4.1. OL2AP Metamodel. Figure 4 shows the main classes and associations that allow creating standard metadata that can be effectively used by approximate query answering system in order to trace the data reduction process and to generate analytical queries based on approximate answers. Notice that this metamodel depends on (a) the *relational* metamodel, that provides an approximate query answering system with the metadata describing the data warehouse logical model (usually, ROLAP), and (b) the *Core* metamodel, that allows to attach a descriptor to any model element (*i.e.,* the element of the database being modelled).

The main classes of the *OL2AP* metamodel are summarized in Table 2. Each instance of class is called metaobject and it represents a construct of the system to be modelled.

As an example, to create the metadata of a relational database, we have to use the *relational* metamodel, which establishes to create a metaobject of the *Table* class for each table of the database.

The steps for the creation of the metaobjects of the *OL2AP* metamodel are as follows:

(i) a metaobject of the class *Reduction* is created to represent the physical database, and the name of this object is the data source name (DSN) used for the physical connection to the database;

(ii) for each relational schema chosen for the data reduction, a metaobject of the class *RSchema* is created, having the name of the schema (*i.e.,* the name of the relational database) and a reference to the physical database it belongs to;

(iii) for each table of a relational schema chosen for the data reduction, a metaobject of the class *RTable* is created, having the name of the table and a reference to the schema it belongs to;

(iv) for each column of a table chosen for the data reduction, a metaobject of the class *RColumn* is created, having the name of the table and a reference to the table it belongs to;

(v) if a table or a column must be tagged, a metaobject of the class *Descriptor* is created, having an arbitrary name and a reference to the model element it belongs to.

TABLE 2: *OL2AP* metamodel classes.

Metamodel	Class	CWM Description
Core	ModelElement	A model element is an element that is an abstraction drawn from the system being modelled.
	TaggedValue	A tagged value allows information to be attached to any model element in the form of a "tagged value" pair; that is, *name = value*.
Relational	Catalog	A catalog is the unit of logon and identification. It also identifies the scope of SQL statements; the tables contained in a catalog can be used in a single SQL statement.
	Schema	A schema is a named collection of tables and collects all the tables of the same relational schema (i.e., a logical database).
	Table	Table is a data structure representing a relation.
	Column	Column is a data structure representing the field of a relation.
OL2AP	Reduction	This class represents a process of reduction of the data stored in a relational database.
	RSchema	This class represents a relational schema chosen for the data reduction.
	RTable	This class represents a table chosen for the data reduction.
	RColumn	This class represents a column whose data have been reduced.
	Descriptor	A descriptor is a tag that can be attached to any element of the model.

In the modelling process, in order to obtain identifiers of the created metaobjects and to ensure correct referencing among these objects, techniques derived from object-oriented database management must be used (cf. [22] for instance).

4.2. Metadata Representation. The metadata are stored into a relational database (cf., the architecture in Figure 1). The logical schema of the relational metadata database is shown in Figure 5. This schema expresses the concept that a data reduction requires a physical connection to a database, which may be composed of several and independent logical schemas. On the turn, a schema is composed of a set of tables, and a table is composed of one or more columns. Each table and each column can be tagged by several descriptors, which are pairs (*name, value*) useful to refer to context-dependent data.

However, such metadata must be exported in web-based environments to be accessed by decision makers since they need to know which data are available for approximate query processing and how to formulate analytical queries.

The business intelligence platform capability matrix [23] has been defined by the Gartner Group in order to establish standard criteria to evaluate systems used by business companies to develop applications supporting decision makers. A set of criteria is related to the information delivery issue. According to these criteria, a platform must provide the ability to publish dashboards to a web-based interface and each user must be allowed to build personal indicators.

To this end, the OMG has defined the XMI format as the physical layer used to store the metadata that are obtained through a serialization process of the created metaobjects. Since it is XML-based, XMI allows high interoperability among business intelligence tools. Therefore, an XMI-compliant file can be suitably transferred via a web service.

5. Case Study

In this section, we illustrate the experimentation executed with an approximate query answering system. The tool, named *Analytical Data Profiling* (ADAP) system, is based on polynomial series approximation and produces sets of coefficients that permit to have knowledge and management of the multivariate data distribution of data warehouse cubes. We used this system as the testing environment of the *OL2AP* Metamodel.

5.1. System Architecture. According to the general architecture shown in Figure 1, the architecture of ADAP is presented. In detail, ADAP is an OLAP tool, whose features are to collect, to organize, and to process large volumes of data stored in a data warehouse, in order to obtain statistical data profiles to be used in approximate query processing.

The main macroactivities supported by ADAP are as follows.

(1) Data Reduction. In this first step, the system calculates the synopses of data. The calculated data are stored in the system database, which represents the main repository accessed in the next analytical processing. ADAP performs read-only accesses to the data warehouse, whenever it is necessary to (re)calculate the data synopses DS.

(2) Approximate Query Processing. In this step, the system performs the computation of aggregate functions in approximate way, by only using the data synopses. The output of the processing consists of scalar values that represent the approximation of aggregate values. However, the system also provides a method to execute queries directly on the data warehouse, every time the user deals with critical factors or when the maximum precision is needed.

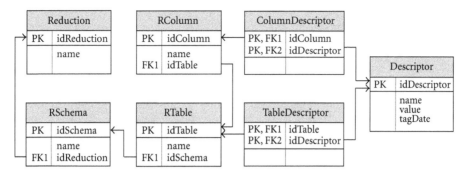

FIGURE 5: Relational schema of the metadata repository.

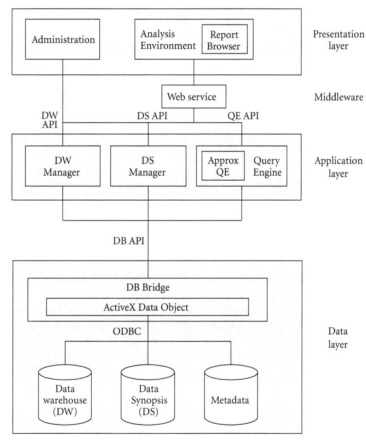

FIGURE 6: ADAP four-level architecture.

In ADAP system, the data reduction process uses the consolidated methodology of orthonormal series approximation (see [24] also) based on Legendre polynomials [12]. Using this method, data synopses are represented by the sets of coefficients of the polynomials, the so-called canonical coefficients.

On the other hand, if using histogram-based methodologies for example, the data synopses are represented by buckets, each of them containing the frequency of values falling within predetermined intervals.

Regardless of the specific methodology, the data synopses carry synthetic information to approximate the multidimensional data distribution of relations. Therefore, the main aggregate functions (such as *count*, *sum*, and *average*) can be computed without accessing the millions-of-records relations of the data warehouse. However, the response may be affected with a small quantity of error.

ADAP has been designed according to a four-level architecture (see Figure 6) and developed according to a modular design, in order to allow the *add-in* of features not yet implemented. The system manages both the data (*i.e.,* the computed coefficients) and metadata (*i.e.,* information on which data in the data warehouse have been reduced).

In the *Presentation* layer, *Administration* is the input component that allows users to select the data warehouse. It receives the metadata of the selected data warehouse

Reduction

idReduction	Name
1	TutorialDSN

RSchema

idSchema	Name	idReduction
1	Tutorial	1

RTable

idTable	Name	idSchema
1	city_ctr_sales	1
2	city_month_sales	1
3	order_detail	1

TableDescriptor

idTable	idDescriptor
1	1
2	2
3	3
1	5
2	6
3	4

Descriptor

idDescriptor	tagDate	Name	Value
1	2012-05-28	degree	27
2	2012-05-30	degree	25
3	2012-05-30	degree	21
4	2012-05-28	cardinality	407529
5	2012-05-30	cardinality	100000
6	2012-05-30	cardinality	200000
7	2012-05-30	min	1
8	2012-05-30	max	100
9	2012-05-30	min	1
10	2012-05-30	max	100
11	2012-05-28	min	1
12	2012-05-28	max	200000
13	2012-05-28	min	1
14	2012-05-28	max	39
15	2012-05-28	min	1
16	2012-05-28	max	1200
17	2012-05-28	min	1
18	2012-05-28	max	10000

RColumn

idColumn	Name	idTable
1	cust_city_id	1
2	cust_city_id	2
3	order_id	3
4	emp_id	3
5	unit_price	3
6	customer_id	3

ColumnDescriptor

idColumn	idDescriptor
1	7
1	8
2	9
2	10
3	11
3	12
4	13
4	14
5	15
5	16
6	17
6	18

FIGURE 7: Example of standard metadata.

(in particular, names of fields and tables) from the *DW Manager* and presents them to the user. Using the *Administration* component, users define the attributes to be involved in the data reduction. When the user ends the selection process, this component asks the *DS Manager* to start the computation of the data synopses on the basis of the selected attributes.

Analysis Environment is the web-based application that allows users to define business indicators to be published in dashboards [25]. First, it loads ADAP metadata via the web service. These metadata define which data are available for approximate query processing. The approximate analysis is executed by accessing only the *Data Synopsis* repository. This kind of analysis returns very fast query answers and the results are visualized in the *Report Browser*, which is the dashboard container. In detail, it gets from the *Analysis Environment* component the user query and starts the analytical processing by calling a public method provided by the web service. At the end of the computation, it reports the results, that can be approximate or real values, and it also shows the response time (in msecs).

In the *Application* layer, *DW Manager* is the only component deputed to access the data warehouse using the *DB Bridge* component. It extracts data and metadata from the data warehouse and distributes them to other components. For the *Administration* component, it extracts the metadata of the selected data warehouse. For the *DS Manager*, it performs a read access to the data warehouse and passes it the dataset containing the data to be used for data reduction.

For the *Query Engine* component, it supports real analyses by executing SQL instructions on the data warehouse.

DS Manager is the basic component with a twofold role: to generate the data synopses (*i.e.,* in our case, the sets of Legendre polynomials' coefficients) and to extract them during the approximate query processing. When storing the coefficients in the *Data Synopsis* database, it also stores further metadata (*i.e.,* which data have been selected by the data warehouse administrator for data reduction).

Query Engine is the basic component that executes OLAP queries. In approximate query processing, its subcomponent, the so-called *Approximate Query Engine*, uses the data synopses and returns the approximate answers. In the other cases, the *Query Engine* translates the query into an SQL instruction to be executed by the *DW manager*.

Finally, the *DW Manager* and the *DS Manager* interact with the *DB Bridge* that is the component that manages the communication with both the DW and DS databases via an ODBC connection, according to metadata.

5.2. Example of Metadata. In the system, there are two basic roles played by users, namely the one played by the data warehouse administrator and that played by the business users.

First, an ODBC connection must be established. Then, the administrator is able to view all the tables (and the related columns) included into the selected data warehouse. At this

```
<CWMOL2AP:RTable xmi.id="a32" name="order_detail">

   <CWM:ModelElement.taggedValue>
     <CWMOL2AP:Descriptor xmi.id="a48" tag="cardinality" value="407529" tagDate="2012-05-28"/>
   </CWM:ModelElement.taggedValue>

  <CWM:Classifier.feature>

   <CWMOL2AP:RColumn xmi.id="a41" name="emp_id">
      <CWM:ModelElement.taggedValue>
        <CWMOL2AP:Descriptor xmi.id="a49" tag="min" value="1" tagDate="2012-05-28"/>
        <CWMOL2AP:Descriptor xmi.id="a50" tag="max" value="39" tagDate="2012-05-28"/>
      </CWM:ModelElement.taggedValue>
   </CWMOL2AP:RColumn>

   <CWMOL2AP:RColumn xmi.id="a38" name="order_id">
      <CWM:ModelElement.taggedValue>
        <CWMOL2AP:Descriptor xmi.id="a51" tag="min" value="1" tagDate="2012-05-28"/>
        <CWMOL2AP:Descriptor xmi.id="a52" tag="max" value="20000" tagDate="2012-05-28"/>
      </CWM:ModelElement.taggedValue>
   </CWMOL2AP:RColumn>

   <CWMOL2AP:RColumn xmi.id="a35" name="unit_price">
      <CWM:ModelElement.taggedValue>
        <CWMOL2AP:Descriptor xmi.id="a53" tag="min" value="1" tagDate="2012-05-28"/>
        <CWMOL2AP:Descriptor xmi.id="a54" tag="max" value="1200" tagDate="2012-05-28"/>
      </CWM:ModelElement.taggedValue>
   </CWMOL2AP:RColumn>

   <CWMOL2AP:RColumn xmi.id="a39" name="customer_id">
      <CWM:ModelElement.taggedValue>
       <CWMOL2AP:Descriptor xmi.id="a55" tag="min" value="1" tagDate="2012-05-28"/>
        <CWMOL2AP:Descriptor xmi.id="a56" tag="max" value="10000" tagDate="2012-05-28"/>
      </CWM:ModelElement.taggedValue>
   </CWMOL2AP:RColumn>

  </CWM:Classifier.feature>
</CWMOL2AP:RTable>
```

FIGURE 8: Part of XMI-compliant file used in approximate query processing.

point, the administrator has only to select a table and to define which columns must be considered for data reduction.

After this, the data reduction process generates the set of coefficients, according to the polynomial approximation degree d chosen by the user.

In this step, the system produces also the metadata according to the *OL2AP* metamodel.

The computed coefficients are stored in the database managed by the approximate query answering system, while the metadata are saved in the central repository of the business intelligence system (cf. Figure 1).

The ADAP system needs to trace also:

(i) the minimum and maximum of each column,

(ii) the number of rows of each table,

because these data will be used by the algorithms performing analytical processing based on approximate responses.

In Figure 7, there are reported the metadata relative to our case study, automatically generated and stored by the ADAP system (cf. Figure 1 and Data layer of Figure 6) according to the settings and choices made by the users through the administration interface. Using these metadata it is possible to know which table and columns have been compressed and, then, available for approximate query processing.

Finally, the metadata can be exported in XML format and used in the web-based interface that allows users to create a business indicator and to obtain fast approximate answers, by choosing any approximation degree x such that $x \leq d$. Furthermore, the use of XML guarantees a high interoperability among the several systems, ensuring

Reduction

idReduction	Name
1	TutorialDSN

RSchema

idSchema	Name	idReduction
1	Tutorial	1

RTable

idTable	Name	idSchema
3	order_detail	1

TableDescriptor

idTable	idDescriptor
1	1
1	2

Descriptor

idDescriptor	tagDate	Name	Value
1	2012-6-4	bucketNo	312000
2	2012-6-4	cardinality	407529
3	2012-6-4	bucketW	1000
4	2012-6-4	bucketW	3
5	2012-6-4	bucketW	100
6	2012-6-4	bucketW	1000
7	2012-6-4	min	1
8	2012-6-4	max	200000
9	2012-6-4	min	1
10	2012-6-4	max	39
11	2012-6-4	min	1
12	2012-6-4	max	1200
13	2012-6-4	min	1
14	2012-6-4	max	10000

RColumn

idColumn	Name	idTable
3	order_id	3
4	emp_id	3
5	unit_price	3
6	customer_id	3

ColumnDescriptor

idColumn	idDescriptor
1	3
2	4
3	5
4	6
1	7
1	8
2	9
2	10
3	11
3	12
4	13
4	14

FIGURE 9: Example of standard metadata in equal-width histograms.

the interaction via web services and, therefore, obtaining a location independence.

The code in Figure 8 is part of the XML file obtained when exporting the metadata represented in Figure 7.

Using these metadata, it is possible to attach a tag to any model element. As an example, we can associate the descriptor (*cardinality*, 407529) to the *order_detail* table in order to state that the cardinality of this reduced table is 407,529 rows. As a further example, we can associate the descriptors (min, 1) and (max, 100) to a given column in order to trace the minimum and the maximum of its domain, respectively.

5.3. Application to Further Methodologies. The *OL2AP* metamodel has been applied also to systems using methodologies to perform the approximate query processing different from the orthonormal series. In particular, we have tested the metamodel on the histogram-based system (see, [10]).

This methodology needs to trace tables and columns involved in the data reduction process, as it happens in polynomials approximation. But, in histogram-based methodology, the number of buckets to be used for data reduction must be also chosen. More precisely, the equal-width histograms first establish the width of the buckets for each column involved in the reduction process, then the frequency in each bucket is computed. On the other hand, the equal-depth histograms first fix the frequency, then the widths of the buckets are computed so as to obtain the same frequency for all the buckets. All these parameters have to

be considered as descriptors to be attached to the model elements.

As a consequence, we observe metadata like those depicted in Figure 9 in case of equal-width histograms. As an example, we have min = 1 and max = 200000 for the domain of *order_id* attribute. Moreover, the fixed bucket width for this attribute is 1000 and, then, we have 200 buckets for *order_id*. In the same way, we compute 13 buckets for *emp_id*, 12 for *unit_price*, and 10 for *customer_id*. Therefore, the total number of buckets, which is a descriptor attached to the *order_detail* table, is $200 \times 13 \times 12 \times 10 = 312000$.

In a similar way, it is trivial to verify the application of the metamodel to other methodologies, since the difference consists only in the creation of specific descriptors as required by each approach.

6. Conclusions

The necessity to decrease the response time in OLAP has led to the exploitation of approximate query answering systems as business intelligence tools able to provide useful information for decision makers, on the basis of fast and approximate answers. However, the current standard for the definition of metadata used by OLAP tools does not include a metamodel to represent *ad hoc* metadata for these systems.

In this paper, we have presented an extension of the standard metamodel that can be used by approximate query answering systems in order to create their own metadata according to the requirements identified by Table 1. The results showed that the metamodel effectively traces which data are available for analytical processing based on approximate methodologies that perform a data reduction. This allows both users to formulate queries based on approximate answers and systems to automatically generate plan for accessing reduced data on the basis of user-defined queries.

References

[1] J. Poole, D. Chang, D. Tolbert, and D. Mellor, *Common Warehouse Metamodel*, John Wiley & Sons, 2002.

[2] A. Sen, "Metadata management: past, present and future," *Decision Support Systems*, vol. 37, no. 1, pp. 151–173, 2004.

[3] Object Management Group, "Common Warehouse Metamodel Specification," vers. 1.1, vol. 1, OMG, Needham, MA, USA, 2003, http://www.omg.org/docs/formal/03-03-02.pdf.

[4] Object Management Group, "XML Metadata Interchange (XMI) Specification," vers. 2.0, OMG, Needham, MA USA, 2003, http://www.omg.org/docs/formal/03-05-02.pdf.

[5] S. Chaudhuri, U. Dayal, and V. Ganti, "Database technology for decision support systems," *Computer*, vol. 34, no. 12, pp. 48–55, 2001.

[6] F. Di Tria, E. Lefons, and F. Tangorra, "Metrics for approximate query engine evaluation," in *Proceedings of the 27th ACM Symposium on Applied Computing (ACM SAC '12)*, pp. 885–887, Riva del Garda, Italy, 2012.

[7] S. Acharya, P. B. Gibbons, V. Poosala, and S. Ramaswamy, "The AQUA approximate query answering system," in *Proceedings of the ACM SIGMOD International Conference on Management of Data*, pp. 574–576, Philadelphia, PA, USA, 1999.

[8] A. Gupta, V. Harinarayan, and D. Quaas, "Aggregate-query processing in data warehousing environments," in *Proceedings of the 21th International Conference on Very Large Data Bases (VLDB '95)*, pp. 358–369, Zurich, Switzerland, 1995.

[9] K. Chakrabarti, M. Garofalakis, R. Rastogi, and K. Shim, "Approximate query processing using wavelets," *The International Journal on Very Large Data Bases*, vol. 10, no. 2-3, pp. 199–223, 2001.

[10] Y. Ioannidis and V. Poosala, "Histogram-based approximation of set-valued query answers," in *Proceedings of the 25th International Conference on Very Large Data Bases (VLDB '99)*, pp. 174–185, Edinburgh, Scotland, 1999.

[11] P. B. Gibbons and Y. Matias, "New sampling-based summary statistics for improving approximate query answers," in *Proceedings of the ACM SIGMOD International Conference on Management of Data*, pp. 331–342, Seattle, Wash, USA, 1998.

[12] E. Lefons, A. Merico, and F. Tangorra, "Analytical profile estimation in database systems," *Information Systems*, vol. 20, no. 1, pp. 1–20, 1995.

[13] J. Spiegel and N. Polyzotis, "TuG synopses for approximate query answering," *ACM Transactions on Database Systems*, vol. 34, no. 1, article 3, 2009.

[14] J. B. Peltzer, A. M. Teredesai, and G. Reinard, "AQUAGP: approximate query answers using genetic programming," in *Proceedings of the 9th European Conference (EuroGP '06)*, pp. 49–60, Budapest, Hungary, April 2006.

[15] C. Jermaine, S. Arumugam, A. Pol, and A. Dobra, "Scalable approximate query processing with the DBO engine," *ACM Transactions on Database Systems*, vol. 33, no. 4, article 23, 2008.

[16] Object Management Group, "XML MetaObject Facility Specification," vers. 1.4, OMG, Needham, MA USA, 2002, http://www.omg.org/docs/formal/02-04-03.pdf.

[17] C. dell'Aquila, F. Di Tria, E. Lefons, and F. Tangorra, "Data reduction for data analysis," in *New Aspects on Computing Research*, C. Cepisca, G. A. Kouzaev, and N. E. Mastorakis, Eds., pp. 204–210, 2008.

[18] F. Di Tria, E. Lefons, and F. Tangorra, "Hybrid methodology for data warehouse conceptual design by UML schemas," *Information and Software Technology*, vol. 54, no. 4, pp. 360–379, 2012.

[19] F. Di Tria, E. Lefons, "GrHyMM: a graph-oriented hybrid multidimensional model," in *Proceedings of the Advances in Conceptual Modeling. Recent Developments and New Directions*, pp. 86–97, Springer, Brussels, Belgium, 2011.

[20] D. Marco, *Building and Managing the Meta Data Repository*, Wiley, 2000.

[21] A. Tannenbaum, *Metadata Solutions*, Addison-Wesley, 2002.

[22] E. Bertino and L. Martino, "Object-oriented database management systems: concepts and issues," *Computer*, vol. 24, no. 4, pp. 33–47, 1991.

[23] K. Schlegel and B. Sood, *Business Intelligence Platform Capability Matrix*, Gartner Research, 2007.

[24] F. Yan, W. C. Hou, Z. Jiang, C. Luo, and Q. Zhu, "Selectivity estimation of range queries based on data density approximation via cosine series," *Data & Knowledge Engineering*, vol. 63, no. 3, pp. 855–878, 2007.

[25] T. Palpanas, P. Chowdhary, F. Pinel, and G. Mihaila, "Integrated model-driven dashboard development," *Information Systems Frontiers*, vol. 9, no. 2-3, pp. 195–208, 2007.

Accountability in Enterprise Mashup Services

Joe Zou[1] and Chris Pavlovski[2]

[1] Centrin Data Systems, 1 Boxing 8th Road, Beijing 100176, China
[2] IBM Global Business Services, 348 Edward Street, Brisbane,
  QLD 4000, Australia

Correspondence should be addressed to Chris Pavlovski; chris_pav@au1.ibm.com

Academic Editor: Xiaoying Bai

As a result of the proliferation of Web 2.0 style web sites, the practice of mashup services has become increasingly popular in the web development community. While mashup services bring flexibility and speed in delivering new valuable services to consumers, the issue of accountability associated with the mashup practice remains largely ignored by the industry. Furthermore, realizing the great benefits of mashup services, industry leaders are eagerly pushing these solutions into the enterprise arena. Although enterprise mashup services hold great promise in delivering a flexible SOA solution in a business context, the lack of accountability in current mashup solutions may render this ineffective in the enterprise environment. This paper defines accountability for mashup services, analyses the underlying issues in practice, and finally proposes a framework and ontology to model accountability. This model may then be used to develop effective accountability solutions for mashup environments. Compared to the traditional method of using QoS or SLA monitoring to address accountability requirements, our approach addresses more fundamental aspects of accountability specification to facilitate machine interpretability and therefore enabling automation in monitoring.

1. Introduction

The recent and rapid expansion of Web 2.0 has considerably placed pressure upon industry to institutionalize new technologies and conform to emerging standards. While agreement on the scope of the term Web 2.0 does vary, O'Reilly provides a commonly accepted definition, noting this to include a range of enhanced services including web services, wikis, blogging, BitTorrents, and syndication [1].

The rapid growth of Web 2.0 has also introduced a number of new design patterns and architectural styles in web development. One of the notable techniques involves mashing up information from existing services to deliver new value-added services. This process effectively involves the drawing of content from several sources to create a new content or service. The resulting web page is then referred to as a mashup of the existing content.

While mashup services bring flexibility and speed in delivering new valuable services to consumers, the legal implications of using this technology are significant. Researchers in law conclude that the development of mashup services is fraught with potential legal liabilities that require careful consideration [2].

The issue of accountability associated with the mashup practice remains largely ignored by the industry. Current formal practices suggest that the mashup developer and original content source owner disclaim any warranties [2]. This appears to be temporarily acceptable since most services from Web 2.0 sites are free to internet users. This means that as long as consumers accept the terms and conditions, the issue of accountability is largely avoided. Notwithstanding, as these services mature to involve some payment, such an approach may no longer be tenable to all parties.

Traditionally, accountability implies that an entity has an obligation for the execution of authority and/or the fulfilment of responsibility [3]. Nonrepudiation of transaction is also a major requirement for a service requester and a service provider. However, in a mashup service scenario, the issue of accountability is more complicated. Firstly, there may be several implicit service providers involved due to the fact that the service is mashed up from a number of sources. Secondly, the content presented may not be delivered by the content originator. Furthermore, the sourced content may be altered or extended during the mashup process. Considering this problem further, does the body who modifies or augments the content assume entire liability for all the repurposed content, including all accuracies and inaccuracies?

This paper is an extended version of earlier work that appears in [4], in particular, providing an implementation scenario. In this paper we consider that the accountability issue in mashup services is a broader and more complex theme when compared to nonrepudiation in an eCommerce transaction. We propose a framework that includes the service or content creator as well as the new owner of the resulting mashed-up service. While accountability issues may not be fully addressable with the current technology, we believe that the first step towards enabling accountability in mashup services is to add more disclosure, trust, and undeniability. This includes identities of all the parties involved and traceability in service composition. We also suggest that the concepts of involved parties and roles are essential in the service ontology model, such as in the Ontology Web Language for Web Services (OWL-S) model [5].

Given that accountability in mashup has not been treated rigorously before, we view the main contributions of this paper as follows.

(1) The underlying mashup accountability issues in practice are analysed with a formal definition for accountability in mashup solutions provided.

(2) A framework and ontology are proposed to model accountability in mashup environments.

(3) An implementation scenario is outlined that applies these methods in practice.

Using these methods, it is hoped that more effective accountability solutions can be prepared on the basis of our framework and model. The remainder of this paper is structured as follows. Section 2 provides background information on the mashup paradigm and related work in the current literature in accountability. In Section 3 we suggest a definition for accountability to address the additional requirements of mashup services. This is followed by a framework and ontology that may be used to model accountability. In Section 5, we illustrate how the framework and ontology can be applied in an implementation scenario. Finally, we summarize our results and observations, discussing areas of further work.

2. Related Work

2.1. Overview of Mashup Services. The term mashup originates from the practice of mixing song samples from two or more sources to produce a new sound track. In the context of the Internet, mashups are websites or applications that combine content from more than one source into an integrated application. This is generally achieved by using third party content provider application programming interfaces (APIs) or open technologies, for instance, Ajax and PHP, and syndicated feeds such as RSS or ATOM. In addition, since the content may be obtained from several sources, intermediate

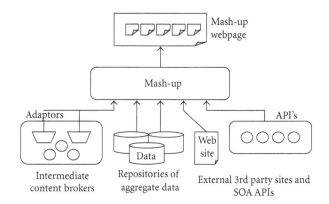

FIGURE 1: Mashup services.

businesses have emerged that act as content brokers. These intermediaries provide access to several content sources from 3rd parties and also supply functions to support the mashup process.

Based on the concept of service composition in Service-Oriented Architecture (SOA), mashup provides flexible and dynamic services with rich experience. This technology also enables a dynamic form of service reusability in contrast to the traditional method of static "cut and paste" reusability. However, since mashup involves the aggregation of another party's content into some new service or application, a number of legal issues are introduced [2]. When legal issues arise, accountability will become the critical concern for the parties involved.

Figure 1 illustrates the fundamental concepts in Web 2.0 mashups, where data and content are drawn from a range of sources to produce a new aggregated content or service. For example, the content may be drawn from local data repositories, from existing local and external web pages, accessed via SOA-based APIs, and from intermediate content brokers.

While mashup applications and services are growing at a rapid rate, currently they appear to be applied in nonmission critical services and are offered to the internet consumer largely as free services. In practice, legal responsibilities are generally avoided by the content provider disclaiming all warranties and liabilities [2].

More recently, industry leaders are accepting mashup as an enterprise tool to enable the creation of so-called situational applications. These types of applications solve business problems such as inventory management, sales, and marketing information management [6]. This emerging approach has been termed "enterprise mashup" and several enterprise tools have been released [7]. Enterprise mashup may be viewed as a Web 2.0 technology that builds upon the flexibility offered by SOA, and having a requirement for increased security.

Although enterprise mashup services hold great promise in delivering a flexible SOA solution in a business context, the lack of accountability in current mashup solutions may render this ineffective in the business environment. As such, as more enterprises embrace this technology in building IT solutions, the issue of accountability will manifest as a key concern for the service stakeholders.

2.2. Related Work on Accountability. The meaning of the term accountability appears to vary considerably and is dependant upon the context. Traditionally the topic of accountability has attracted much interest with focus on the eCommerce transaction. According to Kailar, accountability is "the property whereby the association of a unique originator with an object or action can be proved to a third party" [8]. The definition implies nonrepudiation in an eCommerce transaction. Kailar also proposes a framework for the analysis of communication protocols that require accountability [8, 9].

Bhattacharya and Paul assert that while a digital signature can provide help in enabling accountability in two direct communication nodes, it cannot fully address the accountability issues in multihop message due to the sender's ambiguity problem [10].

In [11], the scope of accountability is broadened to represent the ownership of the responsibility to meet requirements in an end-to-end business process. The authors propose "Accountability Centered Approach" (ACA) for business process engineering. The ACA approach suggests iterative decomposition of accountability to appropriate levels and mapping of subaccountabilities into activities.

A 3D approach in accountability modelling (detect, diagnose, and defuse) is proposed in [12] to discover and eliminate the root cause of problems when violations of service level agreement occur in business processes. The approach adopts Bayesian network reasoning for root cause analysis and service reputation model to address problematic web services.

While existing research on accountability helps traditional eCommerce application and SOA business applications, the issue of accountability in service mashup has not been treated in the literature. In addition, Gerber reviews the implications of using mashups and points out a number of legal issues [2]. This includes copyright misuse, trademark violations, false advertising, contract law issues, patent infringement, warranty, and the rights and privacy of individuals. The author also observes that these legal issues require consideration prior to design or implementation of mashup applications. These issues further motivate the need to address accountability for enterprise mashup services.

Eriksén comprehensively explores the notion of accountability for information and communication technologies [13]. The author cites a general definition of the term accountability as follows: "responsible for giving an account (as of one's acts), answerable," or "capable of being accounted for" [13, 14]. From the analysis of three key articles, the author observes that a common theme prevails in software engineering, which is the characteristic of "making visible and accountable," and also poses the question of "accountability for whom?" These observations further support the notion that accountability for mashup service has a requirement to disclose roles, responsibilities, and current transaction state. Furthermore, Johnson and Mulvey analyze relationships and responsibilities outside the developed IT systems [15].

They focus upon the accountability of system designers with respect to clients, users, and those affected by decision systems, prompting the question "are system designers responsible for the outcomes that result from use of their systems?" Our work addresses visibility through disclosure and identifies for whom the accountability is intended for, with defined roles. In addition, the responsibility aspect is also treated as a key element that requires consideration in accountability.

3. Definition of Accountability

In [3], it is suggested that the term "accountability" is an often used word with no common definition that can be found. The special interest group authors [3] also conduct extensive research of the literature and have provided a definition of accountability in the context of service performance, see Box 1.

We observe that this definition requires strengthening in the multiparty scenario such as mashup service environments. In addition to nonrepudiation, managing trust is also important for entities to collaborate [16]. Moreover, we wish to strengthen this definition with nonrepudiation and trust with one or multiple entities.

In moving towards a definition, we first propose that the essence of accountability involves four elements from an IT perspective, refer to Figure 2. In the original definition of Box 1 a person, group, or organisation can be translated to the concept of identity, whereas execution of authority implies the concept of role. According to Certo, responsibility is an obligation that someone "accepts" and is not allowed to delegate or pass on to someone else [17]. Accepting implies that there is some form of agreement in place. "Answering" and "reporting" relate to disclosure. Assuming liability for results requires a way to clearly demonstrate who has done what. The term assuming liability may be viewed as ambiguous, and considering that trust may vary considerably in a multiparty environment, this needs to be strengthened in order to remove plausible deniability, (i.e., introducing nonrepudiation).

The elements of Figure 2 involve the identity of the involved party, the role the party plays, and the agreed responsibilities in the form of contract, agreement, or signed-off requirements. The last element is the performance outcome, the evidence of who has done what.

We now use a mashup example to demonstrate these accountability elements, see Table 1. In the scenario, Entity B offers a security trading platform to allow their customers to trade various securities globally. It has contracts with different real-time financial data providers to provide price data, which is fed into a charting application provided by a service provider to produce price charts. For a particular trading transaction, customer Alice initiates the trade request with Entity B. This is based on the pricing chart provided by Entity C's charting service, with real-time price input from Entity D.

Using this IT services example, properties of accountability also imply the following:

Accountability refers to the obligation a person, group, or organization assumes for the execution of authority and/or the fulfillment of responsibility. This obligation includes the following:
(i) answering—providing an explanation or justification—for the execution of that authority and/or fulfillment of that responsibility,
(ii) reporting on the results of that execution and/or fulfillment, and
(iii) assuming liability for those results.

Box 1: Accountability for performance.

TABLE 1: Accountability roles in practice.

Identity	Role	Responsibility	Outcome
Alice	Trade requestor	Enter code and bid price. Provide funds for purchase.	The request accepted by Entity B.
Entity B	Trade provider	Display result page with data from Entity C and D. Execute trade requested. Pay Entity C and D fees due.	The trade is executed. Fund transferred from Alice's account.
Entity C	Charting service provider	Provide correct charted pricing indicators.	Chart is displayed and the fee is received from Entity B.
Entity D	Real-time price provider	Provide real-time pricing with integrity.	Data feed is provided and receive fee from B.

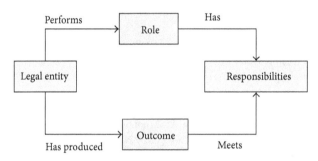

FIGURE 2: Accountability Elements.

(i) clear disclosure of the roles, responsibilities, and transaction status by all parties;

(ii) each party dutifully carry out their obligations;

(iii) there exists readily available evidence of the services rendered;

(iv) the involved parties cannot repudiate services rendered.

These properties reenforce the need for trust and nonrepudiation. However, in a legal sense, an automated IT system is not a legal entity that is accountable. Rather, it is the person, group of people, or company which is legally accountable. In the context of multiple entities involved in a mashup service, we now provide a more formal definition for accountability by extending the definition in [3].

In [3], responsibility is the obligation to perform, while accountability is the liability that one assumes for ensuring that an obligation to perform is fulfilled [3, 18]. In addition, the term authority is the right to act without prior approval from higher management and without challenge from managing peers [3, 18]. The authors point out that authority is assigned, while responsibility is delegated. This implies a

top-down decomposition of authority. Given the bottom-up method of building mashup services, this definition may not strictly apply. Rather, responsibility and authority must be sought and agreed upon between all peer content or service providers, rather than delegated. As pointed out in [17], responsibility is an obligation that is accepted; hence we observe that agreement should be sought. Finally, trust may be established among peers through evidence based on historical behavior and past interactions [16]. Considering these points, we outline the extended definition, by strengthening the definition with multiparty trust and nonrepudiation, making this binding to several parties, see Box 2.

This definition is applicable to both the multiparty service environment (such as mashup) as well as the single party service provider. We also note that the last point of this definition uses the term trusted which also implies that all entities are authenticated. Hence, the accountable service provider would naturally maintain some form of a binding registrar that identifies the subordinate accountabilities present. In order to satisfy this, the approach in [11] would seem to naturally satisfy this condition.

In light of the example and the objective to strengthen the term accountability for the broader context of multiple parties, we observe these additional properties.

(i) Trust: authentication of identities and agreement of accountability between all entities with evidence of behavior.

(ii) Nonrepudiation: undeniable liability with full disclosure (evidence).

4. Service Accountability Framework

Building upon the definitions in this previous section, we now propose a framework, as a metamodel and ontology, for modeling solutions in accountability for the mashup domain.

Accountability in services refers to the obligation that several persons, groups, or organizations assume for the execution and fulfillment of a service. This obligation includes:

(i) Answering, providing an explanation or justification, for the execution of that authority and/or fulfilment of that responsibility;

(ii) Full disclosure on the results of that execution and/or fulfillment;

(iii) Undeniable liability for those result (non-repudiation); and

(iv) Obtaining trusted agreement of accountability from all entities involved in the service, who in turn are bound to the obligations set out above.

Box 2: Accountability for multiple parties.

The metamodel focuses upon the roles and responsibilities from an information systems perspective and is intended for IT developers. The ontology focuses upon the liabilities and agreements aspect of the definition which is useful to establish the contractual terms and definition between the respective parties.

The current literature in IT has placed much focus on the identity and performance outcome elements, which are the most difficult issues to address as that involves trust and nonrepudiation. Security frameworks such as PKI alone cannot address the issues of trust in this computing environment, rather a robust security process framework and security protocol are necessary [19, 20]. As pointed out in [10], digital signatures by themself do not solve the nonrepudiation issue in a multiple party environment due to the sender ambiguity problem (i.e., a party can deny receiving a message by accusing the nonperformance of the intermediary node).

While the identity and performance outcome are essential elements in the accountability framework, the role and responsibility elements are equally important. In fact, we argue that disclosure on the role and responsibility elements is the first step towards an accountability solution. This is because without a clear understanding of the roles and responsibilities by each involved party, the outcome and entity accountable can be disputed.

In a mashup service scenario, the service requester may send a request to a mashup service provider, who in turn forwards the request to the source service provider(s), before aggregating this into a new form for presentation. The issue to observe is that the original service requester may not know the identity of the original service providers. On the other hand, the original service provider is also not aware how their content may be used by the mashup service provider. This motivates the need to find an approach to enable disclosure of roles and responsibilities in mashup services, especially for the enterprise mashup services environment, that are mutually acceptable to all parties involved, whether directly or indirectly. For instance, source content providers may have restrictions on how their content may or may not be used.

We propose a framework for modeling the behavior of mashup services based on SOA and hence briefly visit the fundamentals of this archetype. It is commonly agreed that SOA is an architectural style that involves a triangular relationship amongst three entities: service requester, service provider, and the service registry [21, 22], see Figure 3.

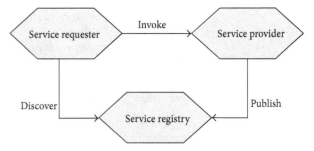

FIGURE 3: SOA Architectural Style and Actors.

While the model captures the essence of the service-oriented architectural model, it may fall short on enabling accountability in service-oriented architectures in the mashup service environment. For instance, this does not address the roles of multiple parties and the associated responsibility of disclosure and nonrepudiation.

In a mashup context, it is important to note that there are multiple service providers involved. There is also the introduction of service source as a separate entity to the provider, although, in some cases the service provider is the same entity as the service source. In practice, the service provider may engage several external content source parties to participate in constructing the service. In this situation, the service provider relies upon the source for accuracies of supplied content. As suggested in [2], there are a number of legal issues that need to be considered prior to developing mashup applications. As such, both the service provider and source are required to assume responsibility to ensure that the mashup service complies with the intended application (and defined terms and conditions).

Disclosure of roles and responsibility, to a large extent, can be enabled by rich service metadata and facilitated by functions provided by the service broker; rich service metadata means adding semantics to allow machine interpretation and reasoning. Currently, the registry (UDDI) provides service metadata in terms of business entities, taxonomy, and reference to service information. The registry is a dynamic name binding service that is syntax based [23]. However, in mashup several sources require identification and these may need to be trusted sources in an accountability sense. We wish to enable semantic meaning, as in OWL-S [23], and suggest a more sophisticated role to facilitate trust by enabling richer metadata to capture aspects such as

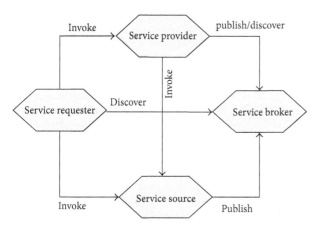

FIGURE 4: Mashup role responsibility.

traceability of service composition and responsibilities for several parties. Using this extended metadata, the service request may be appropriately associated with source content that addresses both the requirement for content and the need for accountability. In some cases, untrusted content will suffice; in other situations such as enterprise mashup full accountability will be necessary.

4.1. Roles and Responsibilities Metamodel. Based upon the previous discussions, we argue that the two identified roles, service requester and service provider, do not adequately represent all the roles involved in mashup service interactions. We now propose a model to depict these relationships. The revised model is shown in Figure 4. This is composed of the additional roles: service source and service broker. The service registry is still implied in this model, residing with the service broker.

Note that the service provider is a special type of role in the mashup environment which plays as both the requester and provider at the same time. The service provider will draw upon several internal and external sources and provide a resultant mashup page to the service requester. When sourcing content from a broker or service source, the provider acts as the requester. The service source publishes a single or discrete set of (common) content sources that may be accessed directly by the service requester or can be built upon and merged with other content source by a mashup service provider.

As pointed out in [2], new intermediary businesses have emerged that aggregate and broker content from several sources, in essence becoming a one stop shop of various content sources for mashup service providers. The broker supplies content to a service provider who is in turn able to mashup and repurpose the content for a service requester. This means that the service requester may discover services from the broker and invoke this from a service provider. Both the service source and broker publish their available services.

The service broker provides several additional benefits: as a trusted brokering agent (notary for unknown sources), monitoring (audit trail and evidence) to address the disclosure and nonrepudiation requirements, rating functions, and

managing a combined registry and repository for multiple sources. Hence, the service broker role can be further refined into detailed roles based on these intermediary functions performed, see Figure 5. The service requester in SOA does not necessarily imply that the entity is a user. This actually refers to the client of the service, which may be another application service or software agent. In an enterprise environment, the participant role in SOA normally represents an organization or party.

The enhanced role interaction model caters for both mashup and traditional service oriented architectures. This helps to understand and define the roles and responsibilities in service metadata. Thus the involved parties and their roles and responsibilities can be discovered and interpreted at runtime and therefore achieve the purpose of disclosure. This model is useful to information systems developers, helping them to identify roles (entities) and responsibilities in an accountable mashup services solution.

4.2. Liabilities and Obligations Ontology. The previous section focused on the roles and responsibilities in a mashup environment, outlining a model from an information systems perspective. This section models the liabilities and obligations from a legal and contractual perspective. This will assist in preparing the engagement basis and contract documents, by identifying the legal entities and artifacts that require consideration when preparing agreements to ensure accountability.

The proposed high-level accountability ontology is illustrated in Figure 6. In this ontology framework, a person or organization is a legal entity that has an identity. A legal entity enters into agreement with other legal entities. The agreement embodies rights and obligations. Rights entail considerations and also imply entitlement for damage if considerations are not met. The obligation sets out the requirements that need to be delivered and penalties if the requirements are not met.

Assigned with the required authority, the legal entity (Figure 6) takes some role, which executes tasks to deliver the requirements. In the context of accountability, the task class has two subclasses, one is service task which provides the intended service; the other is the accountability task which includes disclosure of authority, outcome, and evidence.

OWL-S is the commonly accepted web services ontology language that provides a core set of markup language constructs to describe web service in an unambiguous, machine interpretable form [24]. Thus it will be a natural approach to use those constructs to define the accountability elements in the service metadata. Using the general accountability model in Figure 6, we combine the high level service property constructs from OWL-S [4, 23] (service class and then its property classes: service profile, service model, and service grounding) to address the mashup environment. The extended accountability ontology framework is thus illustrated in Figure 7.

In the context of enterprise mashup environment, a legal entity enters into an agreement with other legal entities in order to participate in a service arrangement through web service interactions. The agreement enables the legal entity to assume a specific web service role to fulfill the obligations

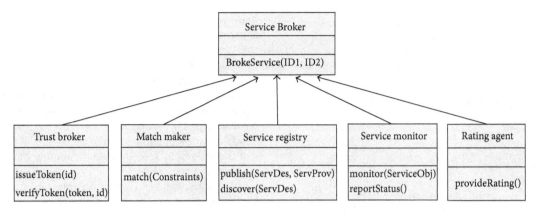

FIGURE 5: Expanded roles and responsibilities.

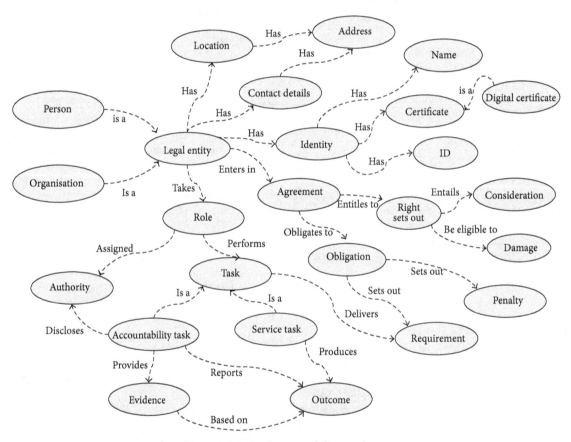

FIGURE 6: General accountability ontology.

while receiving the considerations. As illustrated in Figure 4, the specific web service role can be service requester, service source, service provider, and service broker. This role will carry out tasks to deliver the requirements setout within the obligations. The role performs a task which has two aspects: one is the normal web service and the other is the accountability task. The accountability task includes disclosure and reporting. Disclosure in this context means disclosure of service metadata, providing evidence of the service outcome. Service metadata may include identities of the involved legal entities, roles that they play, reference to the service agreement, and reference to the original content in the

case of mashup service. Service agreement includes terms and conditions of the service.

5. Implementation Scenario

In this section, we demonstrate how to apply the accountability framework and ontology during the development lifecycle of a mashup solution. The example scenario involves a travel agent intending to develop a website that provides travel booking services to online customers. The site will mash up mapping data from a 3rd party together with travel location information in order to present tour routes and destinations

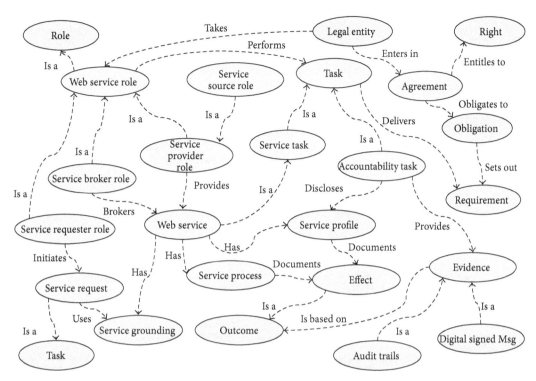

FIGURE 7: Mashup accountability ontology.

on a consolidated map. The metamodel will assist during the software development lifecycle in identifying the roles and responsibilities. The ontology will assist in the preparation of contracts and agreements between the various entities.

5.1. Roles and Responsibilities in Solution Development.

A customer accessing the website is able to select a desired travel plan and confirm a booking. The site will automatically book the air tickets and hotels through the mashed-up APIs provided by independent external airline and hotel businesses. Finally, the solution will also include an electronic commerce transaction to accept payments. Figure 8 illustrates the source and method by which these individual services are pulled together to produce an enterprise mashup service.

The first step in the analysis is to identify the roles and responsibilities associated with each participating entity in the mashup service. During architecture and design, these roles and responsibilities are expanded and mapped to design components, which are subsequently implemented in software. These lifecycle phases are now described.

5.1.1. Requirement Gathering: Allocating Roles and Responsibilities.

Using the roles and responsibilities metamodels from Figures 4 and 5, the mashup service environment is systematically analyzed to identify the specific roles, responsibilities, and expected outcomes for each entity participating in the solution. We conduct an analysis on the service requester, in this case a customer as an example (in other scenarios this may be another external entity).

The service requester has a service invocation relationship with the service provider and indirectly with the service

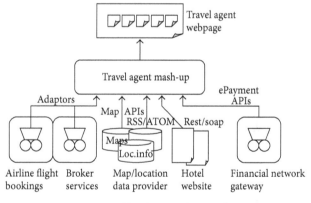

FIGURE 8: Travel booking mashup application.

source (3rd party provider). In this example, there is no need for additional discovery interaction with the service broker as this is managed by the service provider on behalf of the service requester. Based on these interactions, it is necessary for the service requester to supply correct personal information to reserve a booking and ensure that sufficient funds are available to complete the initial transaction booking. Using the metamodel, a similar analysis is conducted for the remaining entities in this scenario. This process will yield an initial high-level accountability model. The completed analysis is shown in Table 2.

5.1.2. Solution Architecture and Design Stage.

The accountability requirements can impose a burden on implementation for the project team. Some key decisions that system

TABLE 2: Accountability model in travel agent mashup solution.

Entity	Role	Responsibility	Outcome
Customer	Service requester	(i) Provide correct personal information for booking. (ii) Provide sufficient funds upon booking confirmation.	Booking and payment submitted.
Travel agent	Mashup service provider	(i) Provide the overall travel booking functionality. (ii) Conform to service source terms and conditions.	Requests submitted to all service sources. Booking receipt provided to customer.
Mapping provider	Service source	(i) Provide map service. (ii) Adhere to service level agreement.	Map service provided.
Location provider	Service source	(i) Provide location information. (ii) Adhere to service level agreement.	Location service provided.
Airline provider	Service source	(i) Provide ticket booking service. (ii) Adhere to service level agreement	Flight ticket booked and receipt provided.
Hotel provider	Service source	(i) Provide hotel booking service. (ii) Adhere to service level agreement.	Hotel booked and receipt provided.
ePayment provider	Service source	(i) Provide payment service. (ii) Adhere to service level agreement.	Travel agent and service sources receive payment.

TABLE 3: Accountability requirements.

Interaction scenario	Accountability requirement
Customer ↔ travel agent	(i) Mutual authentication between customer and travel agent. (ii) Disclose traceability in service composition and the up-to-date booking status upon request. (iii) Provide tamper proof evidences on booking transactions upon request.
Travel agent ↔ mapping service Travel agent ↔ location provider Travel agent ↔ fight provider Travel agent ↔ hotel Travel agent ↔ eCommerce	(i) Mutual authentication between travel agent and the external service sources. (ii) Ensure integrity of the service source. This implies fulfillment of the requirements in the terms and conditions of the service source, ensuring the service providers' copyright and trademarks are not breached. (iii) Service source's reputation is tracked and measured against the agreed quality of the services. . (iv) Provide tamper proof evidences on service transactions upon request.

designers will make during architecture and design revolve around what to leverage from in-house capability, versus what is provided by external service brokers. We analyze this perspective.

Considering the expanded roles and responsibilities the metamodel (Figure 5) highlights the various service broker roles that provide a different accountability capability. For instance, the travel agent is able to use a rating agent to evaluate and track the reputation of the service source. Alternatively, it may engage an external service dynamically to perform this task, reducing the technical complexity of the solution for the travel. This also implies that it will be necessary for service brokers to provide certain accountability capabilities.

Using the initial high-level roles and responsibility identified in Table 2, we now illustrate the expanded accountability requirements for each interaction scenario (Table 3) to address the issues of trust, integrity, disclosure, and nonrepudiation.

5.1.3. Solution Implementation. In the following, we assume the use of a modeling tool such as the control case [25] to capture and expand the accountability requirements listed in Tables 2 and 3. This may then be machine interpreted during solution implementation.

Broadly speaking, there are two categories of requirements identified in Table 3. The first consists of the obligations that form part of the agreement between the different parties. The second category consists of policies that one entity must comply with in order to consume the service provided by the other party. Examples of the first category of requirements are the terms and conditions of the mapping service source, quality of service (QoS) in service level agreements (SLA), and the travel agent's obligation to provide a booking receipt to the customer upon booking confirming. Together with the ontology, these are used to prepare agreements (see Section 5.2). Conversely, ePayment requirements for an authentication scheme, encryption technologies, and digital signature protocols are examples of the second category of requirements.

```
<wsag:ServiceDescriptionTerm wsag:Name="submitBooking"
     wsag:ServiceName="TravelBooking"/>
     <wsag:GuaranteeTerm wsag:Name="Receipt">
     <wsag:ServiceScope>
          <wsag:ServiceName>TravelBooking</wsag:ServiceName>
     </wsag:ServiceScope>
   <wsag:ServiceLevelObjective>supplied</wsag:ServiceLevelObjective>
   </wsag:GuaranteeTerm>
```

ALGORITHM 1: WS-Agreement source.

```
<wsp:Policy          xmlns:wsp=="http://schemas.xmlsoap.org/ws/2004/09/policy"
     xmlns:wsse="http://schemas.xmlsoap.org/ws/2002/12/secext">
     <wsp:ExactlyOne>
      <wsp:All>
          <wsse:SecurityToken>
          <wsse:TokenType>wsse:x509v3</wsse:TokenType>
          </wsse:SecurityToken>
      <wsse:EncryptedParts>
              <wsse:Body />
      </wsse:EncryptedParts>
      <wsse:SignedParts>
              <wsse:Body />
      </wsse:SignedParts>
      </wsp:All>
     </wsp:ExactlyOne>
</wsp:Policy>
```

ALGORITHM 2: WS-Policy source.

WS-Agreement [26] may be used to specify the first category of requirements while WS-Policy framework may be used to specify the second category of requirements. These specifications are designed to enable a service provider to advertise the capabilities that form the basis of an agreement. WS-Agreement also enables a requester to negotiate an agreement with the service for a specified duration; furthermore the agreement can be monitored for compliance in runtime [27]. An example of XML source output of the WS-Agreement for the travel agent's obligation of providing booking receipt is shown in Algorithm 1.

The second category of requirements can generally be expressed in a domain specific policy assertion language and may be attached to the service endpoint through the WS-Policy framework. Algorithm 2 is an example of the ePayment requirements for authentication, encryption and digital signature specified using WS-Policy.

5.2. Preparing Agreements for Accountability. We now describe how the ontology may be used to assist in the preparation and negotiation of contracts and agreements between the various entities involved in the travel agent mashup website project. Some key artifacts include the statement of work (SOW) signed between the travel agent and the IT project delivery team and several agreements between the travel agent and external parties acting as a

service or content sources. Moreover, the SOW determines the functionality to be provided by the website, the roles, and responsibility for delivering those capabilities and thus sets the basis for all other contracts.

5.2.1. Traditional versus Mashup Agreements. Differing from the traditional IT projects, the mashup project presents extra complexity in the area of accountability. The general accountability ontology defined in Figure 6 and the mashup accountability ontology defined in Figure 7 can assist the project team to prepare an SOW that suitably addresses the accountability issue by identifying accountability elements such as entities, roles, responsibilities, and expected outcome in the service arrangement. One important observation to make is that the ontology outlines the need for accountability tasks associated with each service task. The accountability tasks include disclosing authorities, keeping evidences of the service, and reporting service outcome. In this way, the accountability tasks can be categorized as a form of nonfunctional requirements in IT terms, which can then be reflected in the work breakdown structure, service level agreements, pricing, and the service contract with service source or service broker.

A further observation is that the ontology highlights the multiple roles involved in delivering the web services. This means that an SOW for a mashup solution will differ

```
<profile:serviceParameter>
        <profile:serviceParameterName>
                Type_of_Role
        </profile:serviceParameterName>
        <profile:sParameter>
                Mashup Service Provider
        </profile:sParameter>
        </profile:serviceParameterName>
        <profile:serviceParameterName>
                Invoked Service Source
        </profile:serviceParameterName>
        <profile:sParameter rdf:resource=https://hotel.com/
                               OnLineBooking/"/>
        </profile:serviceParameterName>
</profile:serviceParameter>
```

ALGORITHM 3: OWL-S service parameter extension.

from the traditional SOW. In general, the traditional SOW is only required to specify roles and responsibilities of two parties, the project owner and the client (contracts with subcontractors are addressed by additional SOWs). This tenet is supported by Martin, who defines an SOW as "*a narrative description of the products and services to be supplied to the client and the needs and requirements of the contractor to deliver such products and services properly under the contract*" [28]. However, in a mashup case, the SOW definition needs to be broadened to include the roles and responsibilities of all the involved parties including the client, contractor who develops the website, and various service sources. This is because the product and services of the mashup site are not supplied by a single party, rather, by several entities in realtime.

5.2.2. Identifying and Enforcing Accountability. Involved parties are able to apply the ontology to facilitate discovery of accountability statements and clauses. For example, when specifying the hotel booking service within an SOW, based on the ontology in Figure 7, the analyst knows that the hotel operator assumes the web service source role, who performs a service task through a hotel booking web service. A web service has service grounding (information for accessing the service), service process (service logic) and a service profile (service descriptions and service effect). As each service task has associated accountability task, example of accountability statements for the hotel operator could be defined as follows.

(i) Hotel operator is accountable for disclosing the booking service effect and service description metadata that is necessary to locate and access the web service.

(ii) Hotel operator is accountable for providing evidence of the service rendered upon request from the travel agent.

The supplied evidence may be tamper-proof audit trails, service level agreement (SLA) monitoring records, or digitally signed messages. The content and format of the evidence is to be clearly defined in the SOW or in the detailed technical design document referenced by the SOW. Using the ontology in this way prompts the analyst to consider these aspects and include the relevant statements.

Next, the analyst will review the accountability considerations for the travel agent. This is considered in the context of the service provider role, which supplies the travel booking service via the mashup web site. Referring to the ontology, the service provider role is a super type of service source role. In addition to the accountability tasks discussed above, these ontology elements imply that the travel agent is also accountable for disclosing the information in service composition, such as the service profile of all web services provided by the service source roles. The linkage is clearly seen in the ontology as service provider role → web service → service profile. In the example scenario, the roles include the hotel operator, airline, map service, and location information providers.

The mashup service also requires a valid contract with the consumer. This can be normally achieved by notices and "click-through" agreements when a customer registers with the site. Notices and click-through agreements satisfy the basic requirements necessary to establish legally enforceable commercial transactions [29]. The notices and click-through agreements need to be documented as part of the functionality provided by the website in the SOW.

Examining the consumer role in Figure 7, it is clear that a service requester initiates a service request. Based on the ontology, a service request is a special task. A task delivers certain requirements, which are set out in some form of obligations in a client-supplier agreement that stipulates clearly the terms and conditions of the service provided. To hold the consumer accountable in the travel booking service scenario, the agreement is provided online and must be agreed upon before using the service. Upon accepting the agreement, the consumer will be held accountable for the service request. This may be achieved through the consumer's obligation to provide correct payment details and evidence of payment, such as a valid account, payment card, or eCommerce transaction.

To ensure that accountability is upheld in the mashup services, it is necessary that the SOW stipulate several additional areas. This includes privacy, copyright or trademark laws, and the remaining accountability tasks performed by the relevant parties. Where there is no explicit regulation to be applied, but obligations from involved parties are expected, then a valid contract is required to ensure governance by common law. The ontology assists in this legal analysis by identifying the relevant roles, responsibilities, and service tasks.

6. Summary and Conclusions

As mashup technology enters into the mainstream enterprise business, accountability will emerge as a key requirement to be addressed. As pointed out in [2], a number of legal issues require consideration when using mashup solutions. We suggest that it will be increasingly important for mashup service oriented solutions to have an accountability mechanism builtin to facilitate trust and the resolution of the legal issues.

This paper builds upon existing theories by applying trust and nonrepudiation in a multiparty environment for defining accountability. Using this definition, we propose models that may be used by information systems developers to understand the roles and responsibilities that need to be accommodated in a mashup service solution. In addition, the liabilities and obligations are analyzed. The proposed ontology helps to define the various entities and artefacts involved in a mashup service. This can be used to assist in the preparation of agreements that are required between the various entities involved in a mashup service environment. This will also help to define the scope of accountability to be addressed and will further serve to define requirements of the information systems supporting the mashup service solution in order to meet disclosure requirements.

6.1. Further Work. In addition to developing accountability assertion policies that may be included within the WS-* frameworks, there are further extensions that may be studied. For instance, accountability information such as roles and service composition are currently not available in registry services. In other words, there is no information that advises whether the service being discovered is a mashup service. Nor are there details regarding the various service sources involved. An extension may be developed to supply this additional information to the service requester. This may be useful to assist in deciding if the service being discovered is of sufficient integrity (accountable and accurate) to suite the needs of the requester.

One suggested approach to address this requirement is by including the accountability metadata within the OWL-S service property; specifically one may use the *Service Parameter* property as an extension to add the accountability relevant elements into the service profile. Extending the example from Section 5, the sample XML source shown in Algorithm 3 shows the mashup service utilizing a hotel booking service from "hotel.com."

In addition to machine interpretation of the accountability roles and responsibilities, the proposed ontology may also be used to establish a common accountability vocabulary useful to developers and runtime interpretation. The ontology already contributes to the definition and preparation of agreements between the various parties, and extending the ontology for machine interpretation is an area of further work.

Furthermore, as the mashup services based on RESTful web services are becoming mainstream due to the simplicity and performance benefits that the lightweight architecture offers, inevitably we need to adopt RESTful web service semantic description standards to specify the accountability metadata. Another area of further work is using SAWSDL [30] to annotate accountability metadata for RESTful mashup services.

Acknowledgment

The authors would like to thank Yan Wang for his constructive feedback and helpful comments on thier earlier work on accountability in mashup services.

References

[1] T. O'Reilly, *What Is Web 2.0, Design Patterns and Business Models for the Next Generation of Software*, O'Reilly Media, 2005.

[2] R. S. Gerber, "Mixing it up on the web: legal issues arising from internet mashup," *Intellectual Property and Technology Law Journal*, vol. 18, no. 8, 2006.

[3] Performance-Based Management Special Interest Group, *The Performance-Based Management Handbook: Establishing Accountability for Performance*, vol. 3, Oak Ridge Associated Universities, 2001.

[4] J. Zou and C. J. Pavlovski, "Towards accountable enterprise mashup services," in *Proceedings of the IEEE International Conference on e-Business Engineering*, pp. 205–212, Hong Kong, China, October 2007.

[5] D. Martin, M. Burstein, J. Hobbs et al., "OWL-S Semantic Markup for Web Services. W3C Member Submission," 2004, http://www.w3.org/Submission/OWL-S/.

[6] A. Jhingran, "Enterprise information mashups: integrating information, simply," in *Proceedings of the 32nd International Conference on Very Large Data Bases (VLDB '06)*, pp. 3–4, Seoul, Korea, 2006.

[7] R. Smith and SOA, *Enterprise Mashup Services. Part 1: Real-World SOA or Web 2.0 Novelties?* SOA World Magazine, 2007.

[8] R. Kailar, "Reasoning about accountability in protocols for electronic commerce," in *Proceedings of the 1995 IEEE Symposium on Security and Privacy*, IEEE Computer Society, pp. 236–250, May 1995.

[9] R. Kailar, "Accountability in electronic commerce protocols," *IEEE Transactions on Software Engineering*, vol. 22, no. 5, pp. 313–328, 1996.

[10] S. Bhattacharya and R. Paul, "Accountability issues in multihop message communication," in *Proceedings of IEEE Symposium on Application-Specific Systems and Software Engineering and Technology*, pp. 74–81, Richardson, Tex, USA, March 1999.

[11] M. M. Tseng, J. S. Chuan, and Q. H. Ma, "Accountability centered approach to business process reengineering," in *Proceedings of the 31st Annual Hawaii International Conference on System Sciences*, vol. 4, pp. 345–354, January 1998.

[12] Y. Zhang, K. J. Lin, and T. Yu, "Accountability in service-oriented architecture: computing with reasoning and reputation," in *Proceedings of the IEEE International Conference on e-Business Engineering (ICEBE '06)*, pp. 123–131, Shanghai, China, October 2006.

[13] S. Eriksén, "Designing for accountability," in *Proceedings of the second Nordic conference on Human-computer interaction*, vol. 31 of *ACM International Conference Proceeding Series*, pp. 177–186, Aarhus, Denmark, 2002.

[14] *Webster's Ninth New Collegiate Dictionary*, Merriam-Webster, Chicago, Ill, USA, 1991.

[15] D. G. Johnson and J. M. Mulvey, "Accountability and computer decision systems," *Communications of the ACM*, vol. 38, no. 12, pp. 58–64, 1995.

[16] D. Huang and S. Bracher, "Towards evidence-based trust brokering," in *Proceedings of the 1st International Workshop on Value of Security through Collaboration*, pp. 43–50, September 2005.

[17] S. C. Certo, *Principles of Modern Management: Functions and Systems*, William C. Brown Publishers, Ames, Iowa, USA, 2nd edition, 1983.

[18] B. Frost, *Measuring Performance*, Fairway Press, 1998.

[19] C. Ellison and B. Schneier, "Ten risks of PKI: what you're not being told about public key infrastructure," *Computer Security Journal*, vol. 16, no. 1, pp. 1–7, 2000.

[20] B. Schneier, *Secrets & Lies, Digital Security in a Networked World*, John Wiley & Sons, New York, NY, USA, 2000.

[21] Z. Stojanovic and A. Dahanayake, Eds., *Service-Oriented Software System Engineering: Challenges and Practices*, IGI Global, 2005.

[22] K. J. Ma, "Web services: what's real and what's not?" *IEEE IT Professional*, vol. 7, no. 2, pp. 14–21, 2005.

[23] J. Luo, B. Montrose, A. Kim, A. Khashnobish, and M. Kang, "Adding OWL-S support to the existing UDDI infrastructure," in *Proceedings of the IEEE International Conference on Web Services (ICWS '06)*, pp. 153–160, Chicago, Ill, USA, September 2006.

[24] D. Martin, M. Burstein, O. Lassila, M. Paolucci, T. Payne, and S. McIlraith, "Describing web services using OWL-S and WSDL," DAML-S Coalition working document, 2003.

[25] Z. Joe and C. J. Pavlovski, "Modeling architectural non functional requirements: from use case to control case," in *Proceedings of the IEEE International Conference on e-Business Engineering (ICEBE '06)*, pp. 315–322, Shanghai, China, October 2006.

[26] A. Andrieux, K. Czajkowski, K. Keahey et al., "Web services agreement specification (WS-Agreement)," Grid Resource Allocation Agreement Protocol (GRAAP) Working Group, Open Grid Forum, 2005.

[27] B. Margolis and J. Sharpe, *SOA For the Business Developer: Concepts, BPEL, and SCA*, MC Press, 1st edition, 2007.

[28] M. Martin, "Statement of work: the foundation for delivering successful service projects," *PM Network*, vol. 12, no. 10, pp. 54–57, 1998.

[29] J. Matsuura, *Security, Rights, and Liabilities in E-Commerce*, Artech House, Norwood, Mass, USA, 2002.

[30] W3C, "Semantic annotations for WSDL and XML Schema," 2007, http://www.w3.org/TR/sawsdl.

8

How to Safely Integrate Multiple Applications on Embedded Many-Core Systems by Applying the "Correctness by Construction" Principle

Robert Hilbrich

Department Systems Architecture, Fraunhofer FIRST, Kekuléstraße 7, 12489 Berlin, Germany

Correspondence should be addressed to Robert Hilbrich, robert.hilbrich@first.fraunhofer.de

Academic Editor: Michael H. Schwarz

Software-intensive embedded systems, especially cyber-physical systems, benefit from the additional performance and the small power envelope offered by many-core processors. Nevertheless, the adoption of a massively parallel processor architecture in the embedded domain is still challenging. The integration of multiple and potentially parallel functions on a chip—instead of just a single function—makes best use of the resources offered. However, this multifunction approach leads to new technical and nontechnical challenges during the integration. This is especially the case for a distributed system architecture, which is subject to specific safety considerations. In this paper, it is argued that these challenges cannot be effectively addressed with traditional engineering approaches. Instead, the application of the "correctness by construction" principle is proposed to improve the integration process.

1. Introduction

Multicore processors have put an end to the era of the "free lunch" [1] in terms of computer power being available for applications to use. The "end of endless scalability" [2] of single-core processor performance appears to have been reached. Still, the currently available Multicore processors with two, four, or eight execution units—"cores"—indicate just the beginning of a new era in which parallel computing stops being a niche for scientist and starts becoming mainstream.

Multicore processors are just the beginning. With the amount of cores increasing further, *Multicores* become *many-cores*. The distinction between these two classes of parallel processors is not precisely defined. Multicore processors typically feature up to 32 powerful cores. Their memory architecture allows the usage of traditional shared memory programming model without suffering from significant performance penalties.

Many-core processors on the other hand comprise more than 64 rather simple and less powerful cores. With a increasing number of cores, a *scalable* on-chip interconnect between cores on the chip becomes a necessity. Memory access, especially to off-chip memory, constitutes a bottleneck and becomes very expensive. Therefore, traditional shared memory architectures and corresponding programming models suffer from significant performance penalties—unless they are specifically optimized. Comparing their raw performance figures, the approach of having many, but less powerful cores, outperforms processor architectures with less, but more powerful cores [2, 3]. Of course in reality, this comparison is not as clear cut. It largely depends on the software, which has to be able to tap the full performance potential of these chips.

Many-core processors with up to 100 cores on a single chip, such as the Tilera Tile GX family (http://www.tilera .com/products/processors/TILE-Gx_Family) are currently commercially available. However, in order to benefit from these processors, an application has to exhibit sufficient parallelism to "feed" all available cores. Applications with these properties are hard to find among general-purpose software, because most applications have been developed for a single-core processor model. Parallel computing led a niche existence with the exception of its usage in high-performance computing.

In this paper, it is argued that software-intensive embedded systems will benefit from a massively parallel hardware platform. In particular, a new generation of embedded devices will require the increased performance in combination with a small power envelope: *Cyber Physical Systems* [4, 5]. These systems represent a tight integration of computation and physical processes and emphasize the link to physical quantities, such as time and energy. With the environment being composed of many parallel physical processes, why should not embedded systems controlling it, tackle this task with a parallel hardware platform?

Still there is a considerable gap to cover before this vision can be turned into reality. Therefore, this paper looks into several approaches on how to adopt many-core processors in software-intensive embedded systems. In Section 2, several adoption scenarios are described and assessed. Section 3 focuses on the integration of multiple functions and the description of domain-specific trends and developments, which aid the adoption process. Constraints and requirements which have to be addressed when multiple functions are integrated on the same platform are discussed in Section 4. Traditional and state-of-practice integration concepts are described in Section 5. Their shortcomings for many-core processors are used to argue for more formalized approaches in the context of a multifunction integration in Section 6. A case study, current research, and conclusions are contained in Sections 7 and 8.

2. Many-Core Processor Adoption Scenarios

Homogeneous and heterogeneous many-core processors will constitute the dominant processor architectures for all software-intensive embedded systems requiring flexibility and performance. Therefore, the embedded systems engineering community has to develop ways to adopt these new platforms and exploit their capabilities. The new parallel hardware platform offers a new level of processing power in a small power envelope. It enables innovative embedded applications—especially in the shape of next-generation embedded systems which are deeply integrated into the physical processes of the environment—such as *Cyber-Physical Systems* [5].

However, current engineering practices and software architectures for embedded systems are not ready to adopt a massively parallel hardware platform just yet. Current system designs heavily rely on a single-processor model with a serialized execution of tasks. The execution order of tasks is often expressed as task priorities. This approach helps to ensure proper timing by giving exclusive access for a running task to the underlying hardware. If interrupts are disabled, tasks may run to completion without interference. Dynamic scheduling algorithms at run-time focus on assigning priorities to tasks, so that the most important task is selected for execution by a dispatcher component. Albeit the simplicity of the execution model, programmers still struggle to implement complex applications. This is especially the case when quality requirements, such as real-time behavior or functional safety, have to be satisfied. Many-core processors

raise the level of system complexity significantly by offering a parallel execution at run-time. With single-core processors already constituting an engineering challenge for certain applications, how should system engineers and integrators address the increased complexity of many-core processors?

A look on the state-of-practice in embedded systems engineering shows a considerable gap—that is, methodology and tools—that needs to be covered before many-core processors can be adopted in safety-critical domains. Although massively parallel systems have been extensively studied for high-performance computing, the research topic for the embedded domain remains: how to properly adopt massively parallel processors, so that the system performance is maximized and the required changes in legacy software are kept to a minimum. In this paper, this is referred to as the challenge of many-core adoption in embedded systems.

A migration to multi- and many-core processors will need to happen at some point in the future—especially for complex, software-intensive embedded systems. Simply, because there may be no more commercially available single-core processors on the market. Still, there is the chance of a sudden break-through in processor fabrication, which may allow to further increase the clock frequency beyond 5 GHz with only a moderate increase in power usage—thus avoiding the "power wall" [6]. However, at the time of writing, this appears to be unlikely [7]. Therefore, it is only sensible to look at possible multi- and many-core migration paths and analyze their effect on performance and the required changes in the software architecture.

2.1. "Single-Core" Approach. The most simple and straightforward adoption approach is to turn a many-core processor into a single-core processor by disabling all cores except one (see Figure 1). This allows to prolong the applicability of traditional engineering practices and experiences gained in previous projects. The impact on the software layer in terms of necessary changes to adapt to the new platform will be negligible, so that legacy code can be easily ported to the new architecture. For certification purposes, it may be necessary to prove that all remaining cores have been safely disabled so that no interferences at run-time are to be expected.

While this approach comes with a captivating simplicity, it is still a waste of resources, especially processing power, because parallel computing capabilities are not used. Therefore, the overall system performance is bounded by the single-thread performance offered. Given todays performance requirements, this may be sufficient. However, for the future, the single-thread performance will not increase significantly. Even worse, Borkar [7] argues that single-thread performance needs to *decrease* in the future in order to fit a potential 1000-core processor within a reasonable power envelope. Embedded applications may then get less performance in the future.

The "single-core approach" approach requires only minor software changes, but it lacks an *active and conscious migration* to a modern parallel processor architecture. It is a viable first step for specific application domains, for instance to gain a service history and experience for a specific

How to Safely Integrate Multiple Applications on Embedded Many-Core Systems by Applying the "Correctness by Construction" Principle

123

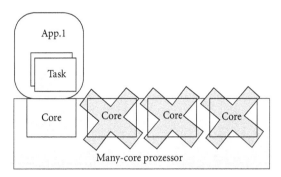

FIGURE 1: "Single-core" approach—disable all cores except one.

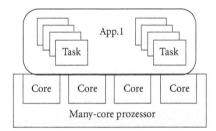

FIGURE 2: Use all cores run a single, parallelized application.

processor in noncritical areas. However, in the long run, the limited single-thread performance will prove to be a major obstacle in providing feature-rich applications.

2.2. Single Application on Multiple Cores. This approach tries to harvest the processing power of a many-core processor by parallelizing a single application running on a many-core processor (see Figure 2). This has a major impact on the software for the specific application. Depending on the application, data-parallel or function-parallel engineering patterns and libraries may help substantially in reducing the parallelization effort.

The impact on the entire system design, that is, the processor in the context of other processors and communication networks with regard to safety and reliability measures, is limited. From the perspective of a system design containing multiple electronic control units (ECUs), migrating to many-core processor within a single ECUs may even prove to be fully transparent—similar to changing the interior of a black box ECU. However, recertification will be necessary for the modified application. Depending on the criticality level, there is a considerable effort to be expected, as the software complexity rises significantly when a parallel execution is allowed.

Using multiple cores from a single application increases its performance and improves the overall processor utilization. Still, the speedup of parallel execution is governed by Amdahl's law [8]. It distinguishes between code to be executed in parallel and code to be executed sequentially. In Amdahl's model, the total execution time is the sum of the execution time of the parallel part and of the the sequential part. By adding more processors, the execution time of the parallel part can be reduced, because the work can be split among several processors. This reduces the total execution time and increases the performance. According to Amdahl's law, an application containing a parallel code portion of 95% and a sequential code portion of 5%, the potential speedup on a processor with 8000 cores in comparison to a single-core processor with the same clock speed is at most 20. It becomes apparent that the performance of the sequential part dominates the speedup. Still, it is the single-thread performance that matters.

With regard to typical embedded applications, a parallel code ratio of 95% seems to be rather unlikely. Most applications are essentially based on processing state machines or they are used in feedback and control loops. In both cases, the potential for parallel execution is rather limited. In this environment, a famous quote by Brooks comes to mind: "The bearing of a child takes nine months, no matter how many women are assigned" [9]. In certain embedded applications, such as digital signal processing, *data parallel* execution instead of *function parallel* execution may be used to increase the parallel portion and to better exploit the parallel performance.

The migration to a single-application spreading over several cores does not have a significant impact on the safety assessment for the electronic control unit containing the Multicore processor. In the context of an entire system architecture, the effects are negligible as the requirements for the implemented function do not change. However, the effort for the development and quality assurance of an application consisting of several task executing in parallel may increase significantly.

2.3. Multiple Applications on Multiple Cores. The discussion of the previous approach showed that the parallelism offered

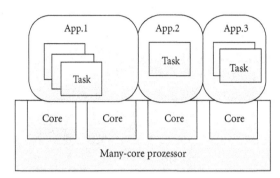

FIGURE 3: Integrate multiple, possibly parallelized applications.

within a single application will not be enough to exploit the potential of many-core processors. Consequently, higher levels of abstraction have to be analyzed for a potential parallel execution as well. The integration of multiple applications on a single many-core processor with each application potentially using multiple cores is a promising approach to harvest the parallel processing power of more than 100 cores on a single chip (see Figure 3).

While this approach offers the most benefits in terms of power and space savings, it is also very challenging throughout the engineering process. All applications need to be carefully analyzed with regard to their resource requirements and deployed to the new parallel hardware platform. Additionally, the entire system design—often consisting of multiple processors and communication networks—needs to be reevaluated as well. Going from two applications on separate single-core processors to the same applications running on a single processor increases the likelihood of interferences and potential fault propagation due to the use of shared resources. This effectively reduces the overall system reliability.

The consolidation of applications on fewer processors *naturally* has to be payed with an increased use of shared resources. In other words, it is the *intrinsic sharing of resources* that enable the much acclaimed benefits of many-core processors in the embedded domain in the first place.

Therefore, the impact on the certification effort is significant. As hardware-based isolation mechanisms between applications, such as dissimilar and incompatible network components, can no longer be used on a single processor, software-based isolation mechanisms have to be applied.

Fuchsen [10] describes necessary approaches to address the certification of multiple functions on Multicore processors in the avionics domain. In short, all "interference channels" have to be analyzed for the effects on the integrity of the isolation between applications. This is especially the case when applications with mixed criticality levels are to be integrated on the same processor.

With multiple applications executing in parallel and competing for the use of shared resources the visibility of the migration challenge being posed by this approach raises. Multiple development teams—at least one for each application—have to be coordinated in order to properly integrate all applications on the same processor *and*

satisfy quality requirements, especially real-time behavior and safety considerations. When teams are even located in separate organizational entities, that is, supplier and original equipment manufacturer (OEM), the integration of multiple application creates another challenge that has to be addressed explicitly.

As it was described in this section, there are various approaches to adopt many-core processors in embedded systems. They differ in migration costs and performance benefits. Each approach has its right to exist, so in the end the choice which approach to take depends on the need for more performance. Fortunately, all approaches are going towards exploiting a parallel execution on some level, so that a stepwise adoption appears to be a sensible choice.

3. Domain-Specific Trends for Embedded Software

Adopting many-core processors by consolidating multiple functions on a single processor is a significant engineering challenge. However, recent developments in the field of domain-specific software architectures clearly demonstrate a trend to address this challenge and ease the migration process. Still it must be noted, that these developments are predominantly a result of the need to reduce development costs for software-intensive embedded systems by requiring interoperability and increasing competition among suppliers. In the following, the avionics domain and the automotive domain will be used as an example to show that the measures taken to support interoperability also help to simplify many-core migration.

3.1. Avionics: Integrated Modular Avionics (IMA) and ARINC 653. Among the dominating trends in the aviation electronics domain (avionics) are increasing functional requirements, the demand for more computer-based systems and the need for a shorter time to market. In the past, avionics systems were based on heterogeneous *federated architectures*. A distinctive feature of these architectures is that each function has its own independent computer and network system—"*one function-one computer*". A major advantage of this approach is that there is fault-containment *by design*—due to the heterogeneity of the components used.

How to Safely Integrate Multiple Applications on Embedded Many-Core Systems by Applying the "Correctness by Construction" Principle

125

Federated architectures, however, exhibit significant drawbacks. First, there are many dedicated resources required, which raises costs for procurement, cooling, maintenance and also increases the space, weight and power (SWaP) requirements. And second, aircraft functionality is artificially separated into independent components with no global control or synchronization, thus rendering the implementation of complex functionality challenging and costly.

Driven by the economic considerations described above, the avionics domain is slowly transitioning from federated avionics architectures to an Integrated Modular Avionics architecture (IMA) [11]. IMA describes the concept of computing modules with standardized components and interfaces to hardware and software. Thus IMA constitutes a logically centralized and shared computing platform, which is physically distributed on the aircraft to meet redundancy requirements. This transition is motivated by the expected benefits of hosting a variety of avionics functions on a single platform—"multifunction integration." More precisely, IMA was developed to reduce space, weight, and power requirements and furthermore to reduce maintenance and certification costs by allowing *incremental* certification of applications with mixed criticality levels [12].

Despite these advantages, the use of common components in IMA architectures significantly increases the probability of common cause errors affecting a variety of aircraft functions. Therefore, federated architectures are still considered to represent the benchmark for fault containment [13].

To consolidate multiple avionics functions on a *single-core processor* and address the challenges introduced by intransparent fault propagation on shared resources, IMA requires the use of *software partitioning*. This is a concept to achieve fault containment in software, independent of the underlying hardware platform.

On a shared computing platform, such as IMA, faults may propagate from one application to another through shared resources, such as a processor, memory, communication channels, or I/O devices. Partitioning isolates faults by means of access control and usage quota enforcement for resources in software.

In avionics safety standards, this is referred to as *partitioning in time and space* [14, page 9]. *Spatial* partitioning ensures that an application in one partition is unable to change private data of another. It also ensures that private devices of a partition, for example, actuators, cannot be used by an application from another partition. *Temporal* partitioning on the other hand guarantees that the timing characteristics and the quality of service of an application, such as a worst case execution time, are not affected by the execution of an application in another partition.

The standardized software API that allows partitions to communicate with the operating system and other partitions is specified in the ARINC 653 standard [15]. It is referred to as APplication EXecutive (APEX) and its underlying terminology is illustrated in Figure 4, which also depicts the relationship between *tasks*, *partitions*, and *applications*, which implement avionic functions.

3.2. Automotive: AUTOSAR. In modern automobiles, the electronic and electric architectures (E/E architectures) are constantly growing to address steadily increasing functional requirements. It is not uncommon for these architecture to encompass over 80 electronic control units (ECU) in a heavily distributed system. These E/E architectures constitute the "nervous system" of modern vehicles.

Traditionally, the design of these architectures focused on ECUs and their role in the entire system. With more and more ECUs being integrated into a single E/E architecture, keeping track of the development became increasingly challenging and costly. At the same time, reusability and exchangeability become important features of embedded software to reduce development costs and vendor lock-in effects.

These challenges lead to the development of AUTOSAR (AUTomotive Open System ARchitecture), (http://autosar.org/), which is an open and standardized automotive software architecture. It is jointly developed by automobile manufacturers, suppliers, and tool developers and tries to pave the way for a paradigm shift. Automotive software should be developed in a function-oriented way—in sharp contrast to the traditional an ineffective ECU-orientation.

AUTOSAR is based on the basic concept of having a standardized *virtual function-bus* (VFB), which facilitates the integration of software components in an existing architecture. This approach significantly streamlines the development of distributed software and improves the manageability of the entire architecture. The realization of an VFB requires an abstraction from the underlying hardware and its communication networks.

The AUTOSAR architecture (Source: http://autosar.org/gfx/AUTOSAR_ECU_softw_arch_b.jpg) is depicted in Figure 5. The architectural part of AUTOSAR specifies a complete *basic software* layer as an *integration platform* for hardware-independent AUTOSAR software applications. Furthermore, AUTOSAR contains a description of software application programming interfaces (APIs) for typical automotive applications. It also defines a complete methodology for the configuration of the basic software and the integration of AUTOSAR software on an ECU.

In Revision 4.0, the use of *software partitioning* was added to AUTOSAR [16, pages 101–107]. According to the standard, partitions are used as "error containment regions" [16, page 103]. Their consistency with regard to spatial aspects (e.g., memory access violation) or temporal aspects (e.g., time budget violation) has to be ensured by the platform.

3.3. How Do These Trends Affect Many-Core Adoption? What can be learned from the trends and developments described above? First of all, it becomes obvious that the embedded industry is actively working towards the design of a system (e.g., an ECU or an IMA board) with *multiple* vendors supplying *different* functions running on the *same* platform with some form of fault containment. This is referred to as a *multitenant processor platform* based on software-partitions and time-sharing of resources. Furthermore, the entire system design often comprises of several distributed processors

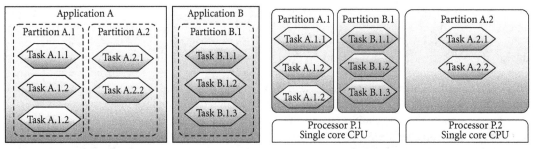

(a) Software architecture (logical view)   (b) Software and hardware mapping (mapping view)

FIGURE 4: ARINC 653 terminology: an *application* is composed of one or more *partitions*. Each partition contains one or more *tasks*, which may execute concurrently. A partition is statically mapped onto a *processor*.

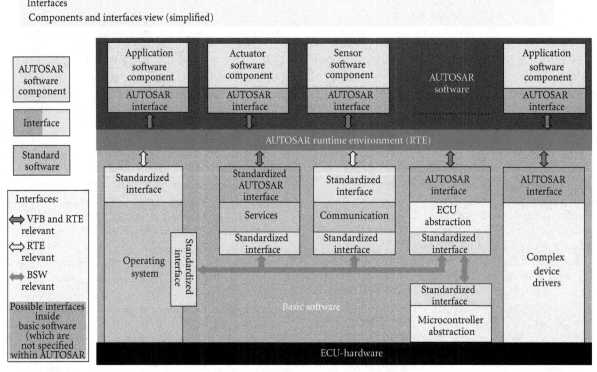

FIGURE 5: The AUTOSAR ECU software architecture.

being connected to each via communication buses. Therefore, it is crucial to design a single multitenant processor platform with respect to other platforms in the same system.

Of course, a multitenant processor platform requires some form of standardization with regard to the hardware and/or operating system layer. Therefore, specific software application programming interfaces (APIs) are mandatory to acquire access to hardware resources. These APIs can also be used to restrict and control the way a function may access the hardware—thus enforcing isolation between separate applications with different criticality levels.

These changes in the engineering process have been initially motivated by the need for increased flexibility and for reduced vendor lock-in effects in order to cut development and maintenance costs. At the same time, multi-tenant system designs significantly facilitate a migration to many-core processors. By using only a standardized set of API calls to

access system resources—instead of processor and operating system specific instruction sets—the software layer seems to be well prepared for a many-core processor environment—at least with regard to application-level parallelism.

This leads to a fundamental question for many-core adoption in software-intensive embedded systems: from the perspective of an application executing within a partition, where is the difference between having multiple partitions on a single-core platform with time-sharing and multiple partitions on a many-core platform allowing for true parallelism?

4. Software Requirements of Embedded Applications

To answer the previous question, it is necessary to take a look at the initial system requirements and compare these to

How to Safely Integrate Multiple Applications on Embedded Many-Core Systems by Applying the "Correctness by Construction" Principle

127

the expected system behavior for each of the aforementioned architectures.

Generally speaking, there are *functional requirements* and *quality requirements*. Functional requirements specify the functionalities that the system has to provide to its users [17, page 15]. Quality requirements on the other hand, define desired attributes of the system, such as performance or reliability [17, pages 15-16]. Software-intensive embedded systems are often used to control and monitor real-world processes so their effectiveness is not only determined by the computational correctness. Instead, quality requirements are often the *primary drivers* of the entire system architecture [18, pages 155-156].

Functional requirements are usually satisfied by the application code within a partition, so in order to asses the equivalence of partitions with time-sharing and partitions executing in parallel, the focus needs to be shifted to quality requirements. For safety-critical embedded systems, quality requirements usually refer to *timing* or *safety* attributes. In some cases, *security* attributes play an important role as well. Timing attributes often comprise of *deadlines* for specific tasks, which have to be met under *all* circumstances. This leads to the requirement of a fully *deterministic* system behavior. The system engineer must to be able to know what the system is doing at all times during the entire lifetime of the system.

Safety-related attributes on the other hand are concerned with the assurance that no human lives are endangered when the system is running. These attributes can be addressed with *run-time monitoring* in addition to *independence* and *redundancy* of resources. These patterns provide protection, so that no single error leads to a system failure with human lives at stake. Safety measures also encompass designated safe states to which the system may transition to in case of a fault at run-time. Finding a safe state is not always trivial. While in some cases shutting down the power supply may be a transition to a safe state ("all offline"), it may be entirely different for a critical avionics component. Therefore, the analysis of safe states and possible transitions to these states is often a mandatory part of a safety assessment for a safety-critical embedded system.

How does a software partitioning approach of applications help to address timing and safety attributes of a system? In general terms, partitioning is a resource assignment to an application. In that sense, it is a vital component for the application and the entire system as its applications cannot execute properly if none or insufficient resources are assigned to it. If an application does not get enough processor time by the partition scheduler in the operation system, it may not be able to produce the results in time so that deadlines may be missed and timing attributes are in jeopardy.

A correct resource assignment is also very important to satisfy safety requirements. If an incorrect assignment creates an unintended interference channel between two separate partitions [10], the isolation between partitions in order to prevent fault propagation is flawed and the integrity of the entire system is endangered.

These quality requirements constitute the many-core migration challenge and lead to the difference between having multiple partitions on a single-core platform with time-sharing and multiple partitions on a many-core platform allowing for true parallelism. With time-sharing, each partition has an exclusive access to all hardware resources during its time slice. The only interruption is to be expected from the operating scheduler when the end of a time slice has been reached. Therefore, the entire system becomes very deterministic as there are no unforeseen waiting times to be expected due to resource contention at run-time. Every application executes as if it were the only application executing on that platform.

The most significant difference to the execution on the many-core platform becomes apparent when a parallel hardware platform effectively invalidates the "exclusive access" assumption. Two applications running in parallel on separate partitions are suddenly competing for resources, which affects the quality attribute of the entire systems. The performance may degrade significantly due to cache thrashing. Concurrent access to resources, such as network interfaces, may lead to nondeterministic waiting times—thus risking the deterministic system behavior. Generally speaking, every processor resource (caches, on-chip interconnect, memory controller, ...), which is now shared between partitions as a result of a parallel execution, constitutes a potential channel for interferences.

How does this affect the software engineering approach? Without parallel execution, applications executing within a partition could be developed and integrated on the platform with only very little knowledge about other partitions. A partition schedule simply defined when to start which partition. With parallel execution, that is, several partitions potentially running at the same time, their integration becomes more challenging. Every partition needs to define, which resources are needed for execution. This encompasses not only processor time, but also on-chip interconnect links, caches, memory controllers, interrupt controllers, CAN bus controllers, and so on—essentially every resource which may be shared and concurrently accessed at runtime. In order to integrate several partitions on a many-core processor platform, these resources requirements need to be aligned, so that no resource is overbooked and resources contention is eliminated.

Also safety analysis for a multi-tenant system becomes more challenging. A single fault within the resources used by one partition may then affect the execution of another partition as well. Shutting down the entire control unit may help to reach a safe state, but on the other hand, this will affect all functions deployed on this processes. In some situations, a fine-grained approach on the partition level may be applicable. If a fault manifests itself in a commonly used resource, all partitions using this resource have to transition to their designated safe state.

Generally speaking, on a parallel hardware platform the resource requirements of each partition need to be compared to the requirements of *every* other partition on the same platform in order to satisfy quality requirements. This *integration effort* increases with an increasing number of partitions and an increased use of shared resources. Therefore, it is safe to assume, that the more the embedded domain embraces many-core architectures, the more challenging the integration will become and the more it will pay off to look at efficient ways to address this integration challenge.

5. Traditional Integration Approaches

The last section described the major challenges of a multifunction integration in order to tap the full performance potential of a many-core hardware platform. Essentially, there are three distinct obstacles to be address during the integration:

(i) identification of *all* shared resources,

(ii) providing sufficient isolation between partitions to prevent fault propagation via shared resources,

(iii) creating and managing an assignment from resources to partitions, so that quality requirements—especially timing—can be satisfied.

The first obstacle can be addressed by a thorough analysis of all applications and the hardware platform. Therefore, it is often necessary to acquire detailed documentation about the processor architecture. With all shared resources being successfully identified, several well-established approaches can be used to ensure isolation. Rushby [13] gives a detailed overview about static and dynamic isolation techniques in the avionics and aerospace domain. In addition to the approaches mentioned by Rushby, highly reliable *hypervisors* can also be used to isolate separate partitions from each other (cf. [19–21]).

The third obstacle turns out to be the most challenging one—especially on many-core processors. This is the case as traditional approaches for an integration of software applications has reached its limits when quality requirements, such as timing properties have to be met. The current practice in the embedded industry can often be described with "timing by accident."

The deployment of partitions onto processors and their operating system schedule—that is, the assignment of resources—is often initially derived from previous project in a similar context. Changes to the resource assignment are realized based on engineering experience and estimations about resource consumption. The initial resource assignment is subsequently analyzed for potentials flaws (see the tool suites from INCHRON (http://www.inchron.com/), TA SIMULATOR (http://www.timing-architects.com/products .html), or SYMTA VISION (http://www.symtavision.com/)). These real-time simulators help to determine whether the priority assignment to tasks and the chosen scheduling algorithm is sufficient to satisfy all real-time requirements. However, this analysis is of NP-complexity and for a larger task set it may take up a significant amount of time in the engineering process.

For low or noncritical applications, it may be sufficient to focus on the *average* case. This approach is often combined with an overprovisioning of resources based on the assumption, that if the worst case scenario occurs, these spare resources will help to mitigate the effects.

The "timing by accident" methodology clearly reaches its limit when a fully deterministic system behavior for highly critical and complex systems is required. In this case, every access to system resources, for example, processor or network interfaces, has to be coordinated based on knowledge at *design time*. Providing spare resources is no longer a viable option, as no deviations from the static operating system schedule are tolerated. The entire system behavior based on the execution patterns of all partitions on a processor has to be defined at design time.

This information is often not gathered during the engineering process and therefore seldom available during the integration. Nevertheless, the process of designing a schedule satisfying all timing requirements of all partitions is very cumbersome, but at the same time a very sensitive matter. Creating a static schedule thus often takes several person months for reasonably complex systems. The complexity of this specific scheduling problem arises not only from the challenge to select tasks so that all deadline are met. Instead the schedule has to mimic the entire system behavior with regard to timing, for example, context switches take a certain amount of time or writing to buffers after a computation finished may take some additional time. It also has to incorporate intra- and interapplication relations, which may affect the order of execution. Furthermore, the execution of some applications may be split into several slices (offline determined preemption), which affects the amount of context switches and thus the timing. And last but not least, it is often necessary to optimize the schedule according to a certain criteria. This is especially beneficial when hypervisor-based systems with a two-level scheduling approaches (for partitions and applications) need be addressed. For these systems, it is a common goal to optimize the schedule for a minimal amount of partition switches to minimize the overhead introduced by the hypervisor. A "timing by accident" approach in which timing is addressed after all functional requirements have been satisfied is not sufficient anymore. Timing is a cross-cutting concern for the entire system design. Therefore, it needs to be addressed and incorporated throughout the entire engineering process [22].

And timing requirements are only a part of the quality requirements, which need to be addressed explicitly for a multi-function integration. The same is true for quality requirements regarding safety. Partitions cannot be freely deployed on the entire system architecture spanning over several processors. Often pairs of partitions need to be mapped on fully *dissimilar* hardware components to avoid a failure due to undetected design errors in the hardware. In some cases with lower criticality requirements, it is sufficient to map partitions on *redundant* hardware nodes. This task can still be accomplished manually up to a problem size of about 20 partitions on 10–15 processors. However, in complex avionics systems, there will be about 100 processors and about 1000 individual functions to be managed in the foreseeable future. A similar trend to increasing number of electronic control units and software components is evident in automotive systems, where more than 80 ECUs in current high-end automobiles are not uncommon.

How to Safely Integrate Multiple Applications on Embedded Many-Core Systems by Applying the "Correctness by Construction" Principle

129

With many-core processors, the engineers face a significant increase in complexity, which cannot be handled manually in an efficient way. The complexity of the hardware increases as there are significantly more shared resources. At the same time, there will be more and more partitions to be migrated to a single processor. With more partitions being integrated on the same platform, more development teams—which are most likely spatially spread over several companies—need to be synchronized. This poses an interesting nontechnical management challenge all by itself. At the same time, the development processes will have to become more agile in order to address the need for a shorter time to market and shorter product evolution cycles.

Generally speaking, the ability to efficiently realize a *temporal* and *spatial* assignment of resources to partitions determines the degree to which important quality attributes can be satisfied. In the end, it also determines the level to which software components can be integrated on the same hardware processor platform. A multi-function integration on a many-core system cannot be done efficiently with the aforementioned traditional approaches. So the research question remains: how to tackle this integration challenge which affects the degree to which the performance of many-core processors can be exploited in software-intensive embedded systems?

A few years ago, the development of complex safety critical software—not entire systems—was confronted with a similar challenge. The application engineers were confronted with a very high system complexity. They had to satisfy challenging functional requirements and of course, there was zero tolerance for defects. This challenge was addressed with a new approach: software development based on *formal methods*. The underlying idea was based on the realization that the correctness of reasonably complex software could no longer be assured by analyzing all possible execution paths. The correctness of a system could not be proven by simply observing its behavior. There were simply too many execution paths, so that each path could not be analyzed and tested without significantly exceeding the project budget.

Instead of analyzing the exhibited behavior of the software after it has been built, this new approach focuses on earlier stages in the development: requirements engineering, design, and implementation. During these stages, the software is *constructed* based on a specific rule-set, which derives the components from formalized requirements—hence its name "*correctness by construction*." This approach has been successfully applied in several case studies and lead to fewer bugs and lower development costs [23–25]. The design space of the entire system is restricted by a construction rule-set, so that a significant amount of implementation errors are circumvented.

The challenge of a *multi-function with mixed-criticality integration on many-core systems* could be properly addressed by a new engineering approach based on similar tactics. The complexity and volatility of the design space simply exceeds the capabilities of traditional integration approaches. Of course, existing "construction rules" for the development of software cannot be used here, because the challenge affects the integration and not the development. So the question is, how to adapt this approach and use it for an *efficient construction* of a resource assignment in a multi-function integration scenario?

6. Integration Based on "Correctness by Construction"

This engineering principle has been pioneered by Chapman and Hall [23, 24] for the development of "high integrity software" [24]. Although it applies to the entire life cycle of a software components, it focuses on the programming aspect. Its goal can be summarized as "*argue the correctness of the software in terms of the manner in which it has been produced ("by construction") rather than just by observing operational behavior*" [24, page 1].

How does this principle help for the multi-function integration? The benefits are desirable, but the adoption of a similar approach for the integration is still the subject of applied research. Up to this point, the following promising strategies have been adapted to the integration challenge based on similar strategies for the prevention and removal of defects in software [24].

Write Right. When quality requirements need to be addressed during the integration, they need to be explicitly expressed and formalized, so that there is no ambiguity about their meaning. Specifications should be distinguished regarding the resources supplied from the hardware and the resource demand from the applications. Typically, these specifications need to contain:

(i) *spatial* parameters (e.g., memory usage, network interface usage, ...),

(ii) *temporal* parameters (e.g., access patterns, tolerated jitter, ...),

(iii) *safety-relevant* parameters (e.g., vendor information, architectural types, ...).

In addition, the hardware architecture of the system with its processing nodes and communication channels have to be modeled as well as the software architecture with all of its applications and their communication intensity.

Step, Do Not Leap. When constructing a resource assignment, typically the questions of "where" and "when" have to be addressed. *Where* does an application get executed—on which resources—and when does it get executed on these resources—its scheduling pattern. In an incremental process, with the question of where ("*mapping*") should be addressed before the question of when ("*scheduling*"). Each constructed mapping should be validated independently whether all spatial and safety-relevant parameters are correctly addressed. In a second step, a schedule gets constructed based on the mapping from the previous step. If a schedule cannot be constructed, feedback should be provided so that the initial mapping can be efficiently adapted accordingly.

Check Here before Going There. Every resource assignment should be checked whether its demand exceeds the resource supply. The distinction between *additive* and *exclusive* resources and the determination of a *resource capacity* is a crucial prerequisite for this validation. While exclusive resources can be acquired by only one application, additive resources can be used by more than one application until their capacity has been reached. However, the differentiation is not as simple as it appears and depends on other parameters as well. For instance, a network interface may typically be used by several applications so it may be categorized as being *additive*. On the other hand, are all applications allowed to access the interface *at the same time*? Do all applications need to have been developed according to same criticality level to avoid an unintended interference channel?

Screws: Use a Screwdriver, Not a Hammer. For the construction of mappings and schedules, a variety of algorithmic approaches in combination with special heuristics can be applied to tackle the challenge of NP-completeness. There is no omnipotent tool being applicable for all integration challenges. Every approach has its advantages in the construction process, but only the combination of all tools significantly boosts the efficiency.

As stated at the beginning of this section, the application of correctness by construction for a multi-function integration on many-core processors is still subject to active research. The next section will give an overview about case studies in which this principle was evaluated in practice.

7. Case Studies and Current Research

A model-based approach for the construction of static operating system schedules was used as an initial study of feasibility [26]. It is based on the underlying assumption that predictable and entirely deterministic real-time behavior for a system—which relies only on periodical tasks with known periods—can be achieved on multi- or many-core processors with static schedules if the following information (or at least an estimation) is available at design time (or configuration time):

(1) *timing characteristics*, for example, worst case execution time (WCET), of all applications and their processes on the underlying hardware platform

(2) *scheduling dependencies* between applications and processes

(3) *off-chip resource* usage patterns of all applications, such as busses or other significant external devices.

All conflicts, which may appear at run-time and lead to unpredictable timing, are resolved statically at design time. Our approach aims to optimize the schedule beforehand rather than troubleshooting afterwards.

A scheduling tool—called *PRECISION PRO*—was developed as a prototype. It automatically generates a valid static schedule for high-level timing characteristics of a given set of applications and a given hardware architecture. In addition to generating solutions, that is, static schedules, for the underlying NP-hard problem, the user is also given

the opportunity to adjust the generated schedules to specific needs and purposes. PRECISION PRO ensures that no hard constraints are violated during the adjustment process. For the sake of simplicity, the input is currently modeled in a textual notation similar to Prolog clauses.

With the help of heuristic approaches [26], PRECISION PRO tries to construct a schedule for the constraints defined in the input model. The input model and the problem specifications have been developed to suit the needs of a safety critical domain: avionics. Therefore, all execution times for software tasks in PRECISION PRO are based on a worst-case analysis. All tasks are executed at run-time with the help of a time-triggered dispatcher. This approach is often overly pessimistic, but still a hard requirement for systems in accordance to avionic safety levels A, B, C, and D.

However, there are other scheduling approaches aimed at optimizing the resource utilization despite having a fixed schedule. On approach is called "slack scheduling." It assigns processor cycles, which are unused to special applications. Another approach to improve resource utilization is based on specifying lower and upper bounds on the execution time. With the help of precedence constraints, a robust schedule can also be constructed, which avoids possible scheduling anomalies [27].

The complexity of the scheduling problem addressed with PRECISION PRO does not only come from determining a fixed schedule for nonpreemptive tasks so that deadlines are met. Instead it tries to capture the timing behavior of the entire systems and let the system engineer construct the desired behavior. Therefore, tasks may be preempted by other tasks if necessary. Tolerated jitter can be specified for each application. Relations between tasks executing on different processors can be incorporated into the schedule as well. Furthermore, the modeled system can also contain other resources despite processing time. These resource may be used exclusively, for example, network bandwidth, or cumulatively, for example, an actuator, by an application. During the construction of a schedule, it is guaranteed that the capacity of these external resources is not exceeded.

Due to the complexity of possible constraint specifications and the use of heuristics, PRECISION PRO focuses on "safe acceptance" for static schedules, that is, a static schedule for a feasible task system may not be found within time, but if a schedule was found, it is guaranteed to satisfy all requirements. Although the worst-case run-time for a complete search is exponential, the heuristics allow for affordable run times. For a real world example consisting of three Multicore processors, about 40 applications, a scheduling hyperperiod of 2000 ms and a 1 ms timeslot, it requires about 800 ms for generating the model from the input data and about 250 ms for searching a valid solution, that is, a feasible static schedule (executed on a virtual machine running Microsoft WindowsXP on a 2.4 GHz dual-core laptop with 4 GB RAM).

The generated schedule and the mapping onto processors and cores is presented in a graphical user interface (see Figure 6(a)). For each processing element, all processes that are executed at a given time within the scheduling period

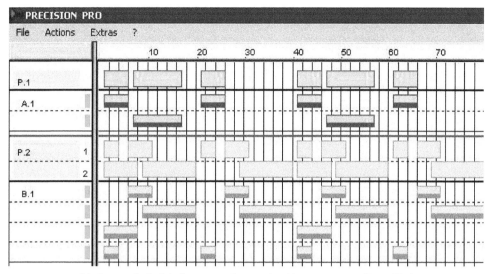

(a) Generated schedule for an example scenario with two processors (P.1 and P.2)

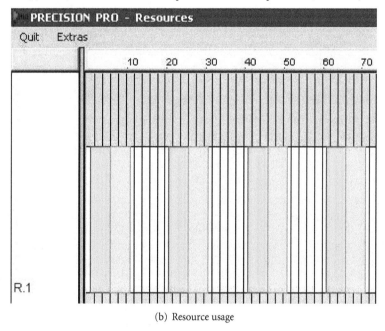

(b) Resource usage

FIGURE 6: PRECISION PRO Output—Figure 6(a) contains the schedules as it was generated for all processes and their mapping onto processors and cores. Figure 6(b) depicts the resource usage of a fictional off-chip resource.

are graphically represented by colored bars in a single row. Relations between processes are indicated by solid lines. Additionally, the usage of external resources is presented in a special *Resource Window* (see Figure 6(b)).

All relevant scheduling information can be exported into an operating system independent ASCII file. This file is usually transformed to satisfy formatting requirements of specific operating systems. After being approved by the certification authority, it is used in the final configuration of the scheduling component in the operating system.

Dynamic scheduling approaches based on fixed or variable priorities represent another common approach for real-time scheduling to allow for exclusive access to the hardware. Although this approach improves resource utilization, it also hides relations between tasks and scheduling constraints by assigning priorities. Priorities express a relationship to other tasks, but they do not capture the intent of the system engineer. Furthermore, with multi- and many-core processors, tasks with different priorities may still be executed at the same time as there may be plenty of cores available. This may not be a problem for systems with less stringent predictability requirements. However, it quickly becomes an issue for safety-critical systems in which predictability and determinism matters. "Correctness-by-Construction" in combination with static scheduling is about making the design decisions explicit, so that they can be reused for other hardware platforms without compromising their integrity.

Generating static schedules for safety critical Multicore systems is only the first step in improving the development

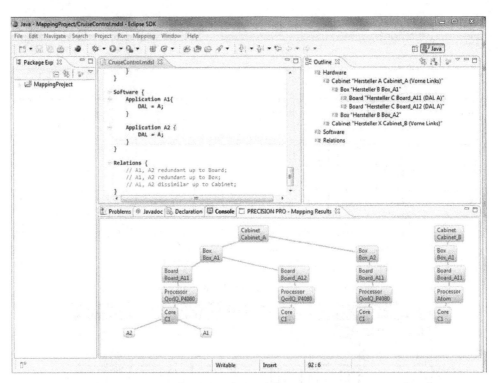

FIGURE 7: Construction of mappings from applications onto processors and cores.

processes and facilitating certification. In addition to PRE-CISION PRO, two supplementary components are currently in development: a *validator* and a *mapper*.

Validator. Due to the importance of an operating system schedule for a safety critical system, special attention has to be given to its verification during certification and official approval—especially, since it was automatically constructed by a software tool. Although PRECISION PRO will—by design—only construct schedules satisfying all constraints, an additional verification step is still necessary, because there may be undetected software bugs in the underlying libraries used by PRECISION PRO, which may eventually lead to the construction of erroneous schedules.

Usually, there are two options for a system engineer who wishes to use tools to automate development processes: either the software tool has to be *qualified*, which is a very intricate and costly task, or the result has to be verified with another, *dissimilar* verification tool (see [14], pages 59–62). (The verification tool does not need to be qualified, as its output is not directly used in the final product.) Here the second option was chosen, so that a special *validator* for static Multicore schedules is currently in development. It uses the output of PRECISION PRO and creates a formal model, which is a deterministic transition system based on time discretization. This model is used for applying model-checking techniques with the linear temporal logic (LTL) model checker UPPAAL (http://www.uppaal.org/).

Model properties, which are checked by the validator—*never claims*, are essentially LTL formulae, which are derived from the original input model of PRECISION PRO. If all properties were successfully checked, that is, no never claim

turned out to be true, the model of the static schedule satisfies all formalized software requirements and the construction was correctly done.

Mapper. Previously, the challenge of mapping from software components, that is, partitions and processes, onto processors and their cores was introduced. Currently, this is often done manually, which may be sufficient for systems with only a few processors. However, it is certainly not a viable approach for complex systems comprising of up to 100 processors, especially, since mapping for safety critical systems does not solely depend on achieving scheduleability, but also on other safety criteria, such as *redundancy*, *dissimilarity* and *independence*.

For instance, the mapping of an application comprising of two *redundant* partitions should not allow these identical partitions to be mapped on the same core or on the same processor. This would clearly lead to a violation of safety requirements, because the underlying hardware usually does not offer *enough* redundancy for the designated assurance level.

It is also common for safety critical applications to comprise of partitions which implement the same functionality, but in a dissimilar fashion. Depending on the criticality level, these partitions may need to be mapped onto *dissimilar* processors and configured to use *dissimilar* communication channels to prevent design errors.

As a result of research conducted in the avionics domain, it became clear that safety related constraints, for example, *"partition A and partition B have to be mapped onto dissimilar/redundant hardware,"* require additional *qualification*. Redundancy and dissimilarity have to be expressed in relation to certain aspects of the underlying hardware. For

How to Safely Integrate Multiple Applications on Embedded Many-Core Systems by Applying the "Correctness by Construction" Principle

133

instance, partition *A* and partition *B* have to be mapped on processors with redundant power supplies and dissimilar communication channels.

By acknowledging the fact that the design of safety-critical embedded systems has to follow complex safety restrictions and regulations, but at the same time it also needs to minimize costs and reduce space, weight and power requirements, a *mapper* is currently in development, which *constructs* feasible mappings that satisfy safety constraints (see Figure 7). These mapping are then used in PRECISION PRO to generate a valid schedule. If such a schedule cannot be found, the *mapper* is requested to modify the initial mapping. PRECISION PRO will help guiding the mapping process by providing elaborate information regarding the degree of capacity utilization for each processor. The mapper may then choose to remove partitions from overutilized processors, so that a schedule can be constructed and all mapping-related safety requirements are met.

8. Conclusions and Discussion

Many-core processors can be used to significantly improve the value of software-intensive systems. A small power envelope in conjunction with unprecedented performance levels—at least in the embedded domain—pave the way for cyber physical systems. Having many, but relatively simple cores requires the exploitation of parallelism on all levels, especially on the application layer and the thread layer. This approach constitutes a significant prerequisite in tapping the full potential of a massively parallel processor. At the same time, this leads to a multi-tenant situation, when multiple functions from different vendors are to be integrated on the same chip. Trends and standardization efforts in key domains, that is, avionics and automotive, already address these challenges arising from the functional requirements. The integrated modular avionics in conjunction with ARINC 653 in avionics and AUTOSAR in the automotive domain provide a standardized abstraction layer, so that software components can be developed relatively independent from the specifics of the underlying processor hardware.

While this helps address the functional correctness of integrating several applications on a many-core processor, quality requirements—especially timing and safety—are not sufficiently addressed. These become especially apparent during the integration. Suddenly applications are competing for resources, which may get congested leading to unpredictable waiting times and jeopardizing the predictable system behavior.

Software partitioning is a well-established concept in operating systems to prevent fault propagation by restricting the access to resources. Partitioning is essentially an assignment from resources to applications. With many-core processors, this assignment can no longer be created manually as there are simply too many resources and too many applications to balance.

"Correctness by construction" is an engineering principle that has been successfully applied in the implementation of highly reliable software. Its fundamentals can also be applied

in the context of multi-function integration on many-core. Formalized requirements and a resource assignment as a result of a *construction process* provide an efficient engineering approach to address the many-core challenge in software-intensive embedded systems.

References

[1] H. Sutter, "The free lunch is over: a fundamental turn toward concurrency in software," *Dr. Dobb's Journal*, vol. 30, no. 3, pp. 202–210, 2005.

[2] A. A. Vajda, *Programming Many-Core Chips*, Springer, 2011.

[3] M. D. Hill and M. R. Marty, "Amdahl's law in the multicore era," *Computer*, vol. 41, no. 7, pp. 33–38, 2008.

[4] E. A. Lee, Cyber-Physical Systems—Are Computing Foundations Adequate?, 2006.

[5] E. A. Lee and S. A. Seshia, *Introduction to Embedded Systems, A Cyber-Physical Systems Approach*, Lee & Seshia, 2011, http://www.lulu.com/.

[6] K. Asanovic, R. Bodik, B. C. Catanzaro et al., The Landscape of Parallel Computing Research: A view from Berkeley, 2006.

[7] S. Borkar, "Thousand core chips—a technology perspective," in *Proceedings of the 44th ACM/IEEE Design Automation Conference (DAC '07)*, pp. 746–749, June 2007.

[8] G. M. Amdahl, "Validity of the single processor approach to achieving large scale computing capabilities," in *Proceedings of the Spring Joint Computer Conference*, pp. 483–485, ACM, April 1967.

[9] F. P. Brooks Jr., *The Mythical Man-Month*, Addison-Wesley Longman Publishing, Boston, Mass, USA, 1995.

[10] R. Fuchsen, "How to address certification for multi-core based IMA platforms: current status and potential solutions," in *Proceedings of the 29th IEEE/AIAA Digital Avionics Systems Conference: Improving Our Environment through Green Avionics and ATM Solutions (DASC '10)*, pp. 5.E.31–5.E.311, October 2010.

[11] C. B. Watkins and R. Walter, "Transitioning from federated avionics architectures to integrated modular avionics," in *Proceedings of the 26th IEEE/AIAA Digital Avionics Systems Conference—4-Dimensional Trajectory-Based Operaions: Impact on Future Avionics and Systems (DASC '07)*, pp. 2.A.1-1–2.A.1-10, October 2007.

[12] RTCA, Integrated Modular Architecture—Development Guidance and Certification Considerations, 2005.

[13] J. Rushby, "Partitioning for avionics architectures: requirements, mechanisms, and assurance," NASA Contractor Report CR-1999-209347, NASA Langley Research Center, 1999, Also to be issued by the FAA.

[14] RTCA, Software Considerations in Airborne Systems and Equipment Certification, 1994.

[15] ARINC, ARINC Specification 653P1-2: Avionics Application Software Standard Interface Part 1—Required Services, 2005.

[16] AUTOSAR, "Layered Software Architecture," 2010, http://autosar.org/download/R4.0/AUTOSAR_EXP_LayeredSoftwareArchitecture.pdf.

[17] K. Pohl, *Requirements Engineering: Grundlagen, Prinzipien, Techniken*, Dpunkt.Verlag GmbH, 2nd edition, 2008.

[18] L. Bass, P. Clements, and R. Kazman, *Software Architecture in Practice*, Addison-Wesley Longman Publishing, Boston, Mass, USA, 1998.

[19] R. Rose, "Survey of system virtualization techniques," Tech. Rep., Oregon State University (OSU), 2004.

[20] M. Rosenblum and T. Garfinkel, "Virtual machine monitors: current technology and future trends," *Computer*, vol. 38, no. 5, pp. 39–47, 2005.

[21] R. Hilbrich and M. Gerlach, "Virtualisierung bei Eingebetteten Multicore Systemen: Integration und Isolation sicherheit-skritischer Funktionen," in *INFORMATIK 2011—Informatik Schafft Communities*, H. U. Heiß, P. Pepper, H. Schlingloff, and J. Schneider, Eds., vol. 192 of *Lecture Notes in Informatics*, Springer, 2011.

[22] E. A. Lee, "Computing needs time," *Communications of the ACM*, vol. 52, no. 5, pp. 70–79, 2009.

[23] A. Hall and R. Chapman, "Correctness by construction: developing a commercial secure system," *IEEE Software*, vol. 19, no. 1, pp. 18–25, 2002.

[24] R. Chapman, "Correctness by construction: a manifesto for high integrity software," in *Proceedings of the 10th Australian workshop on Safety critical systems and software (SCS '05)*, vol. 55, pp. 43–46, Australian Computer Society, Darlinghurst, Australia, 2006.

[25] S. Resmerita, K. Butts, P. Derler, A. Naderlinger, and W. Pree, "Migration of legacy software towards correct-by-construction timing behavior," *Proceedings of the 16th Monterey Conference on Foundations of Computer Software: Modeling, Development, and Verification of Adaptive Systems (FOCS '10)*, Springer, Berlin, Germany, pp. 55–76, 2011.

[26] R. Hilbrich and H. J. Goltz, "Model-based generation of static schedules for safety critical multi-core systems in the avionics domain," in *Proceedings of the 4th ACM International Workshop on Multicore Software Engineering (IWMSE '11)*, pp. 9–16, New York, NY, USA, May 2011.

[27] M. Lombardi, M. Milano, and L. Benini, "Robust non-preemptive hard real-time scheduling for clustered multicore platforms," in *Proceedings of the Design, Automation and Test in Europe Conference and Exhibition (DATE '09)*, pp. 803–808, April 2009.

9

A Comparative Study of Data Transformations for Wavelet Shrinkage Estimation with Application to Software Reliability Assessment

Xiao Xiao and Tadashi Dohi

Department of Information Engineering, Graduate School of Engineering, Hiroshima University, 1-4-1 Kagamiyama, Higashi-Hiroshima 739-8527, Japan

Correspondence should be addressed to Xiao Xiao, xiaoxiao@rel.hiroshima-u.ac.jp

Academic Editor: Chin-Yu Huang

In our previous work, we proposed wavelet shrinkage estimation (WSE) for nonhomogeneous Poisson process (NHPP)-based software reliability models (SRMs), where WSE is a data-transform-based nonparametric estimation method. Among many variance-stabilizing data transformations, the Anscombe transform and the Fisz transform were employed. We have shown that it could provide higher goodness-of-fit performance than the conventional maximum likelihood estimation (MLE) and the least squares estimation (LSE) in many cases, in spite of its non-parametric nature, through numerical experiments with real software-fault count data. With the aim of improving the estimation accuracy of WSE, in this paper we introduce other three data transformations to preprocess the software-fault count data and investigate the influence of different data transformations to the estimation accuracy of WSE through goodness-of-fit test.

1. Introduction

In the field of software reliability engineering, the quantitative assessment of software reliability has become one of the main issues of this area. Especially, people are interested in finding several *software intensity functions* from the software-fault count data observed in the software testing phases, since the software intensity function in discrete time denotes the number of software faults detected per unit time. This directly makes it possible to estimate the number of remaining software faults and the quantitative software reliability, which is defined as the probability that software system does not fail during a specified time period under a specified operational environment. Moreover, these evaluation measures can be used in the decision making such as allocation of development resources and software release scheduling. Therefore, we are interested in developing a high-accuracy estimation method for the software intensity function.

Among over hundreds of software reliability models (SRMs) [1–3], nonhomogeneous Poisson process (NHPP)-based SRMs have gained much popularity in actual software testing phases. In many cases, the NHPP-based SRM is formulated as a parametric model, where the mean value function or its difference in discrete time or derivative in continuous time, called *"software intensity function,"* can be considered as a unique parameter to govern the probabilistic property. One class of parametric NHPP-based SRMs is concerned with modeling the number of software faults detected in testing phases, initiated by Goel and Okumoto [4]. Afterwards, many parametric NHPP-based SRMs were proposed in the literatures [5–8] from various points of view. However, it is well known in the software reliability engineering community that there does not exist a uniquely best parametric NHPP-based SRM which can fit every type of software-fault count data. This fact implies that nonparametric methods without assuming parametric form should be used to describe the software debugging phenomenon which is different in each testing phase.

Apart from the traditional Bayesian framework, some frequentist approaches based on non-parametric statistics were introduced to estimate the quantitative software reliability. Sofer and Miller [9] used an elementary piecewise linear estimator of the NHPP intensity function from the software-fault detection time data and proposed a smoothing technique by means of quadratic programming. Gandy and Jensen [10] applied the kernel-based estimator to estimate the NHPP intensity function in a non-parametric way. Barghout et al. [11] also proposed a kernel-based non-parametric estimation for the order statistics-based SRMs, where the likelihood cross-validation and the prequential likelihood approaches were used to estimate the bandwidth. Wang et al. [12] applied the similar kernel method to the NHPP-based SRMs, where they focused on the local likelihood method with a locally weighted log-likelihood function. By combining the non-parametric estimation with the Bayesian framework, El-Aroui and Soler [13] and Wilson and Samaniego [14] developed non-parametric Bayesian estimation methods. It should be noted that, generally, these non-parametric estimation methods require high computational cost, which, in some cases, may be almost similar to or greater than an effort on model selection in the parametric SRMs.

Another class of non-parametric estimation methods for NHPP-based SRMs is the wavelet analysis-based approach, initiated by Xiao and Dohi [15]. They proposed the wavelet shrinkage estimation (WSE), which does not require solving any optimization problem, so that the implementation of estimation algorithms is rather easy than the other non-parametric methods. They compared their method with the conventional maximum likelihood estimation (MLE) and the least squares estimation (LSE) through goodness-of-fit test. It has been shown that WSE could provide higher goodness-of-fit performance than MLE and LSE in many cases, in spite of its non-parametric nature, through numerical experiments with real software-fault count data.

The fundamental idea of WSE is to remove the noise included in the observed software-fault count data to get a noise-free estimate of the software intensity function. It is performed through the following three-step procedure. First, the noise variance is stabilized by applying the data transformation to the data. This produces a time-series data in which the noise can be treated as Gaussian white noise. Second, the noise is removed using "*Haar-wavelet*" based denoising algorithm. Third, an inverse data transformation is applied to the denoised time-series data, obtaining the estimate of the software intensity function. Among many variance-stabilizing data transformations, the Anscombe transform [16] and the Fisz transform [17] were employed in the previous work [15]. The other well-known square root data transformations are Bartlett transform [18] and Freeman transform [19]. Both Anscombe transform and Freeman transform are actually natural extensions of the Bartlett transform.

This paper focuses on the first step of WSE and aims at identifying and emphasizing the influence that the data transformation exerts on the accuracy of WSE. The remaining part of this paper is planned as follows. In Section 2, we give a preliminary on NHPP-based software reliability modeling. Section 3 is devoted to introduce data transformations. Section 4 describes the WSE for NHPP-based SRMs in details. In Section 5, we carry out the real project data analysis and illustrate numerical examples to examine the effectiveness of the proposed methods. Finally the paper is concluded with future researches in Section 6.

2. NHPP-Based Software Reliability Modeling

Suppose that the number of software faults detected through a system test is observed at discrete time $i = 0, 1, 2, \ldots$. Let Y_i and $N_i = \sum_{k=0}^{i} Y_k$ denote the number of software faults detected at testing date i and its cumulative value, where $Y_0 = N_0 = 0$ is assumed without any loss of generality. The stochastic process $\{N_i : i = 0, 1, 2, \ldots\}$ is said to be a discrete non-homogeneous Poisson process (D-NHPP) if the probability mass function at time i is given by

$$\Pr\{N_i = m\} = \frac{\{\Lambda_i\}^m}{m!} \exp\{-\Lambda_i\}, \quad m = 0, 1, 2, \ldots, \quad (1)$$

where $\Lambda_i = E[N_i]$ is called the mean value function of a D-NHPP and means the expected cumulative number of software faults detected by testing date i. The function $\lambda_i = \Lambda_i - \Lambda_{i-1}$ $(i \geq 1)$ is called the discrete intensity function and implies the expected number of faults detected at testing date i, say $\lambda_i = E[Y_i]$.

MLE is one of the most commonly used parametric estimation method. Let θ denote the vector of parameters in the mean value function $\Lambda_i = \Lambda_i(\theta)$, and $x_i(y_i)$ denote the realization of $N_i(Y_i)$. When n software faults are detected, the log-likelihood function of a D-NHPP is given by

$$\mathcal{LLF}(\theta) = \sum_{i=1}^{n} (x_i - x_{i-1}) \ln[\Lambda_i(\theta) - \Lambda_{i-1}(\theta)] - \Lambda_n(\theta)$$
$$- \sum_{i=1}^{n} \ln[(x_i - x_{i-1})!], \quad (2)$$

where $x_i = \sum_{k=0}^{i} y_k$ and $y_0 = x_0 = 0$. Then, the maximum likelihood estimate of θ, say $\hat{\theta}$, is given by the solution of $\text{argmax}_{\theta} \mathcal{LLF}(\theta)$. Therefore, the estimate of the software intensity function $\lambda_i = \lambda_i(\theta)$ $(i = 0, 1, 2, \ldots)$ can be obtained by $\hat{\lambda}_i = \Lambda_i(\hat{\theta}) - \Lambda_{i-1}(\hat{\theta})$ $(i \geq 1)$ with $\lambda_0 = 0$. In the following sections, we consider the problem of estimating the software intensity function from the noise-involved observation y_i, in a non-parametric way.

3. Variance Stabilizing Data Transformation

It is very familiar to make use of data transformations (DTs) to stabilize the variance of Poisson data. By using DT, the software-fault count data which follow the D-NHPP are approximately transformed to the Gaussian data. The most fundamental data-transform tool in statistics is the *Bartlett transform* (BT) [18]. Let η_i denote the Poisson white noise, that is,

$$Y_i = \lambda_i + \eta_i, \quad i = 1, 2 \ldots, n. \quad (3)$$

A Comparative Study of Data Transformations for Wavelet Shrinkage Estimation with Application to Software
Reliability Assessment

137

TABLE 1: Representative data transformaions.

	Data transformation	Inverse data transformation	Distribution of random variable after DT
BT1 [18]	$B_i = 2\sqrt{Y_i}$	$Y_i = 1/4 \times \{(B_i)^2\}$	$N(2\sqrt{\lambda_i} - 1/4, 1)$
BT2 [18]	$B_i = 2\sqrt{Y_i + 1/2}$	$Y_i = 1/4 \times \{(B_i)^2 - 2\}$	$N(2\sqrt{\lambda_i} + 1/4, 1)$
AT [16]	$S_i = 2\sqrt{Y_i + 3/8}$	$Y_i = 1/4 \times \{(S_i)^2 - 3/2\}$	$N(2\sqrt{\lambda_i} + 1/8, 1)$
FT [19]	$F_i = \sqrt{Y_i + 1} + \sqrt{Y_i}$	$Y_i = 1/4 \times \{(F_i)^2 + (F_i)^{-2} - 2\}$	$N(2\sqrt{\lambda_i}, 1)$

TABLE 2: Representative discrete NHPP-based SRMs.

SRM	Mean value function Λ_i
Geometric (GE)	$\omega\{1 - (1 - p)^i\}$
Negative Binomial (NB)	$\omega\{\sum_{k=1}^{i}((r + k - 1)!/(r - 1)!k!)p^r(1 - p)^{k-1}\}$
Discrete Weibull (DW)	$\omega\{1 - p^{i^r}\}$

Taking the BT, the random variables:

$$B_i = 2\sqrt{Y_i}, \quad i = 1, 2, \ldots, n \quad (4)$$

can be approximately regarded as Gaussian random variables with the normal distribution $N(2\sqrt{\lambda_i} - 1/4, 1)$, so that the realizations:

$$b_i = 2\sqrt{y_i}, \quad i = 1, 2, \ldots, n \quad (5)$$

can be considered as samples from $N(2\sqrt{\lambda_i} - 1/4, 1)$. That is, the transformed realizations b_i ($i = 1, 2, \ldots, n$) by the BT are the ones from the normally distributed random variables:

$$B_i = \lambda_i' + \nu_i, \quad i = 1, 2, \ldots, n, \quad (6)$$

where $\lambda_i' = 2\sqrt{\lambda_i} - 1/4$ is the transformed software intensity function, and ν_i is the Gaussian white noise with unit variance.

Bartlett [18] also showed that

$$b_i = 2\sqrt{y_i + \frac{1}{2}}, \quad i = 1, 2, \ldots, n \quad (7)$$

is a better transformation since it provides a constant variance more closely to 1, even when the mean of Y_i is not large.

The Anscombe transform (AT) [16] is a natural extension of BT and is employed in our previous work [15]. AT is of the following form:

$$s_i = 2\sqrt{y_i + \frac{3}{8}}, \quad i = 1, 2, \ldots, n, \quad (8)$$

where s_i can be considered as observations of Gaussian random variable $S_i = 2\sqrt{Y_i + 3/8}$ with the normal distribution $N(2\sqrt{\lambda_i} + 1/8, 1)$. Freeman and Tukey [19] proposed the following square-root transform (we call it FT), which is also an extension of BT:

$$f_i = \sqrt{y_i + 1} + \sqrt{y_i}, \quad i = 1, 2, \ldots, n. \quad (9)$$

They showed that the variance of Gaussian random variable $F_i = 2\sqrt{Y_i + 1} + \sqrt{Y_i}$ is the nearest to 1 among BT, AT, and FT if the mean of Y_i is small. Recently, these variance stabilization techniques were used to LSE of the mean value function for the NHPP-based SRMs [20]. Table 1 summaries the DTs mentioned above.

As mentioned in Section 1, the first step of WSE is to apply the normalizing and variance-stabilizing DTs to the observed software-fault count data. In this paper, we employ BT, AT, and FT in the first and the third steps of WSE. Then, the target of denoising in the second step of WSE is the transformed data b_i, s_i or f_i ($i = 1, 2, \ldots, n$). Letting b_i', s_i', and f_i' denote the denoised b_i, s_i, and f_i, respectively, the estimate of the original software intensity function λ_i can be obtained by taking the inverse DT of b_i', s_i' and f_i', as given in Table 1.

4. Wavelet Shrinkage Estimation for NHPP-Based SRM

4.1. Haar-Wavelet-Based Denoising Procedure. The Haar-wavelet-based shrinkage technique can be used as a denoising algorithm for the second step of WSE. In general, the noise removal is performed through the following three steps: (i) expanding the transformed time-series data to obtain the empirical wavelet coefficients, (ii) removing the noise included in the empirical wavelet coefficients using thresholding method, and (iii) making use of the denoised coefficients to calculate the estimate of the transformed software intensity function.

4.1.1. Haar Wavelet Transform. The Haar scaling function and the Haar wavelet function are defined as

$$\phi(i) = \begin{cases} 1 & (0 \le i < 1) \\ 0 & (\text{otherwise}), \end{cases}$$

$$\psi(i) = \begin{cases} 1 & \left(0 \le i < \frac{1}{2}\right) \\ -1 & \left(\frac{1}{2} \le i < 1\right) \\ 0 & (\text{otherwise}), \end{cases} \quad (10)$$

TABLE 3: Goodness-of-fit test results for different data transformations. (Threshold level: universal threshold.)

DS1	MSE_1	MSE_2	LL
HBT1(h, ut)	4.180	0.327	-153.759
HBT2(h, ut)	2.401	0.316	-144.850
HAT(h, ut)	2.573	0.317	-145.390
HFT(h, ut)	9.842	0.403	-383.785
HBT1(s, ut)	4.180	0.327	-153.759
HBT2(s, ut)	2.401	0.316	-144.850
HAT(s, ut)	2.573	0.317	-145.390
HFT(s, ut)	3.231	0.320	-148.023
DS2	MSE_1	MSE_2	LL
HBT1(h, ut)	12.449	1.141	-197.109
HBT2(h, ut)	11.600	1.138	-196.904
HAT(h, ut)	11.725	1.138	-196.953
HFT(h, ut)	11.847	1.138	-196.806
HBT1(s, ut)	12.450	1.141	-197.109
HBT2(s, ut)	11.600	1.138	-196.904
HAT(s, ut)	11.725	1.138	-196.953
HFT(s, ut)	11.847	1.138	-196.806
DS3	MSE_1	MSE_2	LL
HBT1(h, ut)	10.159	0.719	-143.181
HBT2(h, ut)	9.055	0.791	-192.903
HAT(h, ut)	9.286	0.793	-193.178
HFT(h, ut)	9.653	0.796	-167.025
HBT1(s, ut)	12.954	1.037	-212.321
HBT2(s, ut)	10.528	1.035	-213.978
HAT(s, ut)	10.813	1.035	-213.496
HFT(s, ut)	11.496	1.037	-213.419
DS4	MSE_1	MSE_2	LL
HBT1(h, ut)	2.065	0.304	-171.605
HBT2(h, ut)	1.781	0.304	-171.491
HAT(h, ut)	1.822	0.304	-171.504
HFT(h, ut)	1.864	0.304	-171.516
HBT1(s, ut)	2.065	0.304	-171.605
HBT2(s, ut)	1.781	0.304	-171.491
HAT(s, ut)	1.822	0.304	-171.504
HFT(s, ut)	1.864	0.304	-171.516
DS5	MSE_1	MSE_2	LL
HBT1(h, ut)	14.013	0.586	-304.198
HBT2(h, ut)	12.781	0.581	-301.073
HAT(h, ut)	12.941	0.581	-301.447
HFT(h, ut)	13.200	0.582	-301.841
HBT1(s, ut)	14.054	0.601	-312.551
HBT2(s, ut)	12.804	0.596	-309.709
HAT(s, ut)	12.968	0.597	-310.005
HFT(s, ut)	13.227	0.598	-310.480
DS6	MSE_1	MSE_2	LL
HBT1(h, ut)	12.707	0.521	-378.932
HBT2(h, ut)	11.899	0.525	-380.497
HAT(h, ut)	12.053	0.526	-380.987

DS6	MSE_1	MSE_2	LL
HFT(h, ut)	12.186	0.526	−381.071
HBT1(s, ut)	13.546	0.585	−423.335
HBT2(s, ut)	12.505	0.584	−421.480
HAT(s, ut)	12.670	0.584	−421.729
HFT(s, ut)	12.810	0.584	−421.866

respectively. By introducing the *scaling parameter j* and *shifting parameter k*, the Haar father wavelet and the Haar mother wavelet are defined by

$$\phi_{j,k}(i) = 2^{-j/2}\phi\left(2^{-j}i - k\right),$$
$$\psi_{j,k}(i) = 2^{-j/2}\psi\left(2^{-j}i - k\right), \tag{11}$$

respectively. Then the target function, transformed software intensity function λ_i' $(i = 1, 2, \ldots, n)$, can be expressed in the following equation:

$$\lambda_i' = \sum_{k=0}^{2^{j_0}-1} \alpha_{j_0,k}\phi_{j_0,k}(i) + \sum_{j=j_0}^{\infty}\sum_{k=0}^{2^j-1} \beta_{j,k}\psi_{j,k}(i), \tag{12}$$

where

$$\alpha_{j_0,k} = \sum_{i=1}^{n}\lambda_i'\phi_{j_0,k}(i), \tag{13}$$

$$\beta_{j,k} = \sum_{i=1}^{n}\lambda_i'\psi_{j,k}(i) \tag{14}$$

are called the scaling coefficients and the wavelet coefficients, respectively, for any primary resolution level $j_0(\geq 0)$. Due to the implementability, it is reasonable to set an upper limit instead of ∞ for the resolution level j. In other words, the highest resolution level must be finite in practice. We use J to denote the highest resolution level. That is, the range of j in the second term of (12) is $j \in [j_0, J]$. The mapping from function λ_i' to coefficients $(\alpha_{j_0,k}, \beta_{j,k})$ is called the Haar wavelet transform (HWT).

Since b_i, s_i or f_i $(i = 1, 2, \ldots, n)$ can be considered as the observation of λ_i', the empirical scaling coefficients $c_{j_0,k}$ and the empirical wavelet coefficients $d_{j,k}$ of λ_i' can be calculated by (13) and (14) with λ_i' replaced by b_i, s_i or f_i. The noises involved in the empirical wavelet coefficients $d_{j,k}$ can be removed by the thresholding method that we will introduce later. Finally, the estimate of λ_i' can be obtained by taking the inverse HWT with denoised empirical coefficients.

4.1.2. Thresholding. In denoising the empirical wavelet coefficients, the common choices of thresholding method are the hard thresholding:

$$\delta_\tau(u) = u1_{|u|>\tau}, \tag{15}$$

and the soft thresholding:

$$\delta_\tau(u) = \text{sgn}(u)(|u| - \tau)_+, \tag{16}$$

for a fixed threshold level $\tau(> 0)$, where 1_A is the indicator function of an event A, $\text{sgn}(u)$ is the sign function of u and $(u)_+ = \max(0, u)$. There are many methods to determine the threshold level τ. In this paper, we use the universal threshold [21] and the "leave-out-half" cross-validation threshold [22]:

$$\tau = \sqrt{2\log n},$$
$$\tau = \left(1 - \frac{\log 2}{\log n}\right)^{-1/2}\tau\left(\frac{n}{2}\right), \tag{17}$$

where n is the length of the observation s_i. Hard thresholding is a "keep" or "kill" rule, while soft thresholding is a "shrink" or "kill" rule. Both thresholding methods and both threshold levels will be employed to work on the empirical wavelet coefficients $d_{j,k}$ for denoising.

4.2. Wavelet Shrinkage Estimation for NHPP-Based SRM. Since the software-fault count data is Poisson data, the preprocessing is necessary before making use of the Haar-wavelet-based denoising procedure. Xiao and Dohi [15] combined data transformation and the standard denoising procedure to propose the wavelet shrinkage estimation (WSE) for the D-NHPP-based SRMs. They call the HWT combined with AT, the Haar-Anscombe transform (HAT). Similarly, we call the HWT combined with BT and FT, the Haar-Bartlett transform (HBT) and the Haar-Freeman transform (HFT), respectively. In the numerical study, we investigate the goodness-of-fit performance of HBT- and HFT-based WSEs and compare them with the HAT-based WSE [15].

5. Numerical Study

5.1. Data Sets and Measures. We use six real project data sets cited from reference [1], where they are named as J1, J3, DATA14, J5, SS1, and DATA8. These data sets are software-fault count data (group data). We rename them for convenience as DS1~DS6 in this paper. Let (n, x_n) denote the pair of the final testing date and the total number of detected fault. Then these data sets are presented by (62, 133), (41, 351), (46, 266), (73, 367), (81, 461), and (111, 481),

TABLE 4: Goodness-of-fit test results for different data transformations. (Threshold level: "leave-out-half" cross-validation threshold.)

DS1	MSE$_1$	MSE$_2$	LL
HBT1(h, lht)	0.112	0.015	−59.704
HBT2(h, lht)	0.131	0.017	−60.634
HAT(h, lht)	0.114	0.014	−60.324
HFT(h, lht)	8.079	0.343	−216.320
HBT1(s, lht)	0.159	0.010	−59.581
HBT2(s, lht)	0.109	0.010	−60.195
HAT(s, lht)	0.115	0.010	−60.118
HFT(s, lht)	0.151	0.010	−59.609
DS2	MSE$_1$	MSE$_2$	LL
HBT1(h, lht)	0.477	0.102	−70.438
HBT2(h, lht)	0.225	0.072	−70.227
HAT(h, lht)	0.263	0.077	−70.663
HFT(h, lht)	0.552	0.125	−71.041
HBT1(s, lht)	0.342	0.027	−69.407
HBT2(s, lht)	0.363	0.030	−69.781
HAT(s, lht)	0.364	0.030	−69.731
HFT(s, lht)	0.351	0.028	−69.446
DS3	MSE$_1$	MSE$_2$	LL
HBT1(h, lht)	0.208	0.032	−55.829
HBT2(h, lht)	0.275	0.041	−56.767
HAT(h, lht)	0.902	0.074	−57.614
HFT(h, lht)	0.323	0.048	−56.411
HBT1(s, lht)	0.573	0.040	−55.847
HBT2(s, lht)	0.486	0.037	−56.649
HAT(s, lht)	0.496	0.037	−56.551
HFT(s, lht)	0.537	0.037	−55.922
DS4	MSE$_1$	MSE$_2$	LL
HBT1(h, lht)	0.288	0.015	−121.008
HBT2(h, lht)	0.132	0.007	−120.942
HAT(h, lht)	0.232	0.013	−121.031
HFT(h, lht)	0.281	0.014	−121.004
HBT1(s, lht)	0.097	0.005	−120.893
HBT2(s, lht)	0.046	0.003	−120.906
HAT(s, lht)	0.050	0.003	−120.907
HFT(s, lht)	0.064	0.004	−120.888
DS5	MSE$_1$	MSE$_2$	LL
HBT1(h, lht)	0.055	0.012	−120.869
HBT2(h, lht)	0.221	0.016	−121.205
HAT(h, lht)	0.228	0.017	−121.195
HFT(h, lht)	0.219	0.017	−120.890
HBT1(s, lht)	0.174	0.007	−120.805
HBT2(s, lht)	0.149	0.006	−120.913
HAT(s, lht)	0.151	0.006	−120.898
HFT(s, lht)	0.158	0.006	−120.806
DS6	MSE$_1$	MSE$_2$	LL
HBT1(h, lht)	0.778	0.025	−166.906
HBT2(h, lht)	0.558	0.017	−166.816
HAT(h, lht)	0.548	0.017	−166.767
HFT(h, lht)	0.540	0.017	−166.673

TABLE 4: Continued.

DS6	MSE$_1$	MSE$_2$	LL
HBT1(s, lht)	0.288	0.009	−166.432
HBT2(s, lht)	0.282	0.009	−166.532
HAT(s, lht)	0.289	0.010	−166.540
HFT(s, lht)	0.294	0.009	−166.440

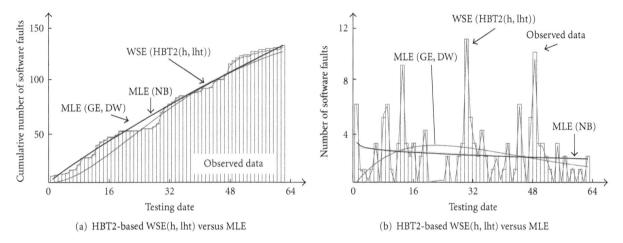

(a) HBT2-based WSE(h, lht) versus MLE

(b) HBT2-based WSE(h, lht) versus MLE

FIGURE 1: Behavior of estimates with MLE and WSE using hard thresholding (DS1).

respectively. We employ the MSE (mean squares error) as the goodness-of-fit measures, where

$$MSE_1 = \frac{\sqrt{\sum_{i=1}^n (\Lambda_i - x_i)^2}}{n},$$

$$MSE_2 = \frac{\sqrt{\sum_{i=1}^n (\lambda_i - y_i)^2}}{n}. \tag{18}$$

Additionally, we calculate LL (Log Likelihood), which is defined as

$$LL = \sum_{i=1}^n (x_i - x_{i-1}) \ln\left[\widehat{\Lambda}_i - \widehat{\Lambda}_{i-1}\right] - \widehat{\Lambda}_n(\theta)$$

$$- \sum_{i=1}^n \ln[(x_i - x_{i-1})!], \tag{19}$$

where $\widehat{\Lambda}_i = \sum_{k=1}^i \widehat{\lambda}_k$ $(i = 1, 2, \ldots, n)$, and $\widehat{\lambda}_i$ is the WSE estimate of the software intensity function λ_i.

5.2. Goodness-of-Fit Test. A total of 16 wavelet-based estimation methods are examined in this paper since the WSE is applied with four thresholding techniques: hard thresholding (h) versus soft thresholding (s); universal threshold (ut) versus "leave-out-half," cross-validation threshold (lht). Let HBT$(\cdot, \cdot)$, HAT$(\cdot, \cdot)$ and HFT$(\cdot, \cdot)$ denote the WSEs based on Haar-Bartlett Transform, Haar-Anscombe Transform and Haar-Freeman Transform, respectively. HBT1$(\cdot, \cdot)$, and HBT2$(\cdot, \cdot)$ correspond to the transforms in (5) and (7), respectively. Additionally, the result of HAT-based WSE was

introduced in [15], but they only showed the results of HAT-based WSE with hard thresholding. Here, we present comprehensively all the results of them for a further discussion.

We present the goodness-of-fit results based on different threshold levels in Tables 3 and 4, respectively. HBT2 provides smaller MSE and larger MLL than the others when "ut" is used, regardless of the thresholding method employed. It is worth mentioning that "ut" provides the same estimates with hard or soft thresholding in three data sets (DS1, DS2, and DS4). This is due to the relatively large value of "ut", since when threshold is set to be 0, the output of thresholding $\delta_\tau(d_{j,k})$ is the wavelet coefficient $d_{j,k}$ itself. In our numerical experiments, "ut" is relatively large in these 3 software-fault count data sets, which result in $\delta_{ut}(d_{j,k}) = 0$ whichever hard or soft thresholding is applied. HBT2 also looks better than the others when software thresholding is applied with "lht." However, when "lht" is combined with hard thresholding, HBT1 (HAT; HFT) possesses the best results in DS3 and DS5 (DS1; DS6), respectively. Since "lht" is considered as a much more proper threshold level than "ut" in analyzing of software-fault count data, we suggest that HBT2 should be selected as an appropriate DT for the WSE.

5.3. Comparison with MLE. Our concern in this section is the comparison of WSE with MLE. We estimate the software intensity function by using three parametric D-NHPP-based SRMs listed in Table 2, where the MLE is applied to estimate the model parameters for comparison. HBT2-based WSE is selected as a representative one among the 16 wavelet-based estimation methods. Figures 1 and 2 depict the estimation behavior of cumulative number of software faults and its increment per testing date (individual number of software

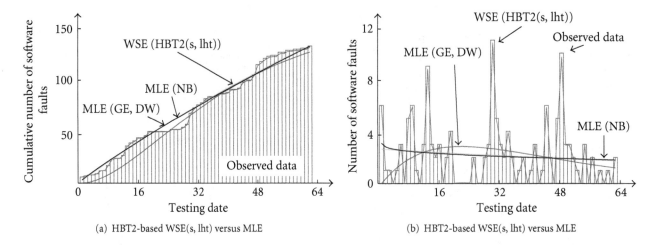

(a) HBT2-based WSE(s, lht) versus MLE   (b) HBT2-based WSE(s, lht) versus MLE

FIGURE 2: Behavior of estimates with MLE and WSE using soft thresholding (DS1).

faults detected per testing date) with DS1. The observed data is plotted in bar graph in both figures. Looking at (i) and (iii) in these figures, it is clear that the parametric D-NHPP-based SRMs with maximum likelihood estimator can fit the real data. However, since the parametric D-NHPP-based SRMs assume the software intensity function as smooth function, they can estimate only the average tendency of the individual number of software faults detected at each testing date, but cannot follow the microscopic fluctuated behavior in (ii) and (iv) of Figures 1 and 2. In other words, the estimation accuracy based on the cumulative number of faults is embedded in "cumulative effects" in (i) and (iii). The experimental results performed here give the potential applicability of the wavelet-based estimation methods with different thresholding schemes. Our methods employed here do not need the expensive computational cost comparing with the MLE (within less than one second to get an estimate). This is a powerful advantage in applying the D-NHPP-based SRMs, in addition to the fact that practitioners do not request much time and effort to implement the wavelet-based estimation algorithms.

6. Concluding Remarks

In this paper, we have applied the wavelet-based techniques to estimate the software intensity function. Four data transformations were employed to preprocess the software-fault count data. Throughout the numerical evaluation, we could conclude that the wavelet-based estimation methods with Bartlett transform $2\sqrt{Y_i}$ have much more potential applicability than the other data transformations to the software reliability assessment practice because practitioners are not requested to carry out troublesome procedures on model selection and to take care of computational efficiency such as judgment of convergence and selecting initial guess of parameters in the general purpose of optimization algorithms. Note that, the result obtained here does not mean that the other data transformations are not good because the performance evaluation was executed only through

goodness-of-fit test. Although the prediction ability of the proposed methods is out of focus of this paper at the present, the predictive performance should be considered and compared in the future.

References

[1] M. R. Lyu, Ed., *Handbook of Software Reliability Engineering*, McGraw-Hill, New York, NY, USA, 1996.

[2] J. D. Musa, A. Iannino, and K. Okumoto, *Software Reliability, Measurement, Prediction, Application*, McGraw-Hill, New York, NY, USA, 1987.

[3] H. Pham, *Software Reliability*, Springer, Singapore, Singapore, 2000.

[4] A. L. Goel and K. Okumoto, "Time-dependent error-detection rate model for software reliability and other performance measures," *IEEE Transactions on Reliability*, vol. R-28, no. 3, pp. 206–211, 1979.

[5] A. L. Goel, "Software reliability models: assumptions, limitations and applicability," *IEEE Transactions on Software Engineering*, vol. SE-11, no. 12, pp. 1411–1423, 1985.

[6] X. Xiao and T. Dohi, "Estimating software reliability using extreme value distribution," in *Proceedings of the International Conference on Advances in Software Engineering and Its Applications (ASEA '11)*, vol. CCIS 257, pp. 399–406, Springer, 2011.

[7] X. Xiao, H. Okamura, and T. Dohi, "NHPP-based software reliability models using equilibrium distribution," *IEICE Transactions of the Fundamentals A*, vol. E95-A, no. 5, pp. 894–902, 2012.

[8] S. Yamada, M. Ohba, and S. Osaki, "S-shaped reliability growth modeling for software error detection," *IEEE Transactions on Reliability*, vol. R-32, no. 5, pp. 475–484, 1983.

[9] A. Sofer and D. R. Miller, "A non-parametric software reliability growth model," *IEEE Transactions on Reliability*, vol. R-40, no. 3, pp. 329–337, 1991.

[10] A. Gandy and U. Jensen, "A non-parametric approach to software reliability," *Applied Stochastic Models in Business and Industry*, vol. 20, no. 1, pp. 3–15, 2004.

[11] M. Barghout, B. Littlewood, and A. Abdel-Ghaly, "A non-parametric order statistics software reliability model," *Software*

A Comparative Study of Data Transformations for Wavelet Shrinkage Estimation with Application to Software Reliability Assessment

143

Testing Verification and Reliability, vol. 8, no. 3, pp. 113–132, 1998.

[12] Z. Wang, J. Wang, and X. Liang, "Non-parametric estimation for NHPP software reliability models," *Journal of Applied Statistics*, vol. 34, no. 1, pp. 107–119, 2007.

[13] M. A. El-Aroui and J. L. Soler, "A bayes nonparametric framework for software-reliability analysis," *IEEE Transactions on Reliability*, vol. 45, no. 4, pp. 652–660, 1996.

[14] S. P. Wilson and F. J. Samaniego, "Nonparametric analysis of the order-statistic model in software reliability," *IEEE Transactions on Software Engineering*, vol. 33, no. 3, pp. 198–208, 2007.

[15] X. Xiao and T. Dohi, "Wavelet-based approach for estimating software reliability," in *Proceedings of the 20th International Symposium on Software Reliability Engineering (ISSRE '09)*, pp. 11–20, IEEE CS Press, November 2009.

[16] F. J. Anscombe, "The transformation of Poisson, binomial and negative binomial data," *Biometrika*, vol. 35, no. 3-4, pp. 246–254, 1948.

[17] M. Fisz, "The limiting distribution of a function of two independent random variables and its statistical application," *Colloquium Mathematicum*, vol. 3, pp. 138–146, 1955.

[18] M. S. Bartlett, "The square root transformation in the analysis of variance," *Journal of the Royal Statistical Society*, vol. 3, no. 1, pp. 68–78, 1936.

[19] M. F. Freeman and J. W. Tukey, "Transformations related to the angular and the square root," *The Annals of Mathematical Statistics*, vol. 21, no. 4, pp. 607–611, 1950.

[20] H. Ishii, T. Dohi, and H. Okamura, "Software reliability prediction based on least squares estimation," *Quality Technology and Quantitative Management Journal*. In press.

[21] D. L. Donoho and J. M. Johnstone, "Ideal spatial adaptation by wavelet shrinkage," *Biometrika*, vol. 81, no. 3, pp. 425–455, 1994.

[22] G. P. Nason, "Wavelet shrinkage using cross-validation," *Journal of the Royal Statistical Society B*, vol. 58, no. 2, pp. 463–479, 1996.

10

Improving Model Checking with Context Modelling

Philippe Dhaussy,[1] Frédéric Boniol,[2] Jean-Charles Roger,[1] and Luka Leroux[1]

[1] Lab-STICC, UMR CNRS 6285, ENSTA Bretagne, 2 rue François Verny, 29806 Brest, France
[2] ONERA, 2 avenue Edouard Belin, 31000 Toulouse, France

Correspondence should be addressed to Philippe Dhaussy, philippe.dhaussy@ensta-bretagne.fr

Academic Editor: Gerardo Canfora

This paper deals with the problem of the usage of formal techniques, based on model checking, where models are large and formal verification techniques face the combinatorial explosion issue. The goal of the approach is to express and verify requirements relative to certain context situations. The idea is to unroll the context into several scenarios and successively compose each scenario with the system and verify the resulting composition. We propose to specify the context in which the behavior occurs using a language called CDL (*Context Description Language*), based on activity and message sequence diagrams. The properties to be verified are specified with textual patterns and attached to specific regions in the context. The central idea is to automatically split each identified context into a set of smaller subcontexts and to compose them with the model to be validated. For that, we have implemented a recursive splitting algorithm in our toolset OBP (Observer-based Prover). This paper shows how this combinatorial explosion could be reduced by specifying the environment of the system to be validated.

1. Introduction

Software verification is an integral part of the software development lifecycle, the goal of which is to ensure that software fully satisfies all the expected requirements. Reactive systems are becoming extremely complex with the huge increase in high technologies. Despite technical improvements, the increasing size of the systems makes the introduction of a wide range of potential errors easier. Among reactive systems, the asynchronous systems communicating by exchanging messages via buffer queues are often characterized by a vast number of possible behaviors. To cope with this difficulty, manufacturers of industrial systems make significant efforts in testing and simulation to successfully pass the certification process. Nevertheless, revealing errors and bugs in this huge number of behaviors remains a very difficult activity. An alternative method is to adopt formal methods, and to use exhaustive and automatic verification tools such as model-checkers.

Model checking algorithms can be used to verify requirements of a model formally and automatically. Several model checkers as [1–5] have been developed to help the verification

of concurrent asynchronous systems. It is well known that an important issue that limits the application of model checking techniques in industrial software projects is the combinatorial explosion problem [6–8]. Because of the internal complexity of developed software, model checking of requirements over the system behavioral models could lead to an unmanageable state space.

The approach described in this paper presents an exploratory work to provide solutions to the problems mentioned above. The proposed approach consists to reduce the set of possible behaviors (and then indirectly the state space) by closing the system under verification with a well-defined environment. For this, we propose to specify the behavior of the entities that compose the system environment. These entities interact with the system. These behaviors are described by use cases (scenarios) called here *contexts*. They describe how the environment interacts with the system. Indeed, in the context of embedded reactive systems, the environment of each system is finite and well known. We claim that it is more efficient to ask the engineers to explicitly and formally express this context, than to search to reduce the state space of the system to explore facing an unspecified environment. In other words, the objective is to circumvent the problem of the combinatorial explosion by restricting the system behavior with a specific surrounding environment describing the different configurations in which one wants to verify the system. Moreover, properties are often related to specific use cases (such as initialization, reconfiguration, and degraded modes) so that it is not necessary for a given property to take into account all possible behaviors of the environment, but only the subpart concerned by the verification. The context description thus allows a first limitation of the explored space search, and hence a first reduction of the combinatorial explosion. The second idea exploited is that, if the context is finite (i.e., there is a noninfinite loop in the context) and in case of safety (invariant) properties, then the two following verification processes are equivalent: (a) compose the context and the system, and then verify the resulting global system; (b) unroll the context into N scenarios (i.e., a sequence of events), and successively compose each scenario with the system and verify the resulting composition. In other words, the global verification problem can be transformed into N smaller verification subproblems.

Our approach is based on these two ideas. This paper presents a DSL (domain-specific language). called CDL (*Context Description Language*) for formally describing the environment of the system to be verified. This language serves to support our approach to reduce the state space. We illustrate our reduction technique with our OBP (*Observer-based Prover*) (OBP is available on http://www.obpcdl.org/.) tool connected to two tools: the first is an academic model checker TINA-SELT (http://projects.laas.fr/tina/) [3] and the second is an explorer called OBP Explorer, integrated in OBP. We illustrate our approach with a partial case study provided by a industrial partner in the aeronautics domain.

This paper is organized as follows: Section 2 presents the related techniques to improve model checking by state reduction. Section 3 presents the principles of our approach for context aware formal verification. Section 4 describes the CDL language for contexts specification and property specification. Our toolset used for the experiments is presented Section 5. In Section 6, we give results on the industrial case study. In Section 7, we discuss our approach and we conclude.

2. Related Works

Model checking is a technique that relies on building a finite model of a system of interest, and checking that a desired property, specified as a temporal logic formula, holds in that model. Since the introduction of this technology in the early 1980s, several model checkers have been developed to help the verification of concurrent asynchronous systems. For example, the SPIN model checker [1] based on the formal language PROMELA allows the verification of LTL properties encoded in "never claim" formalism and further converted into Buchi automata. Since its introduction, model checking has advanced significantly. For instance the state compression method or partial-order reduction contributed

to the further alleviation of combinatorial explosion [9]. In [10], the partial-order algorithm based on a depth-first search (DFS) has been adapted to the breadth first search (BFS) algorithm in the SPIN model checker to exploit interesting properties inherent to the BFS. Partial-order methods [9, 11, 12] aim at eliminating equivalent sequences of transitions in the global state space without modifying the falsity of the property under verification. These methods, exploiting the symmetries of the systems, seemed to be interesting and were integrated into many verification tools (for instance SPIN).

In the same way, the development of more efficient data structure, such as binary decision diagrams (BDD) [13], allows for automatic and exhaustive analysis of finite state models with several thousands of components or state variables.

Another approach deals with compositional verification, for example, assume/guarantee reasoning or design-by-contract techniques. A lot of work exist in applying these techniques to model checking including, for example, [14–17]. These works deal with model checking/analyzing individual components (rather than whole systems) by specifying, considering, or even automatically determining the interactions that a component has or could have with its environment so that the analysis can be restricted to these interactions. Design-by-contract proposes to verify a system by verifying all its components one by one. Using a specific composition operator preserving properties, it allows assuming that the system is verified.

Many other techniques have been proposed for combating state explosion. On-the-fly verification constructs the state space in a demand-driven way, thus allowing the detection of errors without a priori building the entire state space. Distributed verification [18] uses the computing resources of several machines connected by a network, thus allowing to scale up the capabilities of verification tools. In the same objective, methods exploiting heuristic search [19] have been proposed for improving constraint satisfaction problem and more generally for optimizing the exploration for the behaviour of a model to verify.

Combined together, the successful application of these methods to several case studies (see for instance [20] for noncritical application, or [21, 22] for aerospace examples) demonstrates their maturity in the case of synchronous embedded systems. However, if these techniques are useful to find modelling errors, they still suffer from combinatorial explosion in the case of large and complex asynchronous systems (see [23] for an experiment of SPIN on a real asynchronous function showing that the verification does not complete despite all the optimizations mentioned above).

Our approach presented in this paper explores another way for reducing the combinatorial explosion. Conversely to "traditional" techniques in which contexts are often included in the system model, we choose to explicit contexts separately from the model. It is about using the knowledge of the environment of a whole system (or model) to conduct a verification to the end. We propose to formally specify the context behavior in a way that allows a fully automatic divide-and-conquer algorithm.

Another difficulty is about requirement specification. Embedded software systems integrate more and more advanced features, such as complex data structures, recursion, and multithreading. Despite the increased level of automation, users of finite-state verification tools are still constrained to specify the system requirements in their specification language which is often informal. While temporal logic-based languages (example LTL or CTL [6]) allow a great expressivity for the properties, these languages are not adapted to practically describe most of the requirements expressed in industrial analysis documents. Modal and temporal logics are rather rudimentary formalisms for expressing requirements, that is, they are designed having in mind the straight for wardness of its processing by a tool such as a model checker rather than the user-friendliness. Their efficient use in practice is hampered by the difficulty to write logic formula correctly without extensive expertise in the idioms of the specification languages.

In literature, many approaches have been proposed to enable software and hardware engineers to use temporal logic with ease and rigor. For instance [24, 25] proposed a graphical interval logic (RTGIL) allowing visual an intuitive reasoning on real-time systems. From a textual point of view, [26–28] proposed to formulate requirements using textual patterns, that is, textual templates that capture common logical and temporal properties and that can be instantiated in a specific context. They represent commonly occurring types of real-time properties found in several requirement documents for embedded systems. These two approaches have been recently combined by De Francesco et al. in [29]. The authors propose a user-friendly interface with the aim of simplifying the writing of concurrent system properties. This interface supplies a set of patterns from the natural language which are then automatically translated into the mu-calculus temporal logic.

In this paper, we choose to follow this approach. In order to be as simple as possible, we only consider safety properties expressed by using an extension of textual Dwyer's patterns and translated into observer automata and invariants. The work could be extended to other types or properties as proposed in [29]. Such an extension is out of the scope of this article.

3. Context Aware Verification

To illustrate the explosion problem, let us consider the example in Figure 1. We are trying to verify some requirements by model checking using the TINA-SELT model checker [3] and OBP Explorer. We present the results for a part of the S_CP model, which consists in reducing the set of. Then, we introduce our approach based on context specifications.

3.1. An Illustration. We present one part of an industrial case study: the software part of an antiaircraft system (S_CP). This controller controls the internal modes, the system physical devices (sensors, actuators) and their actions in response to incoming signals from the environment. The S_CP system

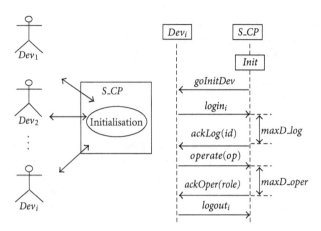

FIGURE 1: *S_CP* system: partial description during the initialization phase.

interacts with devices (*Dev*) that are considered to be *actors* included in the S_CP environment called here *context*.

The sequence diagrams of Figure 2 illustrate interactions between context actors and the *S_CP* system during an initialization phase. This context describes the environment we want to consider for the validation of the *S_CP* controller. This context is composed of several actors *Dev* running in parallel or in sequence. All these actors interleave their behavior. After the initializing phase, all actors Dev_i (i $\in$ [1,...,n]) wait for orders *goInitDev* from the system. Then, actors Dev_i send $login_i$ and receive either *ackLog(id)* (Figures 2(a) and 2(c)) or *nackLog(err)* (Figure 2(b)) as responses from the system. The logged devices can send *operate(op)* (Figures 2(a) and 2(c)) and receive either *ackOper(role)* (Figure 2(a)) or *nackOper(err)* (Figure 2(c)). The messages *goInitDev* can be received in parallel in any order. However, the delay between messages $login_i$ and *ackLog(id)* (Figure 1) is constrained by *maxD_log*. The delay between messages *operate(op)* and *ackOper(role)* (Figure 1) is constrained by *maxD_oper*. And finally all Dev_i send $logout_i$ to end the interaction with the *S_CP* controller.

As example, let's see two requirements on the *S_CP* system. These requirements were found in a document of our partner and are shown in Listings 1 and 2.

The first requirement *R1* is expressed by Listing 1.

We choose to specify this requirement with SELT language for the device *Dev_1*. It is expressed by the following formula:

```
Inv1: []((SM_1_voperateAccepted1) =>
(SM_1_vdevLogged1));
```

SM_1 is a process of *S_CP* and *operateAccepted1* and *devLogged1* are variables of this process. To verify this requirement, we used the TINA-SELT model checker (Figure 3).

Let's see in Listing 2, the second requirement *R2*.

We choose to specify this requirement with an observer automaton (Figure 4). An observer is an automaton which *observes* the set of events exchanged by the system *S* and its context *C* (and thus events occurring in the executions (*runs*) and which produces an event *reject* whenever the

TABLE 1: Table highlighting the verification complexity for the case study with TINA-SELT.

N (Number of devices)	Exploration and model checking time (sec)	Number of LTS configurations	Number of LTS transitions
1	1	22,977	103,354
2	3	172,095	759,094
3	10	718,623	3,127,468
4	27	2,174,997	9,371,560
5	Explosion	—	—

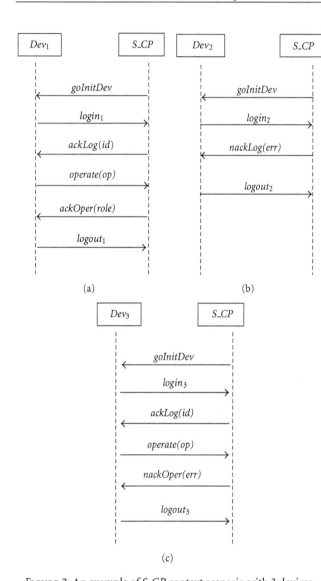

(a)   (b)

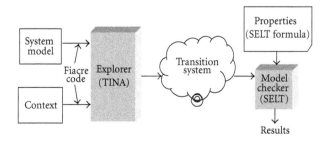

(c)

FIGURE 2: An example of S_CP context scenario with 3 devices.

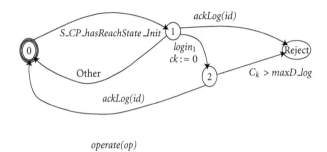

FIGURE 3: Verification with TINA-SELT.

FIGURE 4: Observer automaton for requirement R2.

property becomes false. With observers, the properties we can handle are of safety and bounded liveness type. The accessibility analysis consists of checking if there is a reject state reached by a property observer. In our example, this reject node is reached after detecting the event sequence of S_CP_hasReachState_Init and login₁, in that order, if the sequence of one or more of ackLog is not produced before maxD_log time units. Conversely, the reject node is not reached either if S_CP_hasReachState_Init or login₁ are never received, or if ackLog event above is correctly produced with the right delay. Consequently, such a property can be verified by using reachability analysis implemented in our OBP Explorer.

This observer is checked with OBP Explorer (Figure 5).

In both cases, the system model (Here by system model, we refer to the model to be validated) is translated into Fiacre format [30] to explore all the S_CP model behaviors by simulation, S_CP interacting with its environment (devices). Model exploration generates a labeled transition system (LTS) which represents all the behaviors of the controller in its environment.

3.2. Model Checking Results. Table 1 shows (tests were executed on Linux 32 bits—3 Go RAM computer, with TINA vers.2.9.8 and Frac parser vers.1.6.2.) the TINA-SELT exploration time and the amount of configurations and transitions in the LTS for different complexities (N indicates the number of considered actors). Over four devices, we see a state explosion because of the limited memory of our computer.

Table 2 shows (tests were executed on Linux 32 bits—3 Go RAM computer, with OBP Explorer vers.1.0.) the OBP Explorer exploration analyze time and the amount of configurations and transitions in the LTS. Over three devices,

R1: A device (Dev) can be authorized to execute a command "operate" if it has previously connected to the system.

LISTING 1: Permission requirement for command "operate".

R2: During initialization procedure, S_CP shall associate an identifier to each device (Dev), after login request and before maxD_log time units.

LISTING 2: Initialization requirement for the S_CP system.

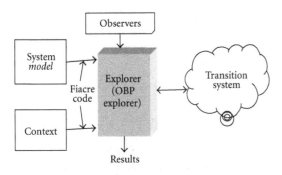

FIGURE 5: Verification with OBP Explorer.

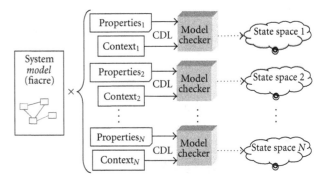

FIGURE 6: Context-aware model checking.

we see also a state explosion because of the limited memory of our computer.

Note that the size of the LTS explored by OBP Explorer for verifying R2 is greater than the size of the related LTS explored by TINA-SELT for verifying R1. This is due to the way chosen for modeling these two requirements. R1 is formalized as a SELT formula, and R2 is modeled as an observer automaton. In the second experiment (R2 with OBP Explorer), the explorer begins by building the synchronized product between the model of the system, each context and the observer automaton. If this automaton contains several locations and several clocks, taking into account the observer as an input of the synchronized product could significantly increase the number of states and transitions explored.

3.3. Combinatorial Explosion Reduction. When checking the properties, a model checker explores all the model behaviors and checks whether the properties are true or not. Most of the time, as shown by previous results, the number of reachable configurations is too large to be contained in memory (Figures 3 and 5). We propose to restrict model behavior by composing it with an environment that interacts with the model. The environment enables a subset of the behavior of the model. This technique can reduce the complexity of the exploration by limiting the scope of the verification to precise system behaviors related to some specific environmental conditions.

This reduction is computed in two stages: contexts are first identified by the user (*context$_i$, $i \in [1, \ldots, N]$*

in Figure 6). They correspond to patterns of use of the component being modeled. The aim is to circumvent the combinatorial explosion by restricting the behavior system with an environment describing different configurations in which one wishes check the requirements. Then each context *context$_i$* is automatically partitioned into a set of subcontexts. Here, we precisely define these two aspects implemented in our approach.

3.3.1. Context Identification. The context identification focuses on a subset of behavior and a subset of properties. In the context of reactive embedded systems, the environment of each component of a system is often well known. It is therefore more effective to identify this environment than trying reduce the configuration space of the model system to explore. The proof relevance is based on a strong hypothesis: *it is possible to specify the sets of bounded behaviors in a complete way.* This hypothesis not formally justified in our work. But, in this approach, the essential idea is *the designer can correctly develop a software only if he knows the constraints of its use.* So, we suppose that the designer is able to identify all possible interactions between the system and its environment.

It's particularly true in the field of embedded systems, with the fact that the designer of a software component needs to know precisely and completely the perimeter (constraints, conditions) of its system for properly developing it.

TABLE 2: Table highlighting the verification complexity for the case study with OBP Explorer.

N (Number of devices)	Exploration and analyze time (sec)	Number of LTS configurations	Number of LTS transitions
1	1	43,828	321,002
2	4	350,256	2,475,392
3	19	1,466,934	6,430,265
4	Explosion	—	—

We also consider second hypothesis. It expresses that the contexts we describe are finite. There are no infinite loops in the interactions between the system and its environment. It is particularly true for instance with command systems or communication protocols.

It would be necessary to study formally the validity of these working hypothesis based on the targeted applications. In this paper, we do not address this aspect that gives rise to a methodological work to be undertaken.

Moreover, properties are often related to specific use cases (such as initialization, reconfiguration, and degraded modes). Therefore, it is not necessary for a given property to take into account all possible behaviors of the environment, but only the subpart concerned by the verification. The context description thus allows a first limitation of the explored space search, and hence a first reduction in the combinatorial explosion.

3.3.2. Context Automatic Splitting. The second idea is to automatically split each identified context into a set of smaller subcontexts (Figure 7). The principle of splitting is as following: each context is represented by an acyclic graph as mentioned earlier. This graph is composed with the model for exploration. In case of explosion, this context is automatically split into several parts taking into account a parameter for the depth in the graph for splitting until the exploration succeeds.

To reach that goal, we implemented a recursive splitting algorithm in our OBP tool. Figure 7 illustrates the function $explore\_mc()$ for exploration of a *model*, with a $context_i$ and model checking of a set of properties pty.

We illustrate one execution of this algorithm in Figures 8 and 9. One context $context_i$, represented by an acyclic graph, is composed with the model S for exploration. In case of explosion, $context_i$ is automatically split into several parts (taking into account a parameter d which specifies the depth in the graph for splitting) until the exploration succeeds. For example in Figure 8, the graph of $context_i$ is split in four graphs $context_{i1}$; $context_{i2}$, $context_{i3}$, and $context_{i4}$. After splitting of $context_i$, the subcontexts are composed with the model for exploration. If exploration fails, one subcontext is split, as $context_{i3}$ into $context_{i31}$ and $context_{i32}$, taking into account parameter d.

In Figure 9, we illustrate $context_i$ which is split into C_{i1}, C_{i2}, and C_{i3} subcontexts and composed with model S. the exploration of $model\|C_{i1}$ successes (we note $\|$ as composition operator). The explorations of $model\|C_{i2}$ and $model\|C_{i3}$ fail. So, C_{i2} (resp., C_{i3}) is split into subcontexts C_{i21} and C_{i22} (C_{i31} and C_{i32} resp.,). In the same way,

C_{i31} is split into subcontexts C_{i311}, C_{i312}, and C_{i313}. This algorithm is executed until all the explorations succeed. Since the property set pty is associated with the context $context_i$, pty is checked during the explorations with all subcontexts. We demonstrated in [31] that the verification of property set (as pty) taking into account of $model\|context_i$ exploration is equivalent union of verifications taking into account each $model\|C_k$ exploration (C_k is each subcontext $C_{i1}, C_{i21}, C_{i22}, C_{i32}, C_{i311}, C_{i312}$, and C_{i313} as illustrated in Figure 9).

The following verification processes are then equivalent: (i) compose the context $context_i$ and the system, and then verify the resulting global system, (ii) partition the context $context_i$ into K_i subcontexts (scenarios), and successively deal each scenario with the model and check the properties on the outcome of each composition. Actually, we transform the global verification problem for $context_i$ into K_i smaller verification subproblems. In our approach, the complete context model can be split into pieces that have to be composed separately with the system model.

In summary, the context aware method provides three reduction axes: the context behavior is constrained, the properties are focused, and the state space is split into pieces. Finally, the N verifications for the set of N contexts is transformed into N' verifications with $N' = \sum_{i=1}^{N} K_i$ small verifications.

The reduction in the model behavior is particularly interesting while dealing with complex embedded systems, such as in avionic systems, since it is relevant to check properties over specific system modes (or use cases) which is less complex because we are dealing with a subset of the system automata. Unfortunately, only few existing approaches propose operational ways to precisely capture these contexts in order to reduce formal verification complexity and thus improve the scalability of existing model checking approaches. The necessity of a clear methodology has also to be identified, since the context partitioning is not trivial, that is, it requires the formalization of the context of the subset of functions under study. An associated methodology must be defined to help users for modeling contexts (out of scope of this paper).

4. CDL Language for Context and Property Specification

We propose a formal tool-supported framework that combines context description and model transformations to assist in the definition of requirements and of the environmental conditions in which they should be satisfied. Thus,

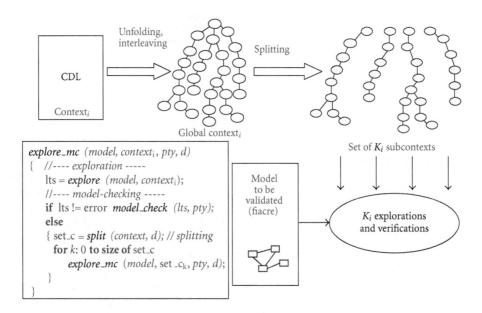

FIGURE 7: Context splitting and verification for each partition (subcontext).

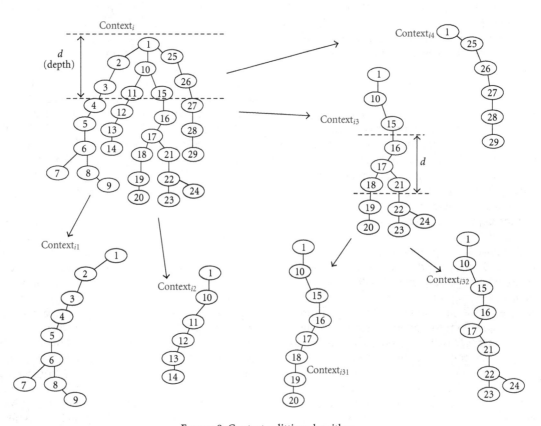

FIGURE 8: Context splitting algorithm.

we proposed [32] a context-aware verification process that makes use of the CDL language. CDL was proposed to fill the gap between user models and formal models required to perform formal verifications. CDL is a (domain specific language) presented either in the form of UML like graphical diagrams (a subset of activity and sequence diagrams) or in a textual form to capture environment interactions.

4.1. Context Hierarchical Description. CDL is based on Use Case Charts of [33] using activity and sequence diagrams. We extended this language to allow several entities (actors) to be described in a context (Figure 10). These entities run in parallel. A CDL (For the detailed syntax, see [34] available on http://www.obpcdl.org/.) model describes, on the one hand, the context using activity and sequence diagrams

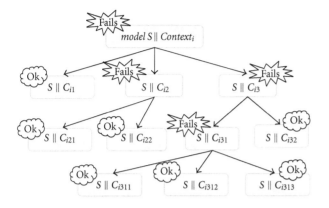

FIGURE 9: An example of context splitting execution.

and, on the other hand, the properties to be checked using property patterns. Figure 10 illustrates a CDL model for the partial use cases of Figures 1 and 2. Initial use cases and sequence diagrams are transformed and completed to create the context model. All context scenarios are represented, combined with parallel and alternative operators, in terms of CDL.

A diagrammatical and textual concrete syntax is created for the context description and a textual syntax for the property expression. CDL is hierarchically constructed in three levels: level 1 is a set of use case diagrams which describes hierarchical activity diagrams. Either alternative between several executions (alternative/merge) or a parallelization of several executions (fork/join) is available. Level 2 is a set of scenario diagrams organized in alternatives. Each scenario is fully described at level 3 by sequence diagrams. These diagrams are composed of lifelines, some for the context actors and others for processes composing the system model. Counters limit the iterations of diagram executions. This ensures the generation of finite context automata.

From a semantic point of view, we can consider that the model is structured in a set of sequence diagrams (MSCs) connected together with three operators: sequence (seq), parallel (par), and alternative (alt). The interleaving of context actors described by a set of MSCs generates a graph representing all executions of the actors of the environment. This graph is then partitioned in such a way as to generate a set of subgraphs corresponding to the subcontexts as mentioned in Section 3.3.

The originality of CDL is its ability to link each expressed property to a context diagram, that is, a limited scope of the system behavior. The properties can be specified with property pattern definitions described in [32, 34]. For checking, properties are linked to one or several context descriptions. Listing 3, we illustrate an example (textual version) of a scenario (scenario_ex) with linked properties: three observer-based properties $P1$, $P2$, and $P3$ (Pi ($i \in [1,...,3]$) property specifying requirement $R2$) and three invariants $Inv1$, $Inv2$, and $Inv1$ ($Invi$ ($i \in [1,...,3]$) property specifying requirement

$R1$). As example, properties $P1$ and $Inv1$ are specified at Section 4.2.

The clause init specifies an initialization with an activity. Actors DEV1, DEV2, and DEV3 are specified with activities, by Listing 4.

In Listing 4, the operators ";" and "[]" are respectively the sequence (seq) and alternative (alt) operators. CDL is designed so that formal artifacts required by existing model checkers could be automatically generated from it. This generation is currently implemented in OBP described briefly in Section 5. The CDL formal syntax and semantics are presented in [35].

4.2. Property Specification Patterns. Property specifying needs to use powerful yet easy mechanisms for expressing temporal requirements of software source code. As example, requirements as $R1$ or $R2$ of the S_CP system described in Section 3.1 can refer to many events related to the execution of the model or environment. Also, a requirement can depends on an execution history that has to be taken into account as a constraint or precondition.

If we want to express these kinds of requirements with a temporal logic based language as LTL or CTL, the logical formulas are of great complexity and become difficult to read and to handle by engineers. So, for the property specification, we propose to reuse the categories of Dwyer patterns [26] and extend them to deal with more specific temporal properties which appear when high-level specifications are refined. Additionally, a textual syntax is proposed to formalize properties to be checked using property description patterns [28]. To improve the expressiveness of these patterns, we enriched them with options (*Prearity*, *Postarity*, *Immediacy*, *Precedence*, *Nullity*, and *Repeatability*) using annotations as [27]. Choosing among these options should help the user to consider the relevant alternatives and subtleties associated with the intended behavior. These annotations allow these details to be explicitly captured. During a future work, we will adapt these patterns taking into account the taxonomy of relevant properties, if this appears necessary.

We integrate property patterns description in the CDL language. Patterns are classified in families, which take into account the timed aspects of the properties to be specified. The identified patterns support properties of answer (*Response*), the necessity one (*Precedence*), of absence (*Absence*), of existence (*Existence*) to be expressed. The properties refer to detectable events like transmissions or receptions of signals, actions, and model state changes. The property must be taken into account either during the entire model execution, before, after, or between occurrences of events. Another extension of the patterns is the possibility of handling sets of events, ordered or not ordered similar to the proposal of [36]. The operators *AN* and *ALL*, respectively, specify if an event or all the events, ordered (Ordered) or not (Combined), of an event set are concerned with the property.

We illustrate these patterns with our case study. The given requirement $R2$ (Listing 2) must be interpreted and can be written with CDL in a property $P1$ as follow (cf. Listing 5). $P1$ is linked to the communication sequence

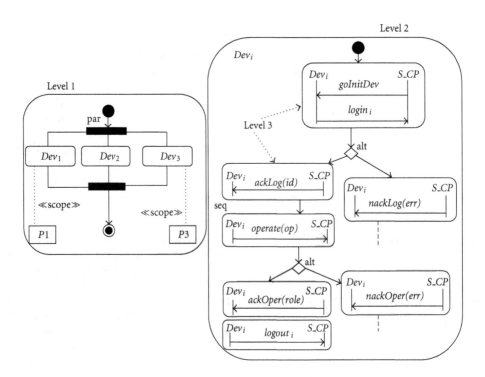

FIGURE 10: S_CP case study; partial representation of the context.

```
cdl scenario_ex is
{
  properties P1, P2, P3        // references to observers
  assert Inv1, Inv2, Inv3      // references to invariants
  init is { initDevs }                   // initialization sequence
  main is { DEV1 || DEV2 || DEV3 }       // body of scenario
}
```

LISTING 3: A CDL scenario with several observer-based properties and invariants.

between the S_CP and device (Dev_1). According to the sequence diagram of Figure 10, the association to other devices has no effect on P1.

P1 specifies an observation of event occurrences in accordance with Figure 10. login1 refers to $login_1$ reception event in the model, ackLog refers to ackLog reception event by Dev_1. S_CP_hasReachState_Init refers a state change in the model under study.

In CDL, we specify properties with events and predicates. For example, the event S_CP_hasReachState_Init is defined with predicate S_CP_State_Init as follows:

```
event S_CP_hasReachState_Init is
{S_CP_State_Init becomes true}
```

The predicate S_CP_State_Init is defined as follows:

```
predicate S_CP_State_Init is {{SM}
1@State_Init}
```

with State_Init as a state of process SM_1.

Invariants are specified with CDL predicats. As example, invariant Inv1 is specified as in Listing 6.

5. OBP Toolset

To carry out our experiments, we used OBP tool (Figure 11). OBP is an implementation of a CDL language translation in terms of formal languages, that is, currently Fiacre [30]. As depicted in Figure 11, OBP leverages existing academic model checkers such as TINA-SELT [3] or simulators such as OBP Explorer. From CDL context diagrams, the OBP tool generates a set of context graphs which represent the sets of the environment runs. Currently, each generated graph is transformed into a Fiacre automaton. Each graph represents a set of possible interactions between model and context. To validate the model under study, it is necessary to compose each graph with the model. Each property on

```
activity DEV1 is
{
    { event send_login1; {event recv_ack_log1 [] event recv_nack_log1}};
    { event send_operate1; {event recv_ack_oper1 [] event recv_nack_oper1}};
    { send logout1 to { SM }1}
}
```

LISTING 4: An CDL activity.

```
Property P1;
    ALL Ordered
        exactly one occurrence of S_CP_hasReachState_Init
        exactly one occurrence of login1
    end
    eventually leads-to [0..maxD_log]
    AN
        one or more occurrence of ackLog (id)
    end
    S_CP_hasReachState_Init may never occurs
    login1 may never occurs
    one of ackLog (id) cannot occur before login1
    repeatability: true
```

LISTING 5: A response pattern from *R2* requirement.

each graph must be verified. In the case of TINA-SELT, the properties are expressed with SELT logic formula [3]. With OBP Explorer, OBP generates an observer automaton [37] from each property for OBP Explorer. With OBP Explorer, the accessibility analysis is carried out on the result of the composition between a graph, a set of observers and the system model as described in [32]. If for a given context, we face state explosion, the accessibility analysis, or model-checking is not possible. In this case, the context is split into a subset of contexts and the composition is executed again as mentioned in Section 3.3.

To import models with standard format such as UML, SysML, AADL, and SDL, we necessarily need to implement adequate translators such as those studied in Top-Cased (http://www.topcased.org/) or Omega (http://www-omega.imag.fr/.) projects to generate Fiacre programs.

6. Experiments and Results

Our approach was applied to several embedded systems applications in the avionic or electronic industrial domain. These experiments were carried out with our French industrial partners. In [32], we reported the results of these experiments. For the *S_CP* case study, we constructed several CDL models with different complexities depending on the number of devices. The tests are performed on each CDL model composed with *S_CP* system.

Table 3 shows the amount of TINA-SELT exploration and model checking (tests with same computer as for Table 1) for checking of requirement *R1* with the use of context splitting. The first column depicts the number *N* of *Dev* asking for login to the *S_CP*. The third one indicates the number of subcontext after splitting by OBP. The other columns depict the exploration time and the cumulative amount of configurations and transitions of all LTS generated during exploration by TINA with context splitting. For example, with 7 devices, we needed to split the CDL context in 56 parts for successful exploration. Without splitting, the exploration is limited to 4 devices by state explosion as shown Table 1. It is clear that device number limit depends on the memory size of used computer.

Table 4 shows the amount of OBP Explorer exploration and analyze (tests with same computer as for Table 2) for checking of requirement *R2* with the use of context splitting. With 7 devices, we needed to split the CDL context in 344 parts for successful exploration. Without splitting, the exploration is limited to three devices by state explosion as shown Table 2.

As mentioned previously in Section 3.2, the size of the LTS explored by OBP Explorer for verifying *R2* is greater than the size of the related LTS explored by TINA-SELT for verifying *R1*. In that case, being able to split the contexts in order to overcome this new source of combinatorial explosion, as proposed by OBP, is of greater importance.

```
predicate Inv1 is
{ ({SM}1:operateAccepted1 = false) or ({SM}1:devLogged1 = true) }
```

LISTING 6: A CDL invariant.

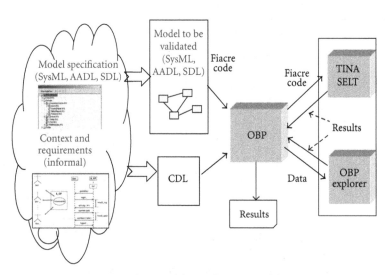

FIGURE 11: CDL model transformation with OBP.

The example given (Figure 1) illustrates a case where there are lots of asynchrony in the behavior of environment actors, causing an explosion in the number of states and thus an increase in the number of contextes generated. We obtain a good performance with this method in case the one hand, the contexts restrict significantly the behavior of the model to be validated (space-complexity reduction) and, secondly, in case the context number is not too large (time-complexity reduction).

Exploration can easily be parallelized. In fact, the splitting method allows contexts to be distributed on machine network. We do not yet implement this parallelization technique, but it can be very effective. Suppose we have a network of N similar machines. We can divide by N time of global exploration. This is an approximation by considering that the context transfer delays and result return delays are negligible compared to the exploration time on a machine. We should take into account the exploration time is not identical for all contexts. But parallelization can significantly improve the proof execution time. For example, in case shown in Table 4, with 20 machines (resp., 100), we can hope to obtain an execution time of approximately 5 minutes (resp. 1 minute) instead of two hours on a single machine. We believe our method of context splitting is complementary with other reduction methods. On some machine, for one subcontext, we can use another technique complementary way.

7. Discussion and Conclusion

CDL is a prototype language to formalize contexts and properties. However, CDL concepts can be implemented in another language. For example, context diagrams are easily described using full UML2. CDL permits us to study our methodology. In future work, CDL can be viewed as an intermediate language. Today, the results obtained using the currently implemented CDL language and OBP are very encouraging. For each case study, it was possible to build CDL models and to generate sets of context graphs with OBP.

During experiments, we noted that some contexts and requirements were often described in the available documentation in an incomplete way. During the collaboration with us, these engineers responsible for developing this documentation were motivated to consider a more formal approach to express their requirements, which is certainly a positive improvement.

In case studies, context diagrams were built, on the one hand, from scenarios described in the design documents and, on the other hand, from the sentences of requirement documents. Two major difficulties have arisen. The first is the lack of complete and coherent description of the environment behavior. Use cases describing interactions between the system (S_CP for instance) and its environment are often incomplete. For instance, data concerning interaction modes may be implicit. CDL diagram development thus requires discussions with experts who have designed the models under study in order to explicate all context assumptions. The problem comes from the difficulty in formalizing system requirements into formal properties. These requirements are expressed in several documents of different (possibly low) levels. Furthermore, they are written in a textual form, and many of them can have several interpretations. Others implicitly refer to an applicable configuration, operational

TABLE 3: Exploration and model checking of $R1$ with TINA-SELT with context splitting using OBP.

Number of devices	Exploration time (sec)	Number of sub-contexts	Number of LTS configurations	Number of LTS transitions
5	112	3	2,233,959	9,875,418
6	2,150	42	32,185,530	158,230,583
7	4,209	56	66,398,542	330,148,458

TABLE 4: Exploration and analyze of $R2$ with OBP Explorer with context splitting using OBP.

Number of devices	Exploration time (sec)	Number of sub-contexts	Number of LTS configurations	Number of LTS transitions
4	954	22	16,450,288	75,362,832
5	1,256	28	33,568,422	156,743,290
6	3,442	242	68,880,326	368,452,864
7	6,480	344	126,450,324	634,382,590

phase, or history without defining it. Such information, necessary for verification, can only be deduced by manually analyzing design and requirement documents and by interviewing expert engineers.

The use of CDL as a framework for formal and explicit context and requirement definition can overcome these two difficulties: it uses a specification style very close to UML and thus readable by engineers. In all case studies, the feedback from industrial collaborators indicates that CDL models enhance communication between developers with different levels of experience and backgrounds. Additionally, CDL models enable developers, guided by behavior CDL diagrams, to structure and formalize the environment description of their systems and their requirements.

One element highlighted when working on embedded software case studies with industrial partners, is the need for formal verification expertise capitalization. Given our experience in formal checking for validation activities it seems important to structure the approach and the data handled during the verifications. That can lead to a better methodological framework, and afterwards a better integration of validation techniques in model development processes. Consequently, the development process must include a step of environment specification making it possible to identify sets of bounded behaviors in a complete way.

Although the CDL approach has been shown scalable in several industrial case studies, the approach suffers from a lack of methodology. The handling of contexts, and then the formalization of CDL diagrams, must be done carefully in order to avoid combinatorial explosion when generating context graphs to be composed with the model to be validated. The definition of such a methodology will be addressed by the next step of this work.

References

[1] G. J. Holzmann, "The model checker SPIN," *IEEE Transactions on Software Engineering*, vol. 23, no. 5, pp. 279–295, 1997.

[2] K. G. Larsen, P. Pettersson, and W. Yi, "UPPAAL in a nutshell," *International Journal on Software Tools For Technology Transfer*, vol. 1, no. 1-2, pp. 134–152, 1997.

[3] B. Berthomieu, P. O. Ribet, and F. Vernadat, "The tool TINA—construction of abstract state spaces for petri nets and time petri nets," *International Journal of Production Research*, vol. 42, no. 14, pp. 2741–2756, 2004.

[4] J. C. Fernandez, H. Garavel, A. Kerbrat, L. Mounier, R. Mateescu, and M. Sighireanu, "Cadp: a protocol validation and verification toolbox," in *Proceedings of the 8th International Conference on Computer Aided Verification(CAV '96)*, pp. 437–440, London, UK, 1996.

[5] A. Cimatti, E. Clarke, F. Giunchiglia, and M. Roveri, "Nusmv: a new symbolic model checker," *The International Journal on Software Tools for Technology Transfer*, vol. 2, no. 4, pp. 410–425, 2000.

[6] E. M. Clarke, E. A. Emerson, and A. P. Sistla, "Automatic verification of finite-state concurrent systems using temporal logic specifications," *ACM Transactions on Programming Languages and Systems*, vol. 8, no. 2, pp. 244–263, 1986.

[7] G. J. Holzmann and D. Peled, "An improvement in formal verification," in *Proceedings of the Formal Description Techniques (FORTE '94)*, pp. 197–211, Chapman & Hall, Berne, Switzerland, October 1994.

[8] S. Park and G. Kwon, "Avoidance of state explosion using dependency analysis in model checking control flow model," in *Proceedings of the 5th International Conference on Computational Science and Its Applications (ICCSA '06)*, vol. 3984 of *Lecture Notes in Computer Science*, pp. 905–911, 2006.

[9] P. Godefroid, "The Ulg partial-order package for SPIN," in *Proceedings of the International Conference on Model Checking Software (SPIN '95)*, Montréal, Quebec, Canada, October 1995.

[10] D. Bošnacki and G. J. Holzmann, "Improving Spin's partial-order reduction for breadth-first search," in *Proceedings of the 12th International SPIN Workshop on Model Checking Software (SPIN '05)*, pp. 91–105, August 2005.

[11] D. Peled, "Combining partial-order reductions with on-the-fly model-checking," in *Proceedings of the 6th International Conference on Computer Aided Verification (CAV '94)*, pp. 377–390, Springer, London, UK, 1994.

[12] A. Valmari, "Stubborn sets for reduced state space generation," in *Proceedings of the 10th International Conference on Applications and Theory of Petri Nets*, pp. 491–515, Springer, London, UK, 1991.

[13] J. R. Burch, E. M. Clarke, K. L. McMillan, D. L. Dill, and L. J. Hwang, "Symbolic model checking: 1020 states and beyond," in *Proceedings of the 5th Annual IEEE Symposium on Logic in Computer Science*, pp. 428–439, June 1990.

[14] E. M. Clarke, D. E. Long, and K. L. Mcmillan, *Compositional Model Checking*, MIT Press, 1999.

[15] C. Flanagan and S. Qadeer, "Thread-modular model checking," in *Proceedings of the 10th International Conference on Model Checking Software (SPIN '03)*, vol. 2648 of *Lecture Notes in Computer Science*, pp. 213–224, 2003.

[16] O. Tkachuk and M. B. Dwyer, "Automated environment generation for software model checking," in *Proceedings of the 18th International Conference on Automated Software Engineering*, pp. 116–129, 2003.

[17] L. De Alfaro and T. A. Henzinger, "Interface automata," in *Proceedings of the 8th Eiropean Engineering Conference and 9th ACM SIGSOFT Symposium on the Foundations of Software Engineering (FSE '01)*, pp. 109–120, ACM Press, September 2001.

[18] J. Barnat, L. Brim, and J. Stříbrná, "Distributed ltl model-checking in spin," in *Proceedings of the 8th International SPIN Workshop on Model Checking of Software (SPIN '01)*, pp. 200–216, Springer, New York, NY, USA, 2001.

[19] S. Edelkamp and S. Schroedl, *Heuristic Search—Theory and Applications*, Academic Press, 2012.

[20] K. Havelund, A. Skou, K. G. Larsen, and K. Lund, "Formal modeling and analysis of an audio/video protocol: an industrial case study using UPPAAL," in *Proceedings of the 18th IEEE Real-Time Systems Symposium*, pp. 2–13, December 1997.

[21] F. Boniol, V. Wiels, and E. Ledinot, "Experiences using model checking to verify real time properties of a landing gear control system," in *Proceedings of the 5th European Congress ERTS Embedded Real Time Software (ERTS '06)*, Toulouse, France, 2006.

[22] T. Bochot, P. Virelizier, H. Waeselynck, and V. Wiels, "Model checking flight control systems: the Airbus experience," in *Proceedings of the 31st International Conference on Software Engineering (ICSE '09)*, pp. 18–27, May 2009.

[23] X. Dumas, P. Dhaussy, F. Boniol, and E. Bonnafous, "Application of partial-order methods for the verification of closed-loop SDL systems," in *Proceedings of the 26th Annual ACM Symposium on Applied Computing (SAC '11)*, W. C. Chu, W. Eric Wong, M. J. Palakal, and C. C. Hung, Eds., pp. 1666–1673, March 2011.

[24] L. E. Moser, Y. S. Ramakrishna, G. Kutty, P. M. Melliar-Smith, and L. K. Dillon, "A graphical environment for the design of concurrent real-time systems," *ACM Transactions on Software Engineering and Methodology*, vol. 6, no. 1, pp. 31–79, 1997.

[25] Y. S. Ramakrishna, L. K. Dillon, L. E. Moser, P. M. Melliar-Smith, and G. Kutty, "Real-time interval logic and its decision procedure," in *Proceedings of the 13th Foundations of Software Technology and Theoretical Computer Science Conference (FSTTCS '93)*, vol. 761 of *Lecture Notes in Computer Science*, pp. 173–192, 1993.

[26] M. B. Dwyer, G. S. Avrunin, and J. C. Corbett, "Patterns in property specifications for finite-state verification," in *Proceedings of the 21st International Conference on Software Engineering*, pp. 411–420, IEEE Computer Society Press, May 1999.

[27] R. L. Smith, G. S. Avrunin, L. A. Clarke, and L. J. Osterweil, "PROPEL: an approach supporting property elucidation," in *Proceedings of the 24th International Conference on Software Engineering (ICSE '02)*, pp. 11–21, St Louis, Mo, USA, May 2002.

[28] S. Konrad and B. H. C. Cheng, "Real-time specification patterns," in *Proceedings of the 27th International Conference on Software Engineering (ICSE '05)*, pp. 372–381, St Louis, Mo, USA, May 2005.

[29] N. De Francesco, A. Santone, and G. Vaglini, "A user-friendly interface to specify temporal properties of concurrent systems," *Information Sciences*, vol. 177, no. 1, pp. 299–311, 2007.

[30] P. Farail, P. Gaufillet, F. Peres et al., "FIACRE: an intermediate language for model verification in the TOPCASED environment," in *Proceedings of the European Congress on Embedded Real-Time Software (ERTS '08)*, Toulouse, France, Janvier 2008.

[31] J. C. Roger, *Exploitation de contextes et d'observateurs pour la validation formelle de modèles [Ph.D. thesis]*, ENSIETA, Université de Rennes I., December 2006.

[32] P. Dhaussy, P. Y. Pillain, S. Creff, A. Raji, Y. Le Traon, and B. Baudry, "Evaluating context descriptions and property definition patterns for software formal validation," in *Proceedings of the 12th IEEE/ACM Conference Model Driven Engineering Languages and Systems (Models '09)*, vol. 5795 of *Lecture Notes in Computer Science*, pp. 438–452, Springer, 2009.

[33] J. Whittle, "Specifying precise use cases with use case charts," in *Proceedings of the International Conference on Satellite Events at the MoDELS (MoDELS '06)*, vol. 3844 of *Lecture Notes in Computer Science*, pp. 290–301, 2006.

[34] P. Dhaussy and J. C. Roger, "Cdl (context description language): syntax and semantics," Tech. Rep., ENSTA, Bretagne, France, 2011.

[35] P. Dhaussy, F. Boniol, and J.-C. Roger, "Reducing state explosion with context modeling for model-checking," in *Proceedings of the 13th IEEE International High Assurance Systems Engineering Symposium (Hase '11)*, Boca Raton, Fla, USA, 2011.

[36] W. Janssen, R. Mateescu, S. Mauw, P. Fennema, and P. Van Der Stappen, "Model checking for managers," in *Proceedings of the International SPIN Workshop on Model Checking of Software*, pp. 92–107, 1992.

[37] N. Halbwachs, F. Lagnier, and P. Raymond, "Synchronous observers and the verification of reactive systems," in *Proceedings of the 3rd International Conference on Algebraic Methodology and Software Technology (AMAST '93)*, M. Nivat, C. Rattray, T. Rus, and G. Scollo, Eds., Workshops in Computing, Springer, Twente, The Netherlands, June 1993.

11

Combining Slicing and Constraint Solving for Better Debugging: The CONBAS Approach

Birgit Hofer and Franz Wotawa

Institute for Software Technology, Graz University of Technology, 8010 Graz, Austria

Correspondence should be addressed to Franz Wotawa, wotawa@ist.tugraz.at

Academic Editor: Zhenyu Zhang

Although slices provide a good basis for analyzing programs during debugging, they lack in their capabilities providing precise information regarding the most likely root causes of faults. Hence, a lot of work is left to the programmer during fault localization. In this paper, we present an approach that combines an advanced dynamic slicing method with constraint solving in order to reduce the number of delivered fault candidates. The approach is called Constraints Based Slicing (CONBAS). The idea behind CONBAS is to convert an execution trace of a failing test case into its constraint representation and to check if it is possible to find values for all variables in the execution trace so that there is no contradiction with the test case. For doing so, we make use of the correctness and incorrectness assumptions behind a diagnosis, the given failing test case. Beside the theoretical foundations and the algorithm, we present empirical results and discuss future research. The obtained empirical results indicate an improvement of about 28% for the single fault and 50% for the double-fault case compared to dynamic slicing approaches.

1. Introduction

Debugging, that is, locating a fault in a program and correcting it, is a tedious and very time-consuming task that is mainly performed manually. There have been several approaches published that aid the debugging process. However, these approaches are hardly used by programmers except for tools allowing to set breakpoints and to observe the computation of variable values during execution. There are many reasons that justify this observation. In particular, most of the debugging tools do not smoothly integrate with the software development tools. In addition, debuggers fail to identify unique root causes and still leave a lot of work for the programmer. Moreover, the approaches can also be computationally demanding, which prevents them from being used in an interactive manner. In this paper, we do not claim to solve all of the mentioned problems. We discuss a method that improves debugging results when using dependence-based approaches like dynamic slicing. Our method makes use of execution traces and the dependencies between the executed statements. In contrast to slicing, we also use symbolic

execution to further reduce the number of potential root causes.

In order to introduce our method, we make use of the program `numfun` that implements a numeric function. The program and a test case are given in Figure 1. When executing the program using the test case, `numfun` returns a value of 10 for variable f, which contradicts the expectations. Since the value for variable g is computed correctly, we only need to consider the dependencies for variable f at position 6. Tracing back these dependencies, we are able to collect statements 6, 4, 3, 2, and 1 as possible fault candidates. Lines 7 and 5 can be excluded because both lines do not contribute to the computation of the value for f. The question now is can we do better? In the case of `numfun`, we are able to further exclude statements from the list of candidates. For example, if we assume that the statement in Line 4 is faulty, the value of y has to be computed in a different way. However, from Statement 7, the value of y = 6 can be derived using the value of z = 6 and the expected outcome g = 12. Knowing the value of y, we are immediately able to derive a value for f = 6 + 6 − 2 = 10 and again we obtain a contradiction with the expected value. As a consequence

```
        // TEST INPUT: a = 2, b = 2, C = 3, d = 3, e = 2
(1) cond = a > 0 & b > 0 c > 0 & d > 0 & e > 0;
(2) if cond {
(3)    x = a ⋆ c;
(4)    y = b ⋆ d;
(5)    z = c ⋆ e;
(6)    f = x + y − a;
(7)    g = y + z;
(8) } else {
(9)    f = 0;
(10)   g = 0; }
        // TEST OUTPUT: f = 12, g = 12
```

FIGURE 1: The program numfun computing a numeric function, the test input, and the expected test output.

the assumption that Line 4 is faulty alone cannot be true and must be retracted.

Using the approach of assuming correctness and incorrectness of statements and proving consistency with the expected values, we are able to reduce the diagnosis candidates to Lines 1, 2, 3, and 6. It is also worth to mention that we would also be able to remove statements 1 and 2 from the list of candidates. For this purpose we only have to check whether a different value of cond would lead to a different outcome or not. For this example, assuming cond to be false also leads to an inconsistency. However, when using such an approach possible alternative paths have to be considered. This extension makes such an approach computationally more demanding.

From the example we are able to summarize the following findings. (1) Using data and control dependences reduces the number of potential root causes. Statements that have no influence on faulty variables can be ignored. (2) During debugging, we make assumptions about the correctness or incorrectness of statements. From these assumptions, we try to predict a certain behavior, which should not be in contradiction with the expectations. (3) Backward reasoning, that is, deriving values for intermediate variables from output variables and other variables, is essential to further reduce the number of fault candidates. In this case, statements are not interpreted as functions that change the state of the program but as equations. The interpretation of statements as equations allows us to compute the input value from the output value. (4) Further reductions of fault candidates can be obtained when choosing alternative execution paths, which is computationally more demanding than considering the execution trace of a failing test case only.

In this paper, we introduce an approach that formalizes findings (1)–(3). However, finding (4) is not taken into consideration, because of the resulting computational overhead. In particular, we focus on providing a methodology that allows for reducing the size of dynamic slices. Reducing the size of dynamic slices improves the debugging capabilities of dynamic slicing. We introduce the basic definitions and algorithms and present empirical results. We gain a reduction of more than 28% compared to results obtained from pure

slicing. Although the approach increases the time needed for identifying potential root causes, the overhead can be neglected at least for smaller programs. It is also worth noting that we do not claim that the proposed approach is superior compared to all other debugging approaches. We belief that a combination of approaches is necessary in practice. Our contribution to the field of debugging is in improving dynamic slicing with respect to the computed number of bug candidates.

This paper is based on previous work [1], where the general idea is explained. Now, we focus on the theoretical foundations and an extended empirical evaluation. In the reminder of this paper, we discuss related work in Section 2. We introduce the basic definitions, that is, the used language, execution traces, relevant slicing, model-based debugging, and the conversion into a constraints system in Section 3. We formalize our approach, named constraints based slicing (CONBAS), in Section 4. In Section 5, we apply CONBAS to several example programs. We show that CONBAS is able to reduce the size of slices for programs with single and double faults without losing the fault localization capabilities. In addition, we apply CONBAS to circuits. In Section 6 we discuss the benefits and limitations of the approach as well as future work. Finally, we conclude the paper in Section 7.

2. Related Research

Software debugging techniques can be divided into fault localization and fault correction techniques. Fault localization techniques focus on narrowing down possible fault locations. They comprise spectrum-based fault localization, delta debugging, program slicing, and model-based software debugging.

   (i) Spectrum-based fault localization techniques are based on an observation matrix. Observation matrices comprise the program spectra of both passing and failing test cases. Harrold et al. [2] give an overview of different types of program spectra. A high similarity of a statement to the error vector indicates a high probability that the statement is responsible for the error [3]. There exist several similarity coefficients to numerically express the degree of similarity, for example, Zoeteweij et al. [4] and Jones and Harrold [5]. Empirical studies [3, 6] have shown that the Ochiai coefficient performs best. Several techniques have been developed that combine spectrum-based fault localization with other debugging techniques, for example, BARINEL [7] and DEPUTO [8].

  (ii) Delta debugging [9] is a technique that can be used to systematically minimize a failure-inducing input. The basic idea of delta debugging is that the smaller the failure-inducing input, the less program code is covered. Zeller et al. [10, 11] adopted delta debugging to directly use it for debugging.

 (iii) Program slicing [12] narrows down the search range of potentially faulty statements by means of data and control dependencies. A slice is a subset of program statements that directly or indirectly influence the values of a given set of variables at a certain program line. A slice behaves like the original program for the variables of interest. Slices will be discussed in detail in Section 2.1.

(iv) Model-based software debugging derives from model-based diagnosis, which is used for locating faults in physical systems. Mayer and Stumptner [13] give an overview of existing model-based software debugging techniques. Some of these techniques will be discussed in detail in Section 2.2.

Fault correction techniques focus on finding solutions to eliminate an observed misbehavior. They comprise, for instance, genetic programming techniques.

Genetic programming deals with the automatic repair of programs by means of mutations on the program code. Arcuri [14] and Weimer et al. [15, 16] deal with this debugging technique. Genetic programming often uses fault localization techniques as a preprocessing step.

In the following, we will discuss techniques that are related to our approach, that is, slicing and model-based debugging, in detail.

2.1. Slicing. Weiser [12] introduced static program slicing as a formalization of reasoning backwards. The basic idea here is to start from the failure and to use the control and data flow of the program in the backward direction in order to reach the faulty location. Static program slices tend to be rather large. For this reason, Korel and Laski [17] introduced dynamic program slicing which relies on a concrete program execution. Dynamic slicing significantly reduces the size of slices. Occasionally, statements which are responsible for a fault are absent in the slice. This happens when the fault causes the nonexecution of some parts of the program. Relevant slicing [18] is a variant of dynamic slicing, which eliminates this problem.

A mentionable alternative to relevant slicing is the method published by Zhang et al. [19]. This method introduces the concept of implicit dependencies. Implicit dependencies are obtained by predicate switching. They are the analog to potential data dependencies in relevant slicing. The obtained slices are smaller since the use of implicit dependencies avoids a large number of potential dependencies.

Sridharan et al. [20] identify data structures as the main reason for too large slices. They argue that data structures provided by standard libraries are welltested and thus they are uncommonly responsible for observed misbehavior. Their approach, called Thin Slicing, removes such statements from slices.

Gupta et al. [21] present a technique that combines delta debugging with forward and backward slices. Delta debugging is used to find the minimal failure-inducing input. Forward and backward slices are computed for the failure-inducing input. The intersection of the forward and backward slices results in the failure-inducing chop. This technique requires a test oracle in contrast to CONBAS.

Zhang et al. [22] introduced a technique that reduces the size of dynamic slices via confidence values. These confidence values represent the likelihood that the corresponding statement computed the correct value. Statements with a high confidence value are excluded from the dynamic slice. Similar to CONBAS, this approach requires only one failing execution trace. However, it requires one output variable with a wrong value and several output variables where the computed output is correct. In contrast, CONBAS requires at least one output variable with a wrong value, but no correctly computed output variables.

Other mentionable work of Zhang et al. includes [23–25]. In [24], they discuss how to reduce the time and space required for saving dynamic slices. In [23], they evaluate the effectiveness of dynamic slicing for locating real bugs and found out that most of the faults could be captured by considering only data dependencies. In [25], they deal with the problem of handling dynamic slices of long running programs.

Jeffrey et al. [26] identify potential faulty statements via value replacement. They systematically replace the values used in statements so that the computed output becomes correct. The original value and the new value are stored as an interesting value mapping pair (IVMP). They state that IVMPs typically occur at faulty statements or statements that are directly linked via data dependences to faulty statements. They limit the search space for the value replacement to values used in other test cases. We do not limit the search space to values used in other test cases. Instead, our constraint solver determines if there exist any values for the variables in an abnormal statement so that the correct values for the test cases can be computed. On the one hand, our approach is computationally more expensive, but on the other hand it does not depend on the quality of other test cases. As Jeffrey et al. stated, the presence of multiple faults can diminish the effectiveness of the value replacement approach. In contrast, the CONBAS approach is designed for handling multiple faults.

Many other slicing techniques have been published. For a deeper analysis on slicing techniques the reader is referred to Tip [27] for slicing techniques in general and to Korel and Rilling [28] for dynamic slicing techniques.

2.2. Model-Based Software Debugging. Our work builds on the work of Reiter [29] and Wotawa [30]. Reiter describes the combination of slicing with model-based diagnosis. Wotawa proves that conflicts used in model-based diagnosis for computing diagnoses are equivalent to slices for variables where the expected output value is not equivalent to the computed one.

Nica et al. [31] suggest an approach that reduces the number of diagnoses by means of program mutations and the generation of distinguishing test cases. Our approach and [31] differ in two major aspects. First, our approach uses the execution trace instead of the source code. Thus, we do not have to explicitly unroll loops. Second, we use a constraint solver to check whether a solution can be found. The diagnosis candidates are previously computed via the hitting set algorithm. In contrast, Nica et al. [31] use a constraint solver to obtain the diagnoses directly.

Wotawa et al. [32] present a model-based debugging approach which relies on a constraint solver as well. They show how to formulate a debugging problem as a constraint satisfaction problem. Similar to [31], they use source code instead of execution traces. Other related work includes research in applying model-based diagnosis for debugging directly, for example, [33, 34] and research in applying constraints for the same purpose, for example, [35].

3. Basic Definitions

In this chapter, we introduce the basic definitions that are necessary for formalizing our approach. Without restricting generality we make some simplifying assumptions like reducing the program language to a C-like language and ignoring arrays and pointers. However, this language is still Turing-complete. The reason for the simplification is to focus on the underlying ideas instead of solving purely technical details. We start this chapter with a brief introduction of the underlying programming language $\mathcal{L}$. We define execution traces and dynamic slices formally. Afterwards, we define test cases and the debugging problem. Finally, we introduce model-based software debugging and the conversion of execution traces into their constraint representation.

3.1. Language. The syntax definition of $\mathcal{L}$ is given in Figure 2. The start symbol of the grammar in Bacchus-Naur form (BNF) is P. A program comprises a sequence of statements B. In $\mathcal{L}$, we distinguish three different types of statements: (1) the assignment statement, (2) the if-then-else statement, and (3) the while statement. In the following, we will refer to if-then-else statements and while statements as conditional statements (or conditionals) and to the conditions in conditional statements as test elements. The right side of an assignment has to be a variable (id). The name of the variable can be any word except a keyword. An expression is either an integer (num), a truth value (true, false), a variable, or two expressions concatenated with an operator. An integer optionally starts with a "−" (if a negative integer is represented) followed by a sequence of digits $(0, 1, \ldots, 9)$. We do not introduce data types, but we assume that the use of Boolean and integer values follow the usual expected type rules. We further assume that comments start with // and go to the end of a line. The program numfun (Figure 1) gives an example for a program written in $\mathcal{L}$.

After defining the syntax of $\mathcal{L}$, we have to define its semantics. In this section, we rely on an operational definition. For this purpose, we introduce an interpretation function $[\![\cdot]\!] : \mathcal{L} \times \Sigma \mapsto \Sigma \cup \{\bot\}$, which maps programs and states to new states or the undefined value $\bot$. In this definition, Σ represents the set of all states. A concrete state $\omega \in \Sigma$ specifies values for the variables used in the program. We call a state also a variable environment. Hence, ω itself is a function $\omega : \text{VARS} \rightarrow \text{DOM}$, where VARS denote the set of variables and DOM its domain comprising all possible values. Note that we also represent $\omega \in \Sigma$ as a set

$$
\begin{aligned}
P &\leftarrow B \\
B &\leftarrow SB \mid \epsilon \\
S &\leftarrow \underline{\text{id}} = E; \mid \texttt{if}\ E\{B\}\ OE\ \mid\ \texttt{while}\ E\ \{B\} \\
OE &\leftarrow \texttt{else}\ \{B\}\ \mid\ \epsilon \\
E &\leftarrow \underline{\text{id}}\ \mid\ \underline{\text{num}}\ \mid\ \underline{\text{true}}\ \mid\ \underline{\text{false}}\ \mid\ EOPE\ \mid\ (E) \\
OP &\leftarrow \underline{+}\ \mid\ \underline{-}\ \mid\ \underline{*}\ \mid\ \underline{/}\ \mid\ \underline{\leq}\ \mid\ \underline{\geq}\ \mid\ \underline{==}\ \mid\ \underline{<>}\ \mid\ \underline{\&}\ \mid\ \underline{|}
\end{aligned}
$$

FIGURE 2: The semantics of the language $\mathcal{L}$.

$\{\ldots, x_i v_i, \ldots\}$, where $x_i \in \text{VARS}$ is a variable and $v_i \in \text{DOM}$ is its value. Further note that in our case $\text{DOM} = \mathbb{Z}^M \cup \mathbb{B}$, where $\mathbb{Z}^M = \{x \mid x \in \mathbb{Z}, \min \leq x \leq \max\}$ is an integer number between predefined minimum and maximum values, and $\mathbb{B} = \{\mathbf{T}, \mathbf{F}\}$ is the Boolean domain.

The definition of the semantics of $\mathcal{L}$ is given in Figure 3. We first discuss the semantics for conditions and expressions. For this purpose, we assume that num (id) represents the lexical value of the token num (id) used in the definition of the grammar. An integer num is evaluated to its corresponding value num$* \in \mathbb{Z}^M$ and the truth values are evaluated to their corresponding values in $\mathbb{B}$. A variable id is evaluated to its value specified by the current variable environment ω. Expressions with operators are evaluated according to the semantics of the used operator. After defining the semantics of the expressions, we define the semantics of the statements in $\mathcal{L}$ in a similar manner. A sequence of statements, that is, the program itself or a sub-block of a conditional or while statement, $S_1 \ldots S_n$ is evaluated by executing the statements S_1 to S_n in the given order. Each statement might change the current state of the program. An assignment statement changes the state for a given variable. All other variables remain unchanged. An if-then-else statement allows for selecting a certain path (via block B_1 or B_2) based on the execution of the condition. A while-statement executes its block B until the condition evaluates to false. Therefore, the formal definition of the semantics is very similar to the semantics definition of an if-then-else statement without else-branch. In order to finalize the definition of the semantics of $\mathcal{L}$, we assume that if a program does not terminate or in case of a division by zero, the semantics function returns $\bot$. Moreover, we further assume that all variable values necessary to execute the program are known and defined in $\omega \in \Sigma$.

When executing the program numfun (Figure 1) on the state

$$\omega_I = \{(a, 2), (b, 2), (c, 3), (d, 3), (e, 2)\}, \tag{1}$$

the semantics function $[\![\cdot]\!]$ on I returns the state

$$
\begin{aligned}
\omega_O = \{&(a, 2), (b, 2), (c, 3), (d, 3), (e, 2), \\
&(\text{cond}, \mathbf{T}), (f, 10), (g, 12)\},
\end{aligned} \tag{2}
$$

where the value for f contradicts the expected value for the same variable.

When obtaining a result that is in contradiction with the expectations someone is interested in finding and fixing

Semantics of expressions:

$$\llbracket \text{num} \rrbracket \omega = \text{num}*$$
$$\llbracket \underline{\text{true}} \rrbracket \omega = \mathbf{T}$$
$$\llbracket \underline{\text{false}} \rrbracket \omega = \mathbf{F}$$
$$\llbracket \text{id} \rrbracket \omega = \omega(\text{id})$$
$$\llbracket \underline{(}E\underline{)} \rrbracket \omega = \llbracket E \rrbracket \omega$$
$$\llbracket E_1 \, \underline{\text{op}} \, E_2 \rrbracket \omega = \begin{cases} \llbracket E_1 \rrbracket \omega + \llbracket E_2 \rrbracket \omega & \text{if } \underline{\text{op}} = '\underline{+}' \\ \llbracket E_1 \rrbracket \omega - \llbracket E_2 \rrbracket \omega & \text{if } \underline{\text{op}} = '\underline{-}' \\ \llbracket E_1 \rrbracket \omega * \llbracket E_2 \rrbracket \omega & \text{if } \underline{\text{op}} = '\underline{*}' \\ \llbracket E_1 \rrbracket \omega / \llbracket E_2 \rrbracket \omega & \text{if } \underline{\text{op}} = '\underline{/}' \\ \llbracket E_1 \rrbracket \omega < \llbracket E_2 \rrbracket \omega & \text{if } \underline{\text{rop}} = '\underline{\leq}' \\ \llbracket E_1 \rrbracket \omega > \llbracket E_2 \rrbracket \omega & \text{if } \underline{\text{rop}} = '\underline{\geq}' \\ \| E_1 \| \omega = \llbracket E_2 \rrbracket \omega & \text{if rop} = '\underline{==}' \\ \llbracket E_1 \rrbracket \omega \neq \llbracket E_2 \rrbracket \omega & \text{if } \underline{\text{rop}} = '\underline{<>}' \\ \llbracket E_1 \rrbracket \omega \wedge \llbracket E_2 \rrbracket \omega & \text{if } \underline{\text{rop}} = '\underline{\&}' \\ \llbracket E_1 \rrbracket \omega \vee \llbracket E_2 \rrbracket \omega & \text{if rop} = '\underline{|}' \end{cases}$$

Semantics of expressions:

$$\llbracket \rrbracket \omega = \omega$$
$$\llbracket S_1 \cdots S_n \rrbracket \omega = \llbracket \cdots S_n \rrbracket (\llbracket S_1 \rrbracket \omega)$$
$$\llbracket \text{id} \, \underline{=} \, E\underline{;} \rrbracket \omega = \omega' \text{with } \omega'(x) = \begin{cases} \llbracket E \rrbracket \omega & \text{if } x = id \\ \omega(x) & \text{otherwise} \end{cases}$$
$$\llbracket \underline{\text{if}} \, E \, \{B_1\} \, \underline{\text{else}} \, \{B_2\} \rrbracket \omega = \begin{cases} \llbracket B_1 \rrbracket \, \omega & \text{if } \llbracket E \rrbracket \, \omega = \text{T} \\ \llbracket B_2 \rrbracket \, \omega & \text{otherwise} \end{cases}$$
$$\llbracket \underline{\text{while}} \, E \, \{B\} \rrbracket \, \omega = \begin{cases} \llbracket B \rrbracket \, \underline{\text{while}} \, E \, \{B\} \, \omega & \text{if } \llbracket E \rrbracket \, \omega = \text{T} \\ \omega & \text{otherwise} \end{cases}$$

FIGURE 3: The semantics of the language $\mathcal{L}$.

the fault, that is, locating the statements that are responsible for the faulty computation of a value and correcting them. Weiser [12] introduced the idea to support this process by using the dependence information represented in the program. Weiser's approach identifies those parts of the program that contribute to faulty computations. Weiser called these parts a slice of the program. In this paper, we use extensions of Weiser's static slicing approach and consider the dynamic case where only statements, which are considered in a particular test run, are executed. In order to define dynamic slices [17] and further on relevant slices [18] we first introduce execution traces.

Definition 1 (execution trace). An execution trace of a program $\Pi \in \mathcal{L}$ and an input state $\omega \in \Sigma$ are a sequence $\langle s_1, \ldots, s_k \rangle$, where $s_i \in \Pi$ is a statement that has been executed when running Π on test input ω, that is, calling $\llbracket \Pi \rrbracket \omega$.

For our running example `numfun`, the execution trace of the input ω_I is illustrated in Figure 4 and comprises the statements 1–7.

We now define dependence relations more formally. For this purpose, we introduce the functions DEF and REF, where DEF returns a set of variables defined in a statement and REF returns a set of variables referenced (or used) in the statement. Note that DEF returns the empty set for conditional statements and a set representing the variable on the left side of an assignment statement. Using these functions we define data dependencies as follows.

Definition 2 (data dependence). Given an execution trace $\langle s_1, \ldots, s_k \rangle$ for a program Π and an input state $\omega \in \Sigma$,

```
(1) cond = a > 0 & b > 0 & c > 0 & d > 0 & e > 0;
(2) if cond
(3) x = a * c;
(4) y = b * d;
(5) z = c * e;
(6) f = x + y - a;
(7) g = y + z;
```

FIGURE 4: The execution trace of `numfun` (Figure 1).

an element of the execution trace s_j is data dependent on another element s_i where $i < j$, that is, $s_i \rightarrow_D s_j$, if and only if there exists a variable x that is element of DEF(s_i) and REF(s_j) and there exists no element s_k, $i < k < j$, in the execution trace where $x \in$ DEF(s_k).

Beside data dependences, we have to deal with control dependences representing the control flow of a given execution trace. In $\mathcal{L}$, there are only if-then-else and while statements that are responsible for the control flow. Therefore, we only have to consider these two types of statements.

Definition 3 (control dependence). Given an execution trace $\langle s_1, \ldots, s_k \rangle$ for a program Π and an input state $\omega \in \Sigma$, an element of the execution trace s_j is control dependent on a conditional statement s_i with $i < j$, that is, $s_i \rightarrow_C s_j$, if and only if the execution of s_i causes the execution of s_j.

In the previous definition the term *cause* has to be interpreted very rigorously. If the condition of the while statement executes to TRUE, then all statements of the outermost sub-block of the while-statement are control dependent. If the condition evaluates to FALSE, no statement is control dependent because the first statement after the while-statement is always executed regardless of the evaluation of the condition. Please note, that we do not consider infinite loops. They are not in the scope of this paper. For if-then-else statements the interpretation is similar. If the condition of an if-then-else statement evaluates to TRUE, the statements of the then-block are control dependent on the conditional statement. If it evaluates to FALSE, the statements of the else-block are control dependent on the conditional statement. Note that in case of nested while-statements or if-then-else statements, the control dependencies are not automatically assigned for the blocks of the inner while-statements or if-then-else statements.

Figure 5 shows the execution trace for our running example where the data and control dependencies have been added. Alternatively, the execution trace including the dependences can be represented as directed acyclic graph, the corresponding execution trace graph (ETG).

In addition to data and control dependencies, we make use of potential data dependencies in relevant slicing [18]. In brief, a potential data dependency occurs whenever the evaluation of a conditional statement causes that some statements which potentially change the value of a variable

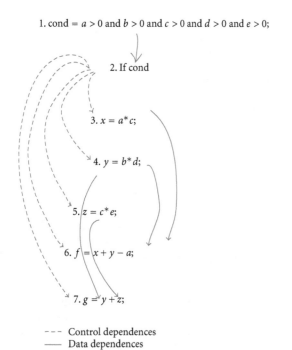

1. cond = $a > 0$ and $b > 0$ and $c > 0$ and $d > 0$ and $e > 0$;

2. If cond

3. $x = a*c$;

4. $y = b*d$;

5. $z = c*e$;

6. $f = x + y - a$;

7. $g = y + z$;

--- Control dependences
— Data dependences

FIGURE 5: The execution trace of numfun (Figure 1) enhanced with data and control dependences.

are not executed. Ignoring such potential data dependencies might lead to slices where the faulty statements are missing.

Definition 4 (potential relevant variables). Given a conditional (while or if-then-else) statement n, the potential relevant variables are a function PR that maps the conditional statement and a Boolean value to the set of all defined variables in the block of n that is not executed because the corresponding condition of n evaluates to TRUE or FALSE.

The previous definition requires all defined variables to be element of the set of potential relevant variables under a certain condition. This means that if there are other while-statements or if-then-else statements in a sub-block, the defined variables of all their sub-blocks must be considered as well. For the sake of clarity Table 1 summarizes the definition of potential relevant variables.

Based on the definition of the potential data dependence set, we define potential data dependences straightforward.

Definition 5 (potential data dependence). Given an execution trace $\langle s_1, \ldots, s_k \rangle$ for a program Π and an input state $\omega \in \Sigma$, an element of the execution trace s_j is potentially data dependent on a test element s_i with $i < j$, which evaluates to TRUE (FALSE), that is, $s_i \rightarrow_P s_j$, if and only if there is a variable $x \in \mathrm{PR}(s_i, \mathrm{TRUE})$ ($x \in \mathrm{PR}(s_i, \mathrm{FALSE})$) that is referenced in s_j and not redefined between i and j.

After defining the dependence relations of a program that is executed on a given input state, we are able to formalize relevant slices, which are used later in our approach.

Definition 6 (relevant slice). A relevant slice S of a program $\Pi \in \mathcal{L}$ for a slicing criterion (ω, x, n), where $\omega \in \Sigma$ is an input state, x is a variable, and n is a line number in the execution trace that comprises those parts of Π, which contribute to the computation of the value for x at the given line number n.

We assume that a statement contributes to the computation of a variable value if there is a dependence relation. Hence, computing slices can be done by following the dependence relations in the ETG. Algorithm 1 RELEVANTSLICE (ET, Π, x, n) computes the relevant slice for a given execution trace and a given variable at the execution trace position n. The program Π is required for determining the potential data dependences.

The relevant slice is likely smaller than the execution trace, where a statement might be executed more often. In our approach, we use relevant slices for restricting the search space for root cause identification.

3.2. The Debugging Problem. Using the definition of $\mathcal{L}$ together with the definition of test cases and test suites, we are able to formally state the debugging problem. Hence, first we have to define test cases and test suites. We do not discuss testing in general. Instead we refer the interested reader to the standard text books on testing, for example, [36]. In the context of our paper, a test case comprises information about the values of input variables and some information regarding the expected output. In principle, it is possible to define expected values for variables at arbitrary positions in the code. For reasons of simplicity, we do not make use of an extended definition.

Definition 7 (test case). A test case t is a tuple (I, O), where $I \in \Sigma$ is the input and $O \in \Sigma$ is the expected output.

A given program $\Pi \in \mathcal{L}$ passes a test case $t = (I, O)$ if and only if $[\![\Pi]\!]I \supseteq O$. Otherwise, we say that the program fails. Because of the use of the $\supseteq$ operator, partial test cases are allowed, which do not specify values for all output variables. If a program passes a test case t, then t is called a passing test case. Otherwise, the test case is said to be a failing test case. Note that we do not consider inconclusive test cases explicitly. In cases where inconclusive test cases exist, we treat them like passing test cases. Since we are only considering failing test cases for fault localization, this assumption has no influence on the final result.

Definition 8 (test suite). A test suite TS for a program $\Pi \in \mathcal{L}$ is a set of test cases.

When using the definition of passing and failing test cases, we are able to partition a test suite into two disjoint sets comprising only positive (PASS), respectively, failing (FAIL) test cases, that is, $\mathrm{TS} = \mathrm{PASS} \cup \mathrm{FAIL}$ and $\mathrm{PASS} \cap \mathrm{FAIL} = \varnothing$. Formally, we define these two subsets as follows:

$$\mathrm{PASS} = \{(I, O) \mid (I, O) \in \mathrm{TS}, [\![\Pi]\!]I \supseteq O\}$$

$$\mathrm{FAIL} = \mathrm{TS}/\mathrm{PASS}, \tag{3}$$

Table 1

Statement n	Cond. E	Potential relevant variables PR
`while` E {	TRUE	$PR(n, \text{TRUE}) = \varnothing$
$\quad B$		
}	FALSE	$PR(n, \text{FALSE}) = \{m \mid m \text{ defined in } B \}$
`if` E {	TRUE	$PR(n, \text{TRUE}) = \{m \mid m \text{ defined in } B_2 \}$
$\quad B_1$		
} `else` {	FALSE	$PR(n, \text{FALSE}) = \{m \mid m \text{ defined in } B_1 \}$
$\quad B_2$		
}		

Require: An execution trace $ET = \langle s_1, \ldots, s_m \rangle$, a variable of interest x, and a certain line
number of the execution trace n.
Ensure: A relevant slice.
  (1) Compute the execution trace ETG using the dependence relations $\rightarrow_C$, $\rightarrow_D$, and $\rightarrow_P$.
  (2) Mark the node s_k in the ETG, where $x \in \text{DEF}(s_k)$ and there is no other
      statement s_i, $k < i \leq n$, $x \in \text{DEF}(s_i)$ in the ETG.
  (3) Mark all test nodes between s_k and s_n, which evaluate to the boolean value B and where
      $x \in \text{PR}(s_k, B)$.
  (4) Traverse the ETG from the marked nodes in the reverse direction of the arcs until no
      new nodes can be marked.
  (5) Let S be the set of all marked nodes.
  (6) Return the set $\{s_i \mid s_i \in S\}$ as result.

ALGORITHM 1: RELEVANTSLICE (ET, Π, x, n).

For a negative test case $t = (I, O) \in \text{FAIL}$, we know that there must be some variables $CV_t = \{x_1, \ldots, x_k\}$, where for all $i \in \{1, \ldots, k\} x_i = v_i \in O$ and $x_i = w_i \in [\![\Pi]\!] I$ follows that $v_i \neq w_i$. We call such variables $x_1, \ldots, x_k$ conflicting variables. The set of conflicting variables for a test case t is denoted by $CV(t)$. If the test case t is a positive test case, the set $CV(t)$ is defined to be empty. Using these definitions, we define the debugging problem.

Definition 9 (debugging problem). Given a program $\Pi \in \mathcal{L}$ and a test suite TS, the problem of identifying the root cause for a failing test case $t \in \text{TS}$ in Π is called the debugging problem.

A solution for the debugging problem is a set of statements in a program Π that are responsible for the conflicting variables $CV(t)$. The identified statements in a solution have to be changed in order to turn all failing test cases into passing test cases for the corrected program.

3.3. Model-Based Debugging. In the introduction, we mentioned that correctness assumptions are the key for fault localization. Therefore, a technique for diagnosis that is based on such assumptions would be a good starting point for debugging. Indeed, such methodology can be found in artificial intelligence. Reiter [29] introduced the theoretical foundations of model-based diagnosis (MBD) where a model that captures the correct behavior of components is used together with observations for diagnosis. The underlying idea of MBD is to formalize the behavior of each

component C in the form $\neg AB(C) \rightarrow \text{BEHAV}(C)$. The predicate AB stands for abnormal and is used to state the incorrectness of a component. Hence, when C is correct, $\neg AB(C)$ has to be true and the behavior of C has to be valid. In debugging, we make use of the same underlying idea. Instead of dealing with components, we now have statements, and the behavior of a statement is given by a formal representation of the statement's source code. We use constraints as a representation language for this purpose.

In the following we adapt Reiter's definition of diagnosis [29] for representing bug candidates in the context of debugging.

Definition 10 (diagnosis). Given a formal representation SD of a program $\Pi \in \mathcal{L}$, where the behavior of each statement s_i is represented as $\neg AB(s_i) \rightarrow \text{BEHAV}(s_i)$ and a failing test case (I, O), a diagnosis Δ (or bug candidate) is a subset of the set of statements of Π such that $SD \cup \{I, O\} \cup \{\neg AB(s) | s \in \Pi \setminus \Delta\} \cup \{AB(s) | s \in \Delta\}$ is satisfiable.

In this definition of a diagnosis, the representation of programs (or execution traces) and failing test cases is not included. Furthermore, a formalism that allows for checking satisfiability is premised. However, the definition exactly states that we have to find a set of correctness assumptions that does not lead to a contradiction with respect to the given test case. We do not want to discuss all the consequences of this definition and refer the interested reader to [29, 37, 38]. In the following, we explain how to obtain a model for a particular execution trace and how to represent failing test cases.

The representation of programs for our model-based approach is motivated by previous work [31, 32]. In [31, 32] all possible execution paths up to a specified size are represented as set of constraints. In contrast, we now only represent the current execution path. In this case, the representation becomes smaller and the modeling itself is much easier since only testing actions and assignments are part of an execution trace. On the contrary, we loose information and we are not able to eliminate candidates that belong to testing actions. Hence, in the proposed approach, we expect improvements of debugging results compared to slicing. Even though we cannot match obtained with model-based debugging approaches like Wotawa et al. [32], our approach requires less runtime.

Modeling for model-based debugging in the context of this paper comprises two steps. In the first step, we convert an execution trace of a program for a given test case to its static single assignment form (SSA) [39]. In the second step, we use the SSA representation and map it to a set of constraints. When using a constraint representation, checking for consistency becomes a constraint satisfaction problem (CSP). A constraint satisfaction problem is a tuple (V, D, CO) where V is a set of variables defined over a set of domains D connected to each other by a set of arithmetic and Boolean relations, called constraints CO. A solution for a CSP represents a valid instantiation of the variables V with values from D such that none of the constraints from CO is violated. We refer to Dechter [40] for more information on constraints and the constraint satisfaction problem.

Now, we explain the mapping of program execution traces into their constraint representations in detail. We start with the conversion into SSA form. The SSA form is an intermediate representation of a program with the property that no two left-side variables share the same name. The SSA form can be easily obtained from an execution trace by adding an index to each variable. Every time a variable is re-defined, the value of the index gets incremented such that the SSA form property holds. Every time a variable is referenced, the current index is used. Note that we always start with the index 0. Algorithm 2 formalizes the conversion of execution traces ET into their SSA form.

The application of the SSA algorithm on the execution trace of our running example numfun delivers the following execution trace:

(1) cond_1 = a_0 > 0 & b_0 > 0 & c_0 > 0 & d_0 > 0 & e_0 > 0,

(2) if cond_1 {,

(3) x_1 = a_0 * c_0,

(4) y_1 = b_0 * d_0,

(5) z_1 = c_0 * e_0,

(6) f_1 = x_1 + y_1 - a_0,

(7) g_1 = y_1 + z_1,

(8) }.

In the second step, the SSA form of the execution trace is converted into constraints. Instead of using a specific language of a constraint solver, we make use of mathematical equations. In order to distinguish equations from statements, we use == to represent the equivalence relation. Algorithm 3 formalizes this conversion. In the algorithm, we make use of a global function index that maps each element of ET to a unique identifier representing its corresponding statement. Such a unique identifier might be the line number where the statement starts. Note that in Algorithm 3 we represent each statement of the execution trace using the logical formula of the form $AB(\cdots) \vee$ Constraint, which is logically equivalent to $\neg AB(\cdots) \rightarrow$ Constraint. Moreover, $\text{CONSTRAINTS}(\text{ET}, (I, O), \text{ssa})$ also converts the given test case.

Applying Constraints $(\text{ET}, (I, O), \text{ssa})$ on the SSA form of the execution trace of the numfun program extracts the following constraints:

$$a\_0 == 2,$$
$$b\_0 == 2,$$
$$c\_0 == 3,$$
$$d\_0 == 3,$$
$$e\_0 == 2,$$
$$f\_1 == 12,$$
$$g\_1 == 12,$$
$$AB(1) \vee (cond\_1 == a\_0 > 0 \wedge b\_0 > 0 \wedge c\_0 \quad (4)$$
$$> 0 \wedge d\_0 > 0 \wedge e\_0 > 0),$$
$$AB(2) \vee (cond\_1),$$
$$AB(3) \vee (x\_1 == a\_0 * c\_0),$$
$$AB(4) \vee (y\_1 == b\_0 * d\_0),$$
$$AB(5) \vee (z\_1 == c\_0 * e\_0),$$
$$AB(6) \vee (f\_1 == x\_1 + y\_1 - a\_0),$$
$$AB(7) \vee (g\_1 == y\_1 + z\_1).$$

4. The CONBAS Algorithm

In this section, we present our approach, CONBAS. The basic idea of CONBAS is to reduce the size of summary slices by computing minimal diagnoses. Minimal diagnoses are computed by combining the statements of the slices of the faulty variables of a single test case as follows. (1) Each diagnosis must contain at least one element of every slice. (2) If there exists a diagnosis that is a proper subset of the diagnosis, the superset diagnosis is skipped. The remaining diagnoses are further reduced with the aid of a constraint solver. For doing so, the execution trace of a failing test case is converted into constraints. The constraint solver checks for satisfiability of the converted execution trace assuming that the statement of the diagnosis is incorrect. Figure 6 gives an overview of the CONBAS approach.

Algorithm 4 explains the CONBAS approach in detail. The function $\text{RUN}(\Pi, t)$ executes a test case t on a program Π. It returns the resulting execution trace ET and the set of conflicting variables CV. The relevant slices are computed for all conflicting variables CV by means of the function $\text{RELEVANTSLICE}(\text{ET}, \Pi, x, n)$ (Algorithm 1), at which $|\text{ET}|$ is established for n. For all conditional statements c in ET the relevant slices SC_c are computed. This is done by computing the relevant slices for all variables contained in the conditions. The function $\text{POSITIONINEXECUTIONTRACE}$

Require: An execution trace ET $= \langle s_1, \ldots, s_m \rangle$.
Ensure: The execution trace in SSA form and a function that maps each variable
to its maximum index value used in the SSA form.
(1) Let *index* be a function mapping variables to integers. The initial integer value
for each variable is 0.
(2) Let ET$'$ be the empty sequence.
(3) **for** $j = 1$ to m **do**
(4)   If s_j is an assignment statement of the form $x = E$ **then**
(5)   Let E' be E where all variables $y \in E$ are replaced with $y\_index(y)$.
(6)   Let $index(x)$ be $index(x) + 1$.
(7)   Add $x\_index(x) = E'$ to the end of the sequence ET$'$.
(8)   **else**
(9)   Let s' be the statement s_j where all variables $y \in E$ are replaced with
$y\_index(y)$.
(10)   Add s' to the end of the sequence ET$'$.
(11)   **end if**
(12) **end for**
(13) Return (ET$'$, *index*).

ALGORITHM 2: SSA(ET).

Require: An execution trace ET $= \langle s_1, \ldots, s_m \rangle$ in SSA form, a test case (I, O),
and a function ssa returning the final index value for each variable.
Ensure: The constraint representation of ET and the test case.
(1) Let CO be the empty set.
(2) **for all** $(x, v) \in I$ **do**
(3)   Add "$(x\_0 == v)$" to CO.
(4) **end for**
(5) **for all** $(y, w) \in O$ **do**
(6)   Add "$(y\_ssa(y) == w)$" to CO.
(7) **end for**
(8) **for** $j = 1$ to m **do**
(9)   **if** s_j is an assignment statement of the form $x = E$ **then**
(10)   Add " $(AB(index(s_j)) \vee (x == E))$" to CO.
(11)   **else**
(12)   Let c be the condition of s_j where $\underline{\&}$ is replaced with $\wedge$ and $\underline{|}$ with $\vee$.
(13)   Add "$(AB(index(s_j)) \vee (c))$" to CO.
(14)   **end if**
(15) **end for**
(16) Return CO.

ALGORITHM 3: CONSTRAINTS (ET, (I, O), ssa).

(c, ET) is used to obtain the line number of c in the execution trace.

The function MINHITTINGSETS (SET OF ALL S_x) returns the set of minimal hitting sets HS of the set of slices S_x. A set d is a hitting set for a set of sets CO if it contains at least one element of every set of CO:

$$d \text{ is hitting set} \iff \forall s \in \text{CO} : s \cap d \neq \{\}. \qquad (5)$$

A hitting set d w.r.t. CO is minimal if there exists no subset of d, which is a valid hitting set w.r.t. CO. Minimal hitting sets can be computed by means of the corrected Reiter algorithm [29, 41].

Bugs causing a wrong evaluation of a condition lead to the wrong (non) execution of statements. In order to handle such bugs, the function EXTENDCONTROLSTATEMENTS(ET, Π) adds a small overhead to each control statement c in the execution trace ET. For each variable v that could be redefined in any branch of c, the statement v=v is added to the execution trace ET. These additional statements are inserted after all statements that are control dependent on c. The inserted statements will be referenced by the line number of c when calling the function *index* in Algorithm 3. The returned execution trace is assigned to ET$_C$. This extension can be compared with potential data dependencies in relevant slicing.

SSA(ET$_C$) (Algorithm 2) transforms the execution trace ET$_C$ into its single static assignment form and also delivers the largest index value for each variable used in

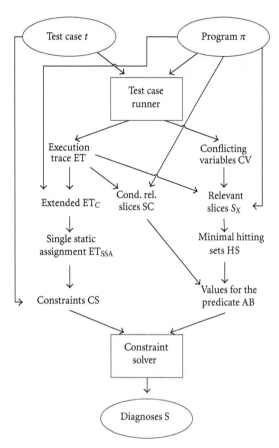

FIGURE 6: The CONBAS approach.

$\{1\}$. The function MINHITTINGSETS($\{\{1,2,3,4,6\}\}$) delivers $\{\{1\},\{2\},\{3\},\{4\},\{6\}\}$ as minimal hitting sets. The resulting constraints are

$$a\_0 == 2,$$
$$b\_0 == 2,$$
$$c\_0 == 3,$$
$$d\_0 == 3,$$
$$e\_0 == 2,$$
$$f\_2 == 12,$$
$$g\_2 == 12,$$
$$AB(1) \vee (cond\_1 == a\_0 > 0 \wedge b\_0 > 0 \wedge c\_0$$
$$> 0 \wedge d\_0 > 0 \wedge e\_0 > 0),$$
$$AB(2) \vee (cond\_1),$$
$$AB(3) \vee (x\_1 == a\_0 * c\_0),$$
$$AB(4) \vee (y\_1 == b\_0 * d\_0),$$
$$AB(5) \vee (z\_1 == c\_0 * e\_0),$$
$$AB(6) \vee (f\_1 == x\_1 + y\_1 - a\_0),$$
$$AB(7) \vee (g\_1 == y\_1 + z\_1),$$
$$AB(1) \vee (x\_2 == x\_1),$$
$$AB(1) \vee (y\_1 == x\_1),$$
$$AB(1) \vee (z\_2 == z\_1),$$
$$AB(1) \vee (f\_2 == f\_1),$$
$$AB(1) \vee (g\_2 == g\_1).$$

(6)

There are five different configurations for the values of AB:

$$AB(1) == \text{true} \wedge AB(2) == \text{true},$$
$$AB(2) == \text{true},$$
$$AB(3) == \text{true},$$
$$AB(4) == \text{true},$$
$$AB(6) == \text{true}.$$

(7)

We only indicate the AB values that are set to true. All other AB variables are set to false. Note that setting $AB(1) ==$ true implies $AB(2) ==$ true since we cannot reason over the correctness of the condition if the computed values used in the condition are wrong. The constraint solver is able to find solutions for all configurations, except for AB(4). Since our approach does only reason on the execution trace and not on all possible paths, $AB(1) ==$ true and $AB(2) ==$ true are satisfiable even though taking the alternative path does not compute the correct value for f.

Algorithm CONBAS terminates if the program Π terminates when executing T. The computational complexity of CONBAS is determined by the computation of the relevant slices, the hitting sets, and the constraint solver. Computing relevant slices only adds a small overhead compared to the execution of the program. Hitting set computation and constraint solving are exponential in the worst case (finite case). In order to reduce the computation time, the computation of hitting sets can be simplified. We only compute hitting sets of the size 1 or 2; that is, we only compute single and double fault diagnoses. Faults with more involved faulty statements are unlikely in practice. Only in cases where the single and double fault diagnoses cannot

the SSA form. CONSTRAINTS (ET_{SSA},t,ssa) (Algorithm 3) converts each statement into its equivalent constraint representation. The statements added in the function EXTENDCONTROLSTATEMENTS (ET, Π) (v=v, in SSA form: $v_{i+1} = v_i$) are concatenated with the predicate AB(j): $AB(j) \vee v_{i+1} = v_i$. The reason for this is that we cannot reason over the variables if the execution path alters. Please note that the required test oracle information can be fully automated extracted from an existing test case.

The result set S represents the set of possible faulty statements. At first, the result set is the empty set. For all minimal hitting sets d in the set of minimal hitting sets HS, we check if the constraint solver is able to find a solution. For this purpose, we set all AB(i) to false except those where the corresponding statements are contained in d. For all conditional statements c where SC_c and d have at least one common element, we set AB(c) to true. The function CONSTRAINTSOLVER(CS $\cup$ AB) calls a constraint solver and returns true if the constraint solver is able to find a solution. If a solution is found, we add all elements of d to the result set S.

We illustrate the application of the algorithm by means of our running example. The function RUN(Π,t) computes the execution trace illustrated in Figure 4 and $\{f\}$ as the set of conflicting variables. The set of relevant slices of the conflicting variables is $\{\{1,2,3,4,6\}\}$. The union of the slices for the variables in the condition in Line 2 is

---

Require: Program Π and failing test case t
Ensure: Dynamic slice S
(1) $[\text{ET}, \text{CV}] = \text{RUN}(\Pi, t)$
(2) **for all** $x \in \text{CV}$ **do**
(3) $S_x = \text{RELEVANTSLICE}(\text{ET}, \Pi, x, |\text{ET}|)$
(4) **end for**
(5) **for all** $c \in \text{ET}$ **do**
(6) $n = \text{POSITIONINEXECUTIONTRACE}(c, \text{ET})$
(7)   **for all** variables x in c **do**
(8) $\text{SC}_x = \text{RELEVANTSLICE}(\text{ET}, \Pi, x, n)$
(9)   **end for**
(10) $\text{SC}_c = \cup \text{SC}_x$
(11) **end for**
(12) $\text{HS} = \text{MINHITTINGSETS}(\text{SETOFALL } S_x)$
(13) $\text{ET}_C = \text{EXTENDCONTROLSTATEMENTS}(ET, \Pi)$
(14) $[\text{ET}_{\text{SSA}}, \text{ssa}] = \text{SSA}(\text{ET}_C)$
(15) $\text{CS} = \text{CONSTRAINTS}(\text{ET}_{\text{SSA}}, t, \text{ssa})$
(16) $S = \{\}$
(17) **for all** $d \in \text{HS}$ **do**
(18) $\forall i \in d : \text{AB}(i) = \text{true}$
(19) $\forall i \notin d : \text{AB}(i) = \text{false}$
(20) $\forall c \ \text{where} \ \text{SC}_c \cap d \neq \{\} : \text{AB}(c) = \text{true}$
(21)   **if** $\text{CONSTRAINTSOLVER}(\text{CS} \cup \text{AB})$ has solution **then**
(22) $S = S \cup d$
(23)   **end if**
(24) **end for**
(25) **return** S

ALGORITHM 4: CONBAS (Π, t).

explain an observed misbehavior, the size of the hitting sets is increased.

5. Empirical Results

This empirical evaluation consists of two main parts. First, we show that CONBAS is able to reduce the size of slices without losing the fault localization capabilities of slicing. We show this for single faults as well as for multiple faults. Second, we investigate the influence of the number of output variables on the reduction result.

We conducted this empirical evaluation using a proof of concept implementation of CONBAS. This implementation accepts programs written in the language $\mathcal{L}$ (see Figure 2). In order to test existing example programs, we have extended this implementation to accept simple Java programs, that is, Java programs with integer and Boolean data types only and without method calls and object orientation. The implementation itself is written in Java and comprises a relevant slicer and an interface to the Minion constraint solver [42]. The evaluation was performed on an Intel Core2 Duo processor (2.67 GHz) with 4 GB RAM and Windows XP as operating system. Because of the used constraint solver, only programs comprising Boolean and integer data types (including arrays of integers) could be handled directly. Note that the restriction to Boolean and integer domains is not a limitation of CONBAS.

For this empirical evaluation, we have computed all minimal hitting sets. We did not restrict the size of the hitting sets. Since we only deal with single and double faults, hitting sets of the sizes 1 and 2 would be sufficient. This reduction would improve our results concerning the number of final diagnoses and the computation time.

For the first part of the empirical evaluation, we use the 10 example programs listed in Table 2. Most of the programs implement numerical functions using conditional statements. The programs *IfExample*, *SumPower*, *TrafficLight*, and *WhileLoops* are borrowed from the JADE project (http://www.dbai.tuwien.ac.at/proj/Jade/). The program *Taste* is borrowed from the Unravel project (http://hissa.nist .gov/unravel/). Table 2 depicts the obtained results. In the table, we present the following data:

(i) the name of the program (Program),

(ii) the fault version (V),

(iii) the number of lines of code (LOC),

(iv) the size of the execution trace (Exec. trace),

(v) the number of constraints (Con.),

(vi) the number of intern variables in the CSP (Int. var.),

(vii) the number of minimal diagnoses that are computed by the hitting set algorithm (Total diag.),

(viii) the number of minimal diagnoses that are satisfiable by the constraint solver (Valid diag.),

Table 2: Results for single faults.

Program	V	LOC	Exec. trace	Con.	Int. var.	Total diag.	Valid diag.	Sum. Slice	Red. Slice	Time
AKSWT	1	12	14	29	8	6	5	6	5	656
	2	12	17	39	11	3	3	6	3	203
	3	12	14	29	8	6	5	6	5	500
	4	12	4	3	2	2	1	2	1	141
	5	12	20	45	12	3	3	6	3	219
ProdSum	1	14	14	29	10	6	6	6	6	469
	2	14	14	31	11	7	6	8	7	469
	3	14	11	22	9	7	5	8	6	453
	4	14	14	31	11	3	3	8	3	203
	5	14	11	22	9	3	2	8	2	188
PowerFunction	1	15	15	25	9	9	8	9	9	625
	2	15	9	9	5	6	5	6	6	359
	3	15	12	16	7	9	7	9	8	578
	4	15	15	23	9	4	4	9	5	250
	5	15	15	23	9	4	4	9	5	266
Multiplication	1	16	13	26	12	10	6	10	7	672
	2	16	14	25	9	8	8	8	8	500
	3	16	10	17	9	4	1	8	2	422
	4	16	11	19	7	6	3	8	3	375
	5	16	16	33	13	4	4	10	4	344
Divide	1	15	24	55	17	10	10	10	10	735
	2	15	26	62	22	12	12	12	12	906
	3	15	13	26	8	8	8	8	8	500
	4	15	10	18	6	4	3	8	3	250
	5	15	7	10	4	6	5	6	5	359
IfExamples	1	7	4	4	2	3	3	3	3	172
	2	8	3	3	2	2	1	2	1	110
	3	14	4	2	1	2	1	3	2	125
SumPowers	1	22	43	89	25	12	7	13	8	1141
	2	22	7	8	4	2	1	6	3	125
	3	22	7	8	4	2	1	6	3	109
	4	22	28	51	15	11	11	12	12	907
	5	22	28	58	17	12	12	13	13	890
TrafficLight	1	17	61	80	12	11	1	11	4	1078
	2	17	44	63	12	6	1	6	2	500
WhileLoops	1	14	52	99	14	7	7	7	7	719
	2	14	12	19	6	6	3	6	3	406
	3	14	52	99	14	7	7	7	7	719
Taste	1	15	10	21	11	4	4	7	5	266
	2	15	10	21	11	4	4	7	5	250
	3	15	28	69	23	6	6	9	7	469
	4	15	25	61	21	6	6	9	7	453
	5	15	19	45	17	6	6	9	7	438
Average		15.1	18.1	34.1	10.4	6.0	4.9	7.7	5.5	454

(ix) the number of statements contained in the union of the relevant slices of all faulty variables (Sum. Slice),

(x) the number of statements in the reduced slice (Red. Slice),

(xi) the time (in milliseconds) required for reducing the slice (Time).

On average, the size of the slice is reduced by more than 28% compared to the size of the corresponding summary slice. Figure 7 illustrates the relation of the program size, the

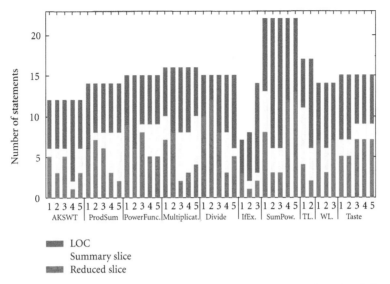

Figure 7: Comparison of the number of statements in total (LOC), in the summary slice and in the reduced slice. The used program variants deal with single faults.

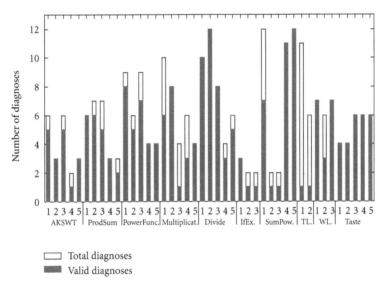

Figure 8: Comparison of the number of minimal diagnoses and the number of valid minimal diagnoses. The used program variants deal with single faults.

summary slice size, and the reduced slice size for the data presented in Table 2.

Figure 8 illustrates the proportion of the number of minimal diagnoses (total diag.) and the number of valid minimal diagnoses (valid diag.) for the data presented in Table 2. The constraint solver reduces about 20% of the number of diagnoses.

In order to estimate the computation time for larger programs, we have investigated if there exists a correlation between the time (in milliseconds) required for Conbas and (1) the LOC, (2) the size of the execution trace (exec. trace), (3) the number of constraints (con.), or (4) the number of diagnoses to be tested for satisfiability (total diag.). We found out that the strongest correlation is between the execution

time and (4). Figure 9 illustrates this correlation. The blue data points represent the data from Table 2. The red line represents the least squares fit as an approximation of the data.

One advantage of Conbas is that it is able to reduce slices of programs that contain two or more faults. In order to demonstrate this, we have performed a small evaluation on double faults. For this, we combined some faults used in the single fault evaluation. The faults were not combined according a particular schema (i.e., masking of faults or avoiding masking of faults). We only made the following restriction: faulty program versions were not combined, where the faults were in the same program line. The reason for this is that two faults in the same line can be seen as one single fault.

TABLE 3: Results for double faults.

Program	V	Faults in Red. Slice	LOC	Sum. Slice	Red. Slice
Taste	6d	2	15	9	6
	7d	2	15	9	6
	8d	2	15	7	4
	9d	2	15	9	5
	10d	2	15	7	4
	11d	2	15	7	4
	12d	2	15	9	6
	13d	2	15	9	6
	14d	2	15	9	6
	15d	2	15	9	2
SumPowers	6d	1	22	6	1
	7d	1	22	12	7
	8d	2	22	13	7
	9d	1	22	6	1
	10d	1	22	6	1
	11d	1	22	12	7
WhileLoops	4d	1	14	6	3
	5d	1	14	7	7
	6d	1	14	6	3
ProdSum	6d	1	14	8	3
	7d	1	14	8	3
	8d	1	14	8	3
	9d	1	14	8	2
	10d	2	14	8	2
	11d	1	14	8	2
Average			16.3	8.2	4.0

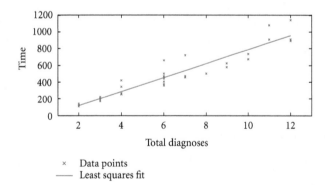

× Data points
— Least squares fit

FIGURE 9: The correlation of the number of diagnoses to be tested (Total diag.) and the computation time (Time, in milliseconds).

Table 3 shows the results obtained when executing CONBAS on these new program versions. The table contains the following data:

(i) the name of the program (Program),

(ii) the fault version (V),

(iii) the number of faults contained in the reduced slice (Faults in Red. Slice),

(iv) the number of lines of code (LOC),

(v) the number of statements contained in the union of the relevant slices of all faulty variables (Sum. Slice),

(vi) the number of statements in the reduced slice (Red. Slice).

It can be seen that sometimes only one of the two faults is contained in the reduced slice. The reason for this is that one fault can be masked by the other fault. CONBAS guarantees that at least one of the faults is contained in the reduced slice. This is not a limitation since a programmer can fix the first bug and then apply CONBAS again on the corrected program. Figure 10 shows the relation of the program size, the summary slice size, and the reduced slice size for the investigated double faults. On average, the summary slice can be reduced by 50%.

In the second part of the empirical evaluation, we investigate if more than one faulty output variable allows for a higher reduction of the summary slice. For this purpose, we use the circuits C17 and C432 of the ISCAS 85 [43] benchmark. The ISCAS 85 circuits describe combinational networks. We have chosen ISCAS 85, because the different circuits of ISCAS 85 have many input and output variables. The circuit C17 has 5 input variables and 2 output variables. The circuit C432 has 36 input variables and 7 output variables. For the evaluation, we have used test cases with different input and output combinations. We used 3 as

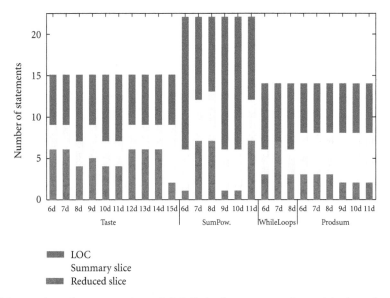

FIGURE 10: Comparison of the number of statements in total (LOC), in the summary slice and in the reduced slice. The used program variants deal with double faults.

TABLE 4: Average results for the Iscas 85 benchmark.

Circuit	LOC	Exec. trace	Con.	Int. var.	Total diag.	Valid diag.	Sum. Slice	Red. Slice
C17	31	14	26	25	12	5.9	9.3	5.1
C432	832	398	646	662	874.5	373.7	328.6	108.3
Average	339.1	161.7	264.5	270	343.8	147.3	132.1	44.8

the upper bound for the number of faulty output variables. In total, we created more than 150 program variants. Table 4 presents the obtained average results for the two circuits of the Iscas 85 benchmark. The column headings are similar to those used in Table 2. An explanation of the column headings can be found as previously mentioned. Conbas is able to reduce the size of the summary slice by 66%.

Now, we want to answer the question if we could yield a higher reduction of the summary slice, when there are more faulty output variables. In order to answer this question, we make use of the Reduction metric, which is defined as

$$ REDUCTION = \left(1 - \frac{Reduced\ Slice}{Summary\ Slice}\right) \times 100\%. \quad (8) $$

We group the tested program variants by the number of faulty output variables and compute the Reduction metric for the program variants. Figure 11 shows the box plots for the different numbers of output variables. It can be seen that two and three faulty output variables yield a better reduction of the slice size than only one output variable. The reason for this is that it is more difficult for the constraint solver to find configurations which meet all of the specified output variables.

6. Discussion and Future Work

Although, Conbas substantially reduces the number of diagnosis candidates with a reduction of about 28% in

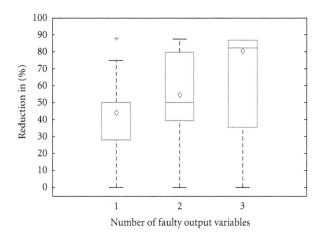

FIGURE 11: Comparison of the Reduction quality for a different number of faulty output variables for the Iscas 85 benchmark. The central lines of the boxes indicate the median of the reduction. The diamonds indicate the arithmetic mean of the reduction. The whiskers extend to the most extreme data points not considered as outliers. Outliers are plotted individually as crosses.

the single fault and 50% in the double fault case, there is still room for improvements. In particular, the current implementation is not optimized both in terms of handling different kinds of program language constructs and time required for performing the analysis. It would benefit from a relevant slicer for Java programs without restrictions on the language's syntax. Currently, only dynamic slicers are available, which might cause root causes to be ignored during the debugging process. Moreover, the combination of slices and constraint solving that is currently used might be improved. Especially, in cases where there are many possible faults, the calls to the external constraint solver slow down the computation, which could be improved by a closely integrated constraint solver.

Apart from these technical issues, there are some open research questions. We start with discussing possible improvements of Conbas that make use of the same underlying ideas but change the way of computing the final results. Instead of computing the hitting sets of the slices, the constraint solver can be directly used to compute all solvable diagnoses of a particular size. Such an approach would restrict the number of constraint solver calls and also the time required for computing the hitting sets for the slices. Such an approach would be very similar to the approaches of Nica and colleagues [31, 32], but it works on execution traces instead of the whole program representation. The expectation is that such an approach would be more efficient. However, there have been no publications on this topic so far.

Another research challenge is to improve Conbas by using information about the evaluation of conditions. We have to analyze if taking the alternative execution path of a condition (e.g., the else path if the condition evaluates to true) could satisfy the test case. If the change leads to a consistent program behavior, a root cause is identified. Otherwise, the condition can be assumed to be correct and removed from the list of fault candidates. The underlying challenge is to make such tests only in cases where infinite loops or infeasible behaviors can be avoided. For example, executing a conditional or a recursive function not as intended might cause a non-terminating behavior. Moreover, it is also important that the computational requirements are not significantly increased.

The empirical evaluation of Conbas, especially in comparison with other approaches, has to be improved. The used programs are rather small. Larger programs that belong to different application domains have to be used for evaluation. The currently used programs implement a variety of functions from state machines to numeric algorithms. Therefore, we believe that the obtained comparison with a pure slicing approach would not change even when using larger programs assuming that the underlying constraint problems can be solved within a reasonable amount of time. However, an empirical study that compares different approaches such as spectrum-based debugging with Conbas would be highly required in order to structure the general research field of automated debugging.

The integration of debugging tools into integrated development environments (IDEs) like Eclipse is another hot topic. Technically, the integration seems to be easy. However, the challenge lies in effectively integrating these tools in an interactive environment such that the time needed for the overall debugging process is reduced. For this purpose, research on human-computer interaction in the context of debugging and program development has to be done. Moreover, user studies with the aim of proving that automated debugging tools really support humans are required. Such studies should go beyond the usual student-based studies that are carried out as part of the course program. Instead, the studies should be carried out using real programmers in their industrial environment. Unfortunately, there are only few user studies in the case of automated debugging available, where [44] is the most recent.

Furthermore, the relationship between testing and debugging has not been sufficiently explored. There is work on this topic that deals with answering the question about the influence on the used test cases for debugging and how to construct test cases to further support debugging. An in-depth analysis of this topic and a well established methodology are still not available. Work in the direction of combining testing and debugging includes [45] and [31]. The latter discusses an approach for actively constructing test cases that allow for distinguishing diagnosis candidates. However, a method for test case construction that optimizes the whole debugging process is not available to the best of our knowledge. Moreover, the impact of such a method on other metrics such as mutation score or coverage criteria is not known and worth being researched.

7. Conclusion

Dynamic program slices are a valuable aid for programmers because they provide an overview of possibly faulty statements when debugging. They are used in many automated debugging techniques as a preprocessing step. However, they are often still too large to be a valuable help.

In this paper, we have introduced the theoretical foundations for an approach which reduces the size of dynamic slices by means of constraint solving. We have formalized the approach for the reduction of slices, named constraint based slicing (Conbas). In an empirical evaluation, we have shown that the size of dynamic slices can be reduced by 28% on average for single faults and by 50% for double faults with the aid of constraint solving. Furthermore, our approach can be used even if there exist multiple faults. We have applied Conbas on circuits of the Iscas 85 benchmark. These circuits contain many data dependencies but lack control dependencies. For these types of programs, Conbas yields a reduction of 66% on average compared to the union of all slices.

The objective behind Conbas is to improve relevant slicing for debugging. Even though other approaches outperform Conbas in certain cases, we point out two application areas where Conbas should be the preferred method to use. First, in case of software maintenance where the root cause for one failing test case has to be identified. In this case, mostly limited knowledge about the program is available. Moreover, the programs themselves are usually large, which makes debugging a very hard task. In such a case, low-cost approaches that require a set of test cases might not be applicable and the application of heavy-weighted approaches might be infeasible because of computational requirements.

Second, in case of programs with a low number of control statements that need a more detailed analysis of data dependences and relationships between variables. In such a case, CONBAS provides the right means for analysis because of handling data dependences and constraints between program variables, which originate from the program statements.

Even though CONBAS cannot solve all debugging problems, we are convinced that CONBAS is a valuable technique for improving the debugging process. Moreover, a combination with other debugging techniques may even increase its fault localization capabilities.

Acknowledgments

The research herein is partially conducted within the competence network Softnet Austria II (http://www.soft-net.at/, COMET K-Projekt) and funded by the Austrian Federal Ministry of Economy, Family and Youth (bmwfj), the province of Styria, the Steirische Wirtschaftsförderungsgesellschaft mbH. (SFG), and the city of Vienna in terms of the center for innovation and technology (ZIT).

References

[1] B. Hofer and F. Wotawa, "Reducing the size of dynamic slicing with constraint solving," in *Proceedings of the 12th International Conference on Quality Software*, 2012.

[2] M. J. Harrold, G. Rothermel, R. Wu, and L. Yi, "An empirical investigation of program spectra," in *Proceedings of the Workshop on Program Analysis for Software Tools and Engineering*, pp. 83–90, ACM, New York, NY, USA, 1998.

[3] R. Abreu, P. Zoeteweij, R. Golsteijn, and A. J. C. van Gemund, "A practical evaluation of spectrum-based fault localization," *Journal of Systems and Software*, vol. 82, no. 11, pp. 1780–1792, 2009.

[4] P. Zoeteweij, R. Abreu, R. Golsteijn, and A. J. C. Van Gemund, "Diagnosis of embedded software using program spectra," in *Proceedings of the 14th Annual IEEE International Conference and Workshops on the Engineering of Computer-Based Systems (ECBS '07)*, pp. 213–220, March 2007.

[5] J. A. Jones and M. J. Harrold, "Empirical evaluation of the tarantula automatic fault-localization technique," in *Proceedings of the 20th IEEE/ACM International Conference on Automated Software Engineering (ASE '05)*, pp. 273–282, ACM Press, November 2005.

[6] R. Abreu, P. Zoeteweij, and A. J. C. Van Gemund, "An evaluation of similarity coefficients for software fault localization," in *Proceedings of the 12th Pacific Rim International Symposium on Dependable Computing (PRDC '06)*, pp. 39–46, Washington, DC, USA, December 2006.

[7] R. Abreu and A. J. C. Van Gemund, "Diagnosing multiple intermittent failures using maximum likelihood estimation," *Artificial Intelligence*, vol. 174, no. 18, pp. 1481–1497, 2010.

[8] R. Abreu, W. Mayer, M. Stumptner, and A. J. C. Van Gemund, "Refining spectrum-based fault localization rankings," in *Proceedings of the 24th Annual ACM Symposium on Applied Computing (SAC '09)*, pp. 409–414, Honolulu, Hawaii, USA, March 2009.

[9] A. Zeller and R. Hildebrandt, "Simplifying and isolating failure-inducing input," *IEEE Transactions on Software Engineering*, vol. 28, no. 2, pp. 183–200, 2002.

[10] H. Cleve and A. Zeller, "Locating causes of program failures," in *Proceedings of the 27th International Conference on Software Engineering (ICSE '05)*, pp. 342–351, ACM Press, New York, NY, USA, May 2005.

[11] A. Zeller, "Isolating cause-effect chains from computer programs," in *Proceedings of the 10th ACM SIGSOFT Symposium on the Foundations of Software Engineering*, pp. 1–10, November 2002.

[12] M. Weiser, "Programmers use slices when debugging," *Communications of the ACM*, vol. 25, no. 7, pp. 446–452, 1982.

[13] W. Mayer and M. Stumptner, "Model-based debugging—state of the art and future challenges," *Electronic Notes in Theoretical Computer Science*, vol. 174, no. 4, pp. 61–82, 2007.

[14] A. Arcuri, "On the automation of fixing software bugs," in *Proceedings of the 30th International Conference on Software Engineering (ICSE '08)*, pp. 1003–1006, New York, NY, USA, May 2008.

[15] W. Weimer, S. Forrest, C. Le Goues, and T. Nguyen, "Automatic program repair with evolutionary computation," *Communications of the ACM*, vol. 53, no. 5, pp. 109–116, 2010.

[16] W. Weimer, T. Nguyen, C. Le Goues, and S. Forrest, "Automatically finding patches using genetic programming," in *Proceedings of the 31st International Conference on Software Engineering (ICSE '09)*, pp. 364–374, May 2009.

[17] B. Korel and J. Laski, "Dynamic program slicing," *Information Processing Letters*, vol. 29, no. 3, pp. 155–163, 1988.

[18] X. Zhang, H. He, N. Gupta, and R. Gupta, "Experimental evaluation of using dynamic slices for fault location," in *Proceedings of the 6th International Symposium on Automated and Analysis-Driven Debugging (AADEBUG '05)*, pp. 33–42, September 2005.

[19] X. Zhang, S. Tallam, N. Gupta, and R. Gupta, "Towards locating execution omission errors," *ACM SIGPLAN Notices*, vol. 42, no. 6, pp. 415–424, 2007.

[20] M. Sridharan, S. J. Fink, and R. Bodik, "Thin slicing," in *Proceedings of the ACM SIGPLAN Conference on Programming Language Design and Implementation (PLDI '07)*, pp. 112–122, ACM, San Diego, Calif, USA, June 2007.

[21] N. Gupta, H. He, X. Zhang, and R. Gupta, "Locating faulty code using failure-inducing chops," in *Proceedings of the 20th IEEE/ACM International Conference on Automated Software Engineering (ASE '05)*, pp. 263–272, New York, NY, USA, November 2005.

[22] X. Zhang, N. Gupta, and R. Gupta, "Pruning dynamic slices with confidence," *ACM SIGPLAN Notices*, vol. 41, no. 6, pp. 169–180, 2006.

[23] X. Zhang, N. Gupta, and R. Gupta, "A study of effectiveness of dynamic slicing in locating real faults," *Empirical Software Engineering*, vol. 12, no. 2, pp. 143–160, 2007.

[24] X. Zhang, R. Gupta, and Y. Zhang, "Efficient forward computation of dynamic slices using reduced ordered binary decision diagrams," in *Proceedings of the 26th International Conference on Software Engineering (ICSE '04)*, pp. 502–511, Los Alamitos, Calif, USA, May 2004.

[25] X. Zhang, S. Tallam, and R. Gupta, "Dynamic slicing long running programs through execution fast forwarding," in *Proceedings of the 14th ACM SIGSOFT International Symposium on Foundations of Software Engineering (SIGSOFT '06)*, pp. 81–91, New York, NY, USA, November 2006.

[26] D. Jeffrey, N. Gupta, and R. Gupta, "Fault localization using value replacement," in *Proceedings of the International Symposium on Software Testing and Analysis (ISSTA '08)*, pp. 167–177, ACM, New York, NY, USA, July 2008.

[27] F. Tip, "A survey of program slicing techniques," *Journal of Programming Languages*, vol. 3, no. 3, pp. 121–189, 1995.

[28] B. Korel and J. Rilling, "Dynamic program slicing methods," *Information and Software Technology*, vol. 40, no. 11-12, pp. 647–659, 1998.

[29] R. Reiter, "A theory of diagnosis from first principles," *Artificial Intelligence*, vol. 32, no. 1, pp. 57–95, 1987.

[30] F. Wotawa, "On the relationship between model-based debugging and program slicing," *Artificial Intelligence*, vol. 135, no. 1-2, pp. 125–143, 2002.

[31] M. Nica, S. Nica, and F. Wotawa, "On the use of mutations and testing for debugging," *Software—Practice and Experience*. In press.

[32] F. Wotawa, M. Nica, and I. Moraru, "Automated debugging based on a constraint model of the program and a test case," *Journal of Logic and Algebraic Programming*, vol. 81, no. 4, pp. 390–407, 2012.

[33] W. Mayer, *Static and hybrid analysis in model-based debugging [Ph.D. thesis]*, School of Computer and Information Science, University of South Australia, 2007.

[34] W. Mayer, R. Abreu, M. Stumptner, and J. C. A. van Gemund, "Prioritising model-based debugging diagnostic reports (DX)," in *Proceedings of the International Workshop on Principles of Diagnosis*, pp. 127–134, 2008.

[35] F. Wotawa and M. Nica, "On the compilation of programs into their equivalent constraint representation," *Informatica*, vol. 32, no. 4, pp. 359–371, 2008.

[36] B. Beizer, *Software Testing Techniques*, Van Nostrand Reinhold, New York, NY, USA, 2nd edition, 1990.

[37] L. Console, D. T. Dupre, and P. Torasso, "On the relationship between abduction and deduction," *Journal of Logic and Computation*, vol. 1, no. 5, pp. 661–690, 1991.

[38] J. de Kleer, A. K. Mackworth, and R. Reiter, "Characterizing diagnoses and systems," *Artificial Intelligence*, vol. 56, no. 2-3, pp. 197–222, 1992.

[39] M. M. Brandis and H. Mossenbock, "Single-pass generation of static single-assignment form for structured languages," *ACM Transactions on Programming Languages and Systems*, vol. 16, no. 6, pp. 1684–1698, 1994.

[40] R. Dechter, *Constraint Processing*, Elsevier Morgan Kaufmann, 2003.

[41] R. Greiner, B. A. Smith, and R. W. Wilkerson, "A correction to the algorithm in reiter's theory of diagnosis," *Artificial Intelligence*, vol. 41, no. 1, pp. 79–88, 1989.

[42] I. P. Gent, C. Jefferson, and I. Miguel, "Minion: a fast, scalable, constraint solver," in *Proceedings of the 17th European Conference on Artificial Intelligence (ECAI '06)*, pp. 98–102, Riva del Garda, Italy, August 2006.

[43] F. Brglez and H. Fujiwara, "A neutral netlist of 10 combinational benchmark circuits and a target translator in fortran," in *Proceedings of the IEEE International Symposium on Circuits and Systems*, pp. 663–698, June 1985.

[44] C. Parnin and A. Orso, "Are automated debugging techniques actually helping programmers?" in *Proceedings of the 20th International Symposium on Software Testing and Analysis (ISSTA '11)*, pp. 199–209, ACM, New York, NY, USA, 2011.

[45] a. González-Sanchez, R. Abreu, H.-G. Hans-Gerhard Gross, and A. van Gemund, "Prioritizing tests for fault localization through ambiguity group reduction," in *Proceedings of the 26th IEEE/ACM International Conference on Automated Software Engineering (ASE '11)*, pp. 83–92, IEEE Computer Society, Washington, DC, USA.

12

Program Spectra Analysis with Theory of Evidence

Rattikorn Hewett

Department of Computer Science, Texas Tech University, Lubbock, TX 79409-3104, USA

Correspondence should be addressed to Rattikorn Hewett, rattikorn.hewett@ttu.edu

Academic Editor: Chin-Yu Huang

This paper presents an approach to automatically analyzing *program spectra*, an execution profile of program testing results for fault localization. Using a mathematical theory of evidence for uncertainty reasoning, the proposed approach estimates the likelihood of faulty locations based on evidence from program spectra. Our approach is theoretically grounded and can be computed online. Therefore, we can predict fault locations immediately after each test execution is completed. We evaluate the approach by comparing its performance with the top three performing fault localizers using a benchmark set of real-world programs. The results show that our approach is at least as effective as others with an average *effectiveness* (the reduction of the amount of code examined to locate a fault) of 85.6% over 119 versions of the programs. We also study the quantity and quality impacts of program spectra on our approach where the quality refers to the spectra *support* in identifying that a certain unit is faulty. The results show that the effectiveness of our approach slightly improves with a larger number of failed runs but not with a larger number of passed runs. Program spectra with support quality increases from 1% to 100% improves the approach's effectiveness by 3.29%.

1. Introduction

Identifying location of faulty software is notoriously known to be among the most costly and time-consuming process in software development [1, 2]. As software gets larger and more complex, the task can be daunting even with the help of debugging tools. Over the decades, many approaches to software fault localization have been studied including diagnostic reasoning [3], program slicing [4], nearest neighbor [5], and statistical analysis [6, 7].

Recent fault localization techniques have focused on automatically analyzing program behaviors observed from the execution of a suite of test cases on the tested program called *program spectra* [8]. For each run of the test case, certain program units (e.g., statements or blocks of code) are executed and result in either a *passed test* (*run*, or *execution*) when the output of the program's execution is the same as the expected output, or a *failed test*, otherwise. A collection of program spectra contains execution profiles that indicate which part of the program is involved in each test run and whether it is passed or failed.

Spectrum-based fault localization basically tries to identify the part of the program whose activity correlates most with the resulting passed or failed test runs. Most existing spectrum-based approaches rely on similarity measures to locate faulty software units by identifying the units that most resemble the spectra error outcomes [9–15]. The technique has been used for fault localization in various applications including the Pinpoint tool [12] for large dynamic online transaction processing systems and AMPLE [16] for objected-oriented software. Spectrum-based fault localization is relatively efficient to compute and does not require modeling of the program under investigation. Therefore, it is a popular fault localization technique that can easily be integrated into testing procedures [10].

The current top three performing spectrum-based fault localizers include *Ochiai* [14], *Jaccard* [12], and *Tarantula* [13]. *Tarantula* uses a heuristic function adapted from a visualization technique while *Jaccard* and *Ochiai* employ different similarity measures, both of which are widely used in other domains such as biology and ecology. While these approaches are useful, most lack theoretical foundation and the ability to immediately incorporate new testing results into the fault localization process. Furthermore, they are not easily extensible to new findings of contributing factors. Our research aims to alleviate these shortcomings.

This paper presents a spectrum-based fault localization technique for pinpointing locations of faulty software units. The approach employs the theory of evidence called Dempster-Shafer Theory [17] for uncertainty reasoning to estimate the likelihood of faulty locations based on evidence gathered from program spectra. Our approach is theoretically grounded and computed online instead of batch. Thus, it allows the prediction of fault locations to be identified immediately as the execution of each test case is completed without having to wait to collect a set of program spectra that is large enough to be statistically valid. Our contribution also includes a study of the influences of the theory of evidence on fault localization effectiveness as well as the influences of the quantity and quality of the program spectra used in the analysis.

The rest of the paper is organized as follows: Section 2 describes preliminary concepts and terminology including basic mechanisms for software fault localization, the three spectrum-based fault localizers used in our comparison study, and the Dempster-Shafer Theory along with its fundamental elements. Section 3 presents our approach to program spectra analysis, an illustration on a small example program, and some characteristic comparisons. Section 4 evaluates the proposed technique and discusses the empirical study using a set of standard benchmarks to compare the proposed method against the other three prominent software fault localizers. Section 5 presents an empirical study to answer questions whether the performance of the proposed approach relies on the quality or quantity of the program spectra or not. Section 6 discusses the work related to fault localization and the method proposed in this paper. Section 7 concludes the paper.

2. Preliminaries

This section describes terms, concepts of spectrum-based fault localization technique, the three fault localizers and the basic foundations of the mathematical theory of evidence.

2.1. Concepts, Terms, and Notations. Following the terminology in [10], a *software failure* occurs when the actual program output, for a given input, deviates from the corresponding specified output. *Software errors*, however, define defects that may or may not cause a failure. Thus, in practice, we may not be able to detect all errors. Defects that result in failures are referred to as *software faults* (or *bugs*).

Program spectra [8] are execution profiles of the program resulting from test runs. In particular, suppose we run m test cases on a program of n units (e.g., statements, blocks, and modules). The *hit spectra* can be represented as an $m \times n$ matrix $R = (r_{ij})$, where $r_{ij} = 1$ if test i involves execution of unit j of the program, otherwise it is 0 (i.e., if test i does not involve execution of unit j). In addition, for each run of test i, we define a corresponding *error* e_i to be 1 if the test failed, and 0, otherwise (i.e., when the test was passed or successful). Program spectra include both the hit spectra and the error. To collect program spectra, we run a suite of test cases and observe execution results where the test can be performed at

TABLE 1: Different types of test run frequency count.

Software Unit	Test run	
	Passed	Failed
Not Executed	a_{00}	a_{01}
Executed	a_{10}	a_{11}

various levels of software units (e.g., code lines or statements, blocks of code, or modules). Much research has studied fault localization in code blocks [9, 15]. Though we illustrate our approach at a code statement (or line) level, the approach is general for application in any level of software unit.

Conceptually, *fault localization* is an attempt to identify a software unit whose behaviors in all relevant test cases are most similar to the errors observed in a given program spectra. To do this, the following notations are defined. For a given test run i and a software unit j, let p and q be a binary variable signifying whether run i involves execution of unit j, and, respectively, whether run i fails or not. Here p is 1 if run i involves execution of unit j, and 0, otherwise. On the other hand, q is 1 if run i fails and 0, otherwise. Next we relate p and q to observations in the program spectra.

For each software unit j, we define the frequency of runs $a_{pq}(j) = |\{i \mid r_{ij} = p, e_i = q\}|$. Recall that r_{ij} represents the result of test run i on unit j (whether it executes unit j or not), and e_i represents the output error of test run i (whether the test is passed or failed). Thus, for a given software unit, we can summarize the interpretations of all possible cases of a_{pq}'s in Table 1. For example, $a_{01}(j)$ represents the number of *failed* test runs (i.e., $q = 1$) that *did not execute* (i.e., $p = 0$) unit j. Note that in general $a_{00}(j)$ is not of interest to fault localization since a successful test run that does not involve the execution of the software unit does not provide any useful information for detecting faults. It does not raise any suspicion that the unit under investigation is faulty nor does it confirm that it is not faulty. On the other hand, $a_{11}(j)$ is an important indicator for identifying faulty units.

2.2. Spectrum-Based Fault Localizers. In spectrum-based fault localization techniques, software units are ranked based on their corresponding *similarity coefficients* (e.g., see [5, 10]). A similarity coefficient of a software unit measures how closely the execution runs of the test cases that involve the considering unit resemble the errors observed [9]. The software unit that has a high similarity to the output errors is assumed to have a high probability that the unit would be the cause of such errors. Thus, a unit with a larger similarity-coefficient value would rank higher in terms of its chance to be faulty. Let S_i denote a similarity coefficient for software unit i.

Next we describe the current top three fault localizers that mainly differ by the similarity coefficient S_i. A popular Tarantula [13] has been shown to be the best performing spectrum-based fault localizer in [18]. Abreu et al. [9] have recently shown that the *Jaccard* coefficient [12] and *Ochiai* coefficient [14] marginally outperform Tarantula. Most similarity coefficients utilize the frequency of occurrences of the result of the test execution that involves a certain code statement. We now describe them in more detail.

Tarantula. The similarity coefficient in Tarantula is adapted from a formula for displaying the color of each program statement to visualize fault locations. For a given code statement i, %*passed*(i) (%*failed*(i)) represents, in percentage, a ratio of the number of passed (failed) test cases that executed i to the total number of the passed (failed) test cases in the overall test suite. Tarantula quantifies *color* value of a given code statement by the following formula:

$$ \text{color} = L + \left(\frac{\text{\%passed}}{\text{\%passed} + \text{\%failed}} \right) * (H - L), \quad (1) $$

where L and H represent low end and a high end color values of the color spectrum, respectively. For example, if a program statement is executed by 10% of the passed test cases and 20% of the failed test cases, its color will be 1/3 of the way from pure red (low end color of value zero) to pure green (high end color of value 120), thus in between red and yellow making it an orange color (of value 40).

Adapting from the above color scheme, the similarity coefficient is defined as follows:

$$ S_i = \frac{\text{\%failed}(i)}{\text{\%failed}(i) + \text{\%passed}(i)}. \quad (2) $$

By using the notation introduced in Section 2.1, we obtain the following:

$$ \text{\%failed}(i) = \frac{a_{11}(i)}{a_{11}(i) + a_{01}(i)}, $$
$$ \text{\%passed}(i) = \frac{a_{10}(i)}{a_{10}(i) + a_{00}(i)}. \quad (3) $$

The numerator in S_i is opposite from that of the color scheme because Tarantula ranks the suspicion of faulty units from those with the highest to the lowest values of $S_i's$. Thus, the higher value of S_i indicates that statement i is more likely to be faulty. Faulty likelihood is influenced by %*failed*. On the contrary, in the color scheme, the lowest color value is represented in pure red to signify that the unit under investigation is the most likely to be faulty.

Jaccard. The Jaccard similarity coefficient [19] is a simple metric that has been used for comparing two binary data objects whose variable values are not equally important (e.g., a positive disease test result is more crucial than a negative one). Chen et al. [12] have applied the Jaccard similarity coefficient for fault localization in a pinpoint tool. The Jaccard coefficient is defined as

$$ S_i = \frac{a_{11}(i)}{a_{11}(i) + a_{01}(i) + a_{10}(i)}. \quad (4) $$

As shown in the formula, the numerator of the Jaccard similarity coefficient uses $a_{11}(i)$ to compare the similarity in frequency of the test cases of interest (i.e., failed tests that execute line i). Furthermore, the denominator omits

$a_{00}(i)$, which provides no valuable information with respect to locating faulty lines. Although the Jaccard coefficient has been shown to improve fault localization performance over Tarantula [9], the difference is marginal. Additional experiments are required to evaluate and draw conclusions.

Ochiai. The Ochiai coefficient [20] has been applied to various domains including ecology and molecular biology [14]. The coefficient is defined as the following:

$$ S_i = \frac{a_{11}(i)}{\sqrt{(a_{11}(i) + a_{01}(i)) * (a_{11}(i) + a_{10}(i))}}. \quad (5) $$

The Ochiai coefficient uses the same contributing factors to measure similarity as those of Jaccard's. However, the denominator has more complex computation. In fault localization application, Abreu et al.'s empirical study [9] has shown that Ochia coefficient yields more superior results than those obtained from Jaccard coefficient. However, there is no intuitive explanation given.

2.3. Mathematical Theory of Evidence. Work in spectrum-based fault localization has mostly concentrated on specifying appropriate similarity coefficients using the information extracted from program spectra. This is quite different from our approach. To provide a theoretical background of the proposed research, we describe the mathematical theory of evidence, also known as the *Dempster-Shafer (D-S) Theory* [17]. The D-S theory allows probability assignment to a set of atomic elements rather than an atomic element. Thus, the D-S theory can be viewed as a generalization of Bayesian probability theory that can explicitly represent ignorance as well as uncertainty [21].

Let $\mathcal{U}$ be a finite set of all hypotheses (atomic elements) in a problem domain. A *mass function* m provides a probability assignment to any $A \subseteq \mathcal{U}$, where $m(\emptyset) = 0$ and $\Sigma_{A \subseteq \mathcal{U}} m(A) = 1$. The mass $m(A)$ represents a belief *exactly* on A. For example, $\mathcal{U} = \{\text{faulty}, \sim\text{faulty}\}$ represents a set of two hypotheses of a suspect being faulty and nonfaulty, respectively. In such a case, the property of the mass function implies that $m(\{\text{faulty}\}) + m(\{\sim \text{faulty}\}) + m(\{\text{faulty}, \sim \text{faulty}\}) = 1$, as $m(\emptyset) = 0$. Thus, mass function is not the same as probability. When there is no information regarding $\mathcal{U}$, $m(\{\text{faulty}, \sim \text{faulty}\}) = 1$, and $m(\{\text{faulty}\}) = m(\{\sim \text{faulty}\}) = m(\emptyset) = 0$. The former (i.e., $m(\{\text{faulty}, \sim \text{faulty}\}) = 1$) deals with a state of ignorance since the hypothesis set includes all possible hypotheses and therefore, its truth is believed to be certain.

For every mass function, there are associated functions of *belief* and *plausibility*. The degree of belief on A, bel(A) is defined to be $\Sigma_{X \subseteq A} m(X)$ and the plausibility of A, pl(A) is $1 - \text{bel}(\sim A) = \Sigma_{X \cap A \neq \emptyset} m(X)$. For example, bel($\{\text{faulty}\}$) = $m(\{\text{faulty}\}) + m(\emptyset) = m(\{\text{faulty}\})$. In general, bel($A$) = $m(A)$ for any singleton set $A \subseteq \mathcal{U}$ and in such a case the computation of bel is greatly reduced. However, bel(A) is not necessary the same as $m(A)$ when A is not a singleton set. Thus, m, bel and pl can be derived from one another. It can be shown that the interval [bel(A), pl(A)] contains probability of A in the classic sense (see [10]). Thus, *belief* and *probability* are different measures. In this paper, we use the terms *likelihood* and *belief* synonymously.

A mass function can be combined using various rules including the popular *Dempster's Rule of Combination*, which is a generalization of the Bayes rule. For $X, A, B \subseteq \mathcal{U}$, a combination rule of mass functions m_1 and m_2, denoted by $m_1 \oplus m_2$ (or $m_{1,2}$) is defined as the following:

$$m_{1,2}(X) = m_1 \oplus m_2(X) = \frac{\sum_{A \cap B = X} m_1(A) m_2(B)}{1 - K}, \quad (6)$$

where $K = \sum_{A \cap B = \varnothing} m_1(A) m_2(B)$ and $m_1 \oplus m_2(\varnothing) = 0$.

The combination rule can be applied in pairs repeatedly to obtain a combination of multiple mass functions. The above rule strongly emphasizes the agreement between multiple sources of evidence and ignores the disagreement by the use of a normalization factor.

3. Proposed Approach

By exploiting program spectra, the proposed approach to the way an automated fault localizer builds on the concepts of Dempster-Shafer theory will be described. Section 3.1 discusses the formulation of mass functions, which are our main contributions. Section 3.2 discusses some characteristics of different fault localizers and how the proposed approach can be extended. Section 3.3 illustrates the approach in a small example along with intuitive justifications.

3.1. Mass Functions and Combination Rule. Mass functions are essential elements in estimating the likelihood of the code statement being faulty based on evidences from the program spectra described in Section 2. For any statement j of a tested program, let $\mathcal{U}_j = \{f_j, \sim f_j\}$, where f_j represents the hypothesis that j is faulty and similarly, $\sim f_j$ for nonfaulty. For each test run, we are concerned with whether the test was successful or not and what code statements were executed during the test. There are two possibilities.

Case 1 (failed test). A failed test that involves the execution of the statement under investigation is evidence that supports that the statement is likely to be faulty. In such a case, the likelihood of the statement being nonfaulty is zero. On the other hand, its likelihood of being faulty can be estimated by a ratio of one over the total number of statements involved in this test run. We can formulate this formally as follows

Recall that in the program spectra, $r_{ij} = 1$ if test i involves execution of unit j of the program, and it is 0, otherwise. Thus, a total number of units executed in test run i can be represented by $\Sigma_j r_{ij}$. We now define m_i, the mass function of failed test i for all possible nonempty subsets of the hypotheses in $\mathcal{U}_j$ as follows:

$$m_i\left(\left\{\sim f_j\right\}\right) = 0, \quad (7)$$

$$m_i\left(\left\{f_j\right\}\right) = \alpha * \left(\frac{r_{ij}}{\Sigma_j r_{ij}}\right), \quad \text{where } 0 < \alpha \leq 1, \quad (8)$$

$$m_i\left(\mathcal{U}_j\right) = 1 - m_i\left(\left\{f_j\right\}\right). \quad (9)$$

The third equation is derived from the property that $m(\varnothing) = 0$ and $\Sigma_{A \subseteq \mathcal{U}} m(A) = 1$. Based on the second equation, it should be easy to see that the likelihood of a statement being faulty can only be influenced by the (failed) test that executes that statement. The parameter α is an adjusted value that represents the strength of the property of "failed test" in determining if statement j is faulty.

Case 2 (passed test). If a test involving the execution of the statement in question is successful, it is evidence that supports that this statement behaves correctly. Thus, the likelihood of it being faulty is zero. On the other hand, the likelihood of this statement being correct (i.e., nonfaulty) can be estimated by a ratio of one over the total number of statements involved in this test run. We now define m_i, the mass function of passed test i for all possible nonempty subsets of the hypotheses in $\mathcal{U}_j$ as follows:

$$m_i\left(\left\{f_j\right\}\right) = 0, \quad (10)$$

$$m_i\left(\left\{\sim f_j\right\}\right) = \beta * \left(\frac{r_{ij}}{\Sigma_j r_{ij}}\right) \quad \text{where } 0 < \beta \leq 1, \quad (11)$$

$$m_i\left(\mathcal{U}_j\right) = 1 - m_i\left(\left\{\sim f_j\right\}\right). \quad (12)$$

It should be easy to see that in this case the likelihood of a statement being correct can only be influenced by the (successful) test that executes it. Analogous to α, the parameter β is an adjusted value that represents the strength of the property of "passed test" in determining if statement j is not faulty.

In general, the appropriate values of the adjusted values α and β are determined empirically since they are likely to depend on the size of the program, the number of tests and the ratios of failed to passed tests (see an example in Section 3.3). The more precision the values of α and β are, the more likely we can discriminate faulty belief values among a large number of software units. In this paper, α and β are estimated conservatively to one and 0.0001, respectively, in order to yield a sufficient power of discrimination for a very large program. The intuitive reason behind this is the fact that when a test fails, we can guarantee the existence of at least one faulty line. Thus, we should give very high strength to such evidence. This justifies α having the highest possible strength of one. However, when a test is successful, there is no guarantee that there is no faulty statement since the particular test may not have executed faulty statements and detected the faults. Thus, a successful test does not contribute to the belief of a statement being faulty as much as a failed test does. Nevertheless, when a statement is executed in a successful test, one may be inclined to believe that the statement is probably not likely to be faulty. As the number of such successful tests increases, we gain more confidence of such belief and thus, the successful test results have a contributing factor (although small) to the belief and cannot be ignored. In practice, the number of failed tests is typically much less than that of successful ones. Thus, each successful test should have less strength compared to that of each failed test. This explains why β takes a very small value that is as close to zero as possible. We conjecture that the larger the size of the program and the smaller ratio of the number of failed tests to the number of successful tests would likely require much smaller β. However, to conclude such a statement requires further experiments.

Recall that a mass function of a singleton set hypothesis is the same as the degree of belief of the hypothesis. Applying one of the above two cases, a mass function is created for each of the supporting evidences (i.e., a test result, which either supports faulty or nonfaulty) of each program statement. Thus, the likelihood of a statement being faulty is estimated by combining the beliefs obtained from corresponding mass functions for each of the supporting pieces of evidence. To define the rule for combining mass functions, suppose that m_1 and m_2 are two distinct mass functions of a particular code statement i. Dempster's rule of combination can be applied as shown below. For readability, we omit i and replace $\{f_i\}$, $\{\sim f_i\}$ and $\mathcal{U}_i$ by f, $\sim f$ and $\mathcal{U}$, respectively.

$$m_{1,2}(f) = \frac{(m_1(f)m_2(f)+m_1(f)m_2(\mathcal{U})+m_1(\mathcal{U})m_2(f))}{1-K},$$

$$m_{1,2}(\sim f) = \frac{m_1(\sim f)m_2(\sim f)+m_1(\sim f)m_2(\mathcal{U})+m_1(\mathcal{U})m_2(\sim f)}{1-K},$$

$$m_{1,2}(\mathcal{U}) = \frac{m_1(\mathcal{U})m_2(\mathcal{U})}{1-K},$$

$$(13)$$

where $K = m_1(f)m_2(\sim f) + m_1(\sim f)m_2(f)$.

This combination rule can be applied repeatedly pairwise until evidence from all test runs has been incorporated into the computation of the likelihood of each statement. Unlike other spectrum-based fault localizers discussed in Section 2.2, instead of ranking the lines based on the similarity coefficient values, our proposed approach ranks the lines based on the corresponding likelihood of them being faulty using the beliefs combined from all of the test evidence.

3.2. Characteristic Comparisons and Generalization. This section discusses and compares some characteristics of the proposed approach with other fault localizers: *Tarantula*, *Jaccard*, and *Ochiai*. Our approach is based on the principle of uncertainty reasoning, while the others are based on similarity coefficients, which share common characteristics. We now describe them below assuming that a code statement in question is given.

Suppose we classify test runs into those that *failed* and those that *executed* the code statement. The coefficient of each of the three localizers reaches its minimum value of zero when there is no test in both groups (i.e., $a_{11} = 0$). This means that there is no association between failed tests and tests that executed the code statement. On the other hand, the coefficient reflects a maximum association with a value one when all tests are in both groups. In other words, there is no failed test that did not execute the statement (i.e., $a_{01} = 0$) and no passed test that executed the statement (i.e., $a_{10} = 0$).

Unlike *Tarantula*, *Jaccard*, and *Ochiai* do not use a_{00} to compute the similarity coefficient. The denominator of the *Jaccard* coefficient represents the "sum" of all *failed* (i.e.,

$a_{11}+a_{01}$) and all *executed* tests (i.e., $a_{11}+a_{10}$) but not both (i.e., excluding a_{11}). On the other hand, the denominator of the *Ochiai* coefficient, which is derived from a geometric mean of $a_{11}/failed$ and $a_{11}/executed$, is a square *root* of a "product" of *executed* and *failed* tests. Thus, the Ochiai coefficient amplifies the distinction between *failed* and *executed* tests more than the Jaccard coefficient. Therefore, the Ochiai coefficient is expected to provide a better discriminator for locating fault units.

Recall that the similarity coefficient of *Tarantula* is *%failed/(%failed + %passed)*. This seems reasonable. However, note that when *%passed* value is zero, the coefficient value is one regardless of the *%failed* value. Suppose that the two code statements both have zero *%passed* but one was executed in one out of 100 failed tests and the other was executed in 90 out of the 100 failed tests. The chance of the latter statement being faulty should be greater than the other but *Tarantula* would rank the two statements as equally likely to be faulty. This explains why *Ochiai* and *Jaccard* can outperform *Tarantula* as reported in [10].

Our approach uses the Dempster-Shafer Theory of Evidence to account for each test run to accumulatively support the hypothesis about the statement. This makes our approach applicable for online computation. As shown in (8), each failed test adds belief to the statement being faulty. Similarly, in (10), each passed test adds belief to the statement being correct. The belief is contributed to by a probability factor that depends on the number of times that the test executed the statement and an overall number of statements executed in that test. Thus, our reasoning is in a finer grain size than the others since it focuses on a specific test (i.e., the mass functions) and the contributing factors are not necessarily expressible in terms of a_{ij}'s as with other similarity coefficients. Thus, it would be interesting to compare the performance among these approaches.

The proposed approach can be generalized to accommodate evidence of new properties. That is, we can, respectively, generalize (8) and (10) to

$$m(\{f_i\}) = \alpha * f, \quad \text{where } 0 < \alpha \le 1,$$
$$m(\{\sim f_i\}) = \beta * g, \quad \text{where } 0 < \beta \le 1, \quad (14)$$

where function f (function g) quantifies evidential support for statement i being faulty (correct). Thus, the proposed approached is easily extensible.

3.3. Illustrated Example. To demonstrate our approach, Algorithm 1 shows a small faulty program introduced in [10]. The program is supposed to sort a list of n rational numbers using a bubble sort algorithm. There is a total of five blocks (the last block corresponding to the body of the `RationalSort` function is not shown here). Block 4 is faulty since when we swap the order of the two rational numbers, their denominators (`den`) need to be swapped as well as the numerators (`num`).

The program spectra can be constructed after running six tests with various inputs as shown in Table 2. Tests 1, 2, and 6 are already sorted and so they result in no error. Test 3 is not sorted but because the input denominators are of the same

```
void rationalsort (
    int n, int* num, int* den)
{
    /* block 1 */
    int i, j, temp;
    for (i = n - 1; i >= 0; i--)   {
        /* block 2 */
        for (j = 0; j < i; j++) {
            /* block 3 */
            if (RationalGT(num[j], den[j],
                num[j + 1], den[j + 1])) {
                /* block 4 */
                temp = num[j];
                num[j] = num[j + 1];
                num[j + 1] = temp;
            }
        }
    }
}
```

ALGORITHM 1: Example of a faulty program.

value, no error occurs. However, double errors occur during Test 4's execution and so errors go undetected and Test 4 is passed. Finally, Test 5 failed since it resulted in erroneous output of $\langle 1/1\ 2/2\ 4/3\ 3/4 \rangle$.

In this small set of program spectra we use the adjusted strength α of value one and the adjusted strength β of value $1/6$ to reflect the ratio of the number of failed test to overall number of test runs. Applying our approach, since Test 1 is a passed test (i.e., error $= 0$), we compute the belief of each hypothesis using the mass functions (10), (11) and (12). For example, the beliefs of hypotheses related to Block 1 after Test 1 are

$$m_1(\{f_1\}) = 0,$$
$$m_1(\{\sim f_1\}) = \beta * \left(\frac{r_{11}}{\Sigma_j r_{1j}} \right) = \left(\frac{1}{6} \right) * \left(\frac{1}{1} \right) = 0.167,\ (15)$$
$$m_1(\mathcal{U}_1) = 1 - m_1(\{\sim f_1\}) = 0.833.$$

Similarly, for Test 2, which is a passed test, we can apply the mass functions (10), (11) and (12) to compute the belief of each hypothesis. For example, the beliefs of hypotheses related to Block 1 after Test 2 are

$$m_2(\{f_1\}) = 0,$$
$$m_2(\{\sim f_1\}) = \beta * \left(\frac{r_{21}}{\Sigma_j r_{2j}} \right) = \left(\frac{1}{6} \right) * \left(\frac{1}{2} \right) = 0.083,$$
$$m_2(\mathcal{U}_1) = 1 - m_2(\{\sim f_1\}) = 0.917.$$
$$(16)$$

Now we can apply the Dempster's rule of combination to update the new beliefs as evidenced by the two tests. For simplicity, we omit the subscript representing software unit

of Block 1. Here $K = m_1(f)m_2(\sim f) + m_1(\sim f)m_2(f) = 0$ and we have

$$m_{1,2}(f) = m_1(f)m_2(f) + m_1(f)m_2(\mathcal{U})$$
$$+ m_1(\mathcal{U})m_2(f) = 0,$$
$$m_{1,2}(\sim f) = m_1(\sim f)m_2(\sim f) + m_1(\sim f)m_2(\mathcal{U})\quad (17)$$
$$+ m_1(\mathcal{U})m_2(\sim f) = 0.236,$$
$$m_{1,2}(\mathcal{U}) = m_1(\mathcal{U})m_2(\mathcal{U}) = 0.764.$$

Next consider Test 3, which is again a passed test. By applying the mass functions (10), (11), and (12), we obtain the following:

$$m_3(\{f_1\}) = 0,$$
$$m_3(\{\sim f_1\}) = \beta * \left(\frac{r_{31}}{\Sigma_j r_{3j}} \right) = \left(\frac{1}{6} \right) * \left(\frac{1}{5} \right) = 0.333,\ (18)$$
$$m_3(\mathcal{U}_1) = 1 - m_3(\{\sim f_1\}) = 0.967.$$

By applying the Dempster's combination rule to $m_{1,2}$ and m_3, we have the following:

$$m_{1,2,3}(f) = m_1(f)m_2(f) + m_1(f)m_2(\mathcal{U})$$
$$+ m_1(\mathcal{U})m_2(f) = 0,$$
$$m_{1,2,3}(\sim f) = m_1(\sim f)m_2(\sim f) + m_1(\sim f)m_2(\mathcal{U})\quad (19)$$
$$+ m_1(\mathcal{U})m_2(\sim f) = 0.262,$$
$$m_{1,2,3}(\mathcal{U}) = m_1(\mathcal{U})m_2(\mathcal{U}) = 0.738.$$

The above belief computation repeats until no more evidence from the test runs is to be considered. Thus, the belief of the hypothesis that Block 1 being faulty is calculated in accumulative fashion. For each block, the process continues for each test to accumulate the new beliefs of each hypothesis until all tests have been considered. Each new test run can be immediately integrated into the fault

TABLE 2: Program spectra and results.

Test input	Block 1	Block 2	Block 3	Block 4	Block 5	Error
(1)⟨⟩	1	0	0	0	0	0
(2)⟨1/4⟩	1	1	0	0	0	0
(3)⟨2/1 1/1⟩	1	1	1	1	1	0
(4)⟨4/1 2/2 0/1⟩	1	1	1	1	1	0
(5)⟨3/1 2/2 4/3 1/4⟩	1	1	1	1	1	1
(6)⟨1/4 1/3 1/2 1/1⟩	1	1	1	0	1	0
No. of matches	1	2	3	4	3	6
Fault Likelihood	0.15	0.17	0.18	0.19	0.18	

TABLE 3: Belief values using different adjusted strengths.

Unit	$\alpha = 0.9, \beta = 0.1$	$\alpha = 0.99, \beta = 0.01$	$\alpha = 1, \beta = 0.0001$
Block 1	0.149	0.1946	0.1999656
Block 2	0.163	0.1962	0.1999816
Block 3	0.170	0.1969	0.1999896
Block 4	0.174	0.1973	0.1999936
Block 5	0.170	0.1969	0.1999896

TABLE 4: Siemens program suite.

Program Name	Versions omitted	No. versions	No. lines	No. test cases
print_tokens	4, 6	7	475	4130
print_tokens2	10	10	401	4115
replace	27, 32	32	512	5542
schedule	3, 5, 6, 7, 8, 9	9	292	2649
schedule2	9	10	297	2710
tcas	38	41	135	1608
tot_info	none	23	346	1052

localization process. It is clear that our approach supports online computing. In this example, Test 5 is the only failed test to which we apply the mass functions (7), (8) and (9).

The final results obtained for the beliefs of each block being faulty are shown in the last row of Table 2. Ranking the beliefs obtained, Block 4 is identified to be the most likely faulty location. This is as expected. In fact, as shown in the second-to-bottom line of Table 2, Block 4 has the highest number of matched executions with the error results obtained from the six tests. Thus, the approach produces the result that is also in line with the concept of finding the block that corresponds most to the error results in the spectra.

As mentioned earlier that the adjusted strength values of α and β can be determined empirically for each specific program to obtain the best discriminative power among beliefs of each software unit. For example, Table 3 shows the belief values obtained for this small program using various adjusted strength values.

As shown in Table 3, all cases of the strength values are able to correctly identify Block 4 as a faulty unit. However, different strength values give different precision on the belief values, which can be critical for large-scale program spectra.

4. Evaluation and Comparison Study

To evaluate our approach, we compare the results of our approach with the top three state-of-the-art spectrum-based fault localizers using a popular benchmark data set.

4.1. Benchmark Data and Acquisition. The Siemens Program Suite [22], which has been widely used as a benchmark for testing fault localizer effectiveness [9–11]. The suite has seven programs with multiple versions that reflect real-world scenarios. Most versions contain a single fault except a few

containing two faults. However, since we typically locate one fault at a time, most studies including ours focus on methods for locating a single fault. The GNU Compiler Collection (GCC) 4.4.0 compiler was used to compile the programs and the GNU Coverage (GCov) extension was used to generate code coverage information to construct the program spectra.

For data preparation, we omit 13 out of a total of 132 faulty program versions due to inappropriate changes in the header file, lack of failure test results, and crash before GCov could produce a trace file. Thus, we use the remaining total of 119 versions in the experiment. Table 4 summarizes the information of the Siemens program suite including the program names, versions excluded and their corresponding number of (faulty) versions, executable lines of code, and test cases.

4.2. Evaluation Metric. Based on the standard method for evaluating fault localizers, we use *effectiveness* [18] as our evaluation metric. Effectiveness is defined to be the percentage of unexamined code (saved efforts) when identifying fault location. More precisely, suppose $P = \langle p_1, p_2, \ldots, p_n \rangle$ is a list of program statements (units, blocks) ranking in a descending order of similarity coefficient or likelihood values. The *effectiveness*, which signifies the reduction of the amount of code examined to locate a single fault in the software, can be specified as

$$\text{effectiveness} = \left(\frac{1-k}{n} \right) * 100\%, \qquad (20)$$

where $k = \min_{1 \le j \le n} \{j \mid p_j \text{ in } P \text{ is actually a faulty line}\}$. In other words, k is the first code statement found in P that actually is faulty. This is an optimistic measure that gives a maximum amount of unexamined code or effectiveness.

Because ranking can result in different findings for fault location, an issue of how to define the effectiveness when multiple lines have the same value of similarity coefficient or belief, can be crucial. Taking the first actual faulty statement found would be too optimistic and taking the last one found would be too pessimistic. Instead, Ali et al. [11] has proposed the *midline* adjustment, which appears to be a practical compromise. The midline takes the average rank of all the statements that have the same measure, which gives

$$\text{midline effectiveness} = \left(\frac{1-\tau}{n}\right) * 100\%, \quad (21)$$

where $\tau = (k + m - 1)/2$, where k is defined above and $m = \max_{1 \leq j \leq n}\{j \mid p_j \text{ in } P \ \& \ p_j\text{'s measure} = p_k\text{'s measure}\}$.

Our experiments employ the *effectiveness* metric in both conventional and adjusted midline measures of effectiveness as described above to compare the performance of our approach with those of other three fault localizers, namely, *Tarantura, Jaccard,* and *Ochiai.*

4.3. Experimental Results. We implemented the four methods in C++. The experimental results show that in a total of 119 versions, our approach gives better or the same *effectiveness* as those of the other three 100% of the time. In fact, in about 40% of all cases, our results have higher effectiveness than those of the rest; specifically they are higher than those of *Tarantura, Jaccard,* and *Ochiai* in 61, 59, and 48 versions, respectively.

Figure 1 shows the results obtained for midline effectiveness, which is less optimistic than the conventional effectiveness. By ranking program versions based on their corresponding effectiveness, Figure 1 compares the average percentages, over all 119 versions, of midline effectiveness obtained by our approach to those of the others. For easy visualization, because *Tarantula* has the lowest performance in all versions, Figure 1 displays the resulting average midline effectiveness of all versions performed by *Tarantula* in increasing order.

As shown in Figure 1, our approach results in slightly higher average midline effectiveness than those of *Tarantula, Jaccard,* and *Ochiai.* In particular, compared with *Tarantula,* our approach approximately shows up to an average of 3% increase in the midline effectiveness. Thus, the proposed approach is competitive with top performing fault localizers.

To see how the midline effectiveness differs from the conventional "optimistic" effectiveness, we compare the results obtained from each metric. Figure 2 shows the average percentages of both types of effectiveness obtained by our approach in each of the programs in the Siemens set. As expected, the midline effectiveness gives slightly less optimistic effectiveness than those of the conventional ones.

Table 5 compares the average effectiveness of overall versions for each approach (in percentages). The numbers after "±" represent variances. The conventional effectiveness is higher than that of the midline effectiveness. All methods perform competitively with no more than 0.5%

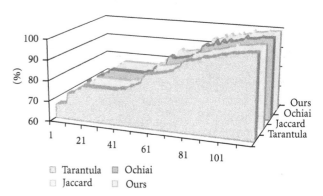

FIGURE 1: Comparison of average midline effectiveness.

TABLE 5: Average effectiveness in percentages.

Fault Localizer	% Avg. effectiveness	% Avg. midline effectiveness
Tarantula	88.10 ± 0.094	86.04 ± 0.088
Jaccard	88.14 ± 0.094	86.07 ± 0.088
Ochiai	88.34 ± 0.093	86.30 ± 0.087
Ours	88.47 ± 0.092	86.53 ± 0.086

difference of the effectiveness and all perform well with over 88% and 86% on the average of the conventional and midline effectiveness, respectively. As shown in Table 5, the proposed method gives the highest average percentage of effectiveness of both types, followed in order by *Ochiai, Jaccard,* and *Tarantula.* The proposed method also shows the least variance, so it performs consistently. However, the differences are marginal.

5. Impacts of Program Spectra

This section studies the impacts of program spectra on the effectiveness of fault localization. In previous sections, although our approach shows promising and competitive results on the Siemens benchmark data, one may question whether it performs well in general, regardless of what program spectra we use. It raises the issue whether the spectra quality or quantity have any impact on the effectiveness of the proposed fault localizer. To better understand how the proposed approach performs under different conditions of program spectra, we further perform our experiments using the same concepts and methodologies introduced in [10]. The effectiveness measure in this section refers to the midline effectiveness described earlier.

5.1. Quality Measure and Impacts. In a collection of program spectra as defined in Section 2, a software unit whose column vector exactly matches with the error vector has more assurance of being faulty. This is because the program fails (represented by a value one in a corresponding error vector entry) if and only if it is executed (represented by a value one in a corresponding entry of the software unit vector).

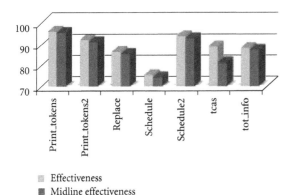

Effectiveness
Midline effectiveness

FIGURE 2: Comparison of two effectiveness measures.

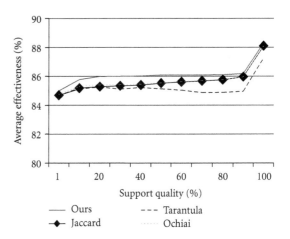

Ours — — — Tarantula
Jaccard ⋯⋯ Ochiai

FIGURE 3: Quality impacts on effectiveness.

Locating faults in such a case can be easily achieved. However, in practice inexact matches are quite common because a program may not fail even when a faulty unit is executed. It is possible to have a faulty unit executed in a successful test run since the run may not involve a condition that introduces errors or the errors may not propagate far enough to result in a program failure. Unfortunately, the ratio between these two cases is often unknown making fault localization more complex and difficult. In fact, the higher the number of successful test runs that involved the execution of software unit i is, the less confident we are that unit i is faulty. In other words, $a_{10}(i)$ is inversely proportional to the support in locating software fault at unit i. On the other hand, as pointed out earlier, fault localization of a software unit is easy if the program fails only whenever it is executed. Thus, the number of failed test runs that involved the execution of software unit i provides support in identifying unit i as faulty. That is, $a_{11}(i)$ is proportional to the support of fault localization at unit i. Based on the above arguments, we define a *support* for locating fault at software unit i, denoted by support (i), as follows:

$$\text{support}(i) = \frac{a_{11}(i)}{a_{11}(i) + a_{10}(i)}. \tag{22}$$

In other words, the percentage of support for locating a faulty software unit is quantified by the ratio of the number of its executions in failed test runs to the total number of its executions. The support measure can be computed using information obtained from the set of program spectra used for locating faults. The higher the support value is, the more confident it is to locate the fault. Therefore, the support measure is an indicator of the quality of the program spectra in facilitating fault localization. When a fault location is known, we can compute the quality of support for locating the fault.

Each faulty version of a program in the benchmark set has an inherent *support,* whose value depends on various attributes including the type of fault and running environments of the test cases as reflected on the resulting program spectra. In the Siemens set, the support values of different faulty units range from 1.4% to 20.3%. We want to see how the quality of program spectra, as indicated by varying support values, impacts the effectiveness of the proposed fault localization approach. To do this, for each given faulty location, a different support value can be obtained by excluding runs that contribute either to a_{11} (to obtain a series of smaller support values) or a_{10} (to obtain a series of larger support values). The passed or failed runs for exclusion are randomly selected from the available set when there are too many choices. In this experiment, each controlled support value is obtained by using the maximum number of relevant runs. For example, suppose a faulty unit is executed in 10 failed and 30 passed runs. A support value of 25% would be generated from all of the available runs instead of say one passed and three failed runs. As observed in [10], although there are alternatives (e.g., setting failed runs to passed or vice versa) for controlling the support values, excluding runs is a preferred method because it maintains integrity and consistency of the data. Using the exclusion method, we obtained support values ranging from 1% to 100% (in a 10% increment).

Figure 3 shows the % of average effectiveness over all 120 faulty program versions for each approach under the study and for the support values ranging from 1% to 100%. As shown in Figure 3, the proposed approach outperformed the rest regardless of the support quality of the program spectra. As support value increases, *Jaccard*'s effectiveness moves toward that of the *Ochiai*, which consistently performed better than *Tarantura*. Each of the approaches provides the effectiveness of at least about 84% even at only 1% of quality support. Comparing these values with 100% of quality support from program spectra, the effectiveness obtained by our approach, *Ochiai, Jaccard,* and *Tarantula* increases by 3.29%, 3.35%, 3.42%, and 2.56%, respectively. The improvement of our proposed approach over *Ochiai,* the second best performing approach, ranges from 0.19% to 0.58%. The small improvements are obtained for higher quality support of 90%–100% and large improvement for lower support values of 20%–50%. This implies that the proposed approach performs more consistently and is more robust to the support quality of the program spectra than the *Ochiai* approach. As expected, the effectiveness of each

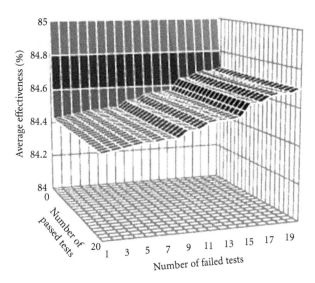

FIGURE 4: Quantity impact on the proposed approach.

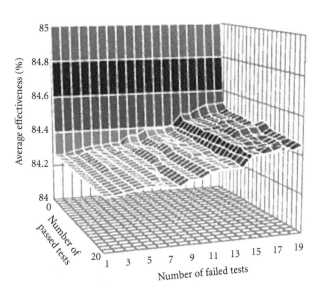

FIGURE 5: Quantity impact on the Ochiai fault localizer.

approach increases as the quality of the program spectra to support fault localization increases. However, for the most part, the impact does not appear to be significant.

5.2. Quantity Impacts. This section investigates the quantity impact of program spectra using our approach. We evaluate the effectiveness by varying the number of passed and failed test runs involved in fault localization across the Siemens benchmark set. The spectra set contains a large number of runs ranging from 1052 to 5542 but it has a relatively small number of failed runs ranging from one to 518. Therefore, it is not possible to have all versions representing all possible cases of passed and failed runs. In our experiments, since interesting effects tend to appear in a small number of runs [10], we have focused on the range of one to 20 of passed and failed runs to maximize the utilization of the number of versions with both types of runs. Consequently, we used 86 of a total of 119 versions in the spectra set.

Figure 4 shows the effectiveness obtained from the proposed approach for the number of passed and failed tests varying from one to 20. Each entry represents an average of effectiveness (in percentages) across 86 selected versions. As shown in Figure 4, we can see that as the number of failed test runs increases, the average effectiveness increases. Thus, adding failed runs appears to improve the effectiveness. However, adding passed runs does not seem to change the average effectiveness obtained by our approach. We also found that the average effectiveness stabilized when the number of runs is around 18.

To gain understanding of our approach compared to others in this aspect, we performed a similar experiment with the *Ochiai* fault localizer. Figure 5 shows the average effectiveness obtained in percentages within the same range of 20 passed and failed tests. As shown in Figure 5, adding more failed runs appears to improve the effectiveness of fault localization when using the *Ochiai* technique. On the other hand, adding the number of passed runs can increase

or decrease the effectiveness especially when the number of passed tests runs toward 20 (from 16). These results obtained by the *Ochiai* localizer agree with those observed by Abreu et al. in [10]. Compared to the *Ochiai* localizer, our approach appears to be slightly more stable and less influenced by the size of passed runs in the benchmark set.

From our experiments on the quantity impact, it is evident that program spectra with more failed runs can slightly improve the effectiveness of fault localization using the proposed method. However, the spectra set with more passed test runs does not seem to have a great impact on its effectiveness. This is rather remarkable and distinct from the *Ochiai* method.

In general, a unit hit by a large number of passed runs should be less suspicious. Therefore, if such a unit were actually faulty, it would be difficult to detect. As a result, the effectiveness obtained by most spectrum-based fault localizers would be decreased. A similar argument applies when there is a large number of runs that can weaken the degree of similarity between the faulty unit and the errors detected from the tests. However, the total number of runs does not seem to impact the effectiveness of our approach. The reason that the proposed approach is not extremely sensitive to the number of passed runs (and thus, overall number of runs) is attributed to the strength parameters that already compensate the large difference between the number of passed and failed runs. Furthermore, performance of any fault localizer is likely to depend on individual programs and sets of program spectra collected for the analysis. Thus, by adjusting different values of strength, our approach can be easily customized to apply to the available data and enhance the fault localization effectiveness.

6. Related Work

Early automated software fault localization work can be viewed as a part of a software diagnostic system [3]. To locate known faults, the system exploits knowledge about faults and their associated possible causes obtained from previous experience. For novel faults, the diagnostic system employs inferences based on the software model that contains program structure and functions along with heuristics to search for likely causes (and locations of faulty units). However, modeling the program behavior and functions is a major bottleneck in applying this technique in practice.

Agrawal et al. [23] introduced the fault localization approach based on *execution slices*, each of which refers to the set of a program's basic blocks executed by a test input. Weiser [4] introduced the concept of a program slice as an abstract used by programmers in locating bugs. Agrawal et al.'s approach assumes that the fault resides in the slice of a failed test and not in the slice of a successful test. By restricting the attention to the statements in the failed slice that do not appear in the successful slice, called *dice*, the fault is likely to be found. However, the technique does not fully exploit program spectra as it only uses a *single* failed (passed) test case's execution slice to locate faults [18]. Consequently, program statements that are executed by one passed test case and a different number of failed test cases would have an equal likelihood to be faulty if both were executed by the failed test case for the considered dice. Our approach, however, makes use of all the test cases in the test suite, both passed or failed, to estimate fault locations.

Recent spectrum-based fault localization techniques include *nearest neighbor queries* [5], *Tarantula* [13], *Jaccard* [12], and *Ochiai* [14]. These approaches use some measure of similarity to compare the units executed in a failed test to those of a passed test. The unit that results in the most similar behaviors to errors in all the test runs is likely to be faulty. Other fault localization techniques employ statistical [6, 7] and neural net models [24] to analyze source codes and program spectra, respectively. However, the performance of the former heavily relies on the quality of data, whereas the latter suffers from classic limitations such as local minima. Unlike these approaches, our approach is not similarity based or statistical based, but estimates the likelihoods or beliefs of units being faulty. The computation is based on a theory that is widely used for reasoning under uncertainty.

7. Discussion and Conclusions

Our approach is fundamentally different from existing methods. Although the results of the proposed approach on the benchmark data are marginally better than state-of-the-art approaches, it should be emphasized that the proposed approach provides useful aspects for software testing in practice. Its ability to do online computation to locate faults as soon as each test run is executed is particularly novel in that testing of large program can be performed more efficiently since it does not have to wait for all testing program spectral data to be completed. The intermediate results obtained can also influence the configuration or design of subsequent tests. This is useful for real-time systems where system configurations tend to be highly adaptable and it is hard to predict the program behaviors.

In summary, this paper presents a spectrum-based approach to fault localization using the Dempster-Shaffer theory of evidence. Other than its competitive performance to state-of-the-art techniques, our approach has several unique benefits. First, it is theoretically grounded and therefore it has a solid foundation for handling uncertainty in fault location. Second, it supports an online computation that allows the prediction of fault locations to be updated immediately as the execution of each test case is completed without having to wait for completion of a large enough set of program spectrum to be statistically valid. Such computation adapts well to real-time systems. Finally, the approach can be extended easily by adding new mass functions to represent additional evidence for use in the probability assignment of faulty hypotheses.

Future work includes more experiments to gain understanding of the characteristics of the proposed approach, for example, what types of program spectra on which the proposed approach would perform best or perform significantly better than the other three approaches, and how we can extend the approach so that it can deal with software with multiple faults. More experiments can be performed to see if different types of software units impact the results. These are among our ongoing and future research.

Acknowledgments

Thanks are due to Adam Jordan for his help on the experiments and to Phongphun Kijsanayothin for his helpful discussion and comments on earlier versions of this paper. The author would also like to thank the reviewers whose comments have helped improve the quality of the paper.

References

[1] B. Hailpern and P. Santhanam, "Software debugging, testing, and verification," *IBM Systems Journal*, vol. 41, no. 1, pp. 4–12, 2002.

[2] I. Vessey, "Expertise in debugging computer programs: an analysis of the content of verbal protocols," *IEEE Transactions on Systems, Man and Cybernetics*, vol. 16, no. 5, pp. 621–637, 1986.

[3] R. Sedlmeyer, W. B. Thompson, and P. E. Johnson, "Diagnostic reasoning in software fault localization," in *Proceedings of the 8th International Joint Conference on Artificial Intelligence*, vol. 1, pp. 29–31, Morgan Kaufmann, San Francisco, Calif, USA, 1983.

[4] M. Weiser, "Programmers use slices when debugging," *Communications of the ACM*, vol. 25, no. 7, pp. 446–452, 1982.

[5] M. Renieres and S. P. Reiss, "Fault localization with nearest neighbor queries," in *Proceedings of the 18th IEEE International Conference on Automated Software Engineering*, pp. 30–39, Providence, RI, USA, 2003.

[6] B. Liblit, M. Naik, A. X. Zheng, A. Aiken, and M. I. Jordan, "Scalable statistical bug isolation," in *Proceedings of the ACM SIGPLAN Conference on Programming Language Design and Implementation*, pp. 15–26, Association for Computing Machinery, New York, NY, USA, 2005.

[7] C. Liu, L. Fei, X. Yan, J. Han, and S. P. Midkiff, "Statistical debugging: a hypothesis testing-based approach," *IEEE Transactions on Software Engineering*, vol. 32, no. 10, pp. 831–848, 2006.

[8] T. Reps, T. Ball, M. Das, and J. Larus, "The use of program profiling for software maintenance with applications to the year 2000 problem," in *Proceedings of the 6th European Software Engineering Conference*, pp. 432–449, Springer, New York, NY, USA, 1997.

[9] R. Abreu, P. Zoeteweij, and A. van Gemund, "An evaluation of similarity coefficients for software fault localization," in *Proceedings of the 12th Pacific Rim International Symposium on Dependable Computing*, pp. 39–46, IEEE Computer Society Press, Riverside, Calif, USA, 2006.

[10] R. Abreu, P. Zoeteweij, and A. van Gemund, "On the Accuracy of Spectrum-based Fault Localization," in *Proceedings of the Testing: Academic and Industrial Conference Practice and Research Techniques (MUTATION '07)*, pp. 89–98, IEEE Computer Society Press, Washington, DC, USA, 2007.

[11] S. Ali, J. H. Andrews, T. Dhandapani, and W. Wang, "Evaluating the accuracy of fault localization techniques," in *Proceedings of the IEEE/ACM International Conference on Automated Software Engineering*, pp. 76–87, IEEE Computer Society Press, Washington, DC, USA, 2009.

[12] M. Y. Chen, E. Kiciman, E. Fratkin, A. Fox, and E. Brewer, "Pinpoint: problem determination in large, dynamic internet services," in *Proceedings of the International Conference on Dependable Systems and Networks (DSN '02)*, pp. 595–604, Berkeley, Calif, USA, 2002.

[13] J. Jones, M. J. Harrold, and J. Stasko, "Visualization of test information to assist fault localization," in *Proceedings of the 24th International Conference on Software Engineering*, pp. 467–477, Association for Computing Machinery, New York, NY, USA, 2002.

[14] A. Meyer, A. Garcia, A. Souza, and C. Souza Jr., "Comparison of similarity coefficients used for cluster analysis with dominant markers in maize (*Zea mays* L)," *Genetics and Molecular Biology*, vol. 27, no. 1, pp. 83–91, 2004.

[15] S. Nessa, M. Abedin, E. W. Wong, L. Khan, and Y. Qi, "Software fault localization using N-gram analysis," in *Proceedings of the 3rd International Conference on Wireless Algorithms, Systems, and Applications*, pp. 548–559, Springer, Berlin, Germany, 2008.

[16] V. Dallmeier, C. Lindig, and A. Zeller, "Lightweight defect localization for Java," in *Proceedings of the 19th European Conference on Object-Oriented Programming*, vol. 3568 of *Lecture Notes in Computer Science*, pp. 528–550, Springer, Glasgow, UK, 2005.

[17] G. Shafer, *A Mathematical Theory of Evidence*, Princeton University Press, Princeton, NJ, USA, 1976.

[18] J. Jones and M. J. Harrold, "Empirical evaluation of the tarantula automatic fault-localization technique," in *Proceedings of the 20th IEEE/ACM International Conference on Automated Software Engineering*, pp. 273–282, Association for Computing Machinery, New York, NY, USA, 2005.

[19] P. Jaccard, "Étude comparative de la distribution florale dans une portion des Alpes et des Jura," *Bulletin de la Société Vaudoise des Sciences Naturelles*, vol. 37, pp. 547–579, 1901.

[20] A. Ochiai, "Zoogeographic studies on the soleoid fishes found in Japan and its neighbouring regions," *Bulletin of the Japanese Society for the Science of Fish*, vol. 22, pp. 526–530, 1957.

[21] J. Pearl, *Causality: Models, Reasoning, and Inference*, Cambridge University Press, 2000.

[22] M. Hutchins, H. Foster, T. Goradia, and T. Ostrand, "Experiments of the effectiveness of dataflow- and control flow-based test adequacy criteria," in *Proceedings of the 6th International Conference on Software Engineering*, pp. 191–200, IEEE Computer Society Press, Sorrento , Italy, 1994.

[23] H. Agrawal, J. R. Horgan, S. London, and W. E. Wong, "Fault localization using execution slices and dataflow tests," in *Proceedings of the 6th International Symposium on Software Reliability Engineering*, pp. 143–151, Toulouse , France, 1995.

[24] W. Wong and Y. Qi, "BP neural network-based effective fault localization," *International Journal of Software Engineering and Knowledge Engineering*, vol. 19, no. 4, pp. 573–597, 2009.

13

Gesture Recognition Using Neural Networks Based on HW/SW Cosimulation Platform

Priyanka Mekala,[1] **Jeffrey Fan,**[1] **Wen-Cheng Lai,**[2,3] **and Ching-Wen Hsue**[2]

[1] *Department of Electrical and Computer Engineering, Florida International University, Miami, FL 33174, USA*
[2] *Department of Electronic Engineering, National Taiwan University of Science and Technology, Taipei 106, Taiwan*
[3] *Department of Engineering, Ming Chi University of Technology, Taipei 243, Taiwan*

Correspondence should be addressed to Priyanka Mekala; pmeka001@fiu.edu

Academic Editor: Christine W. Chan

Hardware/software (HW/SW) cosimulation integrates software simulation and hardware simulation simultaneously. Usually, HW/SW co-simulation platform is used to ease debugging and verification for very large-scale integration (VLSI) design. To accelerate the computation of the gesture recognition technique, an HW/SW implementation using field programmable gate array (FPGA) technology is presented in this paper. The major contributions of this work are: (1) a novel design of memory controller in the Verilog Hardware Description Language (Verilog HDL) to reduce memory consumption and load on the processor. (2) The testing part of the neural network algorithm is being hardwired to improve the speed and performance. The American Sign Language gesture recognition is chosen to verify the performance of the approach. Several experiments were carried out on four databases of the gestures (alphabet signs A to Z). (3) The major benefit of this design is that it takes only few milliseconds to recognize the hand gesture which makes it computationally more efficient.

1. Introduction

In today's world, the field programmable gate array (FPGA) technology has advanced enough to model complex chips replacing custom application-specific integrated circuits (ASICs) and processors for signal processing and control applications. FPGAs are preferred as higher-level tools evolve to deliver the benefits of reprogrammable silicon to engineers and scientists at all levels of expertise. Taking advantage from the current FPGA technology, this paper proposes a hardware/software cosimulation methodology using hardware description language (HDL) simulations on FPGA as an effort to accelerate the simulation time and performance [1, 2].

The conventional software simulation method has more flexibility in terms of parameters variation. The desired simulation parameters can be changed to study the system behavior under various conditions. The major drawback with the conventional approach is the intolerable simulation time. On the other hand, the complete hardware-based approach can provide significant speedup in examining the system behavior, but the flexibility will be nonetheless compromised. In this paper, we attempt to leverage the merits of the software simulation and hardware emulation to retain both the flexibility and performance by adopting a HW/SW-based platform approach [1].

2. Background/Literature Review

The communication between human and machines or between people can be done using gestures called sign language [3]. The use of sign language plays an important role in the means of communication method for the hearing-impaired community [4]. American Sign Language (ASL) is the 3rd most-used language and the choice for most deaf people in the United States. 500,000 and 2,000,000 people use sign language as their major daily communication tool. It seems that 3.68% of the total population is found to be hard of hearing and 0.3% of the total population is functionally deaf, out of a total population of about 268,000,000 (2005) in the US [5].

Gesture recognition is generally based on two different approaches. Primarily, glove-based analysis [6–8] where either mechanical or optical sensors are attached to a glove that transforms finger flexions into electrical signals to determine the hand posture [7]. Currently, the vision-based analysis [9–11] is used mostly, which deals with the way human beings perceive information about their surroundings. The database for these vision-based systems is created by selecting the gestures with predefined meaning, and multiple samples of each gesture are considered to increase the accuracy of the system [10]. In this paper, we have used the vision-based approach for our gesture recognition application.

Several approaches have been proposed previously to recognize the gestures using soft computing approaches such as artificial neural networks (ANNs) [12–16], fuzzy logic sets [17], and genetic algorithms [18]. Some statistical models [6] used for gesture recognition include Hidden Markov Model (HMM) [19, 20] and Finite-State Machine (FSM) [21]. ANNs are the adaptive self-organizing [22, 23] technologies that solved a broad range of problems such as identification and control, game playing and decision making, pattern recognition medical diagnosis, financial applications, and data mining [23, 24] in an easy and convenient manner [25, 26].

Murakami and Taguchi in [12] presented the Japanese Sign Language recognition using two different neural network systems. Back Propagation algorithm was used for learning postures, taken using data gloves, of Japanese alphabet. The system is simple and could successfully recognize a word. The proposed automatic sampling and filtering data proved to help improve the system performance. However, the learning time of both network systems was extremely high varying from hours to days. Maung [13] used the real-time 2D hand tracking to recognize hand gestures for Myanmar Alphabet Language. The system was easy to use and no special hardware was required. The input images were acquired via digitized photographs and the feature vector obtained using histograms of local orientation. This feature vector served as the input to the supervised neural networks system built. Implementing the system in MATLAB tool box made the work easy because of the simplicity in design and easy use of toolbox. However, the tradeoff was the speed in execution time as the time consumed for implementation was high compared to that of other languages.

Bailador et al. [15] presented Continuous Time Recurrent Neural Networks (CTRNNs) real-time hand gesture recognition system. The work was based on the idea of creating specialized signal predictors for each gesture class [15]. The standard Genetic Algorithm (GA) was used to represent the neuron parameters, and each genetic string represents the parameter of a CTRNN. The system is fast, simple, modular, and a novel approach. High recognition rate of 94% is achieved from testing the dataset. This system is limited by the person's movements and activities which caused a higher noise that has significant effect on the results. The dependency of segmentation operation on the predictor proved to greatly affect the segmentation results.

Stergiopoulou and Papamarkos [16] presented static hand-gesture-recognition-based Self-Growing and Self-Organized Neural Gas (SGONG) Network. Digital camera was used for input image. For hand region detection, YCbCr color space was applied and then threshold technique used to detect skin color. SGONG proved to be a fast algorithm that uses competitive Hebbian learning algorithm (the learning starts with two neurons and grows) in which a grid of neurons would detect the exact shape of the hand. However, the recognition rate was as low as 90.45%.

In all the previous works mentioned, they are purely software-based approaches. In order to increase the speed of execution while maintaining the flexibility, we propose an HW/SW approach. General software that can perform gesture recognition is MATLAB, Microsoft Visual C#, Microsoft Visual C++, and Microsoft Visual Basic. The most common software used are MATLAB and Microsoft Visual C# both of which are very powerful tools. MATLAB is chosen over others because it is a high-performance language for technical computing, perfect for speeding up development process as it allows the user to work faster with the features of toolboxes and provides ease and flexibility to the design of the programming. It is a tool of choice for high-productivity research, analysis, and development. It is preferred based on the previous research developed by Maung [13], Maraqa and Abu-Zaiter, [14] and on the review in [25, 26]. It integrates programming, computation, and visualization in user-friendly environment where problems and solutions are presented in common mathematical notation [27]. Also in industry, MATLAB's tool is widely used for high-productivity research, development, and analysis [27].

FPGAs have the advantage of hardware parallelism performing more like concurrent execution of functions. Thus by breaking the paradigm of sequential execution and accomplishing more per clock cycle, the FPGAs exceed the computing power of digital signal processors (DSPs) [28]. Mostly, inputs and outputs of the applications are controlled at the hardware level in order to provide faster response times, and dedicated parts of hardware reduce the power consumption for few complex operations. The programmable silicon indicates no fabrication costs or long lead times for assembly [28]. In general, the software tools provide the programming environment whereas the FPGA-based design is a completely hardware implementation of the application. Processor-based systems often involve several layers of abstraction to help schedule tasks and share resources between multiple processes [28]. The driver layer controls hardware resources and the operating system manages memory and processor bandwidth. FPGAs minimize the reliability concerns with true concurrent execution and dedicated hardware since they do not use the operating system [28].

3. Gesture Recognition Algorithm

The gesture recognition system is mostly classified into three major steps after acquiring the input image from camera(s), videos or even data glove instrumented device. These steps are preprocessing, features estimation and extraction, and classification or recognition [25, 26]. The pre-processing

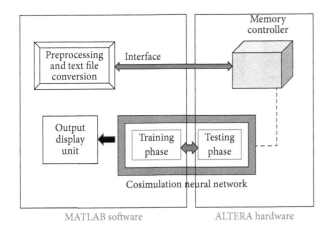

FIGURE 1: System architecture of gesture recognition on hardware/software cosimulation platform.

module of the system developed involves the application of morphological operations and edge detection in order to segment the image into regions of interest. The feature extraction is a very crucial step in the gesture recognition algorithm. Feature vector of the segmented image can be extracted in different ways depending on the application. Different methods are presented that use the skin color, hand shape, hand contour, fingertips position, palm center, and so forth. In our design, the hand shape and magnitude orientation is being considered in order to obtain the feature vector. Thus, the results are not dependent on the skin color or the background of the image gestures obtained.

In our approach, the back propagation is used to train and test the neural network on the cosimulation platform. The interface among the modules of the neural network eases data transfer and controls signals communication. The training phase of the network is done on software platform and the testing phase is done on hardware platform. The data is stored in the memory controller module created using VERILOG HDL and has bus interface for reading and writing back the data to the memory.

Figure 1 shows the system architecture being developed in this paper. MATLAB is used as the software platform and ALTERA-ModelSim 6.3 g_p1 is used as the hardware platform. QUARTUS II (8.1 web edition) design flow is used to simulate and verify the functionality of HDL code. Xilinx ISE 10.1 is used to understand the device and logic utilization, memory design, and test control of the architecture developed.

3.1. Database Generation. The images for database are captured using a Cannon camera which produces image frames of RGB pixels. The ASL alphabet gestures are used to obtain the hand images. The database contains two different subjects with two different backgrounds. Figure 2 shows few of the database sets used in this particular application. The Cannon camera is actually not stationary since it is not in a fixed position but the background is maintained as either black or white. The images are stored in .jpg format. The temporal resolution requirements of the application have to be

considered. The size of the image frame is 640 × 480 pixels. To maintain the resolution and decrease redundancy, the frames are resized to 64 × 64 pixels. Once the input images are obtained, they are converted to grayscale values within a range of 0–255.

The database obtained is read on the computer using MATLAB. The software converts the entire database image frames into text files. These files are stored in the memory of the ALTERA-ModelSim using command "$readmemh." The ALTERA-ModelSim is being called from the MATLAB using HDLDAEMON as shown in Figure 3. HDLDAEMON controls the server that supports interactions with HDL simulators. To communicate with HDL simulators, the server uses one of two interprocess communication methods: shared memory (which is the default) or TCP/IP sockets. Communication through shared memory is usually faster than that of sockets. When using shared memory, the server can communicate with only one HDL simulator at a time, and the HDL simulator must be running on the same host. When using sockets, the server can communicate with multiple HDL simulators simultaneously, running on the same host or other hosts [29].

3.2. Text File Conversion. The grayscale images are converted into text files which contain the hexadecimal value of the pixels. Each image is configured and stored with the appropriate configuration ID. The text file contains 4096 values to be read and stored onto the memory of the ALTERA-ModelSim.

3.3. Memory Controller on ALTERA-ModelSim. The text files obtained from the image files are stored onto another file in the memory locations of the ALTERA-ModelSim. The files contain data represented by hexadecimal values and hence contain 16 digits of length. For every negative edge of the clock cycle, the data is read into the memory location. Figure 4 displays the simulation waveform of the memory controller for the database sets. The value *test_design/k* shows the database set images ranging from 1 to N (the last image depending on the number of database sets considered).

4. Cosimulation Neural Network

Neural networks are based on the parallel architecture of neurons present in human brain. It can be defined as a multiprocessor system with very high degree of interconnections and adaptive interaction between the elements. The choice of neural networks to recognize the gestures automatically is due to the following aspects like adaptive learning (using a set of predefined database sets), self-organization from the training module, real-time operation with parallel computations, and high fault tolerance capability [30, 31].

This paper focuses on recognizing static hand gesture images. Since static hand postures not only can express some concepts, but also can act as special transition states in temporal gestures recognition, thus estimating that static hand postures play an important role in gesture recognition applications. A gesture recognition system takes an image as an input, processes it using a transform that converts the image into a feature vector, which will then be compared with the

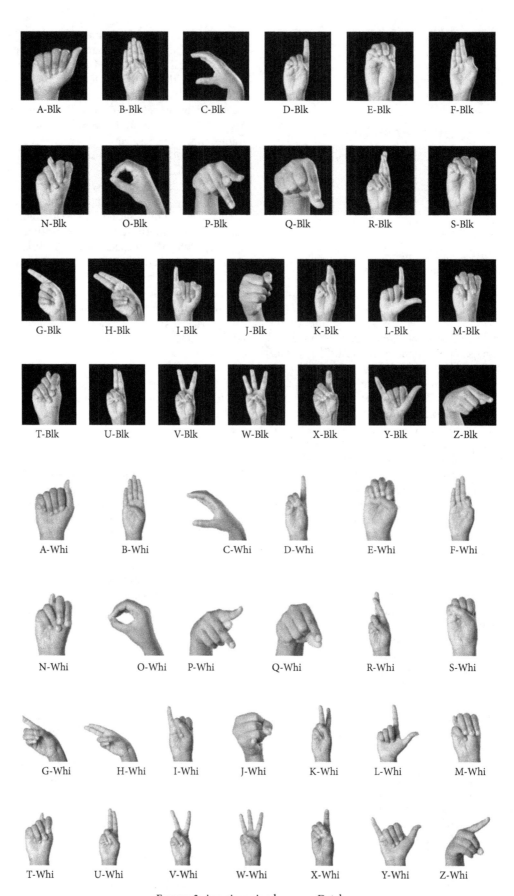

FIGURE 2: American sign language Database.

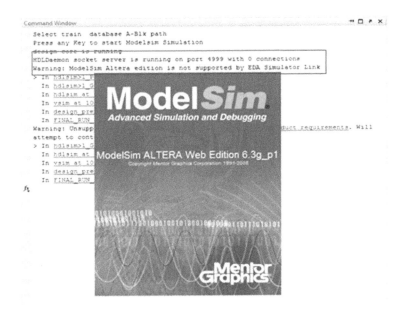

FIGURE 3: HDLDAEMON as the interface between MATLAB and ALTERA-ModelSim.

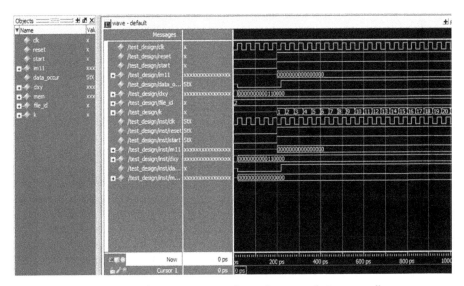

FIGURE 4: Simulation output waveform of memory design controller.

feature vectors of a training set of gestures. A new technique called cosimulation neural network is being adopted. In this method, a part of the neural network is designed on the hardware with dedicated ports. An interface is being introduced among different levels of the neural network to communicate with one another on two different platforms. A simple neural network model is shown in Figure 5 which consists of input layer, hidden layers, and the output layer with different number of neurons (R, S) in each [32].

Our network is built of 16 input neurons in the input layer, 50 neurons in the first hidden layer, 50 neurons in second hidden layer, and 35 neurons in the output layer. The number of neurons selected resulted from the analysis of the features. Since the features extracted from the image to be used for recognition was 16 as discussed later in the Section 4.1, the input layer has 16 neurons. The output is displayed as a visual

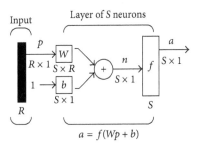

FIGURE 5: Neural network model [32, 37].

representation of the gesture image and hence is a 7×5 (35 neurons) grid display of rows and columns. Since the images are not linearly separable, the hidden layers are necessary

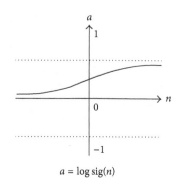

$$a = \log \operatorname{sig}(n)$$

FIGURE 6: Log-sigmoid transfer function [32].

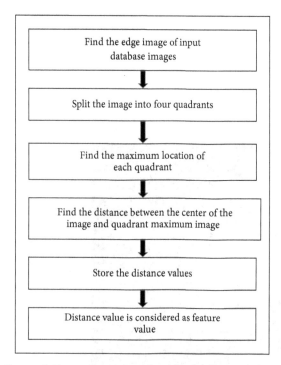

FIGURE 7: Feature Extraction Algorithm for distance values.

for accurate recognition of the gestures. The neural networks with two hidden layers can represent functions with any kind of shapes. It can represent an arbitrary decision boundary to arbitrary accuracy with rational activation functions and can approximate any smooth mapping to any accuracy [33]. Regarding the neurons present in the hidden layers, Geman et al. [34] discuss that there are methods for determining the correct number of neurons to use, such as the following: The number of hidden neurons should be between the size of the input layer and the size of the output layer. The number of hidden neurons should be 2/3 the size of the input layer plus the size of the output layer. The number of hidden neurons should be less than twice the size of the input layer [33]. Hence with some analysis of these methods, the number of hidden neurons is being estimated to be taken as the 2/3 the size of the input layer plus the size of the output layer (i.e., 2/3 times of 16 + 35) which results in 34 neurons and less than twice the output size, that is, 70 neurons. Lawrence

et al. [35] have shown that increasing the number of weights makes it easier for standard back propagation to find a good optimum using oversize networks as it can reduce both training error and generalization error. Hence, the choice of the number of hidden layer neurons was made to be 50 neurons with the above-mentioned criteria and some trial and error computations.

The transfer function (f) may be a linear or a nonlinear function. A particular transfer function is chosen based on the specific requirement of the application. A log-sigmoid function, also known as a logistic function, is used as the transfer function in the network designed. The relationship is as follows:

$$\sigma(t) = \frac{1}{1 + e^{-\beta t}}. \tag{1}$$

In the equation above, β is a slope parameter. This is called the log-sigmoid transfer function depicted in Figure 6. The log-sigmoid transfer function is commonly used in multilayer neural networks that are trained using the back propagation algorithm, since the function is differentiable. The log sigmoid has the similar property to that of the step function, with the addition of a region of uncertainty. A log-sigmoid function in this respect is very similar to that of the input-output relationships of biological neurons, although not exactly the same. Figure 6 is the graph of a log-sigmoid function.

Sigmoid functions are also preferred because it is easy to calculate the derivatives, which is helpful for calculating the weight updates in certain training algorithms.

4.1. Training and Testing. We have used four different sets of data for training and testing of the cosimulation neural network designed. The memory module of the design and the testing of the network are being shifted onto the hardware level to speed up the performance. The neural network contains 16 input neurons; each database image is processed and stored as a feature vector of 16 values. The image is being compressed from 4096 pixel values into 16 feature vector values. The feature extraction algorithm is shown in the flowchart in Figure 7. Once the input preprocessed image is obtained, the edge image is calculated. The edge image is split into four quadrants and the maximum location of each quadrant is calculated. The distance value to be stored as the feature

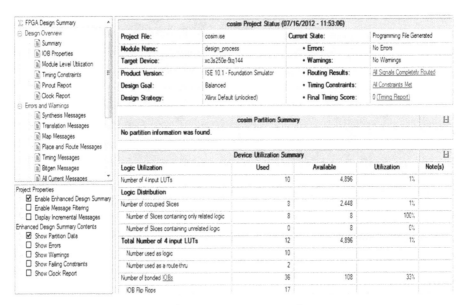

FIGURE 8: Device utilization Summary Report for memory storage.

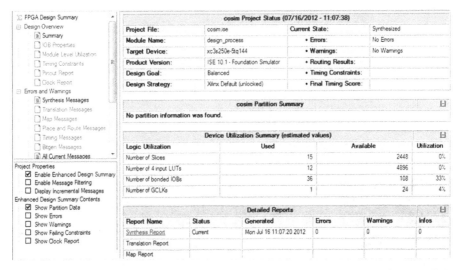

FIGURE 9: Device utilization Summary Report for gesture recognition system test design module.

value is the distance between the center of the image and each quadrant maximum image.

The compression ratio is 256 times that of the input values. Hence, only 0.39% of the image is being used as the feature vector to train and test the neural network designed. As the database set gestures involved in the application may vary very rapidly, it is highly essential to keep the feature vector as low as possible with no tradeoff with respect to accuracy and performance. In this particular application, the feature vector is maintained as 16 bit vector which makes the system memory efficient and also highly redundant.

4.2. Gesture Recognition. Gesture Recognition is widely used in applications like sign language, human-computer interfaces, gaming and animation technology, and so forth. Once a test image is selected, the neural network weights matrix is used to display the recognized gesture on a 7×5 display grid.

5. Device Utilization Factor

To understand the resource constraints, Xilinx ISE simulations are performed. The synthesis report provides the information about the device utilization in detail. Figures 8 and 9 show the report with the representation as defined below [36].

Device Utilization indicates the FPGA elements, such as flip-flops, LUTs, block RAM, and DSP48s.
Estimated indicates the number of FPGA elements that the algorithm might use based on the current directive configurations.

Total indicates the total number of FPGA elements available on the FPGA target.

Percent indicates the percentage of the FPGA elements that the algorithm might use.

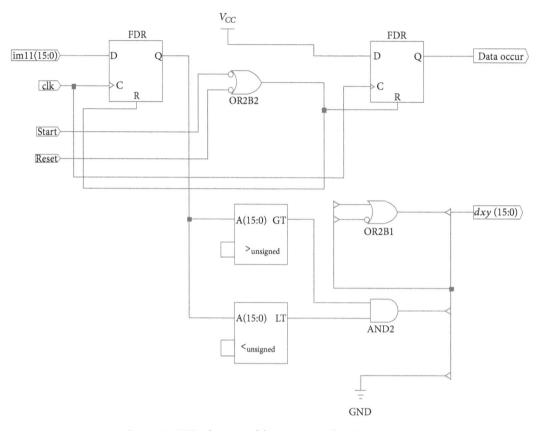

FIGURE 10: RTL schematic of design process flow (screenshot).

FIGURE 11: Simulation result in Xilinx ISE indicating the memory stored.

From the summary reports developed, it is observed that only 33% of the IOBs are being used on the hardware platform. The report is being developed on a Xilinx FPGA SPARTAN 3E with target device XC3S250e-5tql44.

Each image is being read and stored onto the memory of the ALTERA-ModelSim. The RTL schematic design is being shown in Figure 10.

6. Simulation Output

The simulation output of the test design is being shown in Figure 11 run on the Xilinx ISE. The memory *mem[0 : 4095]* loads 4096 values of each image and then processes it to extract features of set of 16 values and stores in *dxy[15 : 0]* as shown. Figures 12, 13, 14, and 15 show the simulation output

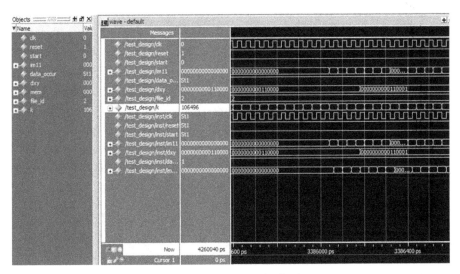

FIGURE 12: Simulation output for database set 1.

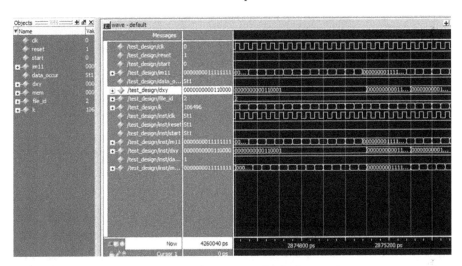

FIGURE 13: Simulation output for database set 2.

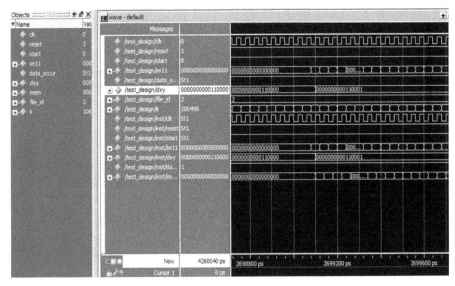

FIGURE 14: Simulation output for database set 3.

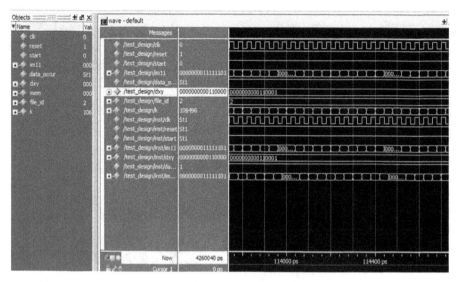

FIGURE 15: Simulation output for database set 4.

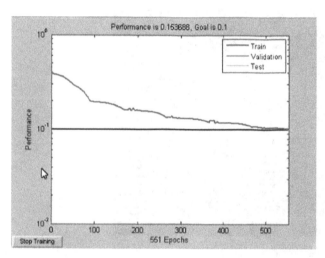

FIGURE 16: Performance curve for gesture recognition using SW (MATLAB software) analysis with reduced database sets for training (screenshot).

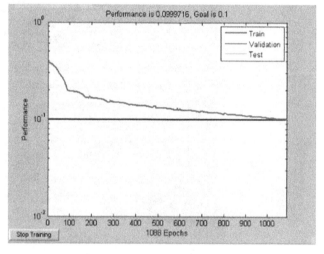

FIGURE 17: Performance curve for gesture recognition using HW/SW cosimulation analysis (screenshot).

for different database sets used for the gesture recognition application. The simulation time took was 164.04 ps to load the memory into the ModelSim and test the system design. The clock is represented by *clk*, memory represented by *mem*, feature vector represented by *dxy*, and the database image file is represented by *im11*. The test_design/k stores 106496 (=4096 × 26) values, which shows 4096 values of each of the 26 alphabet (A to Z) images considered.

7. Results

The cosimulation platform is designed to improve the speed of the application. Current academic and industrial researchers have recently been focusing on analyzing images of people. While researchers are making progress, the problem is hard and many present-day algorithms are complex, slow, or unreliable. The algorithms that run near real-time

require computers that are very expensive relative to the existing hand-held interface devices. The proposed method runs quickly, accurately and fits for the low-power dissipation application. Figure 16 shows the performance curve for gesture recognition using MATLAB software analysis with reduced database sets for training. Figure 17 shows the performance curve for gesture recognition using HW/SW cosimulation analysis (our approach). Figure 18 shows the performance curve for gesture recognition using MATLAB software simulation analysis for complete database sets. To validate the performance of the HW/SW cosimulation network, the mean square error is generated as shown in the performance curves. Epoch-based updating of the weights is performed and mean square error is decreasing at an exponential rate and settling down to an almost constant value as shown in Figure 16. An epoch is the presentation of the entire training set to the neural network once, and for the network to reach the

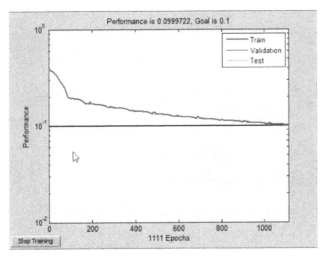

FIGURE 18: Performance curve for gesture recognition using SW (MATLAB) simulation analysis (screenshot).

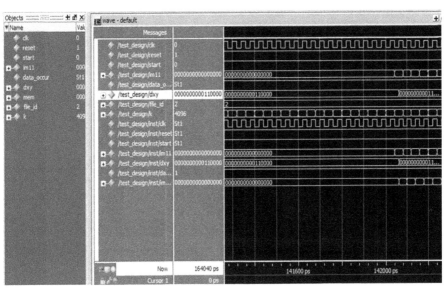

FIGURE 19: System design test output simulation for image gesture alphabet "P."

minimum threshold error the training is done multiple times counted as number of epochs. The maximal weight change in each epoch is decreasing and finally reaches to the least value possible. The epochs involved to reach the steady state are approximately equal (1088 and 1111, resp.) in both cases of Figures 17 and 18, but the decrease in mean square error is at higher exponential rate when compared to Figure 16 making the HW/SW better choice in terms of speed. The higher the exponential rate at which the MSE decreases, the faster the settling time and the faster training is completed.

The algorithm is able to detect the gesture input test image with 100% success rate for all the sign language alphabets (A to Z). The images with black and white background considered provided the same results as the algorithm is designed for uniform background. For users with different skin colors, this algorithm provides the same results as the features used to classify are skin color independent. Figures 19 and 20 depict the output result for the test letter "P." The

influences on major factors like performance, epochs, MSE (mean square error), gradient, and time are being compared to both approaches with various database memories and are tabulated in Table 1.

It is observed from the results tabulated that there is a 10 times decrease in the MSE of the HW/SW cosimulation platform compared to completely SW-based platform. The decrease in MSE is directly related to the increase in the accuracy of the approach adopted. The aim of the back propagation algorithm is to minimize the total error which is the sum of errors (squared difference between the desired and actual outputs) generated by all patterns in the training set. The total error is computed once all patterns in the training set have been presented. One presentation of a training set is known as an epoch. It is normal for many hundreds or thousands of epochs to pass before an acceptable total error is reached. Thus, HW/SW approach reaching a MSE that is 10 times less compared to the SW approach indicates a higher

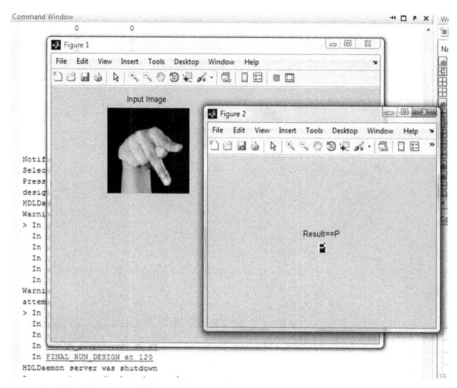

FIGURE 20: Output sign recognition displayed as a grid matrix.

TABLE 1: Comparison of SW versus HW/SW simulation platforms.

	Software simulation (MATLAB)	HW/SW cosimulation (MATLAB and ALTERA-ModelSim Quartus II)
Performance	0.999722	0.999716
Epochs	1111/2000	1088/2000
MSE	0.998182/0.1	0.0999716/0.1
Gradient	0.00269182/1e − 006	0.00204379/1e − 006
Recognition time	0.0058 secs	5.7656e − 004 secs

accurate system with faster training time. Hence, the gain in speed of the system is attained.

Given an input frame for testing the time taken by the network architecture to process and recognize the sign is the single pattern recognition time. The recognition time indicated in the table represents the time taken to recognize the test image (time involved in providing the output gesture identified). From the table, it is clear that the recognition time is reduced by 10.059 times by adopting the HW/SW cosimulation platform instead of completely using the SW-based approach. This implies that the cosimulation network designed is 10 times faster than the existing approach.

Also a 640×480×3 image has been compressed into a 64× 64 image resulting in a compression ratio of 225 times. Then, the compressed image is again being processed to obtain a 16 feature vector which results in a compression ratio of 256 times that of the 64 × 64 reduced input images. This implies that only 0.39% of the reduced image is being used for the recognition system with no tradeoff with respect to accuracy and performance. The simulation time was 164.04 ps to load

the memory into the hardwired memory controller due to reduced data and the hardware design of memory.

References

[1] T. Suh, H. S. Lee, S. Lu, and J. Shen, "Initial observations of hardware/software co-simulation using FPGA in architecture research," in *Proceedings of the Workshop on Architecture Research Using FPGA Platforms in Conjunction with International Symposium on High-Performance Computer Architecture*, Austin, Tex, USA, February, 2006.

[2] X. Ling, Z. Li, J. Hu, and S. Wu, "HW/SW co-simulation platforms for VLSI design," in *Proceedings of the IEEE Asia Pacific Conference on Circuits and Systems (APCCAS '08)*, pp. 578–581, 2008.

[3] M. M. Hasan and P. K. Misra, "Brightness factor matching for gesture recognition system using scaled normalization," *International Journal of Computer Science & Information Technology*, vol. 3, no. 2, pp. 35–46, 2011.

[4] M. P. Paulraj, S. Yaacob, M. S. bin Zanar Azalan, and R. Palaniappan, "A phoneme based sign language recognition

system using skin color segmentation," in *Proceedings of the 6th International Colloquium on Signal Processing and Its Applications (CSPA '10)*, pp. 1–5, May 2010.

[5] P. Mekala, Y. Gao, J. Fan, and A. Davari, "Real-time sign language recognition based on neural network architecture," in *Proceedings of the IEEE International Conference on Industrial Technology & 43rd Southeastern Symposium on System Theory (SSST '11)*, pp. 195–199, Auburn, Ala, USA, March 2011.

[6] S. Mitra and T. Acharya, "Gesture recognition: a survey," *IEEE Transactions on Systems, Man and Cybernetics, Part C*, vol. 37, no. 3, pp. 311–324, 2007.

[7] T. B. Moeslund and E. Granum, "A survey of computer vision-based human motion capture," *Computer Vision and Image Understanding*, vol. 81, no. 3, pp. 231–268, 2001.

[8] J. J. LaViola Jr., *A survey of hand posture and gesture recognition techniques and technology [M.S. thesis]*, NSF Science and Technology Center for Computer Graphics and Scientific Visualization, Providence, RI, USA, 1999.

[9] S. Meena, *A study on hand gesture recognition technique [M.S. thesis]*, Department of Electronics and Communication Engineering, National Institute of Technology, Rourkela, India, 2011.

[10] M. M. Hasan and P. K. Mishra, "HSV brightness factor matching for gesture recognition system," *International Journal of Image Processing*, vol. 4, no. 5, pp. 456–467, 2010.

[11] P. Garg, N. Aggarwal, and S. Sofat, "Vision based hand gesture recognition," *World Academy of Science, Engineering and Technology*, vol. 49, pp. 972–977, 2009.

[12] K. Murakami and H. Taguchi, "Gesture recognition using recurrent neural networks," in *Proceedings of the SIGCHI Conference on Human Factors in Computing Systems: Reaching through Technology*, pp. 237–242, 1999.

[13] T. H. H. Maung, "Real-time hand tracking and gesture recognition system using neural networks," *World Academy of Science, Engineering and Technology*, vol. 50, pp. 466–470, 2009.

[14] M. Maraqa and R. Abu-Zaiter, "Recognition of Arabic Sign Language (ArSL) using recurrent neural networks," in *Proceedings of the 1st IEEE International Conference on the Applications of Digital Information and Web Technologies (ICADIWT '08)*, pp. 478–481, August 2008.

[15] G. Bailador, D. Roggen, and G. Troster, "Real time gesture recognition using continuous time recurrent neural networks," in *Proceedings of the 2nd ICST International Conference on Body Area Networks*, 2007.

[16] E. Stergiopoulou and N. Papamarkos, "Hand gesture recognition using a neural network shape fitting technique," *Engineering Applications of Artificial Intelligence*, vol. 22, no. 8, pp. 1141–1158, 2009.

[17] X. Li, *Gesture Recognition Based on Fuzzy C-Means Clustering Algorithm*, Department of Computer Science, The University of Tennessee Knoxville, 2003.

[18] C. Lien and C. Huang, "The model-based dynamic hand posture identification using genetic algorithm," *Springer Machine Vision and Applications*, vol. 11, no. 3, pp. 107–121, 1999.

[19] R. Yang and S. Sarkar, "Gesture recognition using hidden Markov models from fragmented observations," in *Proceedings of the IEEE Computer Society Conference on Computer Vision and Pattern Recognition (CVPR '06)*, pp. 766–773, June 2006.

[20] M. Elmezain, A. Al-Hamadi, J. Appenrodt, and B. Michaelis, "A hidden Markov model-based isolated and meaningful hand gesture recognition," *International Journal of Electrical and Electronics Engineering*, vol. 3, no. 3, pp. 156–163, 2009.

[21] R. Verma and A. Dev, "Vision based hand gesture recognition using finite state machines and fuzzy logic," in *Proceedings of the IEEE International Conference on Ultra Modern Telecommunications and Workshops (ICUMT '09)*, pp. 1–6, Petersburg, Russia, October 2009.

[22] B. Krose and P. van der Smagtan, *An Introduction to Neural Networks*, The University of Amsterdam, 8th edition, 1996.

[23] A. Chaudhary, J. L. Raheja, K. Das, and S. Raheja, "Intelligent approaches to interact with machines using hand gesture recognition in natural way: a survey," *International Journal of Computer Science & Engineering Survey*, vol. 2, no. 1, 2011.

[24] J. Wu, *Neural Networks and Simulation Methods*, Marcel Dekker, Inc., New York, NY, USA, 1994.

[25] R. Z. Khan and N. A. Ibraheem, "Hand gesture recognition: a literature review," *International Journal of Artificial Intelligence & Applications*, vol. 3, no. 4, 2012.

[26] R. Z. Khan and N. A. Ibraheem, "Survey on gesture recognition for hand image postures," *International Journal of Computer and Information Science*, vol. 5, no. 3, pp. 110–121, 2012.

[27] W. T. Freeman and M. Roth, "Orientation histograms for hand gesture recognition," in *Proceedings of the International Workshop on Automatic Face and Gesture-Recognition*, pp. 296–301, IEEE Computer Society, Zurich, Switzerland, June 1995.

[28] http://www.ni.com/white-paper/6984/en.

[29] https://www.mathworks.com/accesslogin/login.do?uri=http://www.mathworks.com/help/toolbox/edalink/ref/hdldaemon.html.

[30] G. A. Carpenter and S. Grossberg, "The ART of adaptive pattern recognition by a self-organizing neural network," *Computer*, vol. 21, no. 3, pp. 77–788, 1988.

[31] A. R. Omondi and J. C. Rajapakse, *FPGA Implementations of Neural Networks*, Springer, Dordrecht, The Netherlands, 2006.

[32] L. Fausett, *Fundamentals of Neural Networks—Architecture, Algorithms and Applications*, Prentice Hall Publishers, Upper Saddle River, NJ, USA, 1994.

[33] J. Heaton, *Introduction to Neural Networks for JAVA*, Heaton Research, Inc, 2nd edition, 2008.

[34] S. Geman, E. Bienenstock, and R. Doursat, "Neural networks and the bias/variance dilemma," *Neural Computation*, vol. 4, no. 1, pp. 1–58, 1992.

[35] S. Lawrence, C. L. Giles, and A. C. Tsoi, "What size neural network gives optimal generalization? Convergence properties of back propagation," Tech. Rep. UMIACS-TR-96-22 and CS-TR-3617, Institute for Advanced Computer Studies, University of Maryland, 1996.

[36] Xilinx, *XST User Guide*, Xilinx Inc., 2009.

[37] T. Y. Young and K. Fu, *Handbook of Pattern Recognition and Image Processing*, Academic Press, Orlando, Fla, USA, 1986.

14

Applying a Goal Programming Model to Support the Selection of Artifacts in a Testing Process

Andreia Rodrigues da Silva, Fernando Rodrigues de Almeida Júnior, and Placido Rogerio Pinheiro

Graduate Program in Applied Informatics, University of Fortaleza (UNIFOR), Avenue Washington Soares, 1321, 60811-341 Fortaleza, CE, Brazil

Correspondence should be addressed to Placido Rogerio Pinheiro, placidrp@uol.com.br

Academic Editor: Zhenyu Zhang

This paper proposes the definition of a goal programming model for the selection of artifacts to be developed during a testing process, so that the set of selected artifacts is more viable to the reality of micro and small enterprises. This model was based on the IEEE Standard 829, which establishes a set of artifacts that must be generated throughout the test activities. Several factors can influence the definition of this set of artifacts. Therefore, in order to consider such factors, we developed a multicriteria model that helps in determining the priority of artifacts according to the reality of micro and small enterprises.

1. Introduction

According to the Ministry of Science and Technology of Brazil, about 60% of software development enterprises in this country are classified as micro and small enterprises [1, 2]. In order to remain on the market, these companies need to invest significantly in improving the quality of their products because of the inherent complexity of the software development activity, which depends mainly on the interpretation skills of those involved. For that reason, this activity is susceptible to various issues, including the possibility of developing software other than what is expected by the user.

In this context, the test activity is fundamental in supporting the quality assurance of products. However, it is important to note that according to the estimates obtained in recent years, 50% of development costs are allocated to software testing [3] and, in the scenario of micro and small enterprises (MSEs), where resources availability is limited, software testing activities are reduced or, in many cases, eliminated [4], because of the lack of skilled professionals in the area, the variety of techniques existing, and the difficulty of implementing a testing process. These companies do not have the necessary capital to hire such professionals, besides not having the know-how of testing techniques and having much difficulty to deploy a testing process practical enough.

A variety of micro and small enterprises still do not have a formal testing process and even have the ability to implement a process that meets the needs and ensure the correct execution of activities. Generally testing activities, when included in the development process of software these companies are carried out by developers or system analysts. These professionals do not have knowledge about the techniques and testing criteria and, therefore, cannot benefit from the application of the techniques most appropriate to the context of the organization and the characteristics of the software being developed.

About these limitations, it is important to define an approach that is not large or unviable, to allow the utilization of a testing process in these companies. As you can see, the testing process is very expensive and time consuming, spending valuable resources in such activity [5].

Small businesses have unique and distinct characteristics: they develop software generally smaller and less complex; do not have many financial resources; avoid expensive tools, sophisticated and complex procedures; processes and methods are unique [6].

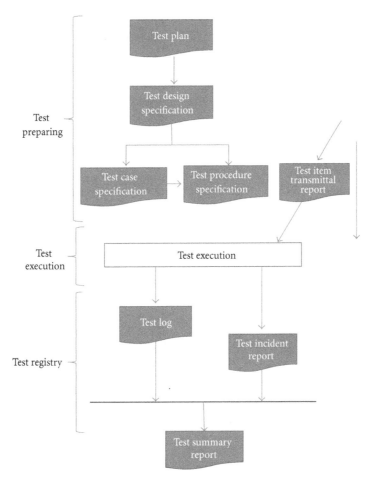

FIGURE 1: Relationship between testing documents.

Thus, from the definition of constraints and objectives expected for a testing process and considering the favorable and unfavorable conditions of the enterprise, it is possible to use operations research techniques such as linear programming, game theory, queuing theory, dynamic programming, risk analysis, goal programming, among others. These techniques and methods provide the decision maker with the possibility of increasing the degree of rationality of the decision, assisting in defining the actions to be taken, since they allow considering various relevant aspects of the decision making process.

The remainder of this paper is organized as follows. Section 2 explains the importance of software testing activity for enterprises in general and how the main standards and maturity models for software address such activities. Section 3 explains the basis of the multicriteria model and how this model can be used for the decision support process. Then, a multicriteria model is defined to support the definition of a software testing methodology in Section 4. Next, Section 5 describes the goal programming model, the proposed model and the results obtained with application from this model. Finally, a conclusion of this work is taken in Section 6.

2. The Importance of Using a Process

Software testing has been covered in the most acknowledged process maturity models and standards, such as CMMI [7], MPS BR [8], ISO/IEC 12207 [9], and ISO/IEC 15504 [10]. All of these maturity models and standards provide a guide to support the definition of a software testing process so that the testing activities are performed in an organized, disciplined manner and based on a set of well-defined activities. However, the definition of that process and the artifacts generated are the responsibility of the company that implements the standard or model and should be in accordance with their needs and the particular characteristics of each project.

Likewise, the evaluation and improvement models of software testing processes, such as Testing Maturity Model [11] and Test Process Improvement [12], were created in order to provide support to companies wishing to improve the testing process. Nevertheless, it is not the purpose of these models to assist the company in the definition of the testing process. However, the ISO/IEC 829 [13] Standard is slightly different from other standards and models because it establishes a set of documents to be generated over the testing activities. Altogether there are eight documents included from planning and specification activities until testing reports, as shown in Figure 1.

3. Related Works

According to [14], although the IEEE 829 can be used to test software products of any size or complexity, for small or low-complexity projects, some proposed documents can be grouped to reduce the management and production cost of documents. Moreover, the content of the documents can also be shortened.

GRASP metaheuristic is applied to the regression test case selection problem, defining an application related to prioritization of tests in [15]. In another work [16], an application for test redundancy detection is developed in a useful way, as a collaborative process between testers and a proposed redundancy detection engine to guide the tester to use valuable coverage information.

4. Fundamentals of Multicriteria

The objective of multicriteria is to reduce the subjectivity in the decision making process, using multiple criteria and application of mathematical calculations. However, it is important to emphasize that the subjectivity factor will always be present in the decision making process since the items to be mathematically evaluated are a result of human opinions. Its focus is, therefore, to support the decision maker in the information analysis and seek the best strategy among existing alternatives.

The adoption of a multicriteria decision support approach in this work is due to the fact that this approach, that is in constant growth, provides the group involved in the decision making process with subsidies required to obtain a solution that best fits the needs of the group [17]. Also, the approach focuses on issues that include qualitative and/or quantitative aspects, based on the principle that the experience and knowledge of people are at least as valuable as the data used for decision making [18]. Another factor that encouraged the adoption of the multicriteria approach in our study was the fact that this method has already been applied in the software engineering field [19–21].

5. A Multicriteria Model to Support the Definition of a Software Testing Methodology for Micro and Small Enterprises

A multicriteria model, developed by Rodrigues et al. [20–23], based on objective and subjective criteria was applied in order to support the prioritization of the artifacts available in the IEEE 829-1998 Standard, selecting the most relevant items for micro and small enterprises.

The model consists of a series of generic steps that were distributed among the three main phases of the decision supporting process: (1) structure, (2) evaluation, and (3) recommendation. However, in the context of our work, we used only the structure phase of the model because other phases were replaced by the goal programming model,

resulting in a hybrid model. The steps of the structure phase are detailed in Table 1.

5.1. Structure. In the step "identify criteria," all the involved actors participated in a conference session to choose the criteria to be analyzed for prioritization of the documents of the IEEE 829-1998 Standard. The criteria selected for the evaluation are shown in Table 2.

In the step "identify actors and their weights," two groups of actors were selected to participate in this decision making process: the first group, consisting of two experts in software testing, and the second group composed of two professionals working in micro and small enterprises.

Then the actors answered a survey composed of three sections covering the characterization of the respondent, the prioritization of the criteria used in the model and the analysis from the point of view of the actor regarding the criteria and documents analyzed. The documents, in turn, represent the alternative solutions in decision making process.

To calculate the weight for a specific actor, a value for each of the answer options was established for each item of the survey. Also an adjustment factor was established for each group of actors, testing experts and professionals working in micro and small enterprises in relation to each of the criteria considered in the model. This is needed to establish a differentiated weight for each group of actors by criterion evaluated in the model. Thus, the weight of each actor consists of the sum of the scores referring to the actor's response to each item of the survey, multiplied by the adjustment factor of the criterion in question, considering the group to which the actor belongs to. The formula applied for obtaining the actor's weight is given below:

$$PA(a, c) = \sum_{i \in A} R_i * F_c, \qquad (1)$$

where $PA(a, c)$ is the actor's weight a for the criterion c, R_i corresponds to the actor's answer for the item i of the survey, F_c corresponds to the multiplication factor of the criterion in question, and A corresponds to the number of items of the survey.

It is worth noting that the actor's weight for the criterion does not vary according to the document being assessed.

In the step "assign prioritization to the criteria," each actor ranked the selected criteria according to their degree of relevance, not by specific document, but for the company's testing process, as shown below:

$$\text{Priority}(a, c_i) \in \{1, \ldots, i, \ldots, n\} \left| \forall c_i, c_j \right| i \neq j$$
$$\Longrightarrow \text{Priority}(a, c_i) \neq \text{Priority}(a, c_j), \qquad (2)$$

where $\text{Priority}(a, c_i)$ is the criterion priority c for the actor a, n is the number of criteria, and $i, j > 0$.

Next, for each criterion, a partial evaluation of the score was made. This partial evaluation is derived by multiplying the values obtained from the viewpoint of the actor for each document, the actor's weight for each criterion and

TABLE 1: Model's steps.

Phase	Step	Description
	(7) Identify criteria	Identifies the criteria to be used to evaluate the artifacts and defines the priority of these criteria.
	(8) Identify actors and their weights	Identifies the actors who will expose their points of view, also considering their roles in the decision making process.
Structure	(9) Assign prioritization to the criteria	Each actor should assign a weight to the criterion, considering the full test process and not only a specific artifact.
	(11) Execute a partial evaluation	During this step, the values are normalized by placing them on the same base (base 1), in order to perform a equality partial evaluation. This evaluation is derived by multiplying the values obtained from the point of view of the actor for each document by the actor's weight and the criteria priority.
	(12) Calculate the general scores of the criteria	It is the calculation of the median obtained using values resulting from the previous step.

TABLE 2: Selected criteria.

Criterion	Description
Difficulty level	Is the level of difficulty to obtain the information necessary to fulfill the artifact low?
Information relevance	Is the information contained in the artifact relevant to the reality of the organization?
Reuse possibility	Is there a high possibility for the information contained in the artifact to be reused?
Effort	Is the effort required to complete the artifact low?
Knowledge	Is the level of knowledge in software testing required to fulfill the artifact appropriately quite low?
Cost	Is the cost for fulfilling the artifact low?

the priority assigned by the actor to the criterion. This multiplication represents the score (E) of each actor for each criterion of each document and will serve for further classification and prioritization of documents, as shown below:

$$E_x(a,c) = [PV_x(a,c)]_1 * [PA(a,c)]_1 * [\text{Priority}(a,c)]_1. \tag{3}$$

It is noteworthy that the values applied for the criteria priority and actor's weight were equalized in order to ensure an equitable evaluation, as shown below

$$[\text{Priority}(a,c)]_1 \in \left\{ \frac{1}{n}, \frac{2}{n}, \ldots, \frac{n}{n} \right\}, \tag{4}$$

where n represents the number of criteria

$$[PA(a,c)]_1 = \frac{\sum_{i \in A} Rx_i * F_c}{m}, \tag{5}$$

where m is the number of actors.

After the results obtained in the partial evaluation for each actor, in the step "calculate the general scores of the criteria" was carried out, the calculation of the arithmetic mean to obtain the final score of each document for each criterion, as shown below:

$$\text{Average}(x,c) = \frac{\sum_{i=1}^{m} E_x}{m}, \tag{6}$$

where E_x is the corresponds to the partial score of the document x_i, determined by the actor a referring to the criterion c, m is the number of actors.

The average value found was used as a basis for the prioritization of the documents during the application of the goal programming model.

6. Goal Programming

In real problems, the occurrence of multiple objectives to be considered at the time of resolution is frequent and mutually conflicting goals are not uncommon.

The goal programming is an extension of linear programming that has emerged as an option to the basic mathematical programming models, allowing to solve, simultaneously, a system of complex goals, rather than a single, simple goal [24].

This is a method that requires an iterative solution procedure by which the decision maker investigates a variety of solutions. However, a peculiarity of goal programming is the impossibility of representing all the goals in a single-objective function (often conflicting or unrelated). Therefore, goal programming considers all the objectives and seeks a solution that least deviates this set and at the same time meets the restrictions of the problem.

The goal programming and the approaches for multicriteria decision support have in common the fact of presenting a series of feasible solutions to the problem so that the decision makers can find/choose the one that best meets their needs and expectations. This similarity between the approaches motivated the creation of the hybrid model for the selection of documents to be produced during the testing activities.

The main idea of goal programming problems is to describe a function for each goal and also set a goal value for each of these. These functions represent the constraints of the problem, and then formulate an objective function that minimizes the sum of the deviations of all goals. The following presents a goal programming model simplified, first presented by Charnes and Cooper [25]:

$$\text{Mininmize} \quad \sum_m (y_m^+ + y_m^-) \tag{7}$$

$$\text{Subject to} \quad f_m(X) - v_m = y_m^+ - y_m^-; \tag{8}$$
for each goal m

$$y_m^+, \ y_m^-, \ x_n \geq 0; \tag{9}$$
$$\forall m, i = 1, \ldots, n,$$

where $X = \{x_1, \ldots, x_n\}$ corresponds to the vector of decision making variables that at the end of the process of resolution of the model will provide a configuration that leads to better results, considering all the goals and constraints applied to the model; $f_m(X)$ is a function $f : \mathfrak{R}^n \to \mathfrak{R}$ that defines the objective of goal m; v_m is the numerical value to be achieved by the goal m; y_m^+ and y_m^- are the positive and negative deviation variables, respectively, that calculate the variation of the goal m. The variable y_j^- represents the absolute value that each goal is below the originally desired and y_j^+ represents the absolute value that each goal is above the originally desired. In order that a negative deviation does not cancel a positive deviation, the model should measure it in absolute terms, and, therefore, the objective function is represented by minimizing the sum of the deviations of each goal.

Note that in the model suggested by Charnes and Cooper [25], we assumed that all objectives and all goals have the same weight.

6.1. *Proposed Goal Programming Model.* The purpose of our work is to decide which documents, among those suggested by the ISO/IEC 829 Standard, presented in Section 2 of this paper, and are more relevant to the reality of micro and small enterprises, in order to make the amount of documents produced during the testing activity more viable to the context of the MSE. These variables are represented by the binary variables u_x, which represent

$$u_x = \begin{cases} 1, & \text{if the document } x \text{ is selected,} \\ 0, & \text{otherwise.} \end{cases} \tag{10}$$

Next, we define the goals for each objective. The goals were defined based on the criteria considered relevant for the selection of artifacts. Each goal relates directly to one of the six selected criteria during the application of the multicriteria model, as shown in Table 2. The definition of the goals can be seen below:

(i) Goal 1—select artifacts whose level of difficulty to obtain the information needed to its completion is low;

(ii) Goal 2—select the artifacts whose information is of most relevance to the reality of the enterprise;

(iii) Goal 3—select the artifacts in which the possibility of reusing the information contained therein is high;

(iv) Goal 4—select artifacts whose effort required to complete them is low;

(v) Goal 5—Select artifacts whose level of knowledge in software testing required to complete them properly is pretty low;

(vi) Goal 6—Select the artifacts whose cost to complete is considered low.

As you can see, the goals defined do not have values directly associated. Therefore, the values obtained using the multicriteria model (step "calculate the general scores of the criteria"), depicted in the previous section, were used as the value of each one of the goal defined herein. Thus, two possible values v_m were established for each goal m associated with a criterion c, and that will be applied to the constraints of inequality (8), according to the section Goal Programming:

(I) $v_m = \sum_{x \in D} E_{x,c}$: summation of the scores of documents to the criterion c;

(II) $v_m = \sum E_{x,c}/|D|$: average of the scores of the documents to the criterion c,

where D represents the set of all documents.

After assignment of values of each goal, the constraint (8) presented in the simplified model of Charnes and Cooper [25], was redefined using the decision variables and the goal values assigned, as shown below:

$$\sum_{x \in D} E_{x,c} * U_x \geq v_m, \tag{11}$$

where x is the document and c is the criterion related to goal m.

Then, the objective function (7) was also redefined by considering that all the positive deviations can be discarded since it is a maximization problem. For a maximization problem it does no matter how much a positive deviation is exceeded, it matters only how to minimize the maximum negative deviations, which represents how much is missed for achieving the goal. Another difference between the objective function redefined and the function originally presented in the simplified model of Charnes and Cooper [25] is the inclusion of weights for each of the goals, which makes the model closer to reality, considering that each goal will have a differentiated factor of relevance according to the particularities of each enterprise. Therefore, we have the following objective function:

$$\text{Minimize} \sum_m w_m y_m^-. \tag{12}$$

Finally, to avoid the obvious solution, which in the context of this work is the use of all the documents in order to achieve all the objectives, it was necessary to add constraint (13), in order to obtain the best subset of n documents,

$$\sum_{x \in D} U_x \leq q, \tag{13}$$

where q is a parameter of the model created with the purpose of limiting the amount of documents used. Thus, if $q = 1$, then the model will define the best document considering all the goals and constraints. If $q = 2$, then the model will define the two best documents, given that the first document was already known after the first run of the model. Therefore, the successive execution with the value of q incremented step by step will result in a formulation of the top ranking documents.

The final model consists of the objective function (12) plus the constraints (9), (11), and (13). The results obtained for the goal values (I) and (II) are presented in the next section:

$$\text{Minimize} \quad \sum_{m} w_m y_m^-,$$

$$\text{Subject to} \quad \sum_{x \in D} E_{x,c} * U_x \geq v_m, \tag{14}$$

$$\sum_{x \in D} U_x \leq q,$$

$$y_m^+, y_m^-, x_i \geq 0; \quad \forall m, i = 1, \ldots, n.$$

7. Application of Hybrid Model for the Selection of Test Artifacts

The proposed testing methodology for micro and small software development companies is based on the ISO 829, with regard to the standard documentation to be developed during the planning and execution of the tests. We chose to use this standard as a basis for this work, given that, in addition to presenting a set of documents that can be adapted for specific organizations or projects, this standard provides a set of information relevant to the testing of software.

The adaptation of ISO 829 with the purpose of enabling its use in micro and small enterprises was based on Crespo (2003). According to Crespo (2003), although the IEEE 829 can be used for testing of software products of any size or complexity, for the projects of small or low complexity, some proposed that documents can be grouped so as to decrease the manageability and production cost of documents. Furthermore, document content may also be abbreviated.

That way, the proposed methodology was defined with the support of experts in software testing and professionals engaged in micro and small enterprises through the hybrid approach involving multiple criteria and goal programming technique, as presented in the following section.

7.1. Application of Multicriteria Model in the Prioritization of Documents Made Available by ISO 829. Initially the multicriteria model was applied to the documentation provided by the IEEE 829-1998, aiming at obtaining a goal value to each of the documents and, thus, supporting the selection of the items most relevant to the needs of micro and small enterprises through the application of goal programming model. The structuring phase of the multicriteria model consists of the steps of identifying criteria, identification of the actors and their weights, and realization of partial evaluation.

During the stage of identification of criteria, all actors participated in a section for the choice of the criteria to be considered for prioritization of documents of IEEE 829-1998. Two groups of actors were selected to be part of this decision making process. The first group consists of 2 (two) experts in software testing, and the second group consists of 2 (two) professionals working in micro and small enterprises.

These actors have responded to a questionnaire consisting of 3 (three) sections, covering the characterization of the interviewee, the prioritization of criteria used in the model, and the analysis of the actor's point of view against the criteria and analysed documents. The documents, in turn, represent the decision making process solution alternatives.

The calculation of the actor's weight was obtained through the sum of the score corresponding to each of the items of the questionnaire. For example, in the case of the item of the questionnaire that considers the degree of the actors, each one of the options: bachelor, specialization, masters, and Ph.D., corresponds to a specific score, ranging between 0.25; 0.50; 0.75; 1.0, respectively. The weight of each actor is presented in Table 3.

Still regarding the weight of the actor, each criterion was established with the support of experts and through conferences, a factor that is differentiated for each group (experts and practitioners of micro and small enterprises), which multiplied the weight of the actor obtained previously, corresponds to the actor's weight to the criterion in question. Table 4 presents the factor defined for each criterion and a group of actors.

To facilitate the understanding, the calculation of the final weight of one of the actors participating in the process in relation to the relevance of information is presented below:

$$PA(a, c) = \sum_{i \in A} Rx_i * F_c, \tag{15}$$

so PA(Professional MPE 2, Relevance of information) = $(1 + 1 + 1 + 0,75) * 0,66 = 2,475$.

Then each actor ranked the selected criteria as your perception of their priority for the process as a whole, as can be seen in Table 5.

Continuing the process, for each criterion, we performed a partial evaluation of the score. This partial evaluation is the result of the multiplication of the values obtained from the point of view of the actor for each document, the actor's weight, and priority of the criterion. It is worth mentioning that the values applied to priority and weight of the actor, were equalized, aiming to ensure equal assessment. Thus, whereas the priority value presented in Table 5, for the professional actor MPE 2 regarding the criterion "relevance of information" is 4, for the calculation of partial evaluation, we have

$$[\text{Priority}(a, c)]_1 \in \left\{ \frac{1}{n}, \frac{2}{n}, \ldots, \frac{n}{n} \right\}, \tag{16}$$

TABLE 3: Actor's weight.

Criteria	Expert 1	Expert 2	Professional MPE 1	Professional MPE 2
Difficulty level	0,99	0,7425	3,25	3,75
Information relevance	2,49	1,8675	2,145	2,475
Reuse possibility	1,5	1,125	1,0725	1,2375
Effort	1,98	1,485	1,625	1,875
Knowledge	3	2,25	0,52	0,6
Cost	0,48	0,36	2,6975	3,1125

TABLE 4: Adjustment factor per criterion and group of actors.

Group of professionals	Difficulty level	Information relevance	Reuse	Effort	Knowledge	Cost
Professionals in micro and small enterprises	1	0,66	0,33	0,5	0,16	0,83
Expert in software testing	0,33	0,83	0,5	0,66	1	0,16

where n represents the amount of criteria, so: Priority (Professional MPE 2, Relevance of information) = 4/6, Priority (Professional MPE 2, Relevance of information) = 0,66.

Similarly, the actor's weight was also standardised. Therefore, standardisation of professional actor weight MPE 2, presented in Table 3, for the relevance of the information, is shown below:

$$[\mathrm{PA}(a,c)]_1 = \frac{\sum_{i \in A} Rx_i * F_c}{4}, \qquad (17)$$

so PA(Professional MPE 2, Relevance of information) = 2,475/4, PA (Professional MPE 2, Relevance of information) = 0,61.

Finally, the calculation of partial evaluation representing the score obtained for the test plan document of professional actor MPE 2, with respect to the criterion "relevance of information," is presented below:

$$E_x(a,c) = [\mathrm{PV}_x(a,c)]_1 * [\mathrm{PA}(a,c)]_1 * [\mathrm{Priority}\,(a,c)]_1,$$

$E_{\text{test plan}}(\text{Professional MPE 2, Relevance of information})$

$$= [1 \times 0,61 \times 0,66],$$

$E_{\text{test plan}}(\text{Professional MPE 2, Relevance of information})$

$$= 0,40. \qquad (18)$$

After the result was obtained in partial evaluation for each actor, the average calculation was performed to obtain the final score of each document for each criterion. Thus, for the test plan document, criterion "relevance information," considering the scores of all the actors, we have

$E_{\text{test plan}}(\text{Expert 1, Relevance of information})$

$$= [1 * 0,62 * 0,5] = 0,31,$$

$E_{\text{test plan}}(\text{Expert 2, Relevance of information})$

$$= [1 \times 0,46 * 0,5] = 0,23,$$

$E_{\text{test plan}}(\text{Professional MPE 1, Relevance of information})$

$$= [1 * 0,53 * 1] = 0,53,$$

$E_{\text{test plan}}(\text{Professional MPE 2, Relevance of information})$

$$= [1 * 0,61 * 0,66] = 0,40,$$

$\mathrm{ME}(\text{test plan, Relevance of information}) = 0,3675.$

$$(19)$$

Table 6 presents the result of the average of each document and criteria. This result, as shown in Section 5.1, the value of goal of each criterion was evaluated in the model obtained based on:

(I) $v_m = \sum_{x \in D} E_{x,c}$: summation of the scores of documents to the criterion c;

(II) $v_m = \sum E_{x,c}/|D|$: average of the scores of the documents to the criterion c.

The value corresponding to the sum of the scores of documents for each criterion, as well as the average of the scores of the calculated documents was obtained based on the presented values.

Finally, the goal programming model structured based on the results obtained through the application of multicriteria model is presented below. The average of the priorities assigned to each criteria by the actors involved in the decision process was used as the weight of the criteria in the objective function of goal programming model. Likewise, as shown in

TABLE 5: Priorities criteria by actor.

Criteria	Expert 1	Expert 2	Professional MPE 1	Professional MPE 2
Difficulty level	5	2	4	1
Information relevance	3	3	6	4
Reuse possibility	1	4	1	2
Effort	6	5	3	5
Knowledge	2	1	2	3
Cost	4	6	5	6

TABLE 6: Overall score of the criteria.

Document	Calculation of scores of the criteria					
	Difficulty level	Information relevance	Reuse possibility	Effort	Knowledge	Cost
Test plan	0,000	1,493	0,335	0,495	0,000	0,080
Test design specification	0,062	1,182	0,103	0,804	0,250	0,090
Test case specification	0,206	1,493	0,166	0,495	0,250	0,080
Test procedure specification	0,542	1,493	0,166	0,203	0,250	0,642
Test log	0,966	0,311	0,000	0,513	0,462	0,732
Test incident report	0,966	1,493	0,000	1,089	0,368	1,420
Test summary report	0,218	1,493	0,000	1,195	0,344	0,948

Section 5.1, the model was carried out twice with different amounts of target. The first run used as target value for each criterion, the overall mean score of each document for each criterion, as can be seen below in the constraint definition R_Crit_0

$$\text{Minimize} \quad \text{obj} : 0.5Yn\_Dif + 0.667Yn\_Rel + 0.333Yn\_Reu + 0.792Yn\_Esf + 0.333\ Yn\_Con + 0.875Yn\_Cst + id173$$

$$\text{Subject to} \quad R\_Crit\_0 : Yn\_difficulty + 0.015U\_EPjT + 0.052U\_ECT + 0.135U\_EPT + 0.242U\_HT$$

$$+ 0.242U\_RIT + 0.055U\_RRT - Yp\_difficulty = 0.1058571 \tag{20}$$

$$R\_numDocs : E\_EPjT + E\_ECT + E\_EPcT + E\_HT + E\_RIT + E\_RRT + E\_PT = 6.$$

In the second run, the value of the summation of the scores of each general document for each criteria was used as the target value for the constraint R_Crit_0. In this case, the value 0.1058571 was replaced by 0.8468571. The following are the results of applying the hybrid model to support the decision of the test artifacts selection.

In the second run, the value of the summation of the scores of each general document for each criteria was used as the target value for the constraint R_Crit_0.

7.2. Computational Results. The proposed model was solved using the software IBM ILOG OPL 6.3, assigned to the academic community. Two scenarios were performed using the sum (I) and the average (II) as the goal values. The results are shown in Figure 2.

We can note that the prioritization of the documents was carried out satisfactorily, considering the two goal values options established. However, the application of the model using the average as a goal value obtained a result closer to what had already been obtained by applying a multicriteria

model and evaluation of the actors involved in decision making process presented by Rodrigues [26]. This result is possibly more feasible because it includes documents produced during the main stages of the testing activity. On the other hand, the result that considered as a goal value of the summation could be more interesting for an enterprise in which the documents produced for the stage of execution and evaluation of the tests are of higher priority than those documents produced for the planning stage of tests.

8. Conclusion and Future Works

This paper proposed a hybrid model for prioritization of documents to be produced during the software testing activity in an enterprise. The purpose of applying the model to obtain the prioritization of the documents available on IEEE 829 [13] Standard is to establish a set of documents that may be considered, possibly closer to the reality of micro and small enterprises when they are not able to produce all documents suggested by the IEEE 829.

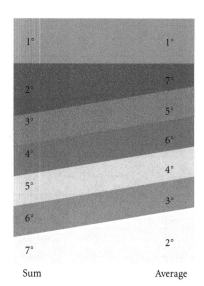

FIGURE 2: Comparison of results using as goals the sum (I) and average (II).

The application of the proposed model met the goal of prioritization while at the same time allowed to replace the way enterprises define, often using an evaluation without criteria formally established, the documents that are part of the scope of their processes. Thus, the application of a decision support model attempts to decrease the subjectivity, with which decisions are made, but it is important to note, not necessarily the result of decision making will be exactly equal to the result obtained with application of the prioritization model. However, future works, it is essential that the differences among the results obtained with the application of the model and the judgments expressed by the participants involved in the decision making process are evaluated, with the purpose of adjusting the model as close as possible to the reality.

Although the proposed approach aims the prioritization of documents to form a testing process, we believe that it can be applied to different prioritization problems, such as prioritization of use cases to perform peer review.

Acknowledgments

The first and second authors would like to thank FUNCAP—Foundation for Support in Scientific and Technological Development State of Ceará—that has been financially sponsored this work, and the third author would like to thank CNPq—National Counsel of Technological and Scientific Development, via Grant no. 305844/2011-3. The authors also acknowledge IBM for making the IBM ILOG CPLEX Optimization Studio available to the academic community.

References

[1] MCT. Ministério da Ciência e Tecnologia. Qualidade e Produtividade no Setor de Software Brasileiro: Result-ados da pesquisa, 2005, http://www.mct.gov.br/index.php/content/view/3253/Pesquisa_2005.html.

[2] SEPIN (Secretaria de Política de Informática), MCT (Ministério da Ciência e Tecnologia), Qualidade e Produtividade no Setor de Software—Resultados da Pesquisa, 2005, http://www.mct.gov.br/index.php/content/view/3253/Pesquisa_2005.html.

[3] S. Wagner and T. Seifert, "Software quality economics for defect-detection techniques using failure prediction," *ACM Software Engineering Notesn*, vol. 30, no. 4, pp. 1–6, 2005.

[4] A. Rodrigues, A. Bessa, and P. R. Pinheiro, "Barriers to implement test process in small-sized companies," *Communications in Computer and Information Science*, vol. 112, no. 2, pp. 233–242, 2010.

[5] P. Laplante, F. Belli, J. Gao et al., "Software test automation," *Advances in Software Engineering*, vol. 2010, Article ID 163746, 2 pages, 2010.

[6] L. E. S. Sartori, *Melhoria do processo de teste para pequenas empresas [M.S. Dissertação]*, Departamento de Ciência da Computação, Centro Universitário Eurípides de Marília, Fundação de Ensino Eurípides Soares da Rocha, 2005.

[7] "SEI (Software Engineering Institute). CMMI for Development (CMMI-DEV), Version 1.3," Tech. Rep. CMU/SEI-2010-TR-033, Software Engineering Institute, Carnegie Mellon University, Pittsburgh, Pa, USA, 2010.

[8] SOFTEX (Associação para Promoção da Excelência do Software Brasileiro—SOFTEX), MPS.BR—Guia Geral, 2011, http://www.softex.br.

[9] R. Singh, "ISO/IEC draft international standard 12207, software life-cycle processes," *IFIP Transactions A*, no. 55, pp. 111–113, 1994.

[10] ISO/IEC 15504, *Information Technology—Software Process Assessment, Parts 19*, International Organization for Standardization and the International Electrotechnical Commission, Geneva, Switzerland, 2003.

[11] I. Burnstein, T. Suwanassart, and R. Carlson, "Developing a testing maturity model for software test process evaluation and improvement," in *Proceedings of the 1996 IEEE International Test Conference*, pp. 581–589, Washington, DC, USA, October 1996.

[12] T. Koomen and P. O. L. M, *Test Process Improvement: A Practical Step-By-Step Guide to Structured Testing*, Addison-Wesley, 1999.

[13] IEEE Standard 829-1998: Standard for Software Test Documentation, IEEE Press.

[14] A. N. Crespo, O. J. Silva, C. A. Borges, C. F. Salviano, M. Argollo, and M. Jino, "Uma metodologia para teste de Software no Contexto da Melhoria de Processo," in *III Simpósio Brasileiro de Qualidade de Software (SBQS '04)*, Brasília, Brazil, 2004.

[15] C. L. B. Maia, R. A. F. Carmo, F. G. Freitas, G. A. L. Campos, and J. T. Souza, "Automated test case prioritization with reactive GRASP," *Advances in Software Engineering*, vol. 2010, Article ID 428521, 18 pages, 2010.

[16] N. Koochakzadeh and V. Garousi, "A tester-assisted methodology for test redundancy detection," *Advances in Software Engineering*, vol. 2010, Article ID 932686, 13 pages, 2010.

[17] C. A. Bana e Costa, J. M. De Corte, and J. C. Vansnick, "MACBETH," *International Journal of Information Technology and Decision Making*, vol. 11, no. 2, pp. 359–387, 2012.

[18] Â. M. A. Schmidt, *Processo de apoio à tomada de decisão—abordagens: AHP e MACBETH [M.S. Dissertação]*, UFSC, Florianópolis, Brazil, 1995, http://www.eps.ufsc.br/disserta/engait95.html.

[19] F. Gonçalves, G. S. Márcia et al., "Multicriteria model for selection of automated system tests," in *Proceedings of the International Conference on Research and Practical Issues of Enterprise Information Systems (CONFENIS '06)*, Viena, Áustria, 2006.

[20] A. Rodrigues, P. R. Pinheiro, M. M. Rodrigues, A. B. Albuquerque, and F. M. Gonçalves, "Towards the selection of testable use cases and a real experience," *Communications in Computer and Information Science*, vol. 49, pp. 513–521, 2009.

[21] A. Rodrigues, P. P. Rogerio, M. M. Rodrigues, C. A. Albuquerque, and F. M. Gonçalves, "Applying a multicriteria model for selection of test use cases: a use of experience," *International Journal Social and Humanistic Computing*, vol. 1, pp. 246–260, 2010.

[22] A. Rodrigues, C. A. Albuquerque, P. P. Rogerio, A. Bessa, A. Diego, and M. Thiago, "Uma abordagem de teste de software para micro e pequenas empresas," in *Proceedings of the 4th International Conference on Research and Practical Issues of Enterprise Information Systems*, 2010.

[23] A. Rodrigues, P. R. Pinheiro, and A. Albuquerque, "The definiton of a testing process to small-sized companies: the Brazilian scenario," in *7th International Conference on the Quality of Information and Communications Technology, QUATIC 2010*, pp. 298–303, Porto, Portugal, October 2010.

[24] A. C. Hax and D. Candea, *Production and Inventory Management*, Prentice-Hall, 1984.

[25] A. Charnes and W. W. Cooper, "Goal programming and multiple objectives optimizations," *European Journal of Operational Research*, vol. 1, pp. 39–54, 1977.

[26] A. Rodrigues, *Uma metodologia de testes em software para micro e pequenas empresas estruturada em multicritério [M.S. dissertation]*, Graduate Program in Applied Informatics, University of Fortaleza, 2011.

Permissions

The contributors of this book come from diverse backgrounds, making this book a truly international effort. This book will bring forth new frontiers with its revolutionizing research information and detailed analysis of the nascent developments around the world.

We would like to thank all the contributing authors for lending their expertise to make the book truly unique. They have played a crucial role in the development of this book. Without their invaluable contributions this book wouldn't have been possible. They have made vital efforts to compile up to date information on the varied aspects of this subject to make this book a valuable addition to the collection of many professionals and students.

This book was conceptualized with the vision of imparting up-to-date information and advanced data in this field. To ensure the same, a matchless editorial board was set up. Every individual on the board went through rigorous rounds of assessment to prove their worth. After which they invested a large part of their time researching and compiling the most relevant data for our readers. Conferences and sessions were held from time to time between the editorial board and the contributing authors to present the data in the most comprehensible form. The editorial team has worked tirelessly to provide valuable and valid information to help people across the globe.

Every chapter published in this book has been scrutinized by our experts. Their significance has been extensively debated. The topics covered herein carry significant findings which will fuel the growth of the discipline. They may even be implemented as practical applications or may be referred to as a beginning point for another development. Chapters in this book were first published by Hindawi Publishing Corporation; hereby published with permission under the Creative Commons Attribution License or equivalent.

The editorial board has been involved in producing this book since its inception. They have spent rigorous hours researching and exploring the diverse topics which have resulted in the successful publishing of this book. They have passed on their knowledge of decades through this book. To expedite this challenging task, the publisher supported the team at every step. A small team of assistant editors was also appointed to further simplify the editing procedure and attain best results for the readers.

Our editorial team has been hand-picked from every corner of the world. Their multi-ethnicity adds dynamic inputs to the discussions which result in innovative outcomes. These outcomes are then further discussed with the researchers and contributors who give their valuable feedback and opinion regarding the same. The feedback is then collaborated with the researches and they are edited in a comprehensive manner to aid the understanding of the subject.

Apart from the editorial board, the designing team has also invested a significant amount of their time in understanding the subject and creating the most relevant covers. They scrutinized every image to scout for the most suitable representation of the subject and create an appropriate cover for the book.

The publishing team has been involved in this book since its early stages. They were actively engaged in every process, be it collecting the data, connecting with the contributors or procuring relevant information. The team has been an ardent support to the editorial, designing and production team. Their endless efforts to recruit the best for this project, has resulted in the accomplishment of this book. They are a veteran in the field of academics and their pool of knowledge is as vast as their experience in printing. Their expertise and guidance has proved useful at every step. Their uncompromising quality standards have made this book an exceptional effort. Their encouragement from time to time has been an inspiration for everyone.

The publisher and the editorial board hope that this book will prove to be a valuable piece of knowledge for researchers, students, practitioners and scholars across the globe.

List of Contributors

Naser Ezzati- Jivan and Michel R. Dagenais
Department of Computer and Software Engineering, Ecole Polytechnique de Montreal, C.P. 6079, Station Downtown, Montreal, Quebec, Canada H3C 3A7

Michael F. Dossis
Department of Informatics and Computer Technology, School of Kastoria, Higher Technological Education Institute of Western Macedonia, Fourka Area, 52100 Kastoria, Greece

Onur Derin and Prasanth Kuncheerath Ramankutty
ALaRI, Faculty of Informatics, University of Lugano, 6904 Lugano, Switzerland

Paolo Meloni
Department of Electrical and Electronic Engineering, Faculty of Engineering, University of Cagliari, 09123 Cagliari, Italy

Emanuele Cannella
LIACS, Leiden University, 2333 CA Leiden, The Netherlands

Andrea Bosin
Dipartimento di Fisica, Universita degli Studi di Cagliari, Complesso Universitario di Monserrato, 09042 Monserrato, Italy
Istituto Nazionale di Fisica Nucleare (INFN), Complesso Universitario di Monserrato, Sezione di Cagliari, 09042 Monserrato, Italy

Etiel Petrinja and Giancarlo Succi
Center for Applied Software Engineering, Free University of Bozen/Bolzano, 39100 Bolzano/Bozen, Italy

Francesco Di Tria, Ezio Lefons and Filippo Tangorra
Dipartimento di Informatica, Universita degli Studi di Bari Aldo Moro, Via Orabona 4, 70125 Bari, Italy

Joe Zou
Centrin Data Systems, 1 Boxing 8th Road, Beijing 100176, China

Chris Pavlovski
IBM Global Business Services, 348 Edward Street, Brisbane, QLD 4000, Australia

Robert Hilbrich
Department Systems Architecture, Fraunhofer FIRST, Kekulestraße 7, 12489 Berlin, Germany

Xiao Xiao and Tadashi Dohi
Department of Information Engineering, Graduate School of Engineering, Hiroshima University, 1-4-1 Kagamiyama, Higashi-Hiroshima 739-8527, Japan

Philippe Dhaussy, Jean-Charles Roger and Luka Leroux
Lab-STICC, UMR CNRS 6285, ENSTA Bretagne, 2 rue Francois Verny, 29806 Brest, France

Frederic Boniol
ONERA, 2 avenue Edouard Belin, 31000 Toulouse, France

Birgit Hofer and Franz Wotawa
Institute for Software Technology, Graz University of Technology, 8010 Graz, Austria

Rattikorn Hewett
Department of Computer Science, Texas Tech University, Lubbock, TX 79409-3104, USA

Priyanka Mekala and Jeffrey Fan
Department of Electrical and Computer Engineering, Florida International University, Miami, FL 33174, USA

Wen-Cheng Lai
Department of Electronic Engineering, National Taiwan University of Science and Technology, Taipei 106, Taiwan
Department of Engineering, Ming Chi University of Technology, Taipei 243, Taiwan

Ching-Wen Hsue
Department of Electronic Engineering, National Taiwan University of Science and Technology, Taipei 106, Taiwan

Priyanka Mekala and Jeffrey Fan
Department of Electrical and Computer Engineering, Florida International University, Miami, FL 33174, USA

Wen-Cheng Lai
Department of Electronic Engineering, National Taiwan University of Science and Technology, Taipei 106, Taiwan
Department of Engineering, Ming Chi University of Technology, Taipei 243, Taiwan

Ching-Wen Hsue
Department of Electronic Engineering, National Taiwan University of Science and Technology, Taipei 106, Taiwan

Andreia Rodrigues da Silva, Fernando Rodrigues de Almeida Junior and Placido Rogerio Pinheiro
Graduate Program in Applied Informatics, University of Fortaleza (UNIFOR), Avenue Washington Soares, 1321, 60811-341 Fortaleza, CE, Brazil

Printed in the USA
CPSIA information can be obtained
at www.ICGtesting.com
JSHW052021301024
72690JS00004B/128

9 781632 402936